100 BULLETS
SPLIT SECOND CHANCE

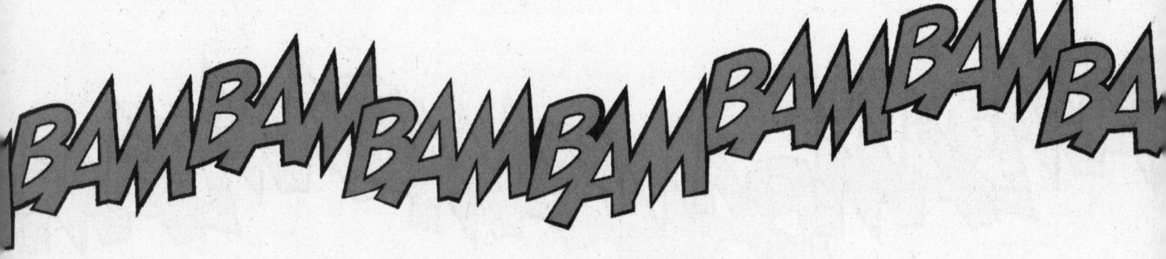
BAMBAMBAMBAMBAMBAMBA

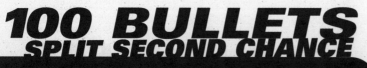

100 BULLETS
SPLIT SECOND CHANCE

BRIAN AZZARELLO Writer EDUARDO RISSO Artist
GRANT GOLEASH Colorist CLEM ROBINS Letterer
DAVE JOHNSON Covers
100 BULLETS CREATED BY BRIAN AZZARELLO

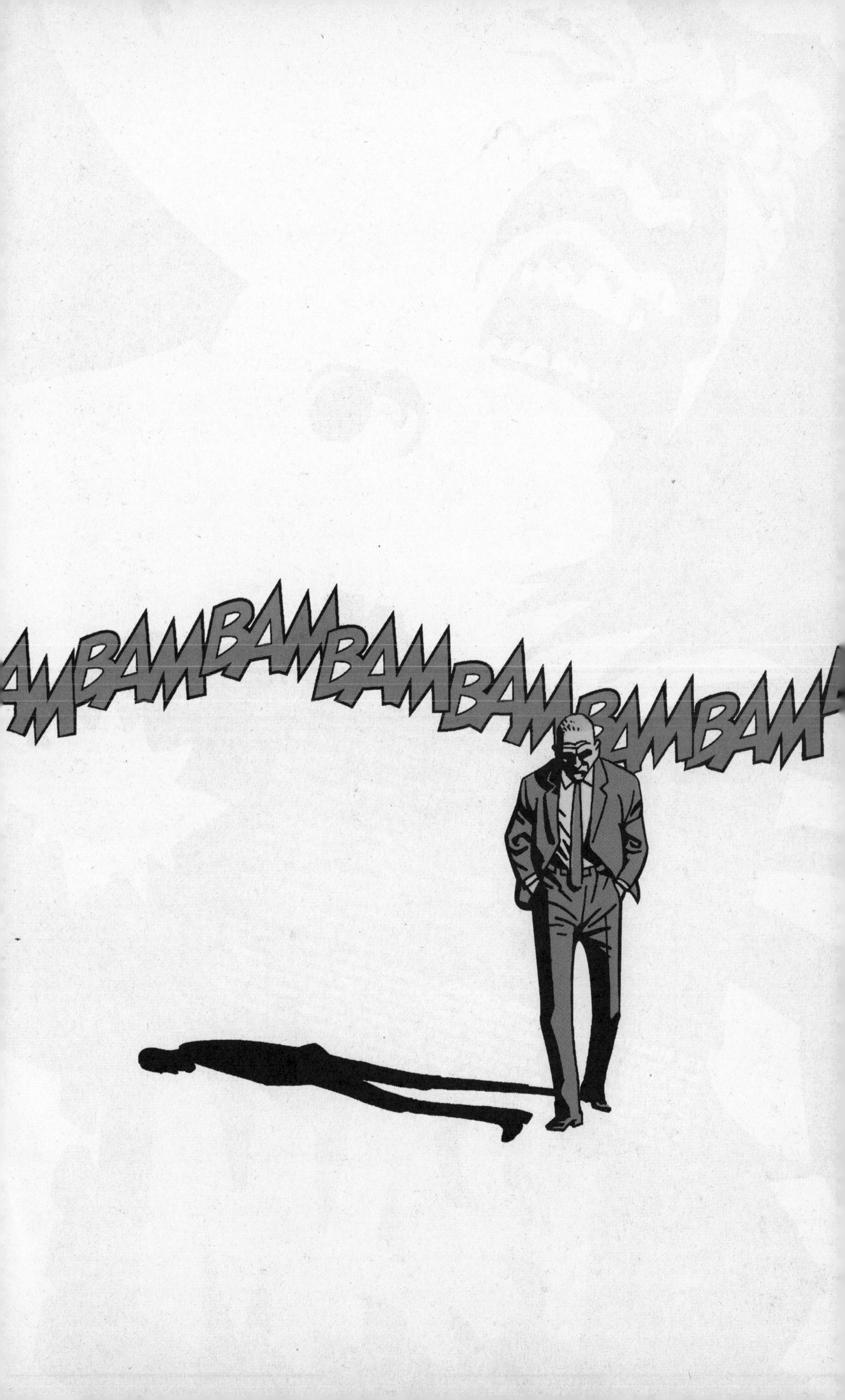
BAMBAMBAMBAMBAMBAM

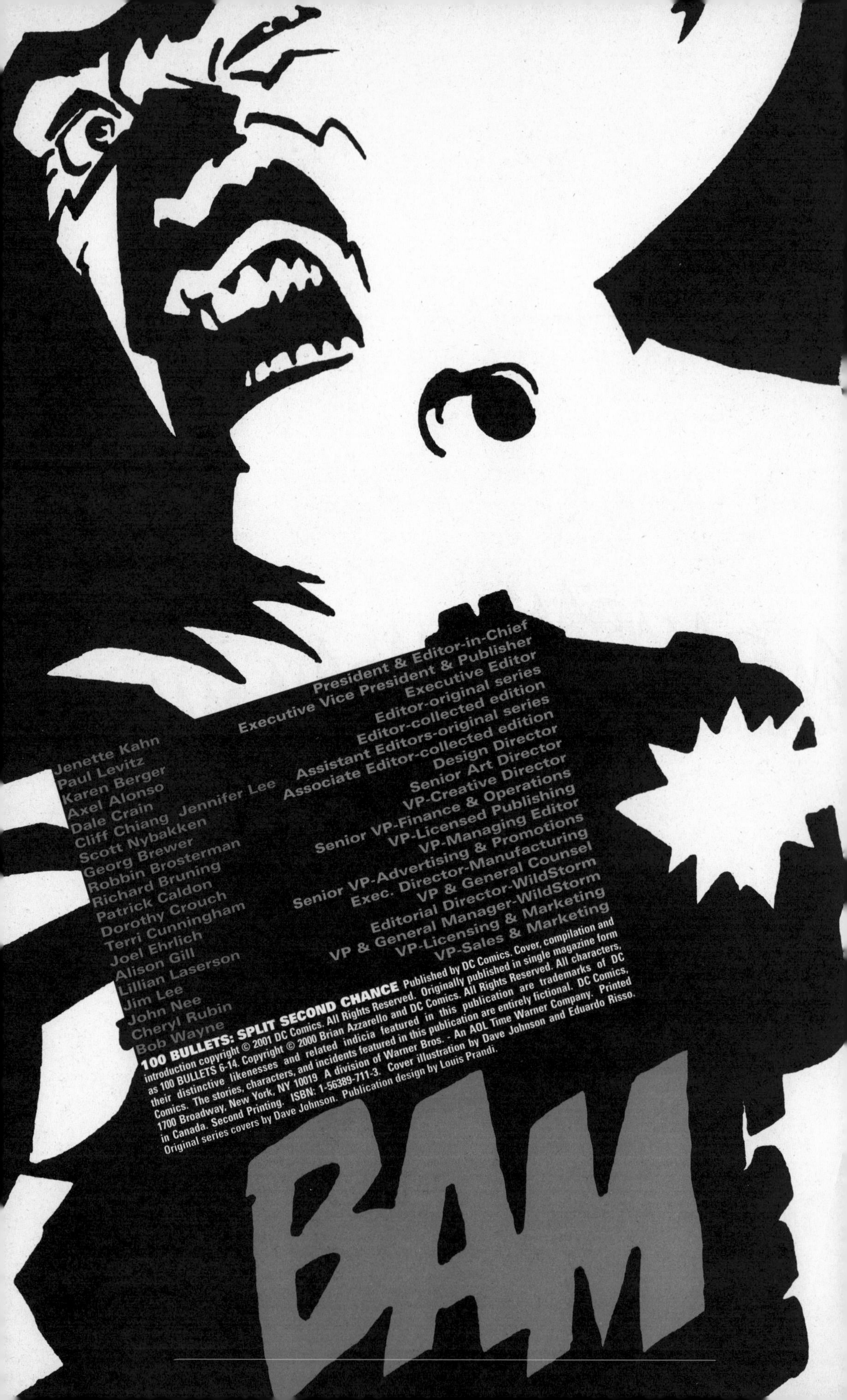

President & Editor-in-Chief
Executive Vice President & Publisher
Executive Editor
Editor-original series
Editor-collected edition
Assistant Editors-original series
Associate Editor-collected edition
Design Director
Senior Art Director
VP-Creative Director
VP-Finance & Operations
Senior VP-Licensed Publishing
VP-Managing Editor
VP-Advertising & Promotions
Senior VP-Advertising & Promotions
Exec. Director-Manufacturing
VP & General Counsel
Editorial Director-WildStorm
VP & General Manager-WildStorm
VP-Licensing & Marketing
VP-Sales & Marketing

Jenette Kahn
Paul Levitz
Karen Berger
Axel Alonso
Dale Crain
Cliff Chiang Jennifer Lee
Scott Nybakken
Georg Brewer
Robbin Brosterman
Richard Bruning
Patrick Caldon
Dorothy Crouch
Terri Cunningham
Joel Ehrlich
Alison Gill
Lillian Laserson
Jim Lee
John Nee
Cheryl Rubin
Bob Wayne

100 BULLETS: SPLIT SECOND CHANCE Published by DC Comics. Cover, compilation and introduction copyright © 2001 DC Comics. All Rights Reserved. Originally published in single magazine form as 100 BULLETS 6-14. Copyright © 2000 Brian Azzarello and DC Comics. All Rights Reserved. All characters, their distinctive likenesses, and incidents featured in this publication are entirely fictional. DC Comics, Comics. The stories, characters, and related indicia featured in this publication are trademarks of DC 1700 Broadway, New York, NY 10019 A division of Warner Bros. - An AOL Time Warner Company. Printed in Canada. Second Printing. ISBN: 1-56389-711-3. Cover illustration by Dave Johnson and Eduardo Risso. Original series covers by Dave Johnson. Publication design by Louis Prandi.

Introduction

Let's start with a couple of confessions.

When I first became aware of 100 BULLETS, I didn't like it. The covers were annoying, and the interior artwork didn't grab me either.

The second confession is that I never really gave it a close look, and I certainly never read it.

Now, I've got a lot of defects of character. I expend an awful lot of energy on a daily basis in order to lose these shortcomings — and one of the most pernicious of these flaws is contempt prior to investigation.

In this particular case, I figured this book was just another one of the current spate of crypto-crime comics — a subgenre that includes everything from bad Spillane pastiche to nihilist bullshit that acts like it's about something, but turns out to be nothing more than a stream of shuck and jive that isn't about anything but itself.

I don't exactly recall why I bothered to get past my feelings and actually *read* an issue of 100 BULLETS, but whatever the reason, I read the second arc in the series — and I was sinker, line and hooked.

I went back and read everything from the beginning, and fuck, this stuff is just terrific — in, among others, a particularly comic-book way. 100 BULLETS looks and reads like it was written and drawn by *one* man — or, at the very least, two guys with as symbiotic a relationship as Simon & Kirby, or Kurtzman & Elder.

It certainly never feels like the work of one guy who lives in Chicago, writing scripts for another guy who lives in Argentina — two guys who I have to assume don't spend a lot of time together bonding.

Some years back, somebody, I don't recall who, described my stuff as "public transportation dialogue." I assume this was said with derogatory or, at the very least, condescending intentions. For my part, I took it as a compliment. It meant, at least to me, that my characters talked like people you may not know, or even *want* to know — but are unavoidable in the landscape in which we live.

Brian Azzarello writes public transportation dialogue, too — and he writes the kind of characters one can neither ignore nor avoid. Brian's work compares favorably with several of the best crime writers out there today — precisely because he doesn't write nostalgic horseshit about guns, goons and gals, or pretentious dreck filled with contemporary slang that's already old school.

Brian writes a world I recognize — filled with those unavoidable and unforgettable characters — and Eduardo Risso does one serious fuck of a job visualizing that world. In an industry filled with louts trying to pass off bad drawing as cartooning, Eduardo is a consummate cartoonist. Without aping either of them, he manages to remind me simultaneously of Kurtzman and Toth — two extraordinary cartoonists who created convincing worlds with a minimum of detail.

If I hear one more asshole justify sloppy laziness with that old saw, "Less is more," one more time, it's going to be tower and rifle week for me — time once again for the Charles Joseph Whitman invitational. Less is only more if the less you've got is beautiful. In other words, boil it down to its simplest terms, then write and draw the fuck out of it. That's what Brian and Eduardo do, and beautifully, too.

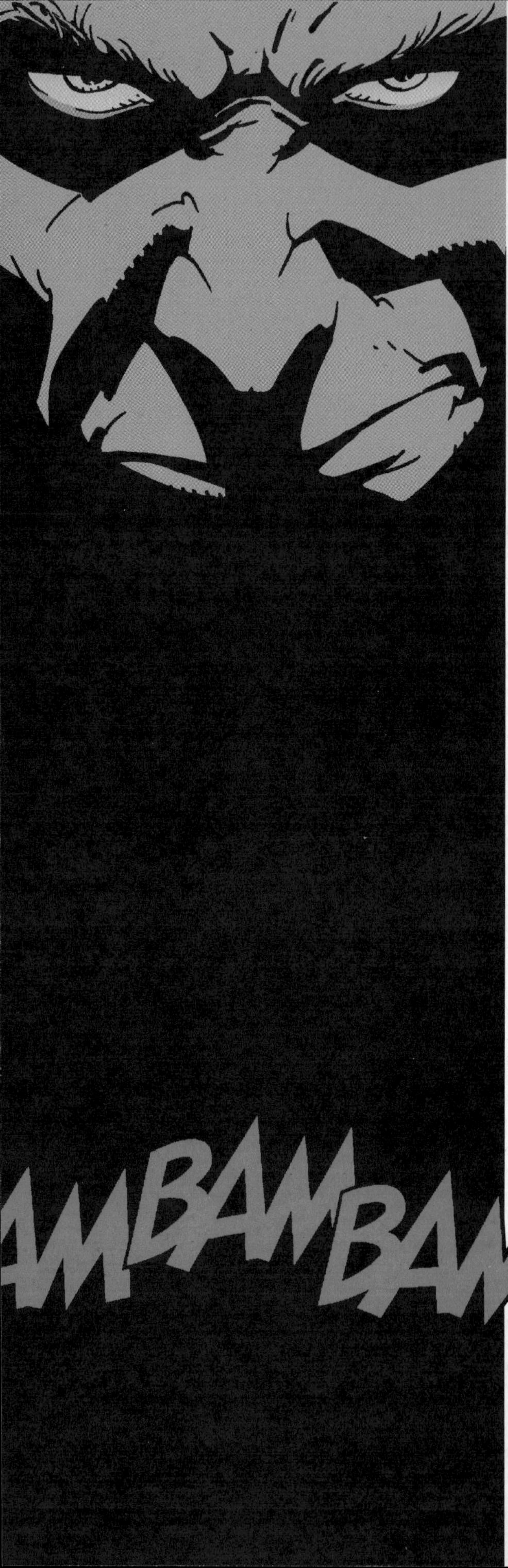
BAM BAM BAM BAM

The text and visuals are stripped down to their barest essentials — creating a synchronous package that is contemporary comics at its finest.

And about those covers. Okay — one more example of contempt prior to investigation. What David Johnson — I don't know him at all, let alone well enough to call him "Dave" — has going on here is a technical *tour de force* that does everything we demand of covers. They sell the book, they capture the tone, and they convey the idea and theme of the interior art without stepping on anybody's toes.

So for "annoyed," read "envious."

In closing, I hope I'm not speaking out of turn when I relate, in part, a conversation that I had with Axel Alonso, the man who did such a terrific job editing the original issues collected in this trade paperback. I have to assume this chat played no small part in my being asked to write this introduction.

Axel mentioned, in very general terms, that Brian had long-term goals for 100 BULLETS, with threads being let out to be slowly tied together. Now, maybe I've just finally stopped caring about comics in the way I used to — as individual chapters in extended picaresque novels — but when I watch, for example, Ricky Jay, or David Blaine, I don't want to know how they're doing it — I just want to be dragged to the edge of belief with my sense of wonder intact.

That's exactly how I feel about what Brian and Eduardo have achieved with 100 BULLETS. I don't give a damn where Brian and Eduardo are going, nor do I want to know what they've got planned. I just want to continue being dragged along by the beautiful synthesis of text and narrative, grateful to have a comic book that I can savor on a monthly basis.

Thanks are overdue to both of these guys for producing the most exciting comic book in years.

— Howard Chaykin

Howard Chaykin has written and drawn comics for more than twenty years. His breakthrough creation, American Flagg! *set a new standard in graphic storytelling with its frenetic, absorbing pace and whip-smart dialogue — characteristics Chaykin brought to later projects like DC's THE SHADOW, BLACKHAWK, and most recently JLA: SECRET SOCIETY OF SUPER-HEROES, as well as VERTIGO's PULP FANTASTIC and his own black-hearted noir miniseries,* Black Kiss.

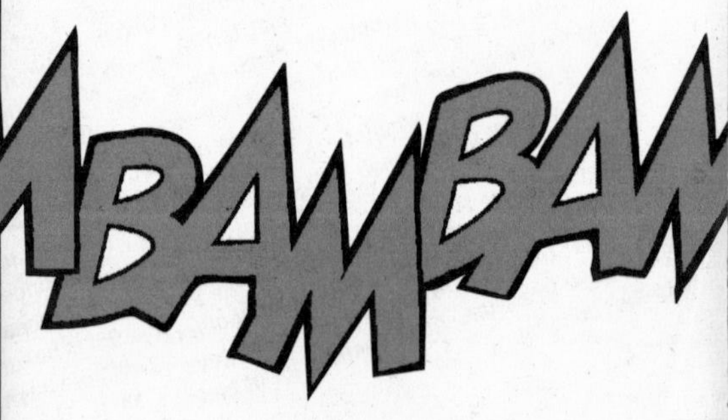

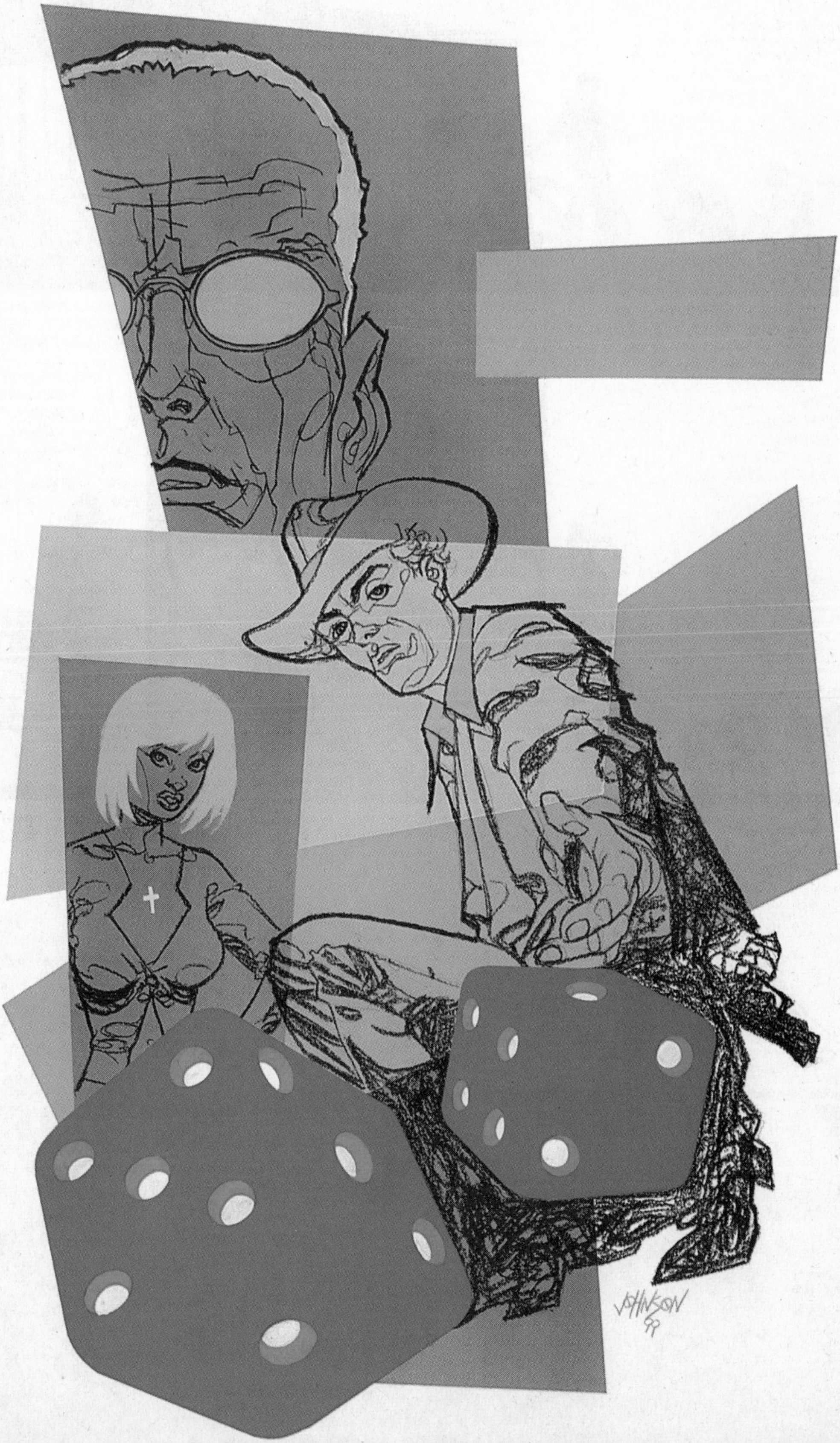
JOHNSON 99

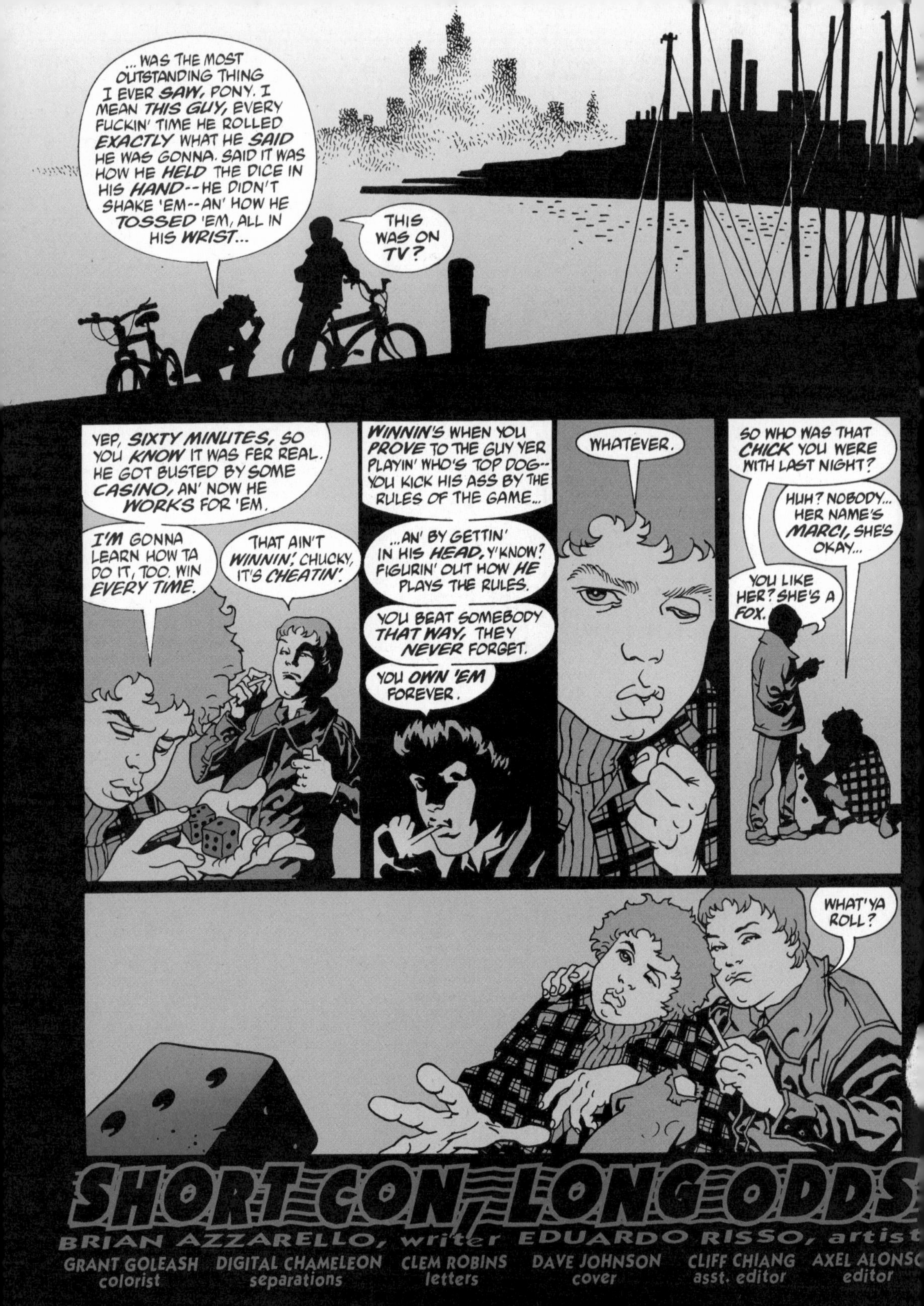
...WAS THE MOST OUTSTANDING THING I EVER SAW, PONY. I MEAN THIS GUY, EVERY FUCKIN' TIME HE ROLLED EXACTLY WHAT HE SAID HE WAS GONNA. SAID IT WAS HOW HE HELD THE DICE IN HIS HAND--HE DIDN'T SHAKE 'EM--AN' HOW HE TOSSED 'EM, ALL IN HIS WRIST...
THIS WAS ON TV?
YEP, SIXTY MINUTES, SO YOU KNOW IT WAS FER REAL. HE GOT BUSTED BY SOME CASINO, AN' NOW HE WORKS FOR 'EM.
I'M GONNA LEARN HOW TA DO IT, TOO. WIN EVERY TIME.
THAT AIN'T WINNIN', CHUCKY, IT'S CHEATIN'.
WINNIN'S WHEN YOU PROVE TO THE GUY YER PLAYIN' WHO'S TOP DOG--YOU KICK HIS ASS BY THE RULES OF THE GAME...
...AN' BY GETTIN' IN HIS HEAD, Y'KNOW? FIGURIN' OUT HOW HE PLAYS THE RULES.
YOU BEAT SOMEBODY THAT WAY, THEY NEVER FORGET.
YOU OWN 'EM FOREVER.
WHATEVER.
SO WHO WAS THAT CHICK YOU WERE WITH LAST NIGHT?
HUH? NOBODY... HER NAME'S MARCI, SHE'S OKAY...
YOU LIKE HER? SHE'S A FOX.
WHAT'YA ROLL?
SHORT CON, LONG ODDS
BRIAN AZZARELLO, writer EDUARDO RISSO, artist
GRANT GOLEASH colorist
DIGITAL CHAMELEON separations
CLEM ROBINS letters
DAVE JOHNSON cover
CLIFF CHIANG asst. editor
AXEL ALONSO editor

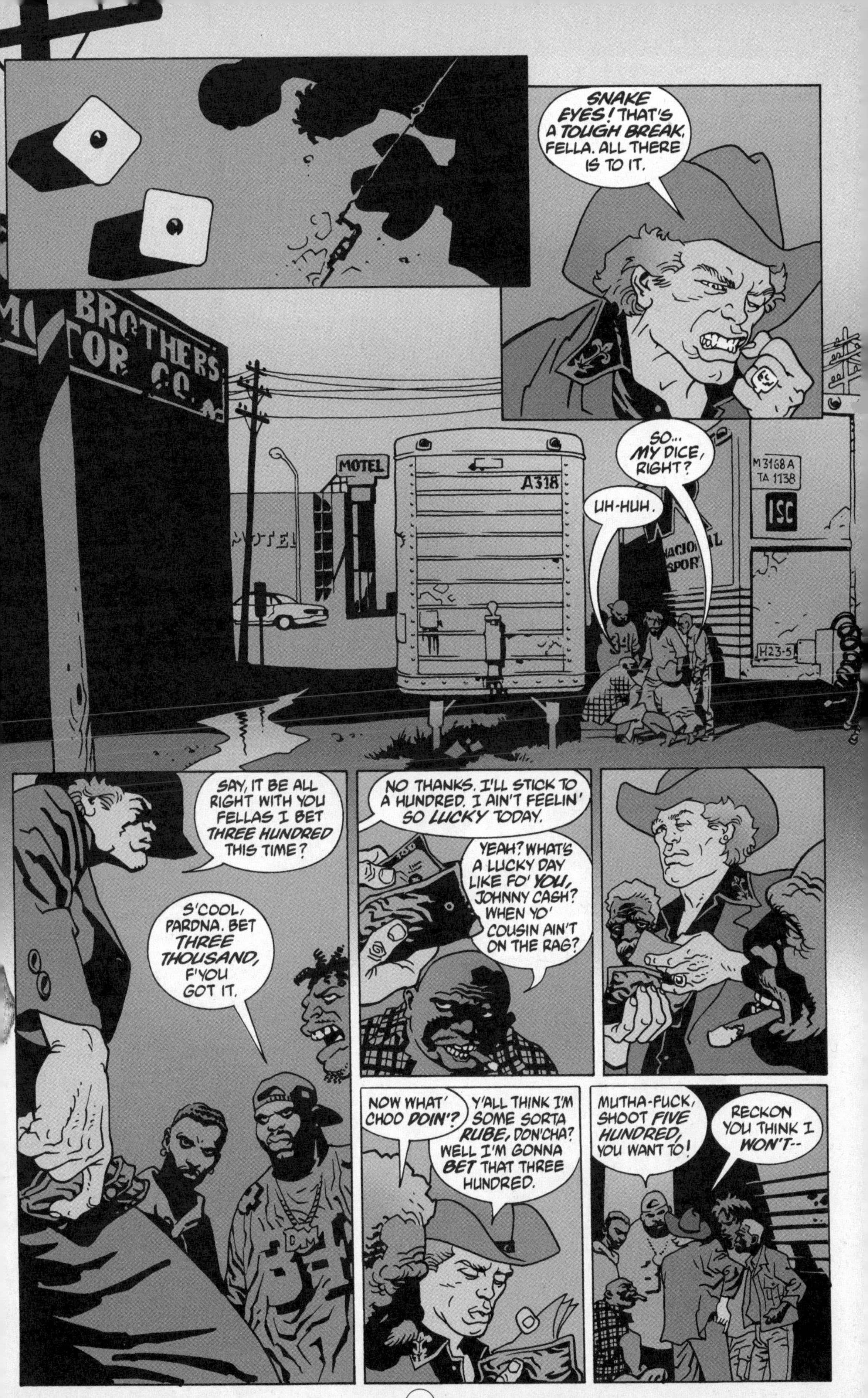
SNAKE EYES! THAT'S A TOUGH BREAK, FELLA. ALL THERE IS TO IT.
BROTHERS
TOR CO.
MOTEL
A318
M 3168 A
TA 1138
ISC
SO... MY DICE, RIGHT?
UH-HUH.
H23-5
SAY, IT BE ALL RIGHT WITH YOU FELLAS I BET THREE HUNDRED THIS TIME?
S'COOL, PARDNA. BET THREE THOUSAND, F'YOU GOT IT.
NO THANKS. I'LL STICK TO A HUNDRED. I AIN'T FEELIN' SO LUCKY TODAY.
YEAH? WHAT'S A LUCKY DAY LIKE FO' YOU, JOHNNY CASH? WHEN YO' COUSIN AIN'T ON THE RAG?
NOW WHAT' CHOO DOIN'?
Y'ALL THINK I'M SOME SORTA RUBE, DON'CHA? WELL I'M GONNA BET THAT THREE HUNDRED.
MUTHA-FUCK, SHOOT FIVE HUNDRED, YOU WANT TO!
RECKON YOU THINK I WON'T--

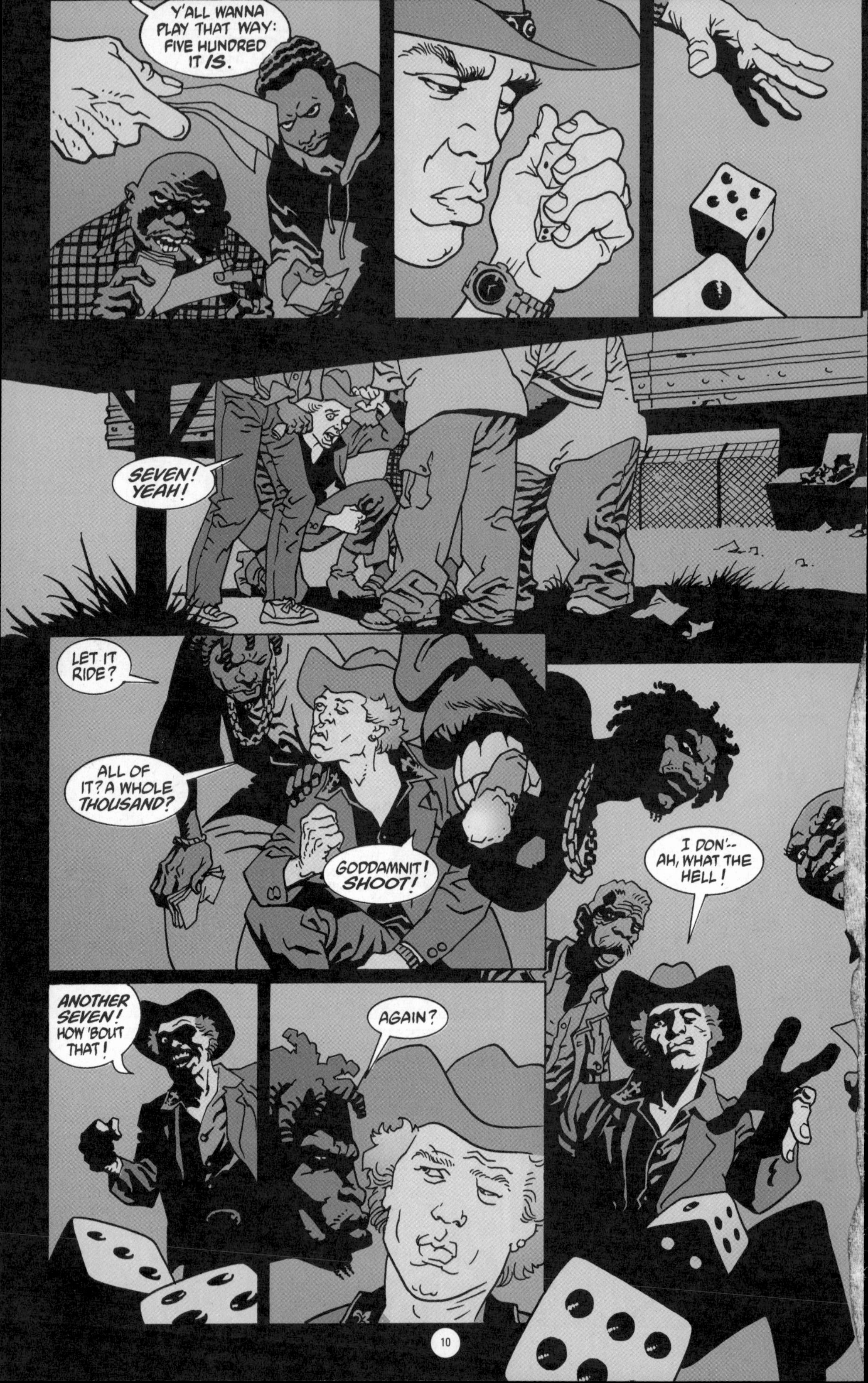
Y'ALL WANNA PLAY THAT WAY: FIVE HUNDRED IT IS.
SEVEN! YEAH!
LET IT RIDE?
ALL OF IT? A WHOLE THOUSAND?
GODDAMNIT! SHOOT!
I DON'-- AH, WHAT THE HELL!
ANOTHER SEVEN! HOW 'BOUT THAT!
AGAIN?

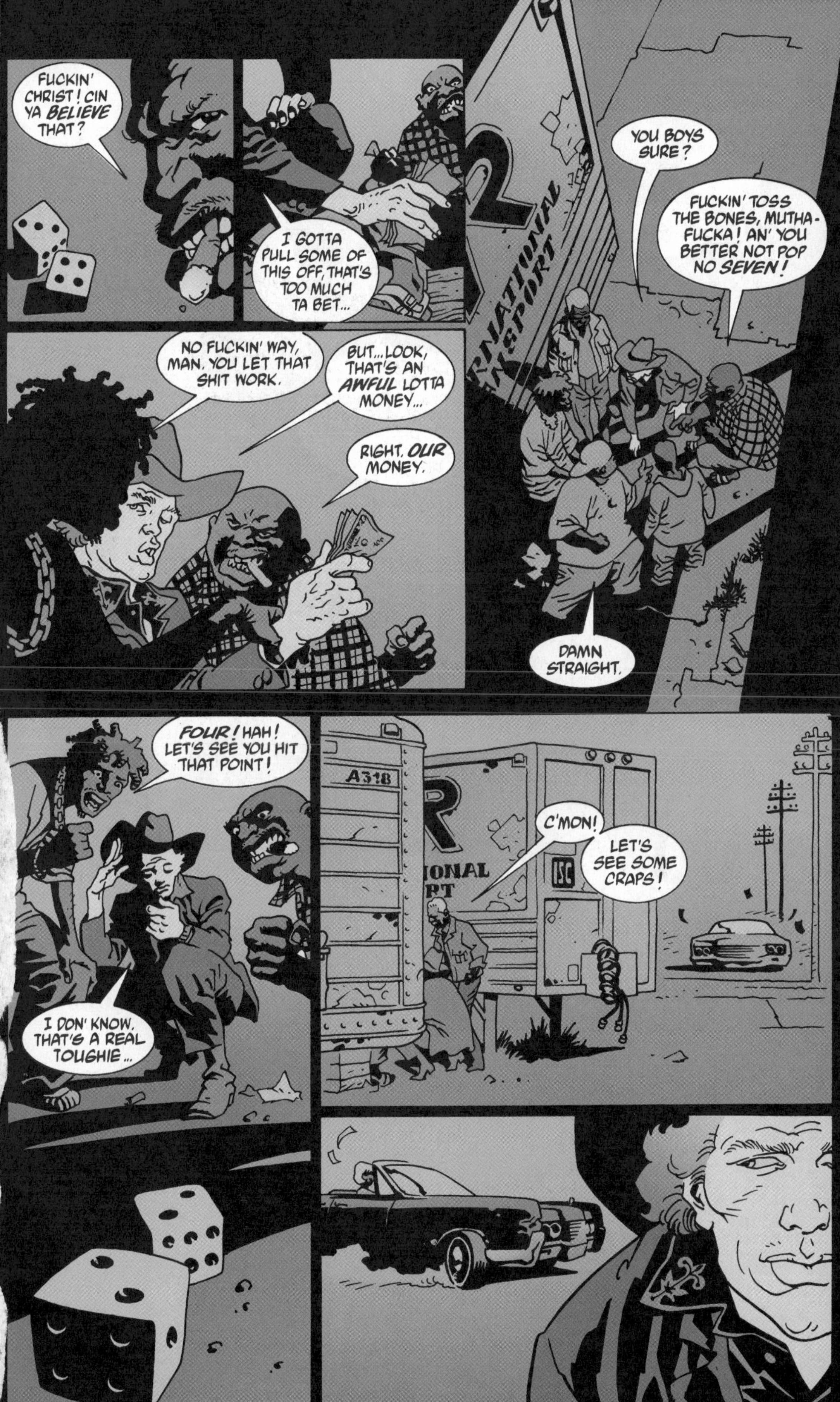
FUCKIN' CHRIST! CIN YA BELIEVE THAT?
I GOTTA PULL SOME OF THIS OFF, THAT'S TOO MUCH TA BET...
YOU BOYS SURE?
FUCKIN' TOSS THE BONES, MUTHA-FUCKA! AN' YOU BETTER NOT POP NO SEVEN!
NO FUCKIN' WAY, MAN. YOU LET THAT SHIT WORK.
BUT...LOOK, THAT'S AN AWFUL LOTTA MONEY...
RIGHT. OUR MONEY.
DAMN STRAIGHT.
FOUR! HAH! LET'S SEE YOU HIT THAT POINT!
I DON' KNOW. THAT'S A REAL TOUGHIE...
C'MON!
LET'S SEE SOME CRAPS!

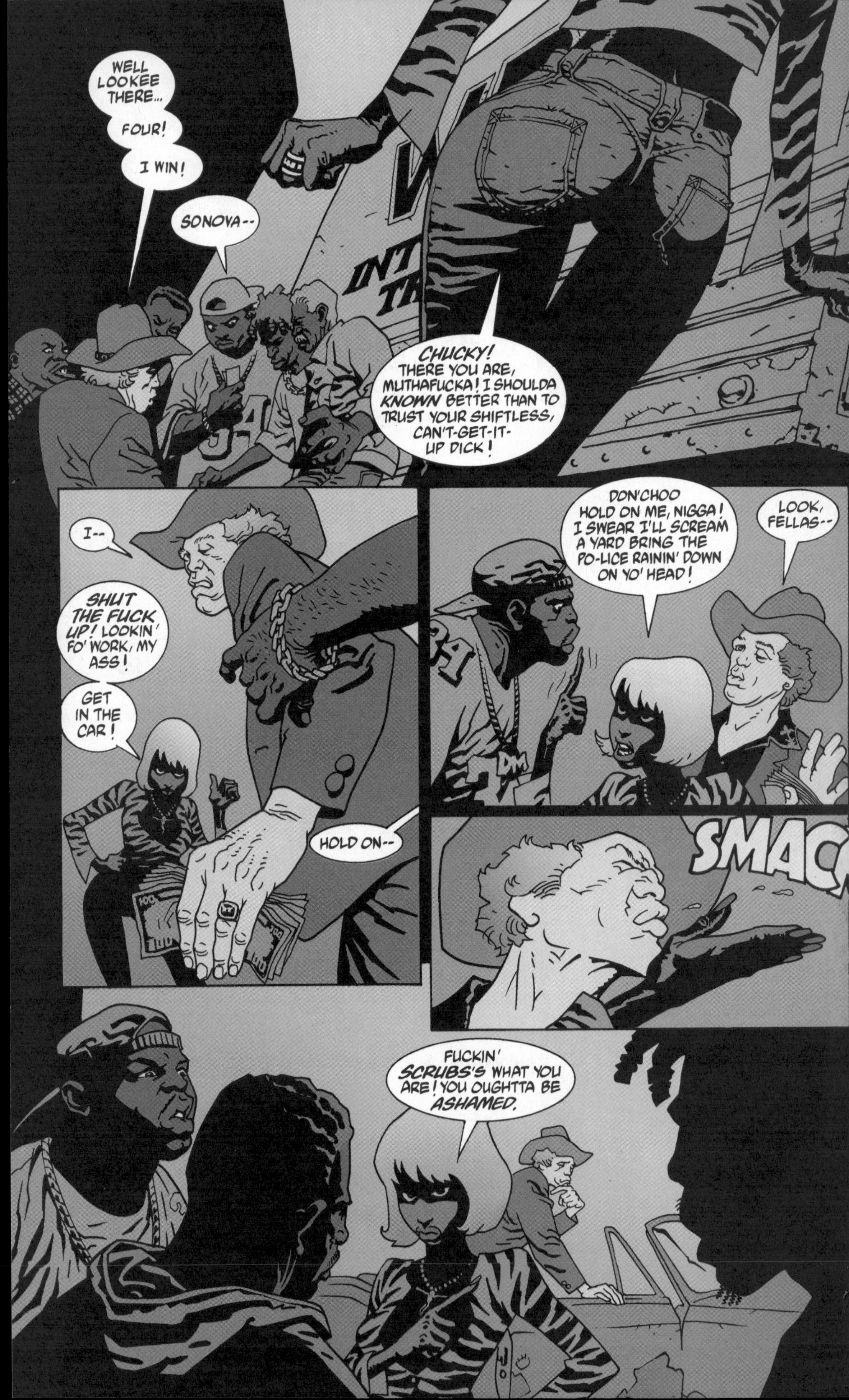
WELL LOOKEE THERE...
FOUR!
I WIN!
SONOVA--
CHUCKY! THERE YOU ARE, MUTHAFUCKA! I SHOULDA KNOWN BETTER THAN TO TRUST YOUR SHIFTLESS, CAN'T-GET-IT-UP DICK!
I--
SHUT THE FUCK UP! LOOKIN' FO' WORK, MY ASS!
GET IN THE CAR!
HOLD ON--
DON'CHOO HOLD ON ME, NIGGA! I SWEAR I'LL SCREAM A YARD BRING THE PO-LICE RAININ' DOWN ON YO' HEAD!
LOOK, FELLAS--
SMAC
FUCKIN' SCRUBS'S WHAT YOU ARE! YOU OUGHTTA BE ASHAMED.

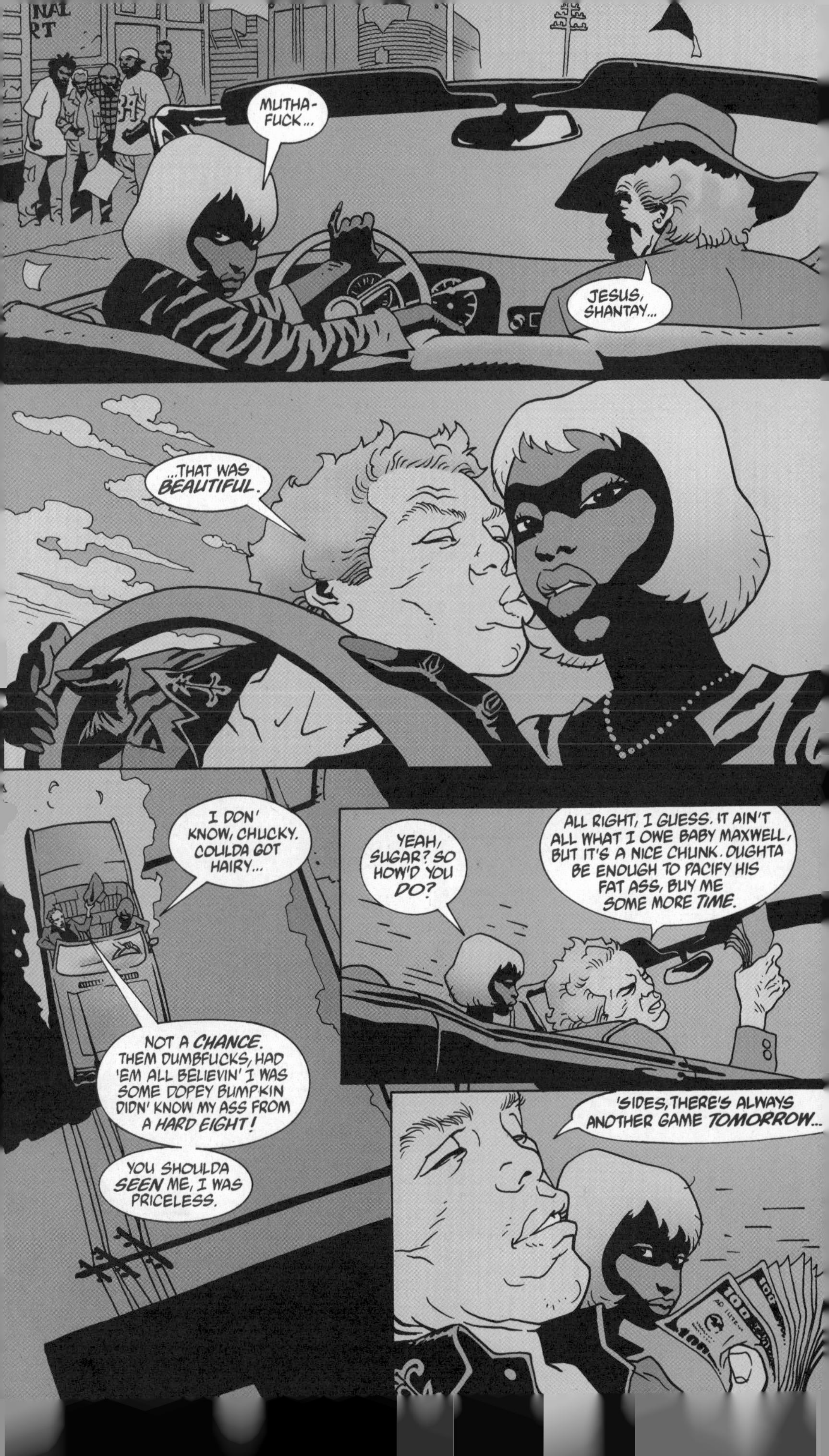
MUTHA-FUCK...
JESUS, SHANTAY...
...THAT WAS BEAUTIFUL.
I DON' KNOW, CHUCKY. COULDA GOT HAIRY...
NOT A CHANCE. THEM DUMBFUCKS, HAD 'EM ALL BELIEVIN' I WAS SOME DOPEY BUMPKIN DIDN' KNOW MY ASS FROM A HARD EIGHT!
YOU SHOULDA SEEN ME, I WAS PRICELESS.
YEAH, SUGAR? SO HOW'D YOU DO?
ALL RIGHT, I GUESS. IT AIN'T ALL WHAT I OWE BABY MAXWELL, BUT IT'S A NICE CHUNK. OUGHTA BE ENOUGH TO PACIFY HIS FAT ASS, BUY ME SOME MORE TIME.
'SIDES, THERE'S ALWAYS ANOTHER GAME TOMORROW...

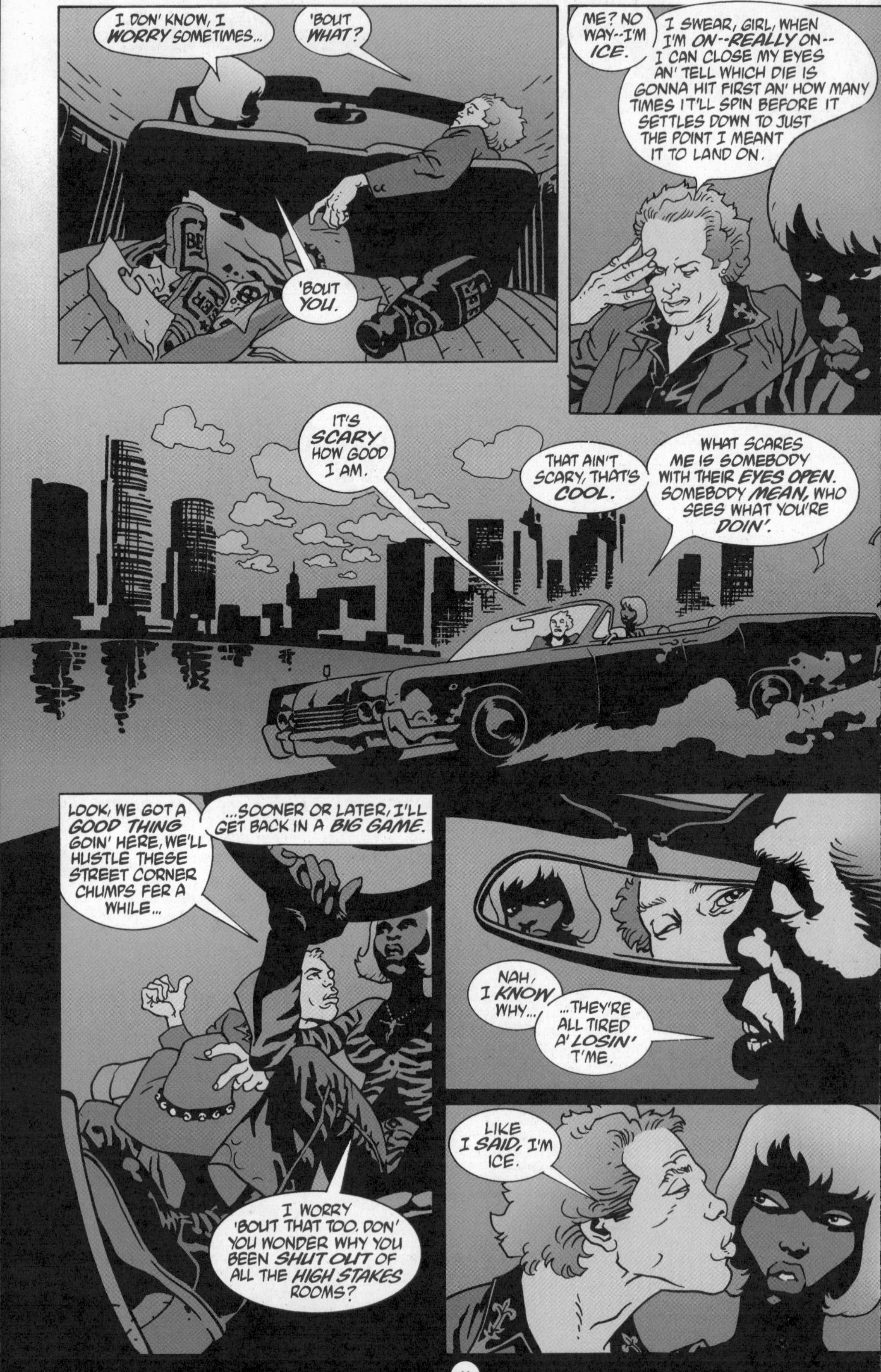
I DON' KNOW, I WORRY SOMETIMES...
'BOUT WHAT?
'BOUT YOU.
ME? NO WAY--I'M ICE.
I SWEAR, GIRL, WHEN I'M ON--REALLY ON--I CAN CLOSE MY EYES AN' TELL WHICH DIE IS GONNA HIT FIRST AN' HOW MANY TIMES IT'LL SPIN BEFORE IT SETTLES DOWN TO JUST THE POINT I MEANT IT TO LAND ON.
IT'S SCARY HOW GOOD I AM.
THAT AIN'T SCARY, THAT'S COOL.
WHAT SCARES ME IS SOMEBODY WITH THEIR EYES OPEN. SOMEBODY MEAN, WHO SEES WHAT YOU'RE DOIN'.
LOOK, WE GOT A GOOD THING GOIN' HERE, WE'LL HUSTLE THESE STREET CORNER CHUMPS FER A WHILE...
...SOONER OR LATER, I'LL GET BACK IN A BIG GAME.
I WORRY 'BOUT THAT TOO. DON' YOU WONDER WHY YOU BEEN SHUT OUT OF ALL THE HIGH STAKES ROOMS?
NAH, I KNOW WHY...
...THEY'RE ALL TIRED A' LOSIN' T'ME.
LIKE I SAID, I'M ICE.

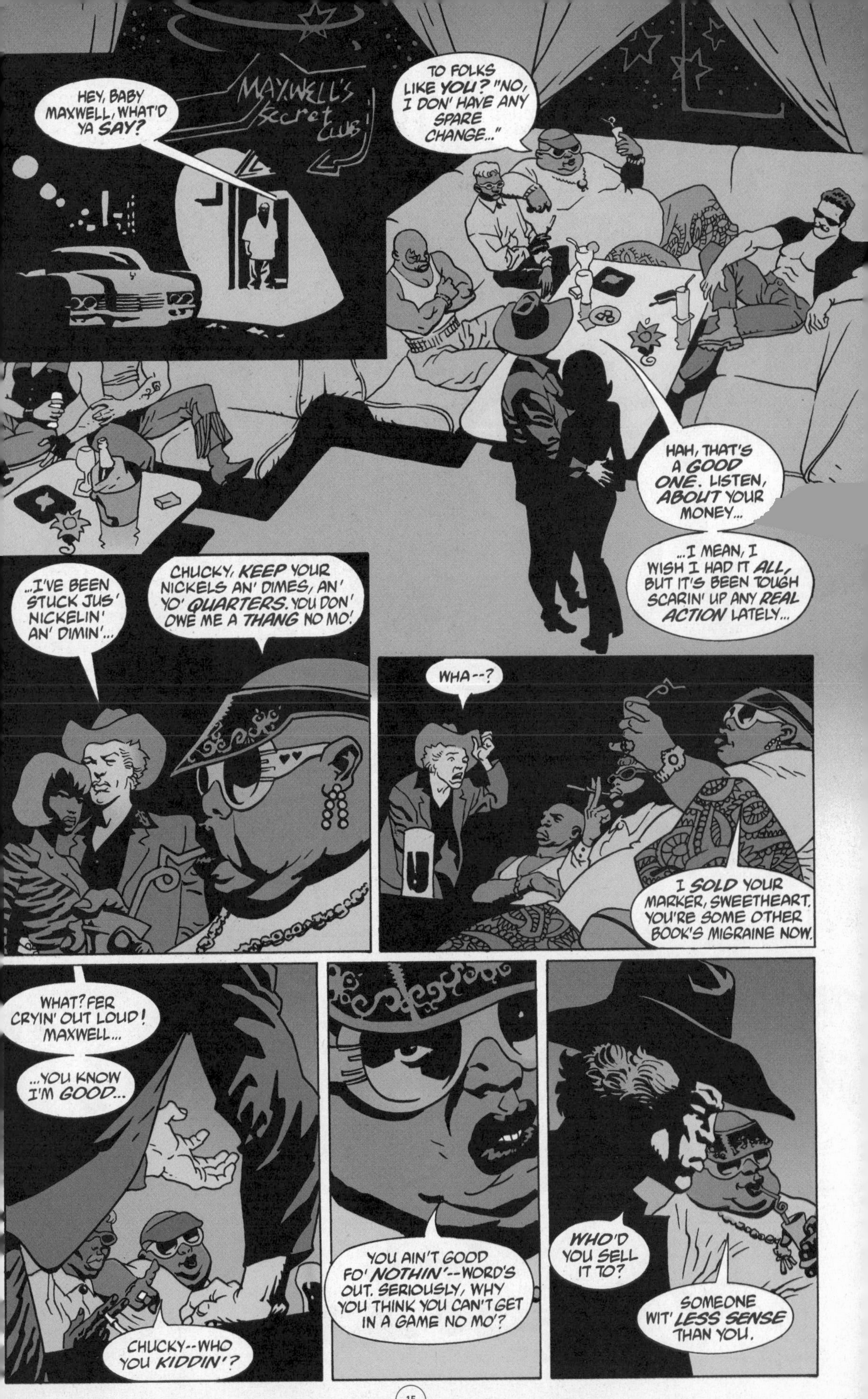
MAXWELL'S secret CLUB
HEY, BABY MAXWELL, WHAT'D YA SAY?
TO FOLKS LIKE YOU? "NO, I DON' HAVE ANY SPARE CHANGE..."
HAH, THAT'S A GOOD ONE. LISTEN, ABOUT YOUR MONEY...
...I MEAN, I WISH I HAD IT ALL, BUT IT'S BEEN TOUGH SCARIN' UP ANY REAL ACTION LATELY...
...I'VE BEEN STUCK JUS' NICKELIN' AN' DIMIN'...
CHUCKY, KEEP YOUR NICKELS AN' DIMES, AN' YO' QUARTERS. YOU DON' OWE ME A THANG NO MO'.
WHA--?
I SOLD YOUR MARKER, SWEETHEART. YOU'RE SOME OTHER BOOK'S MIGRAINE NOW.
WHAT? FER CRYIN' OUT LOUD! MAXWELL...
...YOU KNOW I'M GOOD...
CHUCKY--WHO YOU KIDDIN'?
YOU AIN'T GOOD FO' NOTHIN'--WORD'S OUT. SERIOUSLY, WHY YOU THINK YOU CAN'T GET IN A GAME NO MO'?
WHO'D YOU SELL IT TO?
SOMEONE WIT' LESS SENSE THAN YOU.

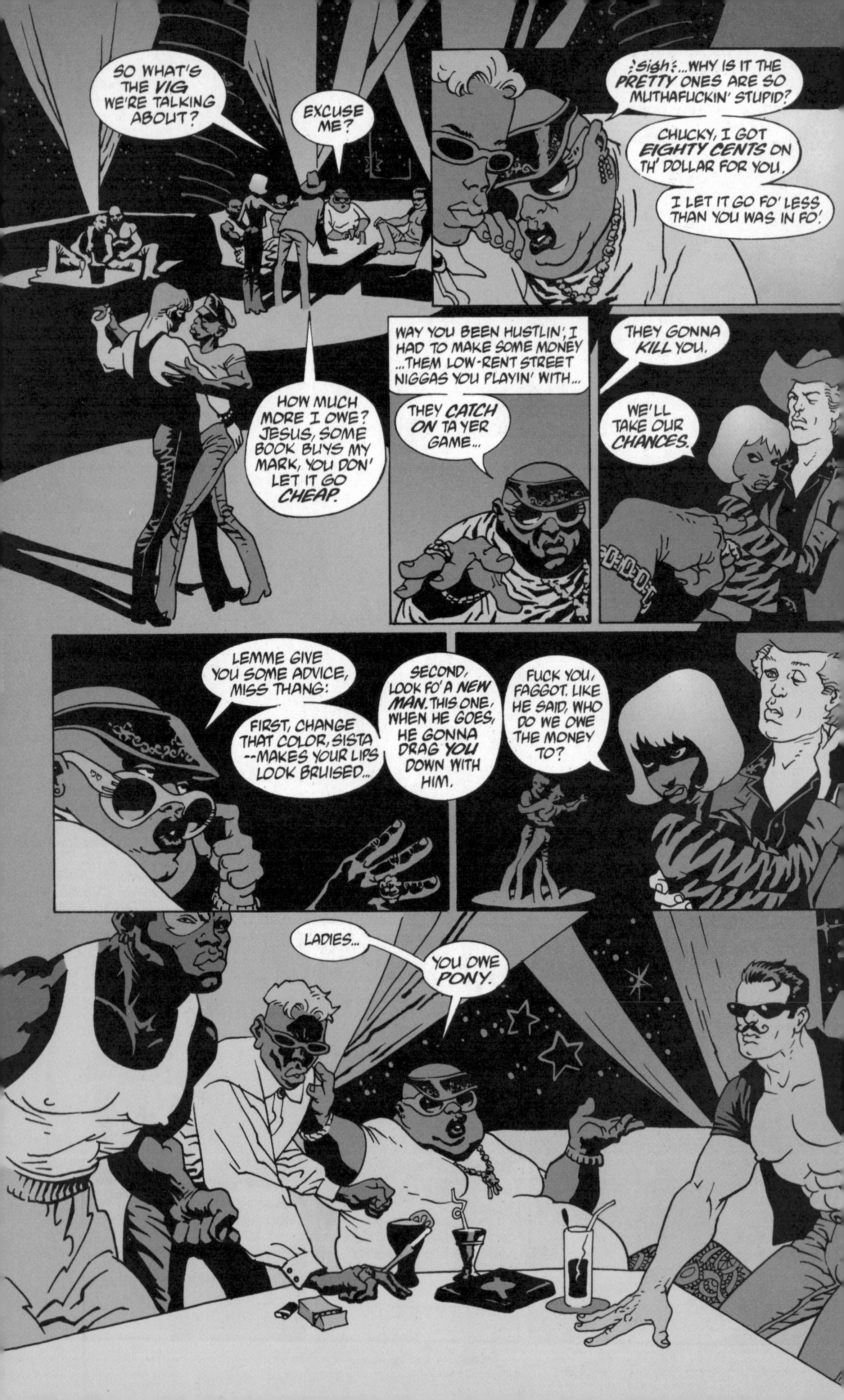
SO WHAT'S THE VIG WE'RE TALKING ABOUT?
EXCUSE ME?
:Sigh:...WHY IS IT THE PRETTY ONES ARE SO MUTHAFUCKIN' STUPID?
CHUCKY, I GOT EIGHTY CENTS ON TH' DOLLAR FOR YOU.
I LET IT GO FO' LESS THAN YOU WAS IN FO'.
HOW MUCH MORE I OWE? JESUS, SOME BOOK BUYS MY MARK, YOU DON' LET IT GO CHEAP.
WAY YOU BEEN HUSTLIN', I HAD TO MAKE SOME MONEY ...THEM LOW-RENT STREET NIGGAS YOU PLAYIN' WITH...
THEY CATCH ON TA YER GAME...
THEY GONNA KILL YOU.
WE'LL TAKE OUR CHANCES.
LEMME GIVE YOU SOME ADVICE, MISS THANG:
FIRST, CHANGE THAT COLOR, SISTA --MAKES YOUR LIPS LOOK BRUISED...
SECOND, LOOK FO' A NEW MAN. THIS ONE, WHEN HE GOES, HE GONNA DRAG YOU DOWN WITH HIM.
FUCK YOU, FAGGOT. LIKE HE SAID, WHO DO WE OWE THE MONEY TO?
LADIES...
YOU OWE PONY.

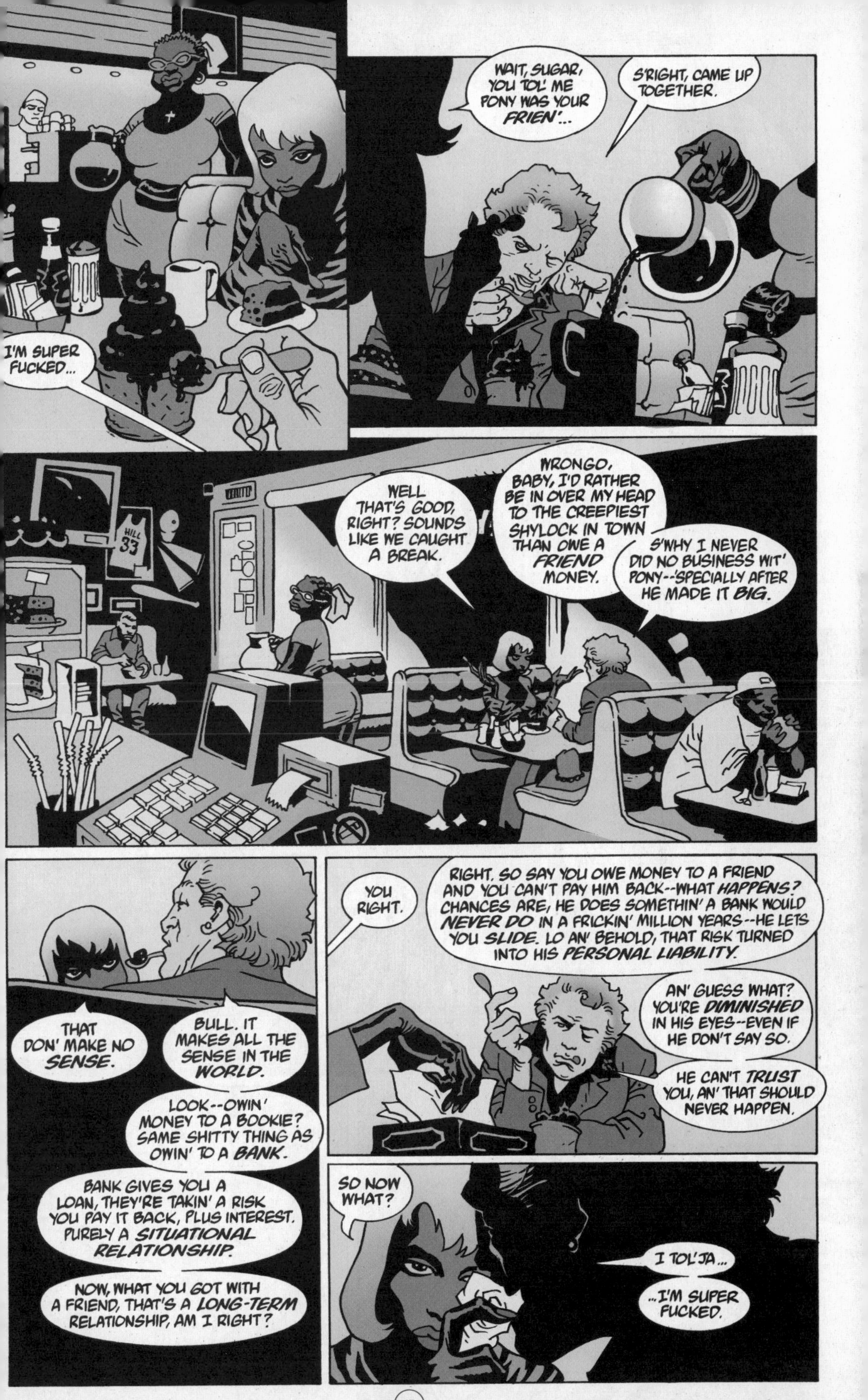
I'M SUPER FUCKED...
WAIT, SUGAR, YOU TOL' ME PONY WAS YOUR FRIEN'...
S'RIGHT, CAME UP TOGETHER.
WELL THAT'S GOOD, RIGHT? SOUNDS LIKE WE CAUGHT A BREAK.
WRONGO, BABY, I'D RATHER BE IN OVER MY HEAD TO THE CREEPIEST SHYLOCK IN TOWN THAN OWE A FRIEND MONEY.
S'WHY I NEVER DID NO BUSINESS WIT' PONY--'SPECIALLY AFTER HE MADE IT BIG.
HILL 33
THAT DON' MAKE NO SENSE.
BULL. IT MAKES ALL THE SENSE IN THE WORLD.
LOOK--OWIN' MONEY TO A BOOKIE? SAME SHITTY THING AS OWIN' TO A BANK.
BANK GIVES YOU A LOAN, THEY'RE TAKIN' A RISK YOU PAY IT BACK, PLUS INTEREST. PURELY A SITUATIONAL RELATIONSHIP.
NOW, WHAT YOU GOT WITH A FRIEND, THAT'S A LONG-TERM RELATIONSHIP, AM I RIGHT?
YOU RIGHT.
RIGHT. SO SAY YOU OWE MONEY TO A FRIEND AND YOU CAN'T PAY HIM BACK--WHAT HAPPENS? CHANCES ARE, HE DOES SOMETHIN' A BANK WOULD NEVER DO IN A FRICKIN' MILLION YEARS--HE LETS YOU SLIDE. LO AN' BEHOLD, THAT RISK TURNED INTO HIS PERSONAL LIABILITY.
AN' GUESS WHAT? YOU'RE DIMINISHED IN HIS EYES--EVEN IF HE DON'T SAY SO.
HE CAN'T TRUST YOU, AN' THAT SHOULD NEVER HAPPEN.
SO NOW WHAT?
I TOL'JA...
...I'M SUPER FUCKED.

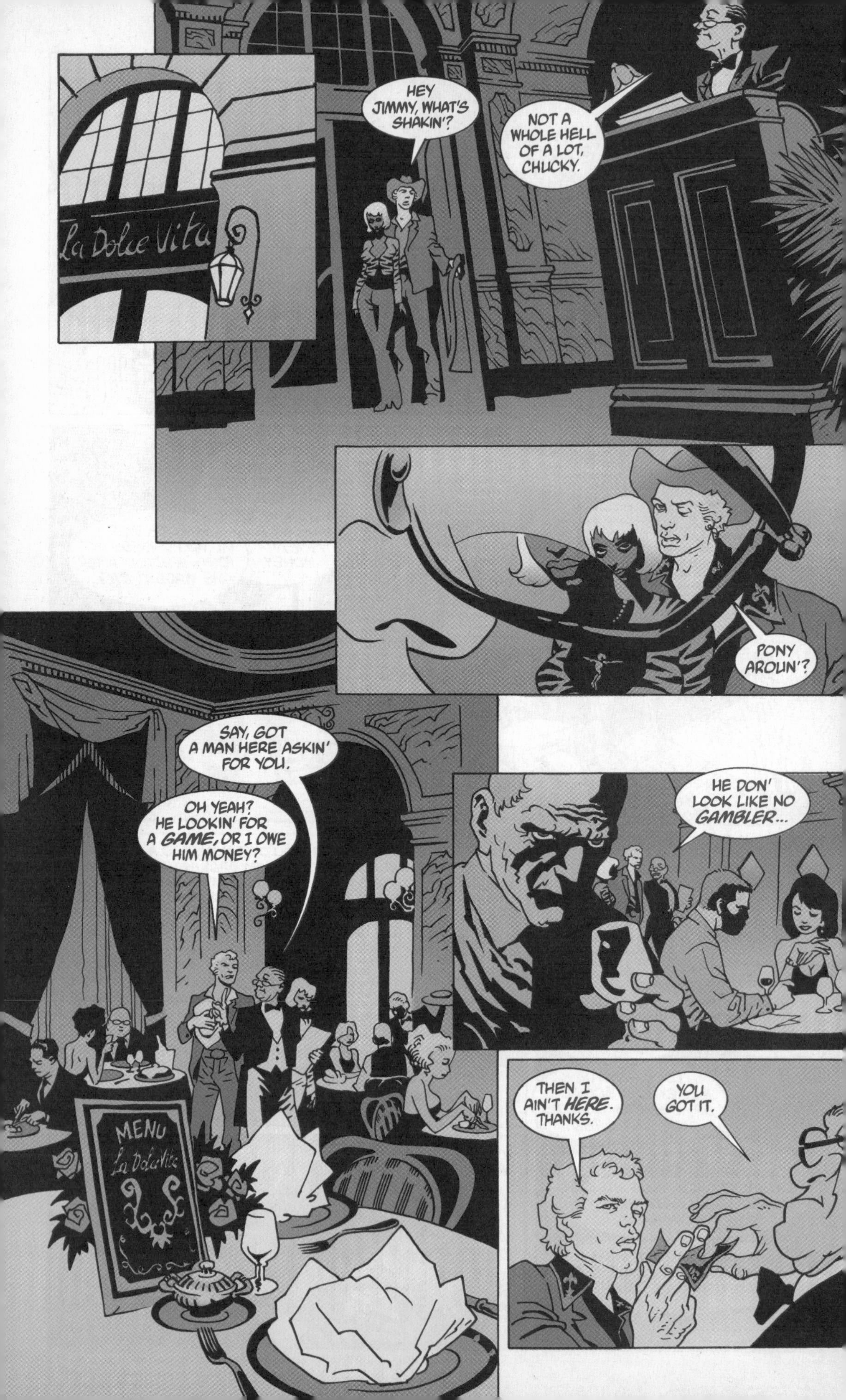
La Dolce Vita
HEY JIMMY, WHAT'S SHAKIN'?
NOT A WHOLE HELL OF A LOT, CHUCKY.
PONY AROUN'?
SAY, GOT A MAN HERE ASKIN' FOR YOU.
OH YEAH? HE LOOKIN' FOR A GAME, OR I OWE HIM MONEY?
HE DON' LOOK LIKE NO GAMBLER...
MENU
La Dolce Vita
THEN I AIN'T HERE. THANKS.
YOU GOT IT.

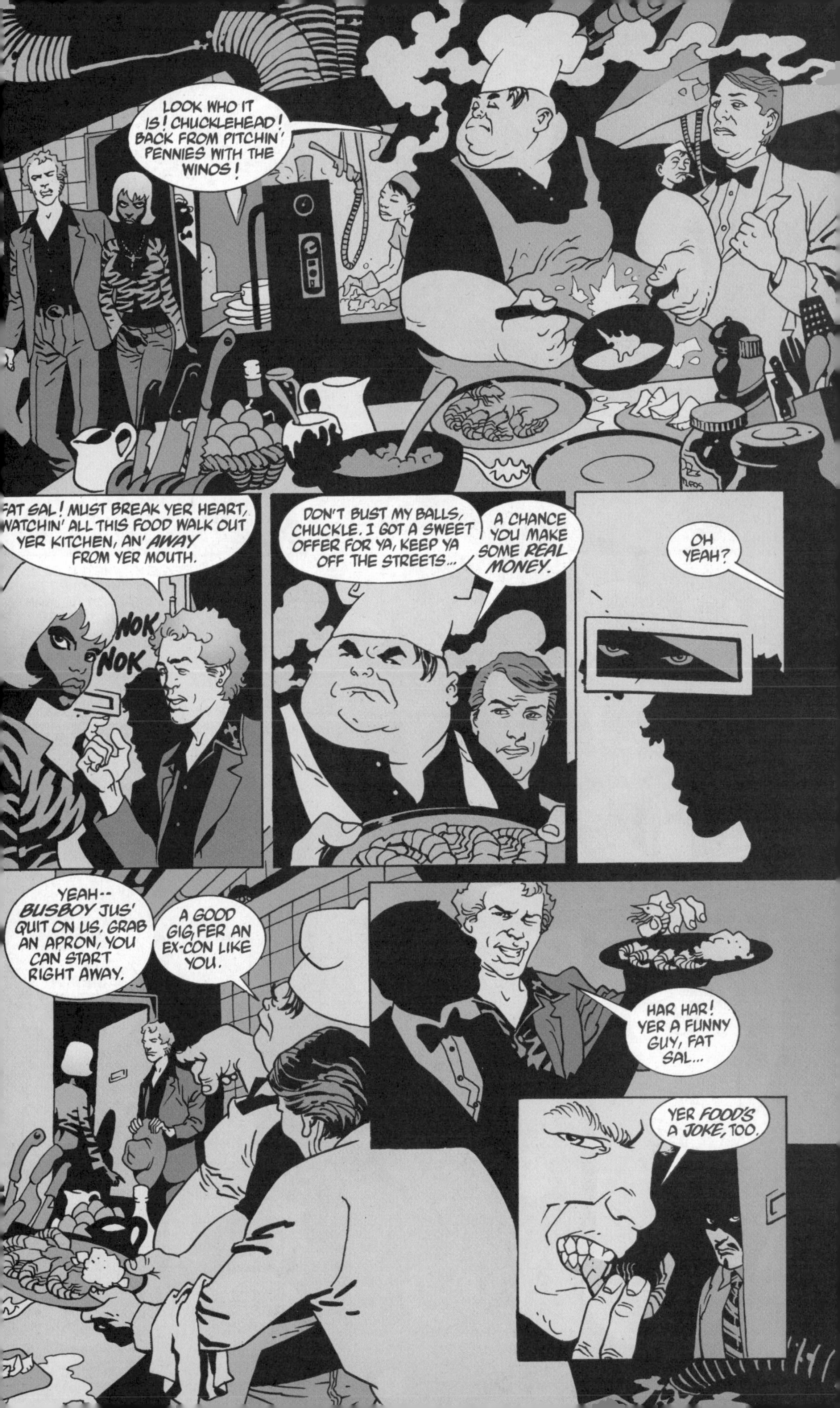
LOOK WHO IT IS! CHUCKLEHEAD! BACK FROM PITCHIN' PENNIES WITH THE WINOS!
FAT SAL! MUST BREAK YER HEART, WATCHIN' ALL THIS FOOD WALK OUT YER KITCHEN, AN' AWAY FROM YER MOUTH.
NOK NOK
DON'T BUST MY BALLS, CHUCKLE. I GOT A SWEET OFFER FOR YA, KEEP YA OFF THE STREETS...
A CHANCE YOU MAKE SOME REAL MONEY.
OH YEAH?
YEAH-- BUSBOY JUS' QUIT ON US. GRAB AN APRON, YOU CAN START RIGHT AWAY.
A GOOD GIG, FER AN EX-CON LIKE YOU.
HAR HAR! YER A FUNNY GUY, FAT SAL...
YER FOOD'S A JOKE, TOO.

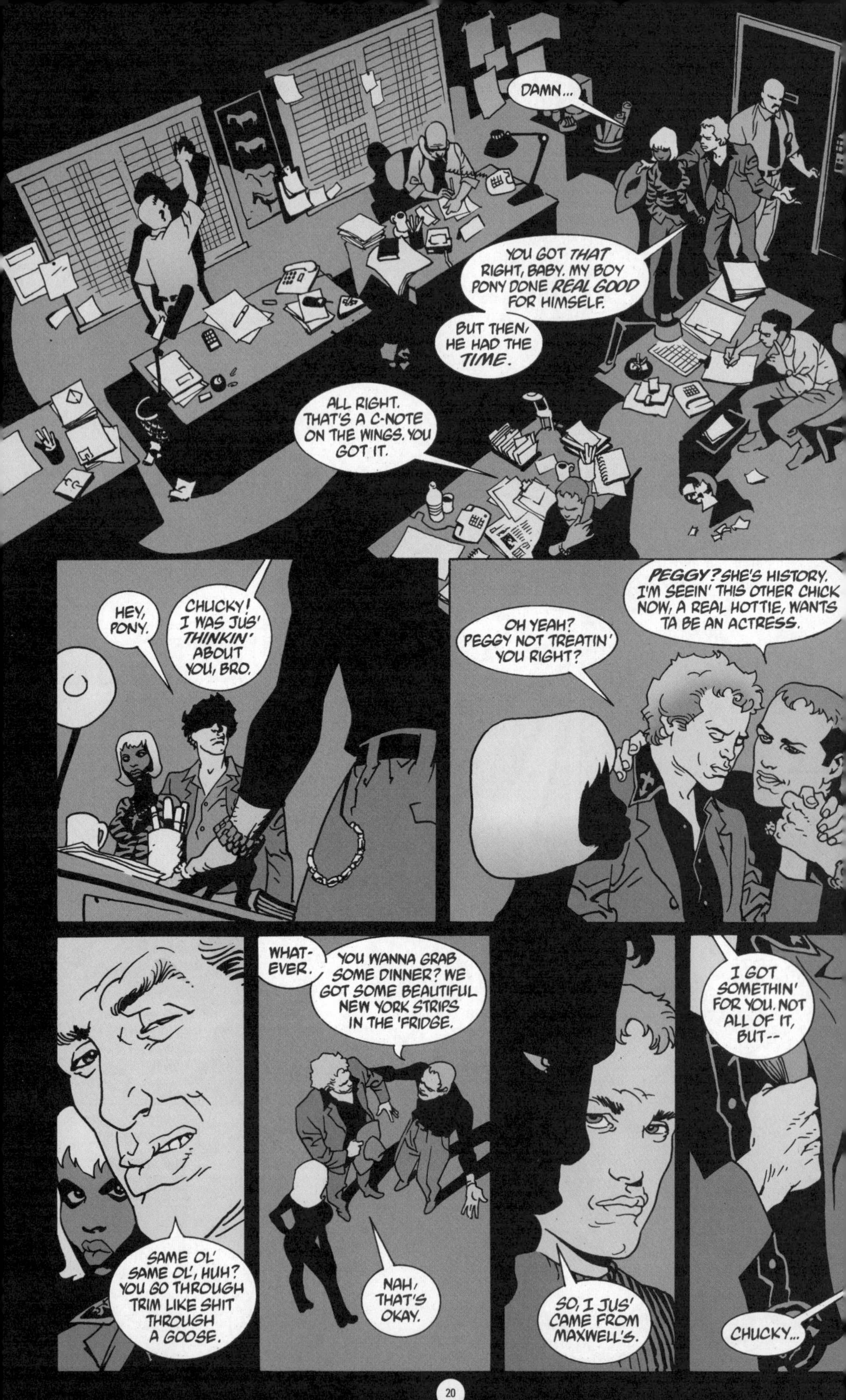
DAMN...
YOU GOT THAT RIGHT, BABY. MY BOY PONY DONE REAL GOOD FOR HIMSELF.
BUT THEN, HE HAD THE TIME.
ALL RIGHT. THAT'S A C-NOTE ON THE WINGS. YOU GOT IT.
HEY, PONY.
CHUCKY! I WAS JUS' THINKIN' ABOUT YOU, BRO.
OH YEAH? PEGGY NOT TREATIN' YOU RIGHT?
PEGGY? SHE'S HISTORY. I'M SEEIN' THIS OTHER CHICK NOW, A REAL HOTTIE, WANTS TA BE AN ACTRESS.
SAME OL' SAME OL', HUH? YOU GO THROUGH TRIM LIKE SHIT THROUGH A GOOSE.
WHAT-EVER.
YOU WANNA GRAB SOME DINNER? WE GOT SOME BEAUTIFUL NEW YORK STRIPS IN THE 'FRIDGE.
NAH, THAT'S OKAY.
SO, I JUS' CAME FROM MAXWELL'S.
I GOT SOMETHIN' FOR YOU. NOT ALL OF IT, BUT--
CHUCKY...

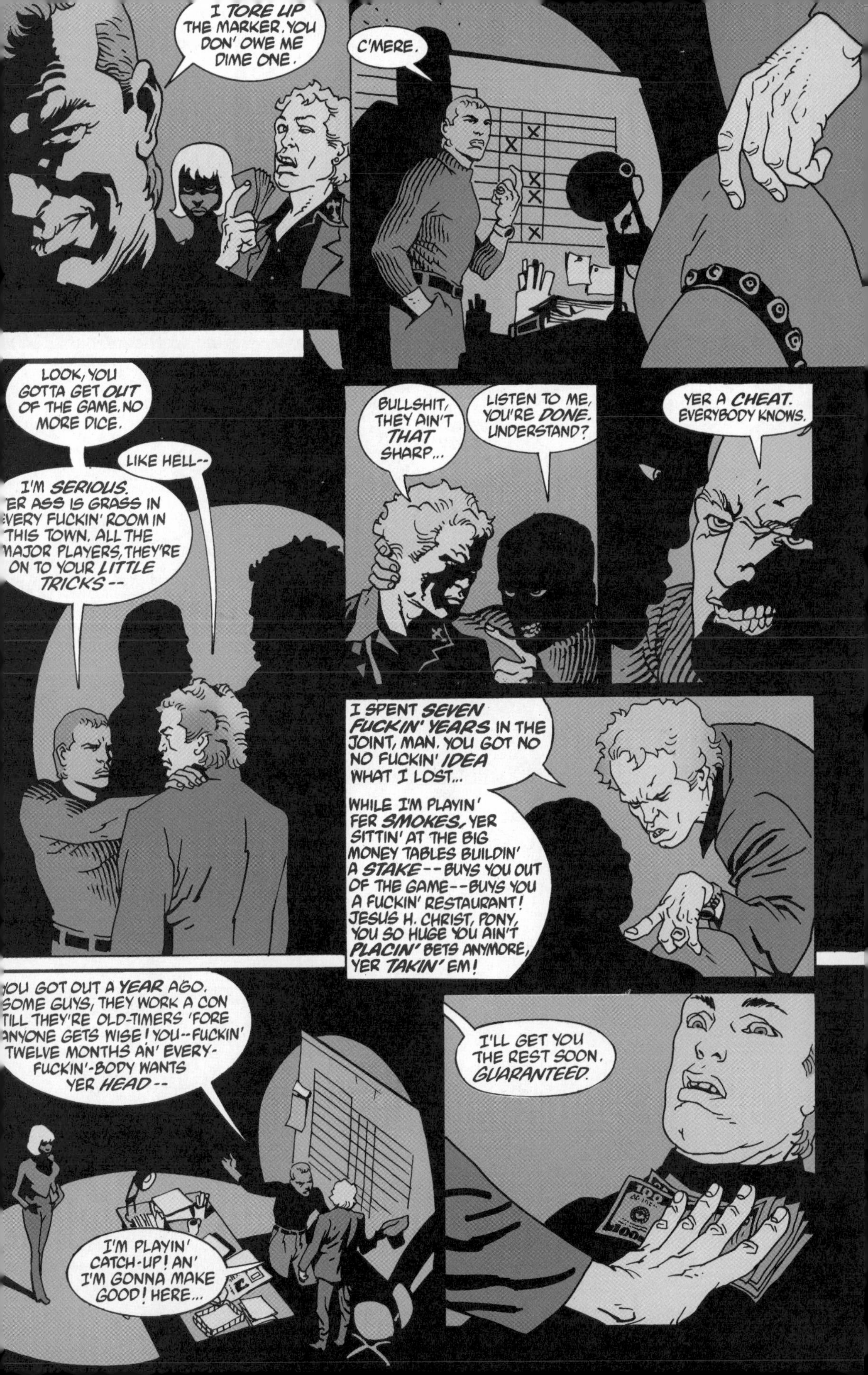
I TORE UP THE MARKER. YOU DON' OWE ME DIME ONE.
C'MERE.
LOOK, YOU GOTTA GET OUT OF THE GAME. NO MORE DICE.
LIKE HELL--
I'M SERIOUS. YER ASS IS GRASS IN EVERY FUCKIN' ROOM IN THIS TOWN. ALL THE MAJOR PLAYERS, THEY'RE ON TO YOUR LITTLE TRICKS--
BULLSHIT, THEY AIN'T THAT SHARP...
LISTEN TO ME, YOU'RE DONE. UNDERSTAND?
YER A CHEAT. EVERYBODY KNOWS.
I SPENT SEVEN FUCKIN' YEARS IN THE JOINT, MAN. YOU GOT NO NO FUCKIN' IDEA WHAT I LOST...
WHILE I'M PLAYIN' FER SMOKES, YER SITTIN' AT THE BIG MONEY TABLES BUILDIN' A STAKE--BUYS YOU OUT OF THE GAME--BUYS YOU A FUCKIN' RESTAURANT! JESUS H. CHRIST, PONY, YOU SO HUGE YOU AIN'T PLACIN' BETS ANYMORE, YER TAKIN' EM!
YOU GOT OUT A YEAR AGO. SOME GUYS, THEY WORK A CON TILL THEY'RE OLD-TIMERS 'FORE ANYONE GETS WISE! YOU--FUCKIN' TWELVE MONTHS AN' EVERY-FUCKIN'-BODY WANTS YER HEAD--
I'M PLAYIN' CATCH-UP! AN' I'M GONNA MAKE GOOD! HERE...
I'LL GET YOU THE REST SOON. GUARANTEED.

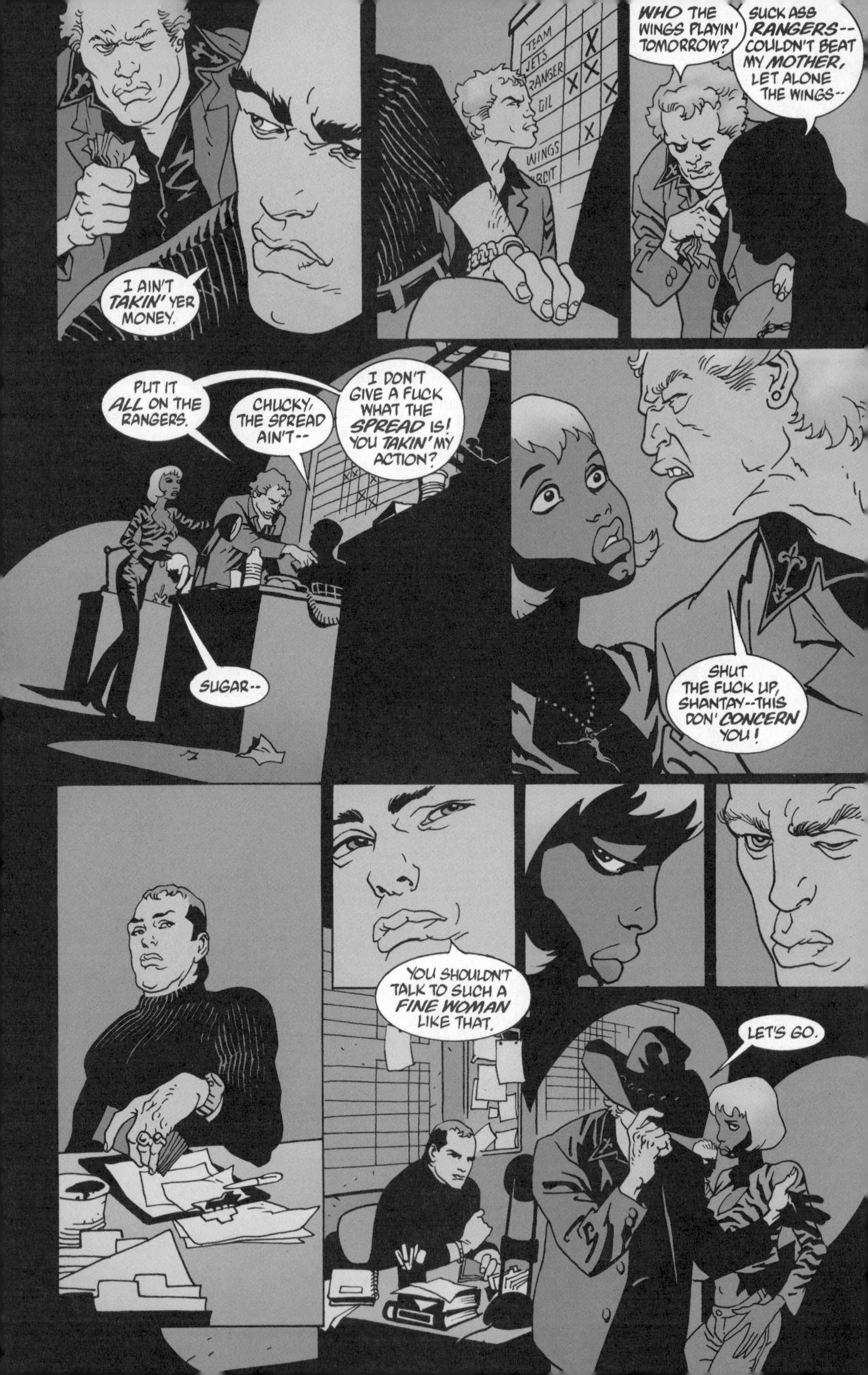
I AIN'T TAKIN' YER MONEY.
TEAM
JETS
RANGER
OIL
WINGS
WHO THE WINGS PLAYIN' TOMORROW?
SUCK ASS RANGERS-- COULDN'T BEAT MY MOTHER, LET ALONE THE WINGS--
PUT IT ALL ON THE RANGERS.
CHUCKY, THE SPREAD AIN'T--
I DON'T GIVE A FUCK WHAT THE SPREAD IS! YOU TAKIN' MY ACTION?
SUGAR--
SHUT THE FUCK UP, SHANTAY--THIS DON' CONCERN YOU!
YOU SHOULDN'T TALK TO SUCH A FINE WOMAN LIKE THAT.
LET'S GO.

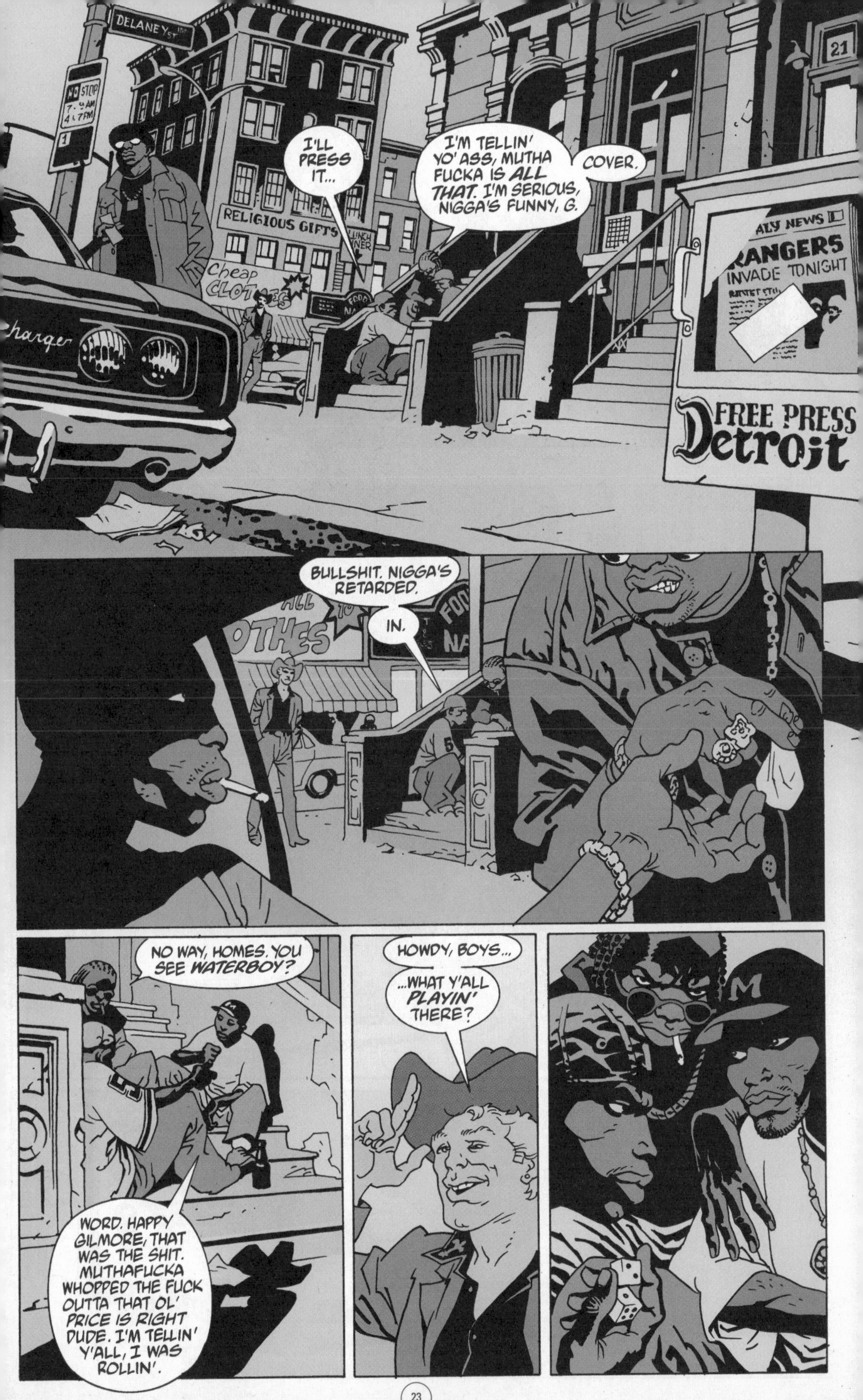

DELANEY ST
NO STOP 7-9AM 4-7PM
RELIGIOUS GIFTS
I'LL PRESS IT...
I'M TELLIN' YO' ASS, MUTHA FUCKA IS ***ALL THAT.*** I'M SERIOUS, NIGGA'S FUNNY, G.
COVER.
RANGERS INVADE TONIGHT
FREE PRESS Detroit
BULLSHIT. NIGGA'S RETARDED.
IN.
NO WAY, HOMES. YOU SEE ***WATERBOY?***
WORD. HAPPY GILMORE, THAT WAS THE SHIT. MUTHAFUCKA WHOPPED THE FUCK OUTTA THAT OL' PRICE IS RIGHT DUDE. I'M TELLIN' Y'ALL, I WAS ROLLIN'.
HOWDY, BOYS...
...WHAT Y'ALL ***PLAYIN'*** THERE?

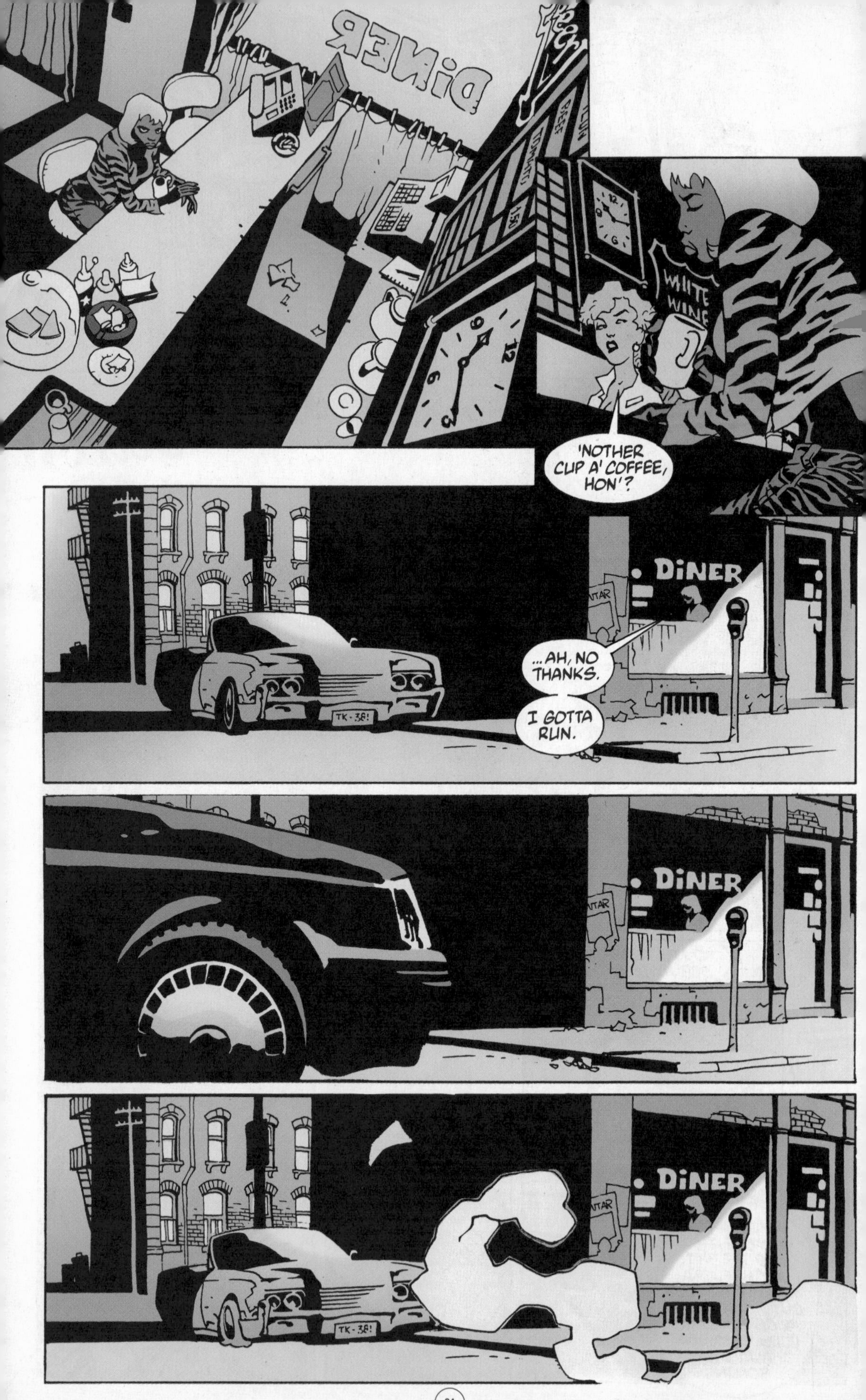
DINER
'NOTHER CUP A' COFFEE, HON'?
DINER
...AH, NO THANKS.
I GOTTA RUN.
TK-38!
DINER
DINER
TK-38!

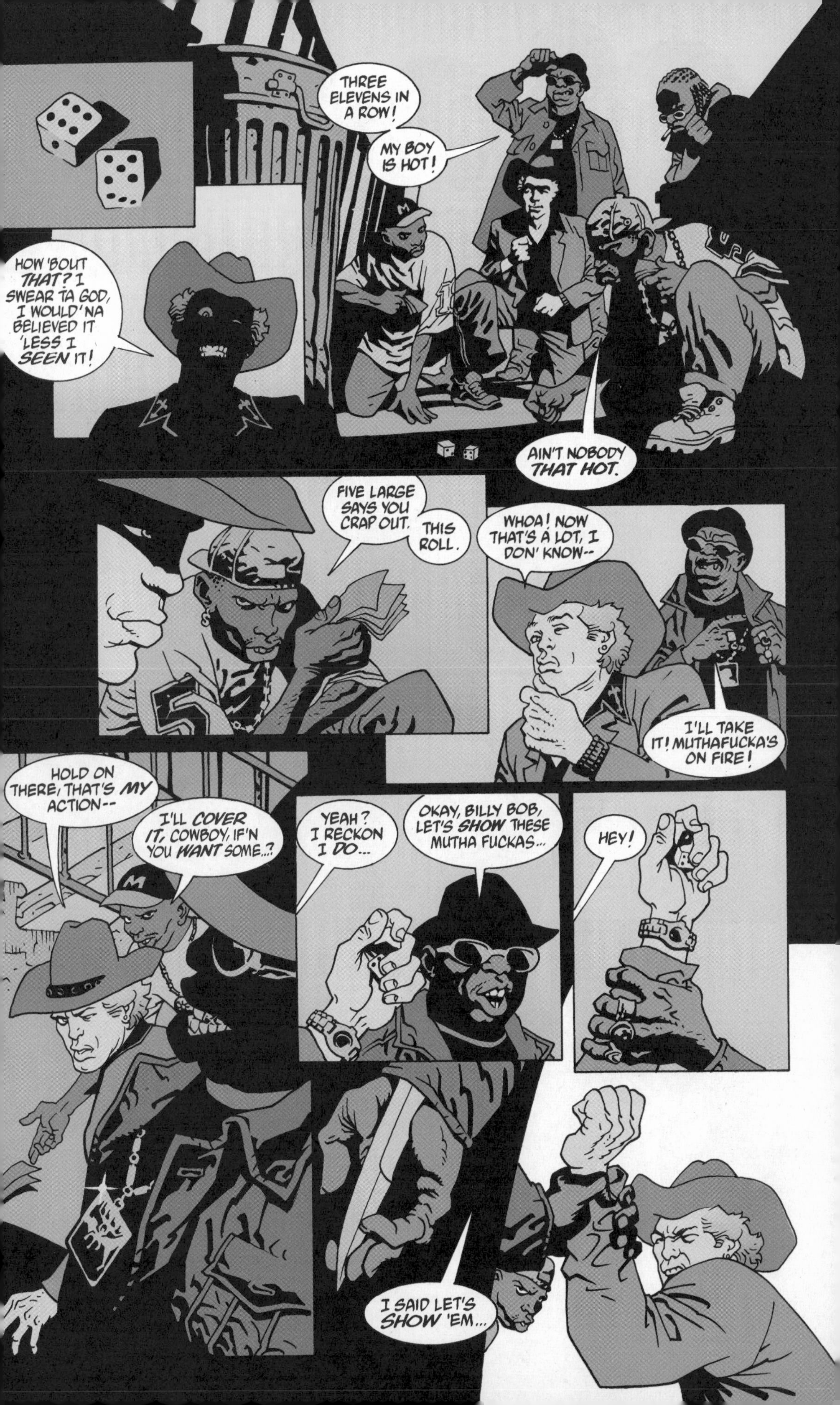

THREE ELEVENS IN A ROW!
MY BOY IS HOT!
HOW 'BOUT THAT? I SWEAR TA GOD, I WOULD'NA BELIEVED IT 'LESS I SEEN IT!
AIN'T NOBODY THAT HOT.
FIVE LARGE SAYS YOU CRAP OUT.
THIS ROLL.
WHOA! NOW THAT'S A LOT, I DON' KNOW--
I'LL TAKE IT! MUTHAFUCKA'S ON FIRE!
HOLD ON THERE, THAT'S MY ACTION--
I'LL COVER IT, COWBOY, IF'N YOU WANT SOME..?
YEAH? I RECKON I DO...
OKAY, BILLY BOB, LET'S SHOW THESE MUTHA FUCKAS...
HEY!
I SAID LET'S SHOW 'EM...

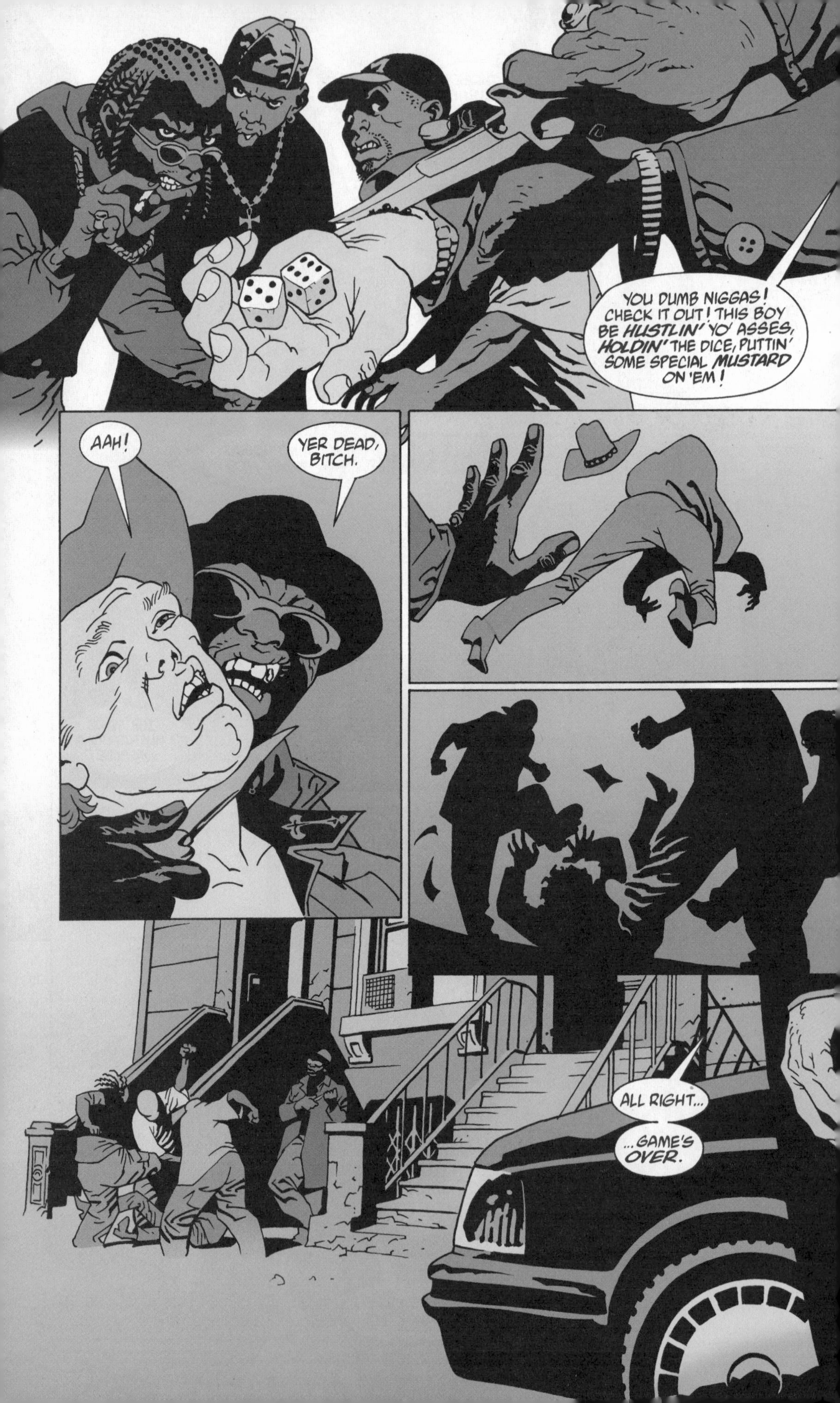
YOU DUMB NIGGAS! CHECK IT OUT! THIS BOY BE HUSTLIN' YO' ASSES, HOLDIN' THE DICE, PUTTIN' SOME SPECIAL MUSTARD ON 'EM!
AAH!
YER DEAD, BITCH.
ALL RIGHT...
...GAME'S OVER.

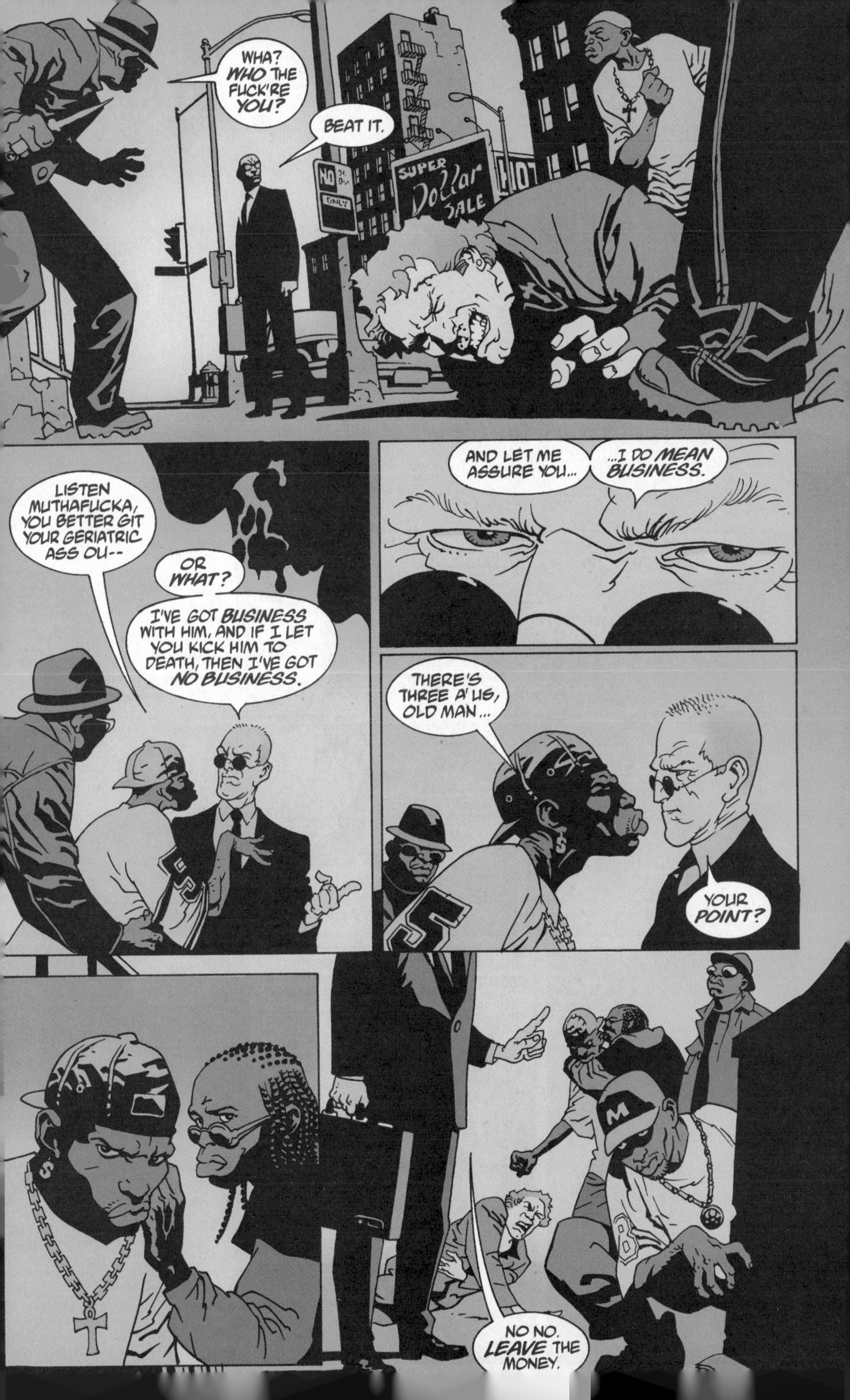
WHA? WHO THE FUCK'RE YOU?
BEAT IT.
SUPER Dollar SALE
LISTEN MUTHAFUCKA, YOU BETTER GIT YOUR GERIATRIC ASS OU--
OR WHAT?
I'VE GOT BUSINESS WITH HIM, AND IF I LET YOU KICK HIM TO DEATH, THEN I'VE GOT NO BUSINESS.
AND LET ME ASSURE YOU...
...I DO MEAN BUSINESS.
THERE'S THREE A' US, OLD MAN ...
YOUR POINT?
NO NO. LEAVE THE MONEY.

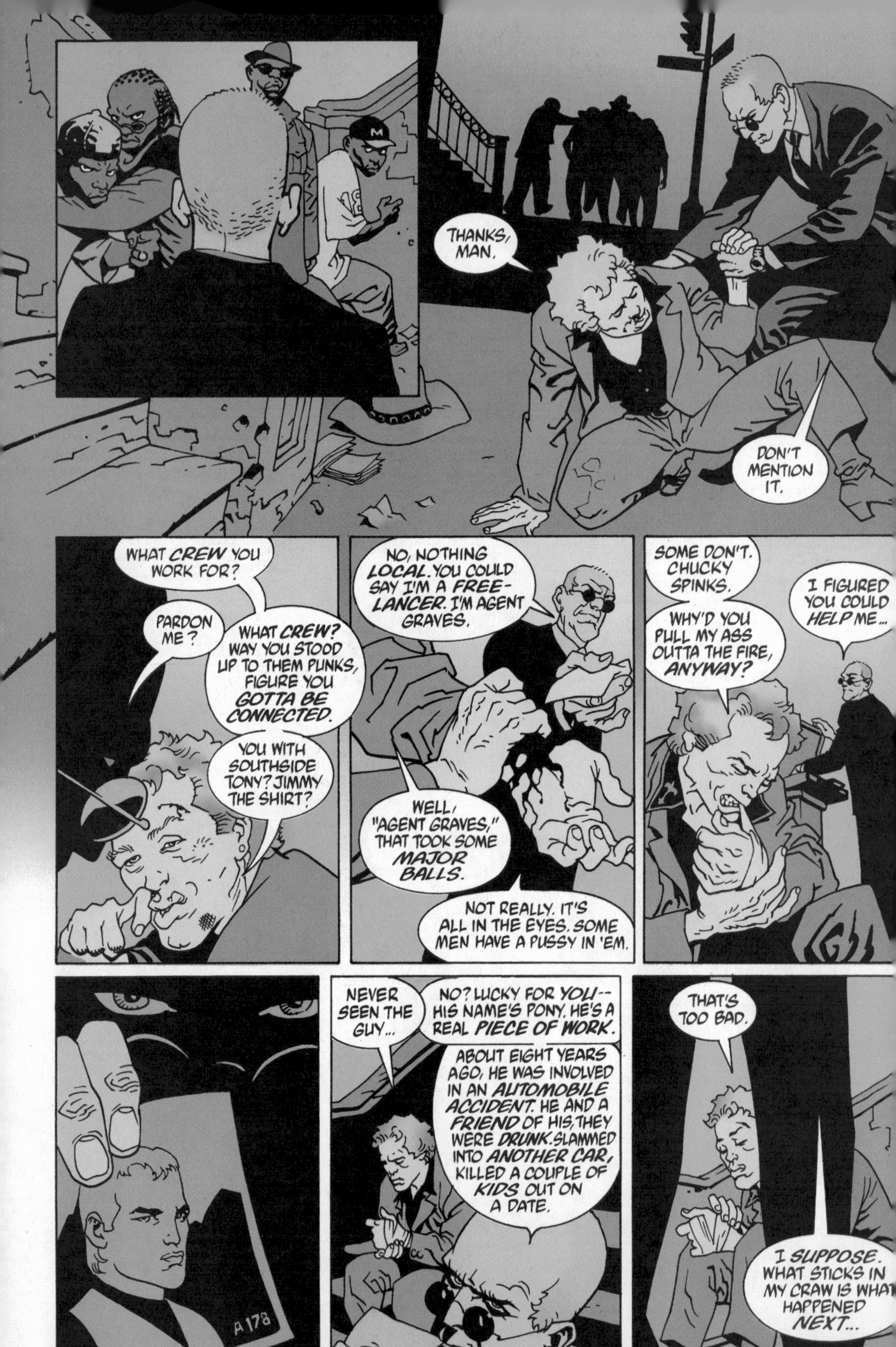
THANKS, MAN.
DON'T MENTION IT.
WHAT CREW YOU WORK FOR?
PARDON ME?
WHAT CREW? WAY YOU STOOD UP TO THEM PUNKS, FIGURE YOU GOTTA BE CONNECTED.
YOU WITH SOUTHSIDE TONY? JIMMY THE SHIRT?
NO, NOTHING LOCAL. YOU COULD SAY I'M A FREE-LANCER. I'M AGENT GRAVES.
WELL, "AGENT GRAVES," THAT TOOK SOME MAJOR BALLS.
NOT REALLY. IT'S ALL IN THE EYES. SOME MEN HAVE A PUSSY IN 'EM.
SOME DON'T. CHUCKY SPINKS.
WHY'D YOU PULL MY ASS OUTTA THE FIRE, ANYWAY?
I FIGURED YOU COULD HELP ME...
A 178
NEVER SEEN THE GUY...
NO? LUCKY FOR YOU-- HIS NAME'S PONY. HE'S A REAL PIECE OF WORK.
ABOUT EIGHT YEARS AGO, HE WAS INVOLVED IN AN AUTOMOBILE ACCIDENT. HE AND A FRIEND OF HIS, THEY WERE DRUNK. SLAMMED INTO ANOTHER CAR, KILLED A COUPLE OF KIDS OUT ON A DATE.
THAT'S TOO BAD.
I SUPPOSE. WHAT STICKS IN MY CRAW IS WHAT HAPPENED NEXT...

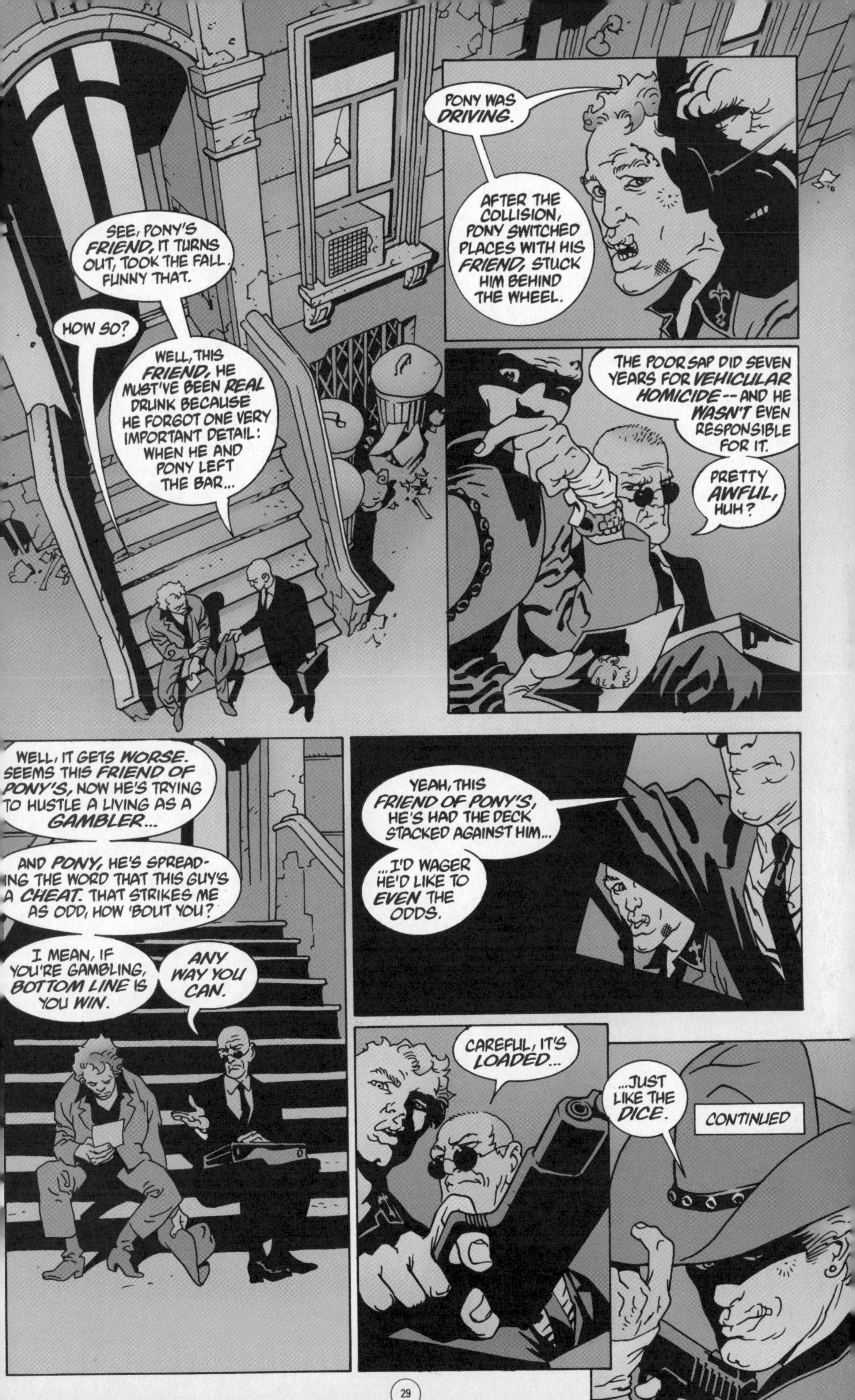
SEE, PONY'S FRIEND, IT TURNS OUT, TOOK THE FALL. FUNNY THAT.
HOW SO?
WELL, THIS FRIEND, HE MUST'VE BEEN REAL DRUNK BECAUSE HE FORGOT ONE VERY IMPORTANT DETAIL: WHEN HE AND PONY LEFT THE BAR...
PONY WAS DRIVING.
AFTER THE COLLISION, PONY SWITCHED PLACES WITH HIS FRIEND, STUCK HIM BEHIND THE WHEEL.
THE POOR SAP DID SEVEN YEARS FOR VEHICULAR HOMICIDE -- AND HE WASN'T EVEN RESPONSIBLE FOR IT.
PRETTY AWFUL, HUH?
WELL, IT GETS WORSE. SEEMS THIS FRIEND OF PONY'S, NOW HE'S TRYING TO HUSTLE A LIVING AS A GAMBLER...
AND PONY, HE'S SPREADING THE WORD THAT THIS GUY'S A CHEAT. THAT STRIKES ME AS ODD, HOW 'BOUT YOU?
I MEAN, IF YOU'RE GAMBLING, BOTTOM LINE IS YOU WIN.
ANY WAY YOU CAN.
YEAH, THIS FRIEND OF PONY'S, HE'S HAD THE DECK STACKED AGAINST HIM...
...I'D WAGER HE'D LIKE TO EVEN THE ODDS.
CAREFUL, IT'S LOADED...
...JUST LIKE THE DICE.
CONTINUED

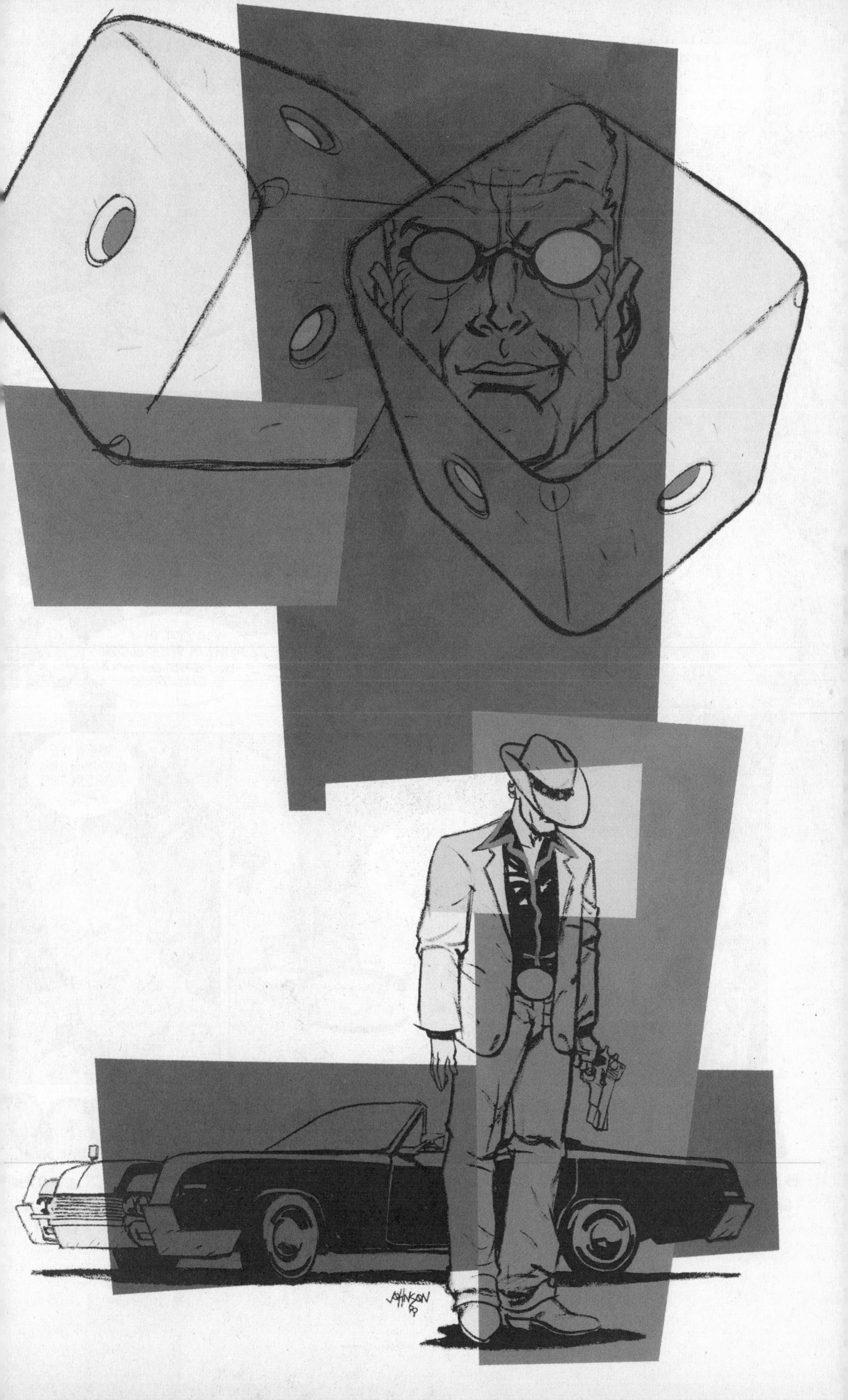
JOHNSON
99

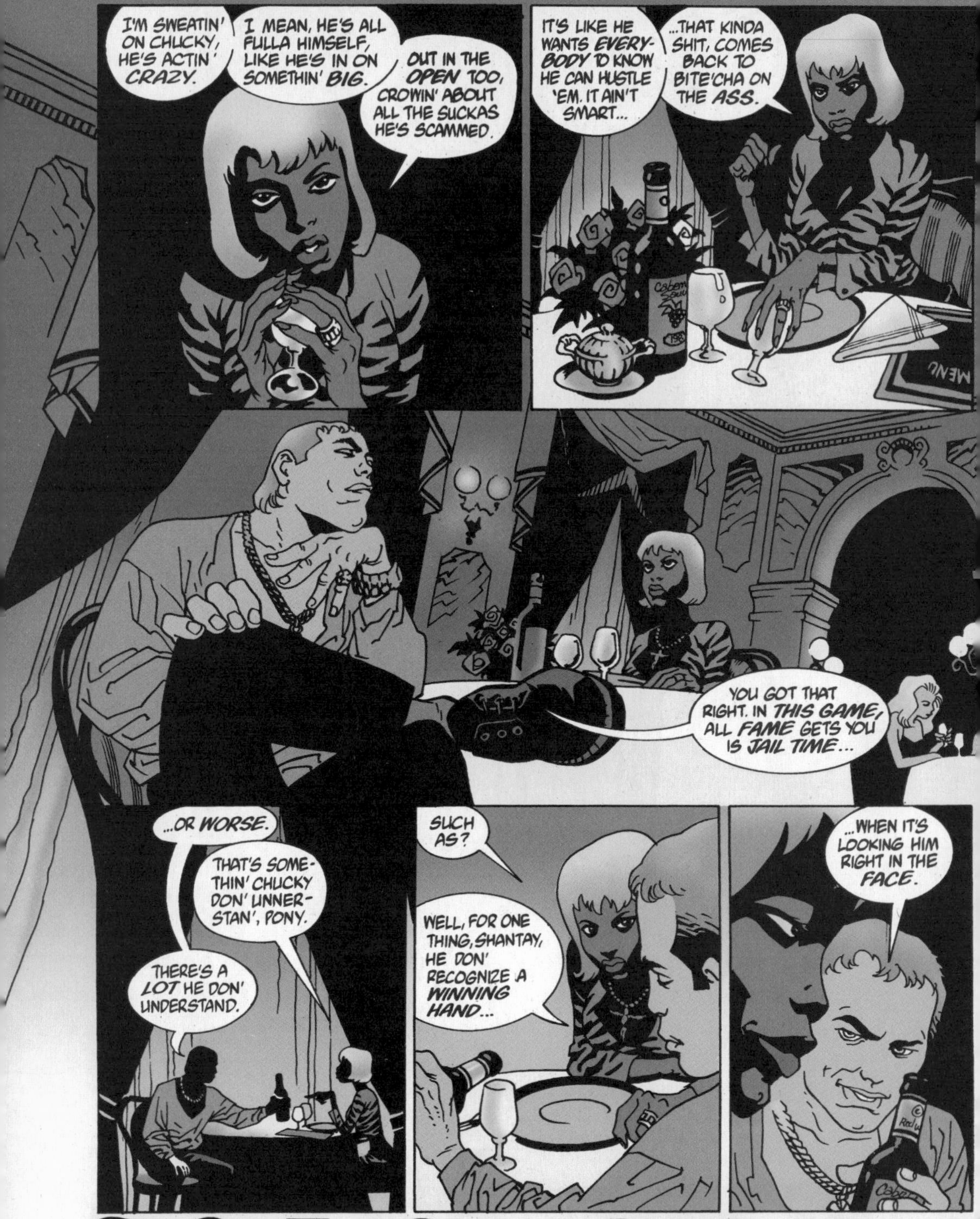
I'M SWEATIN' ON CHUCKY, HE'S ACTIN' CRAZY.
I MEAN, HE'S ALL FULLA HIMSELF, LIKE HE'S IN ON SOMETHIN' BIG.
OUT IN THE OPEN TOO, CROWIN' ABOUT ALL THE SUCKAS HE'S SCAMMED.
IT'S LIKE HE WANTS EVERY-BODY TO KNOW HE CAN HUSTLE 'EM. IT AIN'T SMART...
...THAT KINDA SHIT, COMES BACK TO BITE'CHA ON THE ASS.
YOU GOT THAT RIGHT. IN THIS GAME, ALL FAME GETS YOU IS JAIL TIME...
...OR WORSE.
THAT'S SOME-THIN' CHUCKY DON' UNNER-STAN', PONY.
THERE'S A LOT HE DON' UNDERSTAND.
SUCH AS?
WELL, FOR ONE THING, SHANTAY, HE DON' RECOGNIZE A WINNING HAND...
...WHEN IT'S LOOKING HIM RIGHT IN THE FACE.

SHORT CON, LONG ODDS

BRIAN AZZARELLO, writer **EDUARDO RISSO, artis**

GRANT GOLEASH colorist · DIGITAL CHAMELEON separations · CLEM ROBINS letters · DAVE JOHNSON cover · CLIFF CHIANG asst. editor · AXEL ALONSO editor

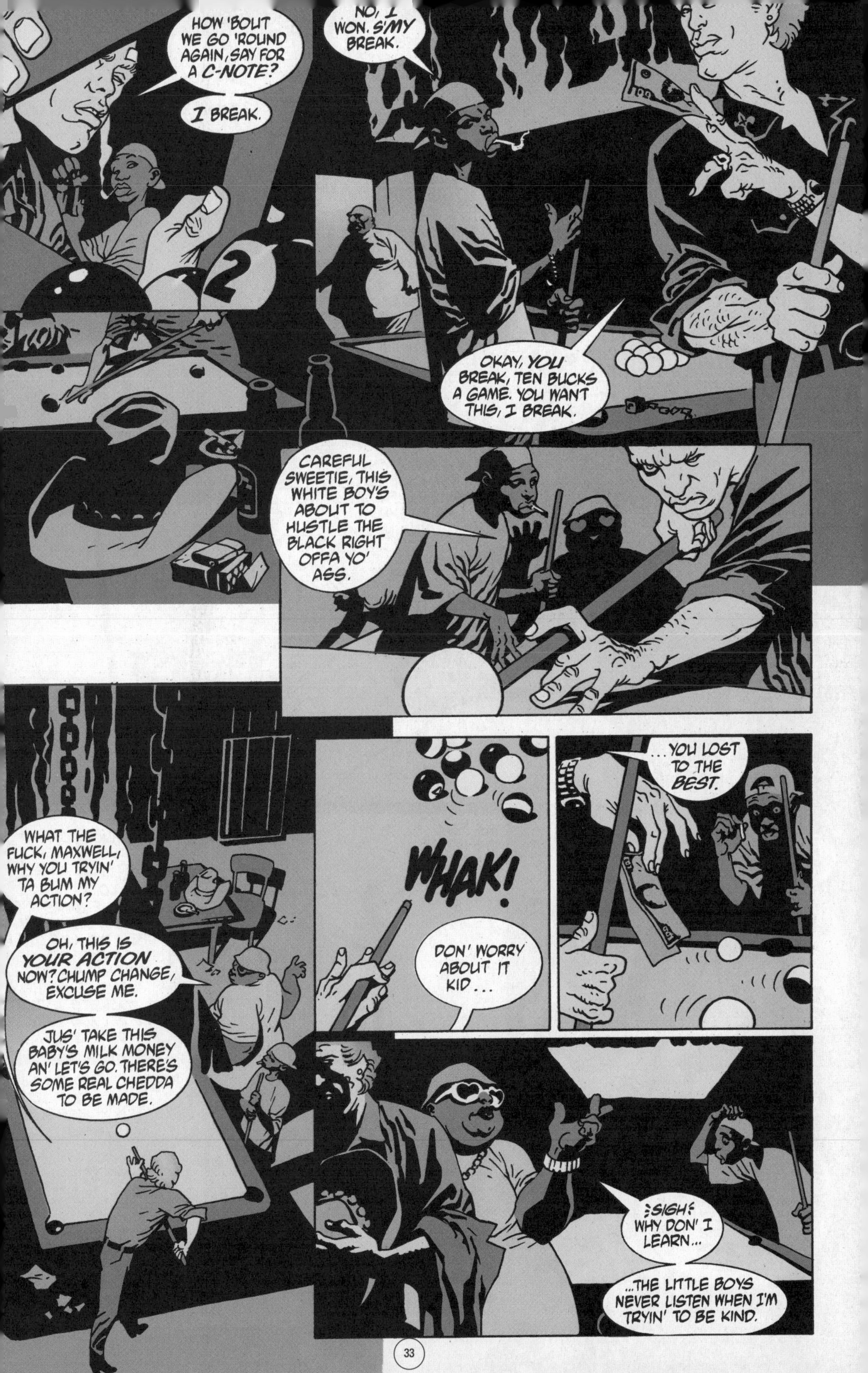
HOW 'BOUT WE GO 'ROUND AGAIN, SAY FOR A C-NOTE?
I BREAK.
NO, I WON. S'MY BREAK.
OKAY, YOU BREAK, TEN BUCKS A GAME. YOU WANT THIS, I BREAK.
CAREFUL SWEETIE, THIS WHITE BOY'S ABOUT TO HUSTLE THE BLACK RIGHT OFFA YO' ASS.
WHAT THE FUCK, MAXWELL, WHY YOU TRYIN' TA BUM MY ACTION?
OH, THIS IS YOUR ACTION NOW? CHUMP CHANGE, EXCUSE ME.
JUS' TAKE THIS BABY'S MILK MONEY AN' LET'S GO. THERE'S SOME REAL CHEDDA TO BE MADE.
WHAK!
DON' WORRY ABOUT IT KID...
...YOU LOST TO THE BEST.
SIGH WHY DON' I LEARN...
...THE LITTLE BOYS NEVER LISTEN WHEN I'M TRYIN' TO BE KIND.

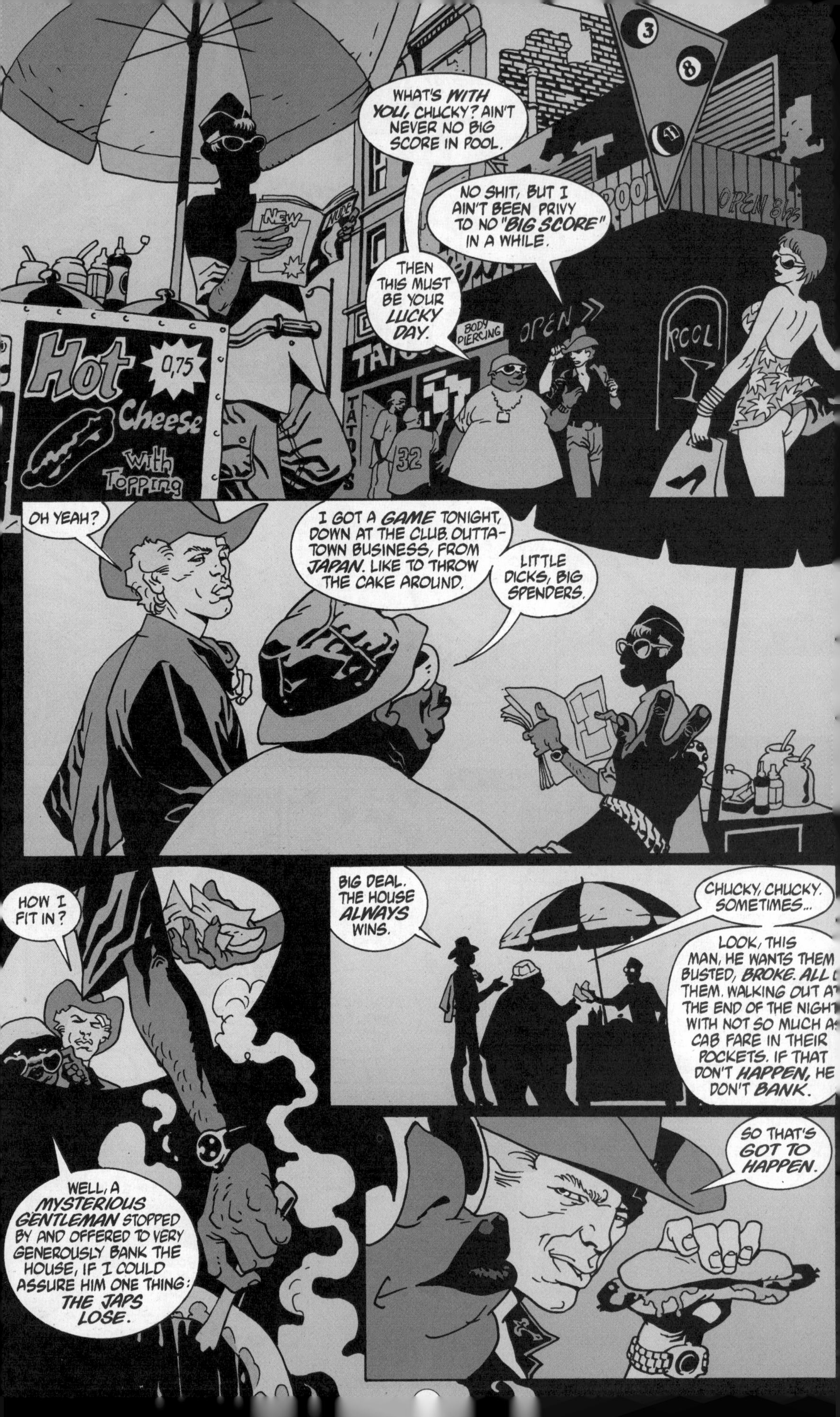
WHAT'S WITH YOU, CHUCKY? AIN'T NEVER NO BIG SCORE IN POOL.
NO SHIT, BUT I AIN'T BEEN PRIVY TO NO "BIG SCORE" IN A WHILE.
THEN THIS MUST BE YOUR LUCKY DAY.
NEW
NUDE
Hot
0,75
Cheese
With Topping
BODY PIERCING
TATOO
OPEN
POOL
OPEN 8PM
32
OH YEAH?
I GOT A GAME TONIGHT, DOWN AT THE CLUB. OUTTA-TOWN BUSINESS, FROM JAPAN. LIKE TO THROW THE CAKE AROUND.
LITTLE DICKS, BIG SPENDERS.
HOW I FIT IN?
BIG DEAL. THE HOUSE ALWAYS WINS.
CHUCKY, CHUCKY. SOMETIMES...
LOOK, THIS MAN, HE WANTS THEM BUSTED, BROKE. ALL OF THEM. WALKING OUT AT THE END OF THE NIGHT WITH NOT SO MUCH AS CAB FARE IN THEIR POCKETS. IF THAT DON'T HAPPEN, HE DON'T BANK.
WELL, A MYSTERIOUS GENTLEMAN STOPPED BY AND OFFERED TO VERY GENEROUSLY BANK THE HOUSE, IF I COULD ASSURE HIM ONE THING: THE JAPS LOSE.
SO THAT'S GOT TO HAPPEN.

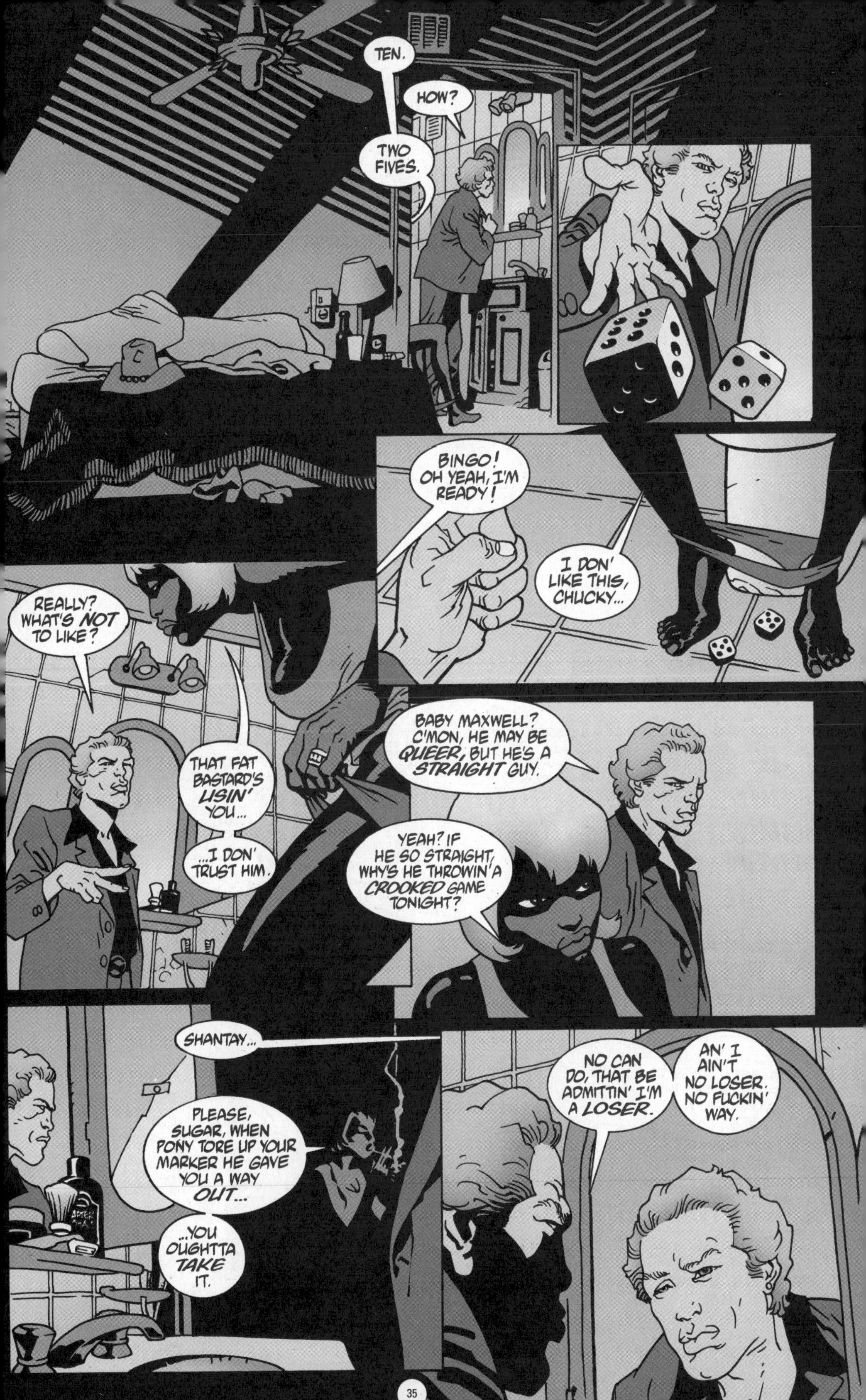
TEN.
HOW?
TWO FIVES.
BINGO! OH YEAH, I'M READY!
I DON' LIKE THIS, CHUCKY...
REALLY? WHAT'S NOT TO LIKE?
THAT FAT BASTARD'S USIN' YOU...
...I DON' TRUST HIM.
BABY MAXWELL? C'MON, HE MAY BE QUEER, BUT HE'S A STRAIGHT GUY.
YEAH? IF HE SO STRAIGHT, WHY'S HE THROWIN' A CROOKED GAME TONIGHT?
SHANTAY...
PLEASE, SUGAR, WHEN PONY TORE UP YOUR MARKER HE GAVE YOU A WAY OUT...
...YOU OUGHTTA TAKE IT.
NO CAN DO, THAT BE ADMITTIN' I'M A LOSER.
AN' I AIN'T NO LOSER. NO FUCKIN' WAY.

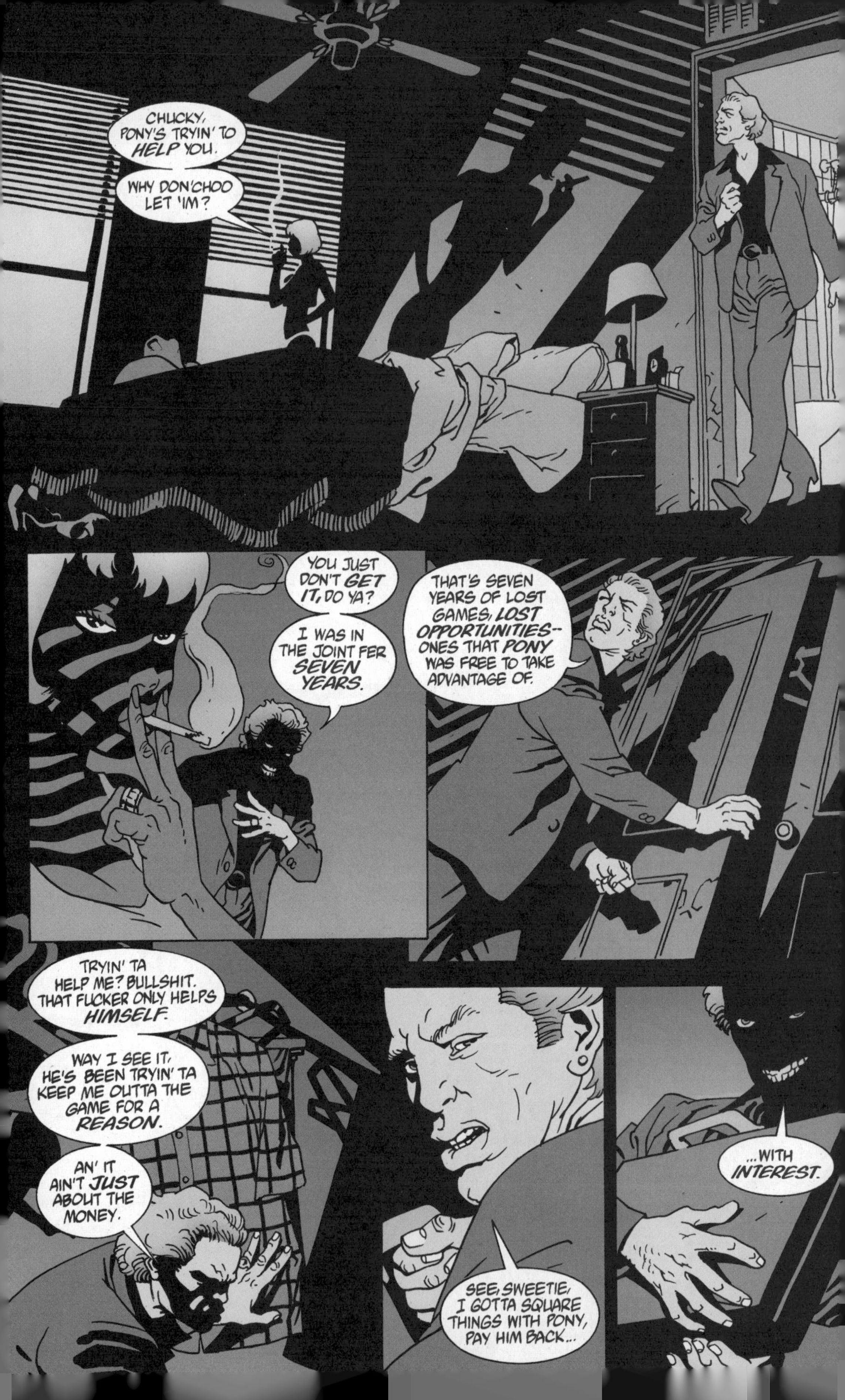
CHUCKY, PONY'S TRYIN' TO HELP YOU.
WHY DON'CHOO LET 'IM?
YOU JUST DON'T GET IT, DO YA?
I WAS IN THE JOINT FER SEVEN YEARS.
THAT'S SEVEN YEARS OF LOST GAMES, LOST OPPORTUNITIES-- ONES THAT PONY WAS FREE TO TAKE ADVANTAGE OF.
TRYIN' TA HELP ME? BULLSHIT. THAT FUCKER ONLY HELPS HIMSELF.
WAY I SEE IT, HE'S BEEN TRYIN' TA KEEP ME OUTTA THE GAME FOR A REASON.
AN' IT AIN'T JUST ABOUT THE MONEY.
SEE, SWEETIE, I GOTTA SQUARE THINGS WITH PONY, PAY HIM BACK...
...WITH INTEREST.

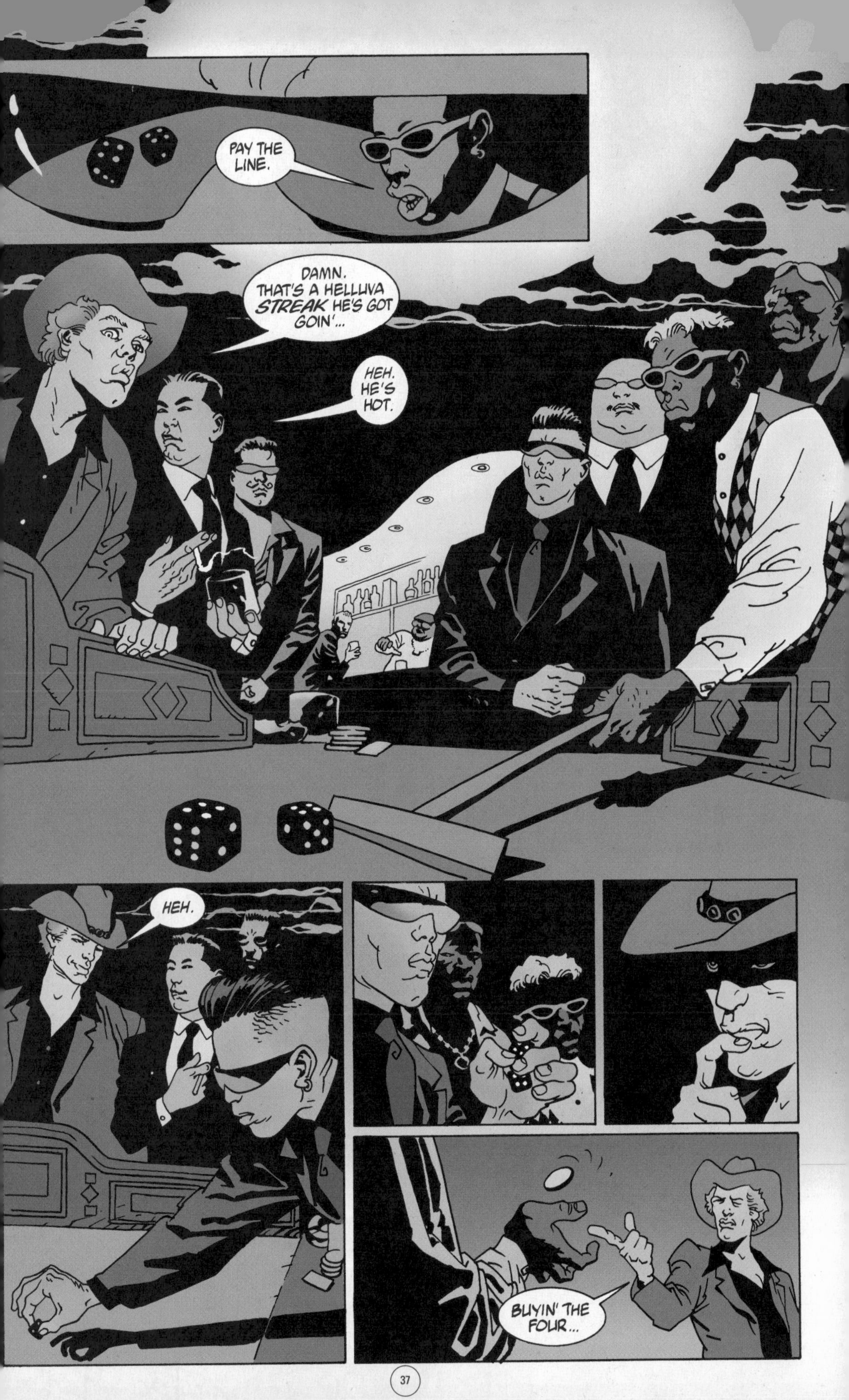
PAY THE LINE.
DAMN. THAT'S A HELLUVA STREAK HE'S GOT GOIN'...
HEH. HE'S HOT.
HEH.
BUYIN' THE FOUR...

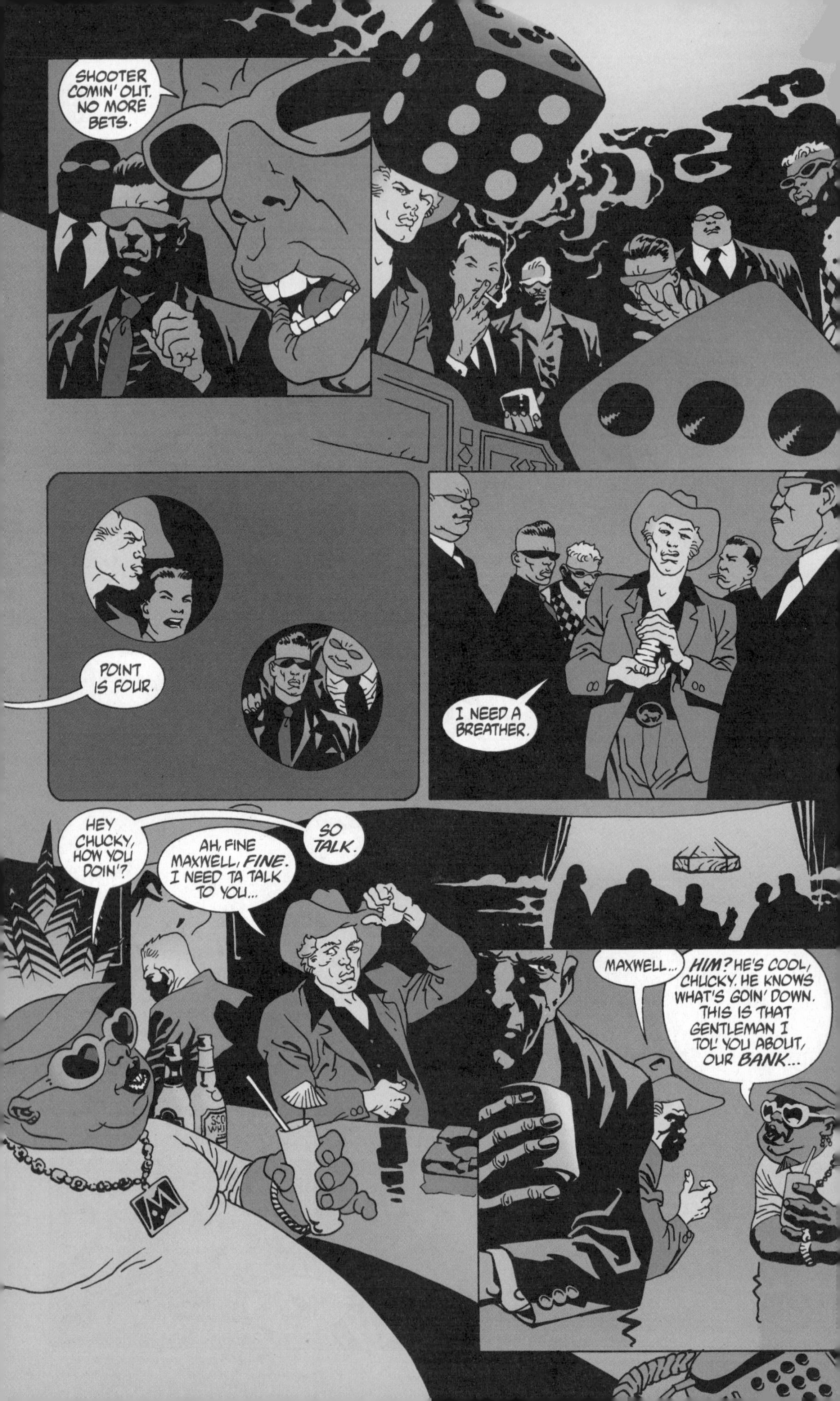
SHOOTER COMIN' OUT. NO MORE BETS.
POINT IS FOUR.
I NEED A BREATHER.
HEY CHUCKY, HOW YOU DOIN'?
AH, FINE MAXWELL, FINE. I NEED TA TALK TO YOU...
SO TALK.
MAXWELL...
HIM? HE'S COOL, CHUCKY. HE KNOWS WHAT'S GOIN' DOWN. THIS IS THAT GENTLEMAN I TOL' YOU ABOUT, OUR BANK...

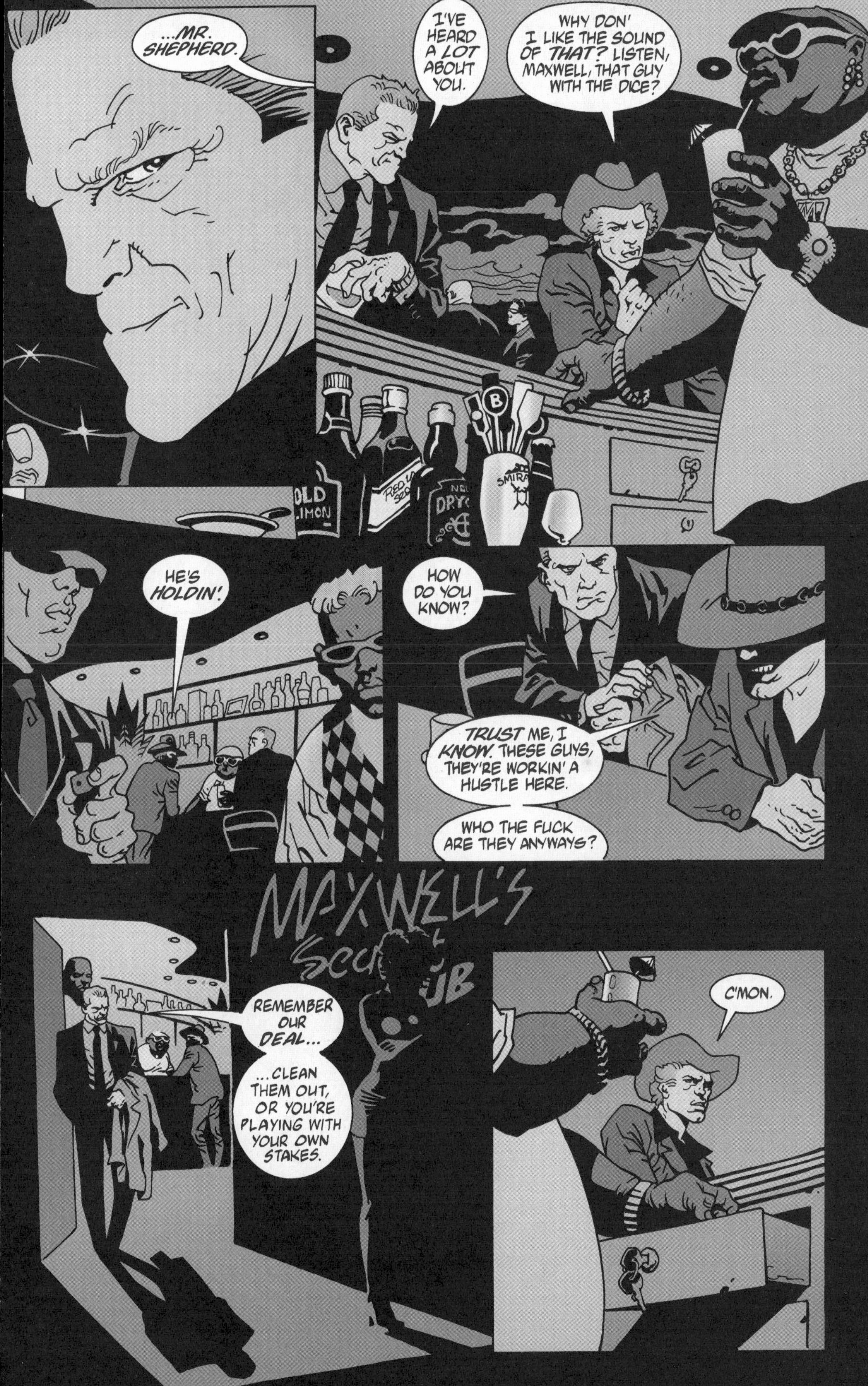
...MR. SHEPHERD.
I'VE HEARD A LOT ABOUT YOU.
WHY DON' I LIKE THE SOUND OF THAT? LISTEN, MAXWELL, THAT GUY WITH THE DICE?
HE'S HOLDIN'.
HOW DO YOU KNOW?
TRUST ME, I KNOW. THESE GUYS, THEY'RE WORKIN' A HUSTLE HERE.
WHO THE FUCK ARE THEY ANYWAYS?
REMEMBER OUR DEAL...
...CLEAN THEM OUT, OR YOU'RE PLAYING WITH YOUR OWN STAKES.
C'MON.

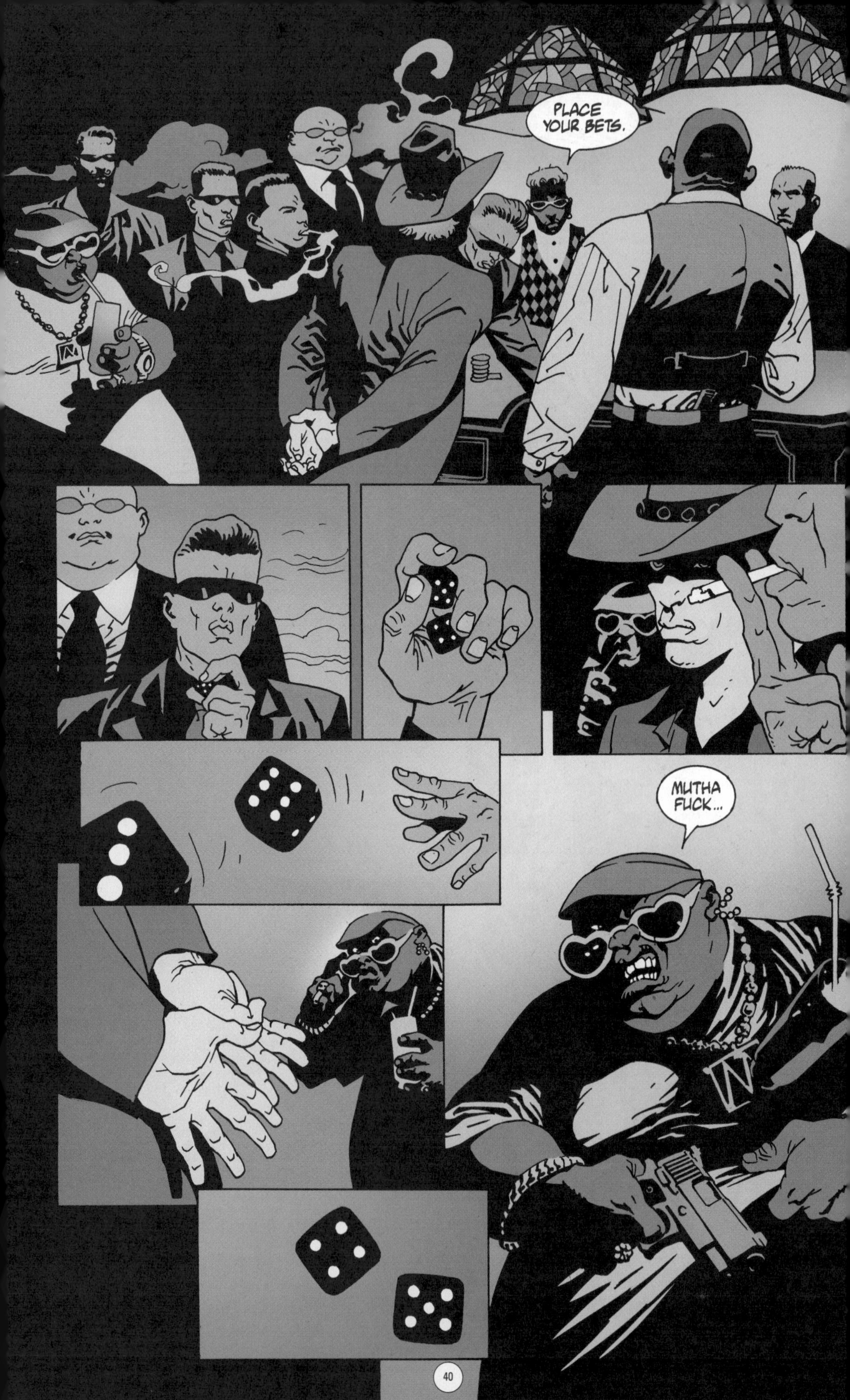
PLACE YOUR BETS.
MUTHA FUCK...

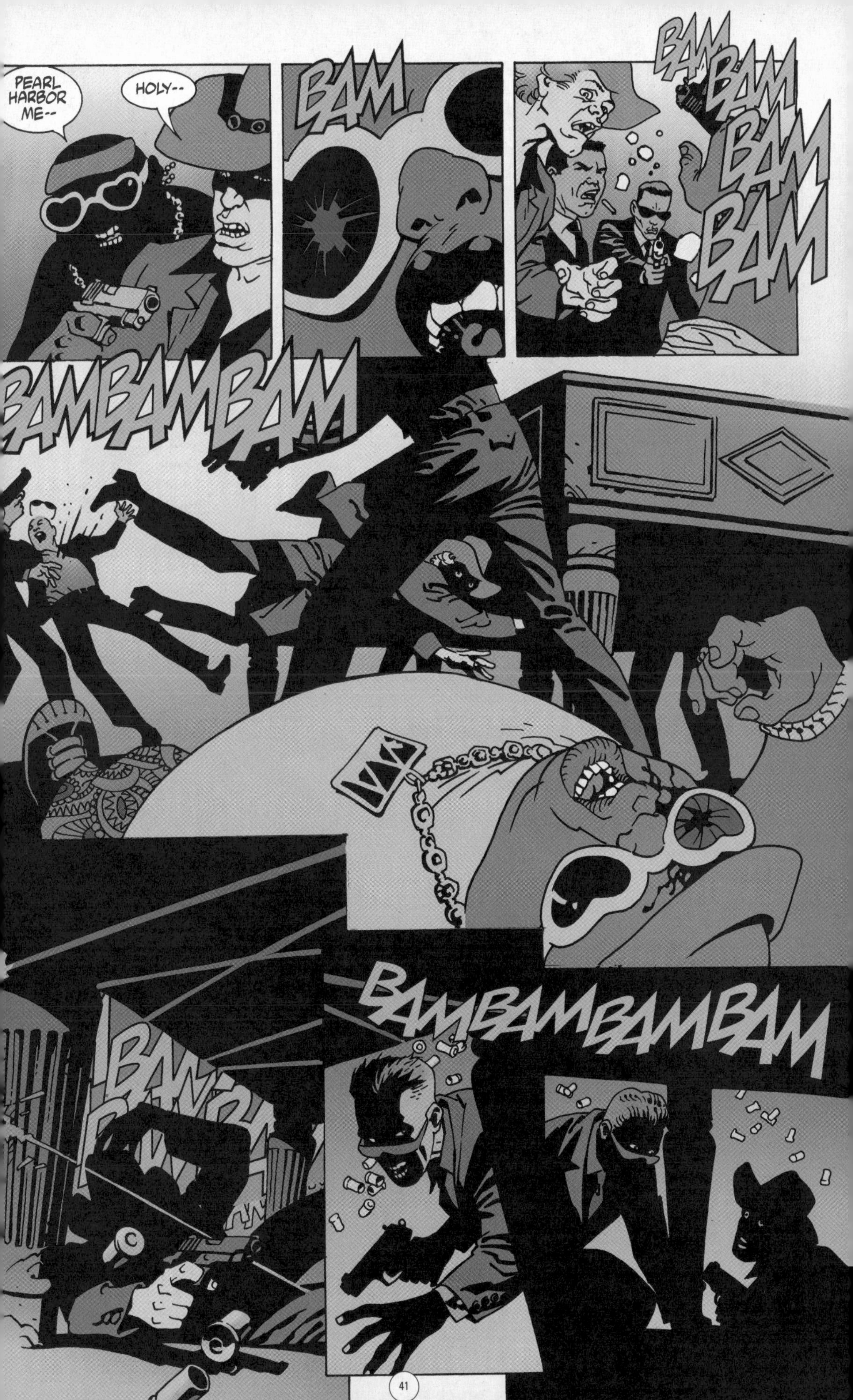

PEARL HARBOR ME--
HOLY--
BAM
BAM BAM BAM BAM
BAMBAMBAM
BAMBAMBAMBAM

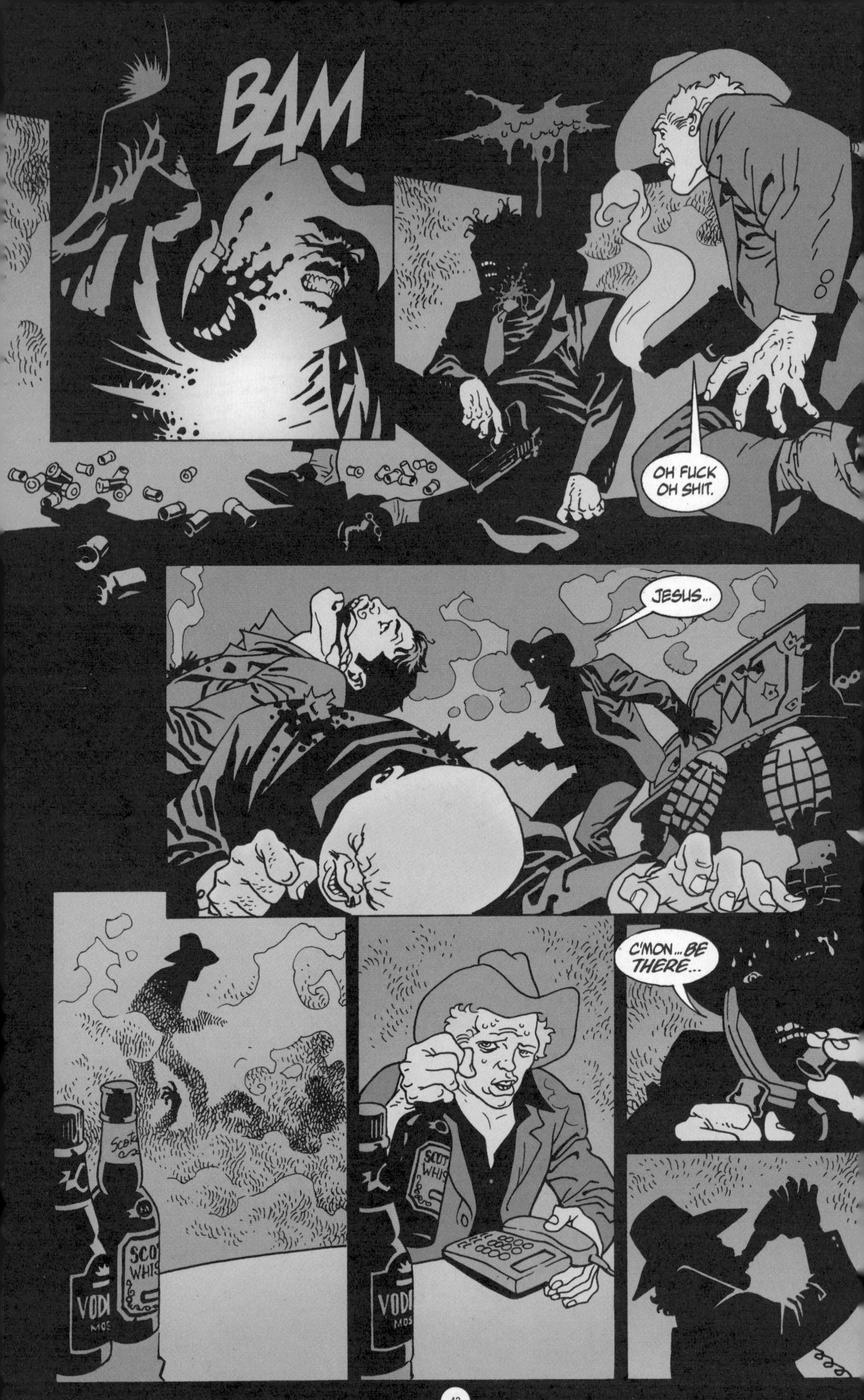

BAM
OH FUCK OH SHIT.
JESUS...
C'MON... BE THERE...

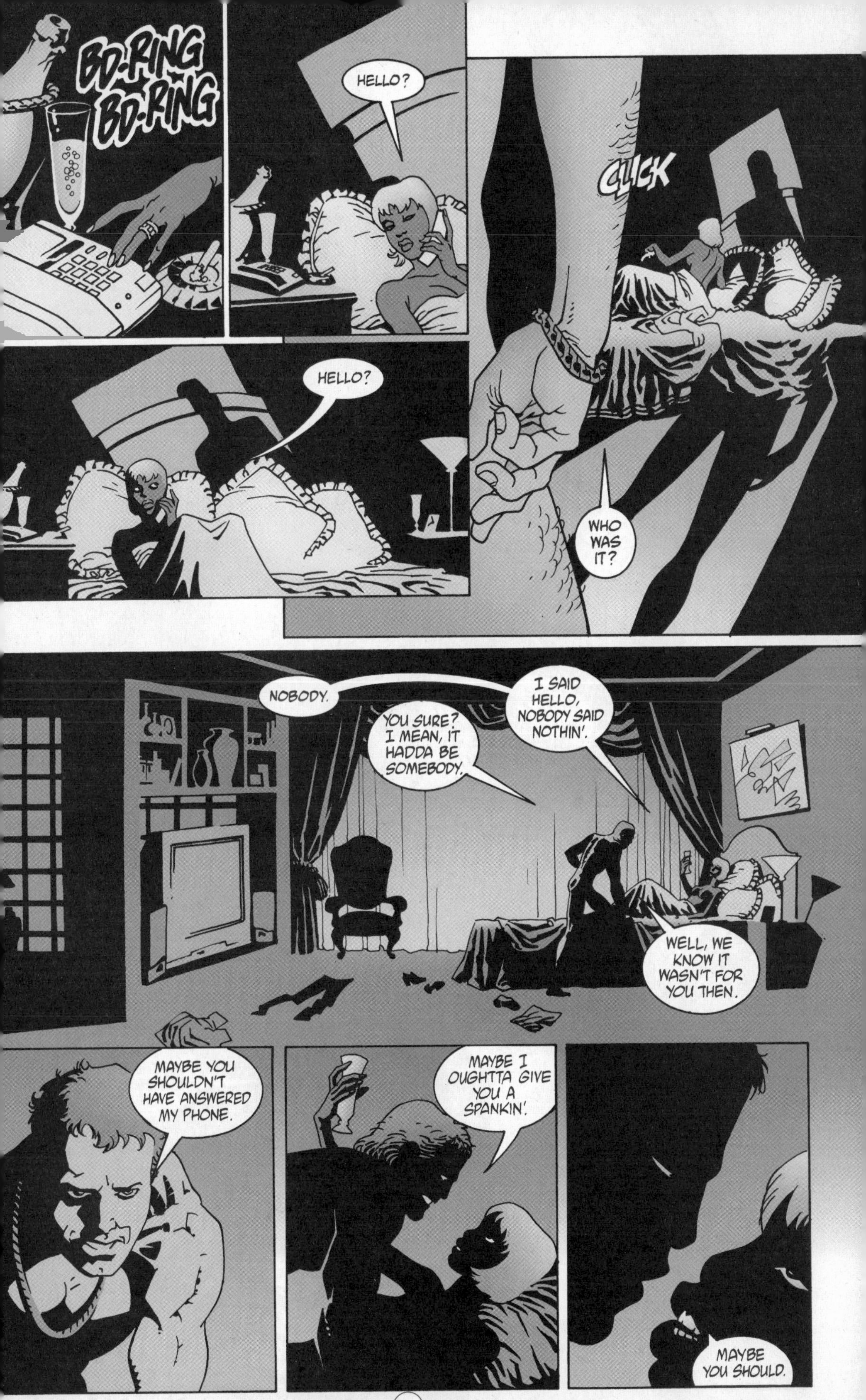
BD-RING BD-RING
HELLO?
CLICK
HELLO?
WHO WAS IT?
NOBODY.
I SAID HELLO, NOBODY SAID NOTHIN'.
YOU SURE? I MEAN, IT HADDA BE SOMEBODY.
WELL, WE KNOW IT WASN'T FOR YOU THEN.
MAYBE YOU SHOULDN'T HAVE ANSWERED MY PHONE.
MAYBE I OUGHTTA GIVE YOU A SPANKIN'.
MAYBE YOU SHOULD.

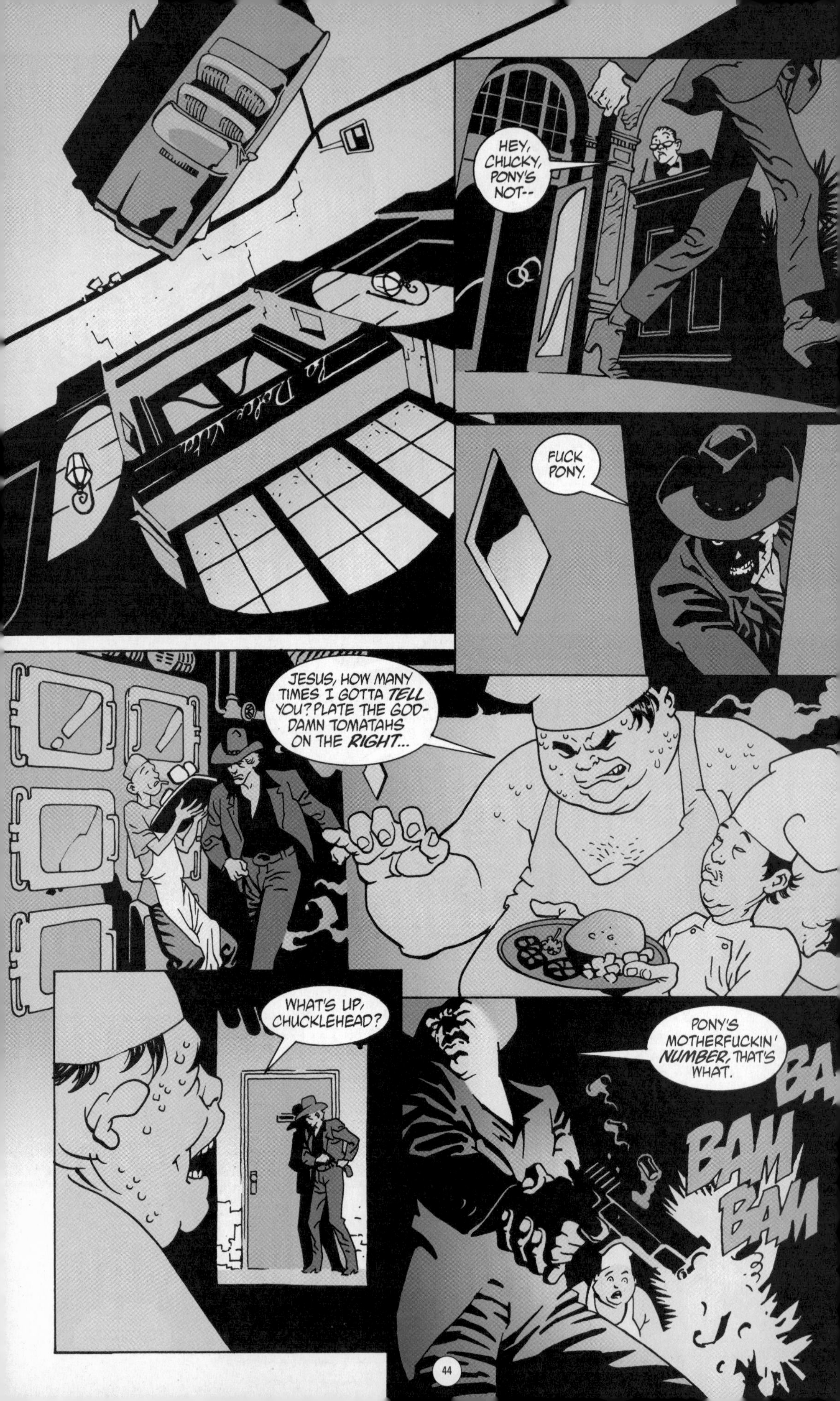

HEY, CHUCKY, PONY'S NOT--
FUCK PONY.
JESUS, HOW MANY TIMES I GOTTA *TELL* YOU? PLATE THE GOD-DAMN TOMATAHS ON THE *RIGHT*...
WHAT'S UP, CHUCKLEHEAD?
PONY'S MOTHERFUCKIN' *NUMBER*, THAT'S WHAT.
BAM BAM BAM

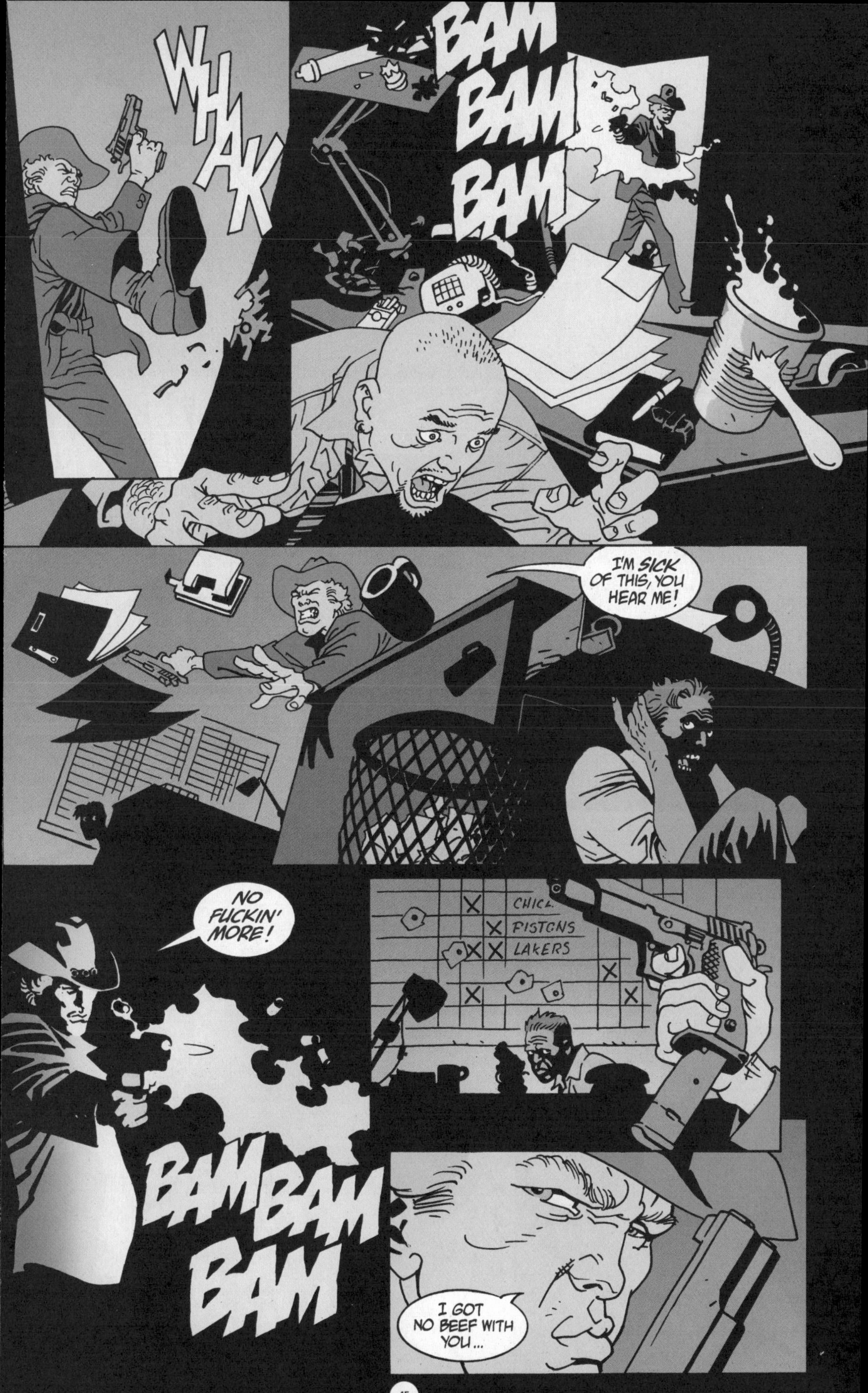
WHAK
BAM BAM BAM
I'M SICK OF THIS, YOU HEAR ME!
NO FUCKIN' MORE!
CHIC
PISTONS
LAKERS
BAM BAM BAM
I GOT NO BEEF WITH YOU...

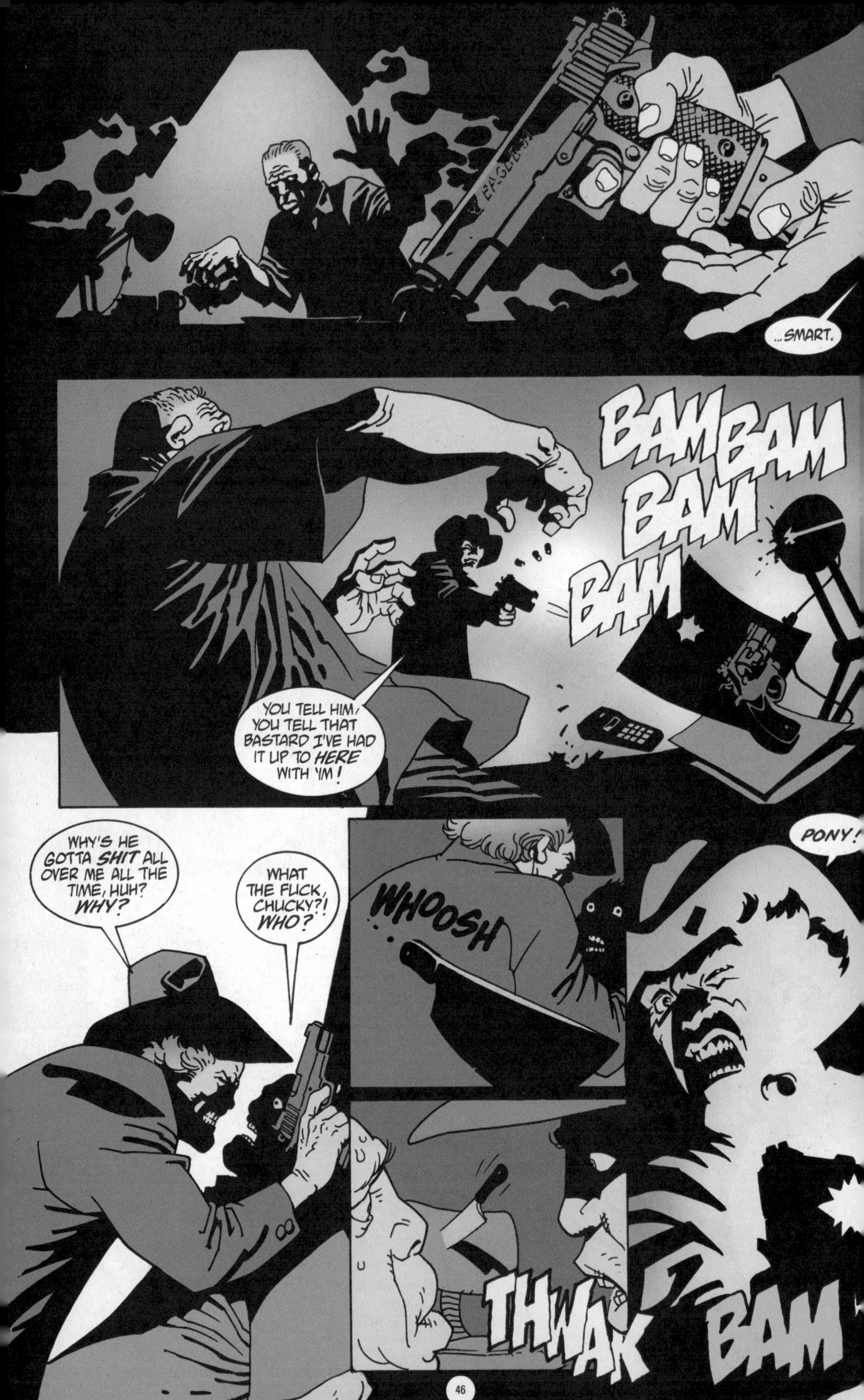
...SMART.
BAM BAM
BAM
BAM
YOU TELL HIM, YOU TELL THAT BASTARD I'VE HAD IT UP TO HERE WITH 'IM!
WHY'S HE GOTTA SHIT ALL OVER ME ALL THE TIME, HUH? WHY?
WHAT THE FUCK, CHUCKY?! WHO?
WHOOSH
PONY!
THWAK
BAM

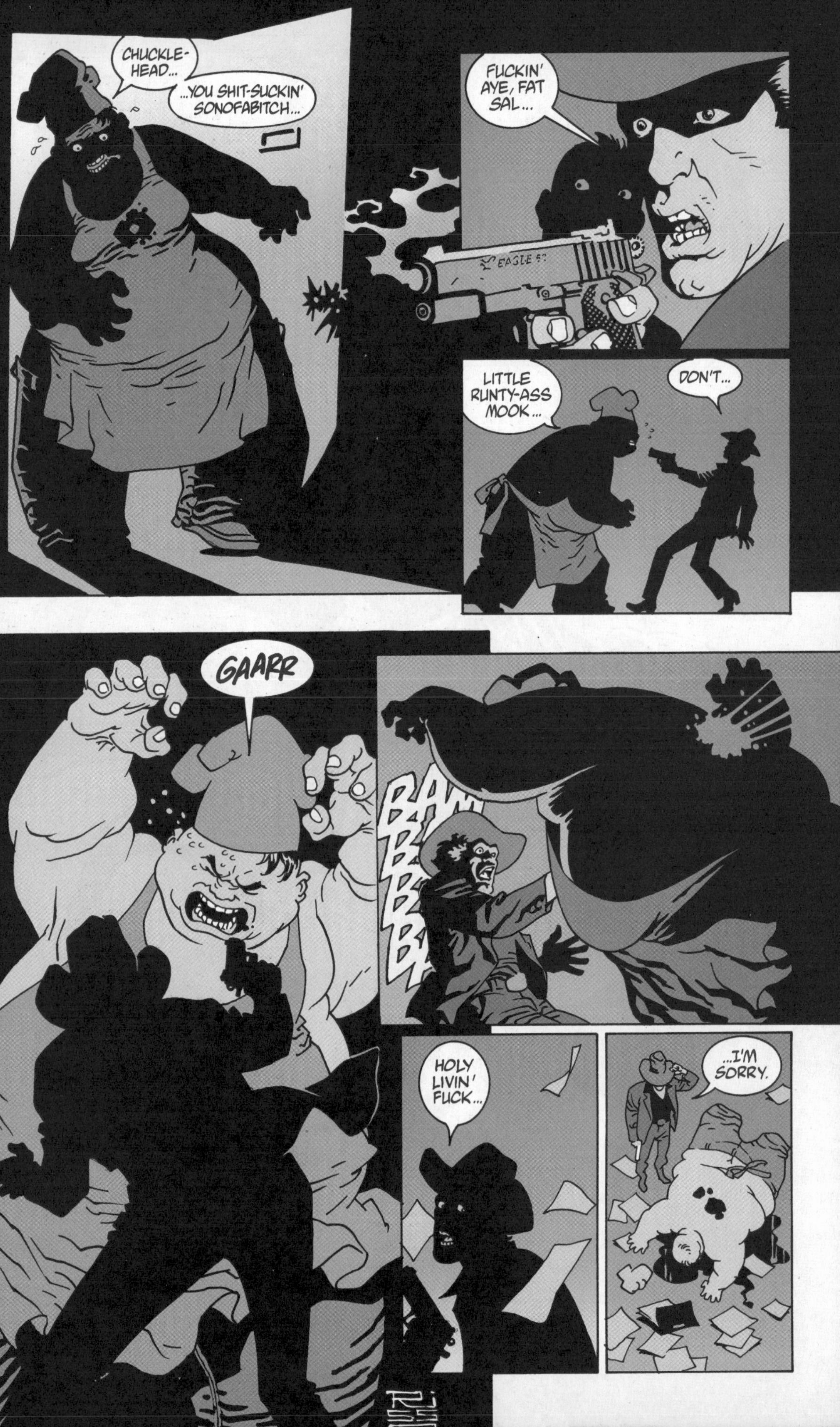
CHUCKLE-HEAD...
...YOU SHIT-SUCKIN' SONOFABITCH...
FUCKIN' AYE, FAT SAL...
EAGLE 57
LITTLE RUNTY-ASS MOOK...
DON'T...
GAARR
BAM
HOLY LIVIN' FUCK...
...I'M SORRY.

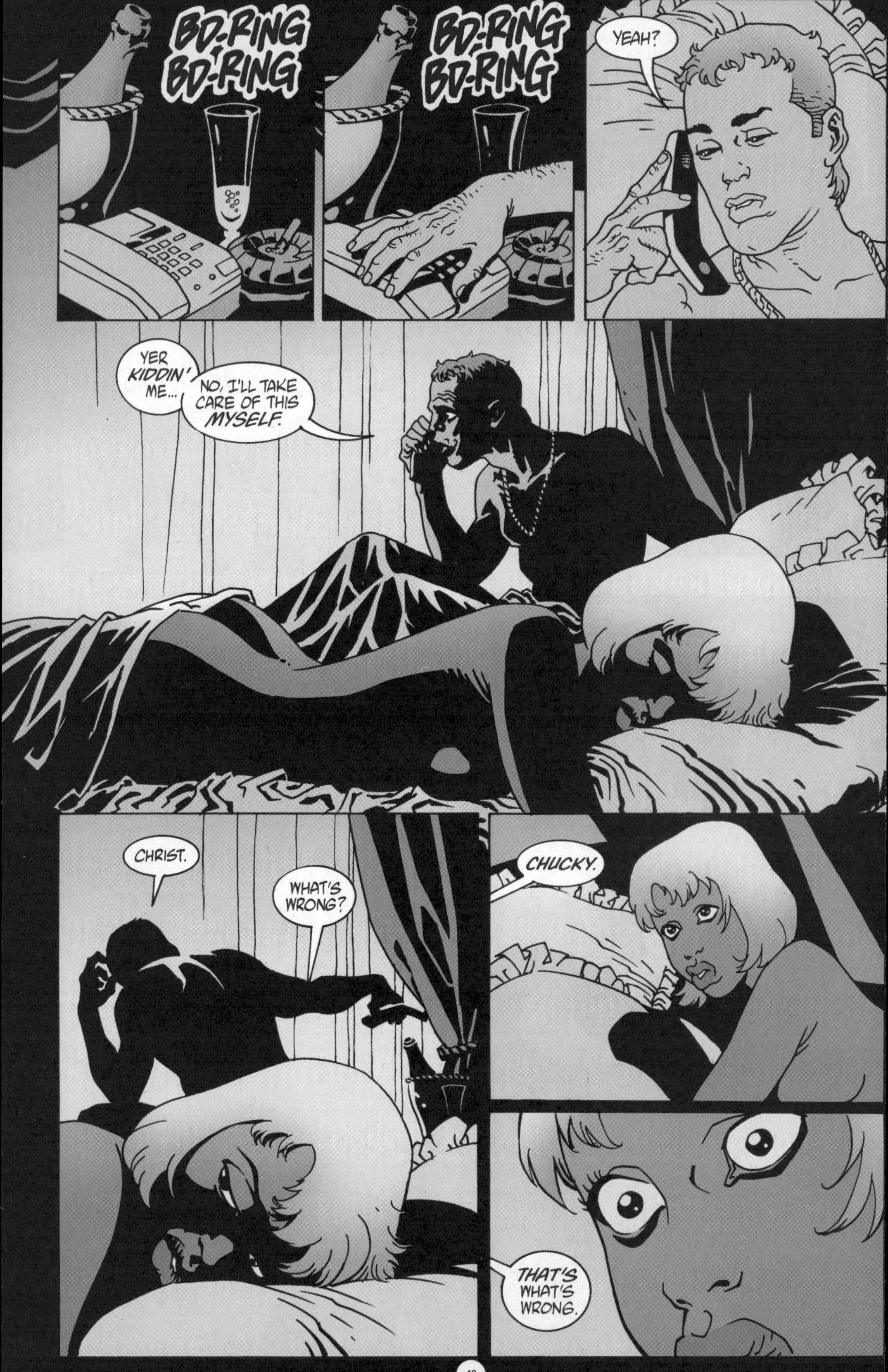
BD-RING BD-RING
BD-RING BD-RING
YEAH?
YER KIDDIN' ME...
NO, I'LL TAKE CARE OF THIS MYSELF.
CHRIST.
WHAT'S WRONG?
CHUCKY.
THAT'S WHAT'S WRONG.

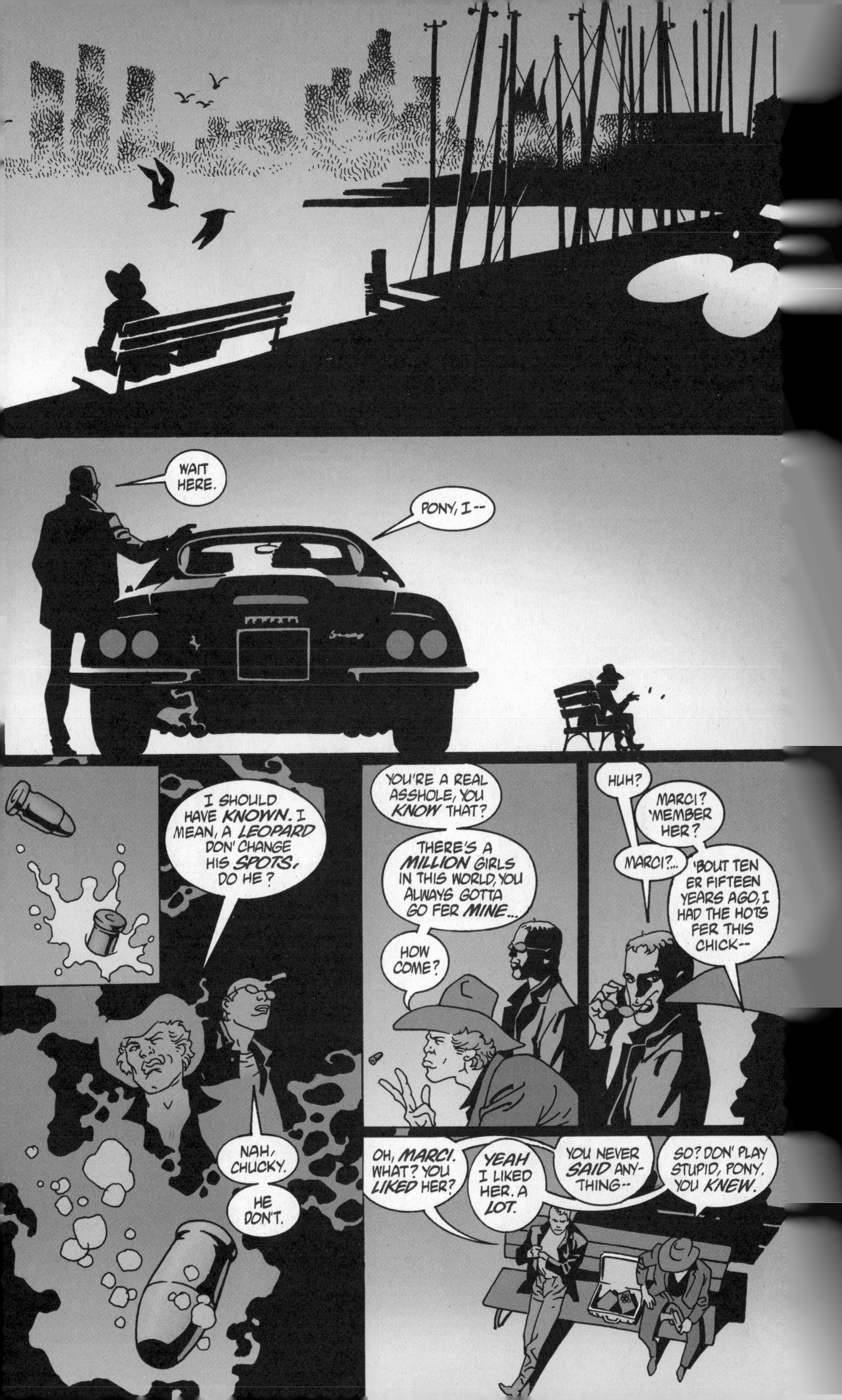
WAIT HERE.
PONY, I--
I SHOULD HAVE KNOWN. I MEAN, A LEOPARD DON' CHANGE HIS SPOTS, DO HE?
NAH, CHUCKY.
HE DON'T.
YOU'RE A REAL ASSHOLE, YOU KNOW THAT?
THERE'S A MILLION GIRLS IN THIS WORLD, YOU ALWAYS GOTTA GO FER MINE...
HOW COME?
HUH?
MARCI? 'MEMBER HER?
MARCI?...
'BOUT TEN ER FIFTEEN YEARS AGO, I HAD THE HOTS FER THIS CHICK--
OH, MARCI. WHAT? YOU LIKED HER?
YEAH I LIKED HER. A LOT.
YOU NEVER SAID ANYTHING--
SO? DON' PLAY STUPID, PONY. YOU KNEW.

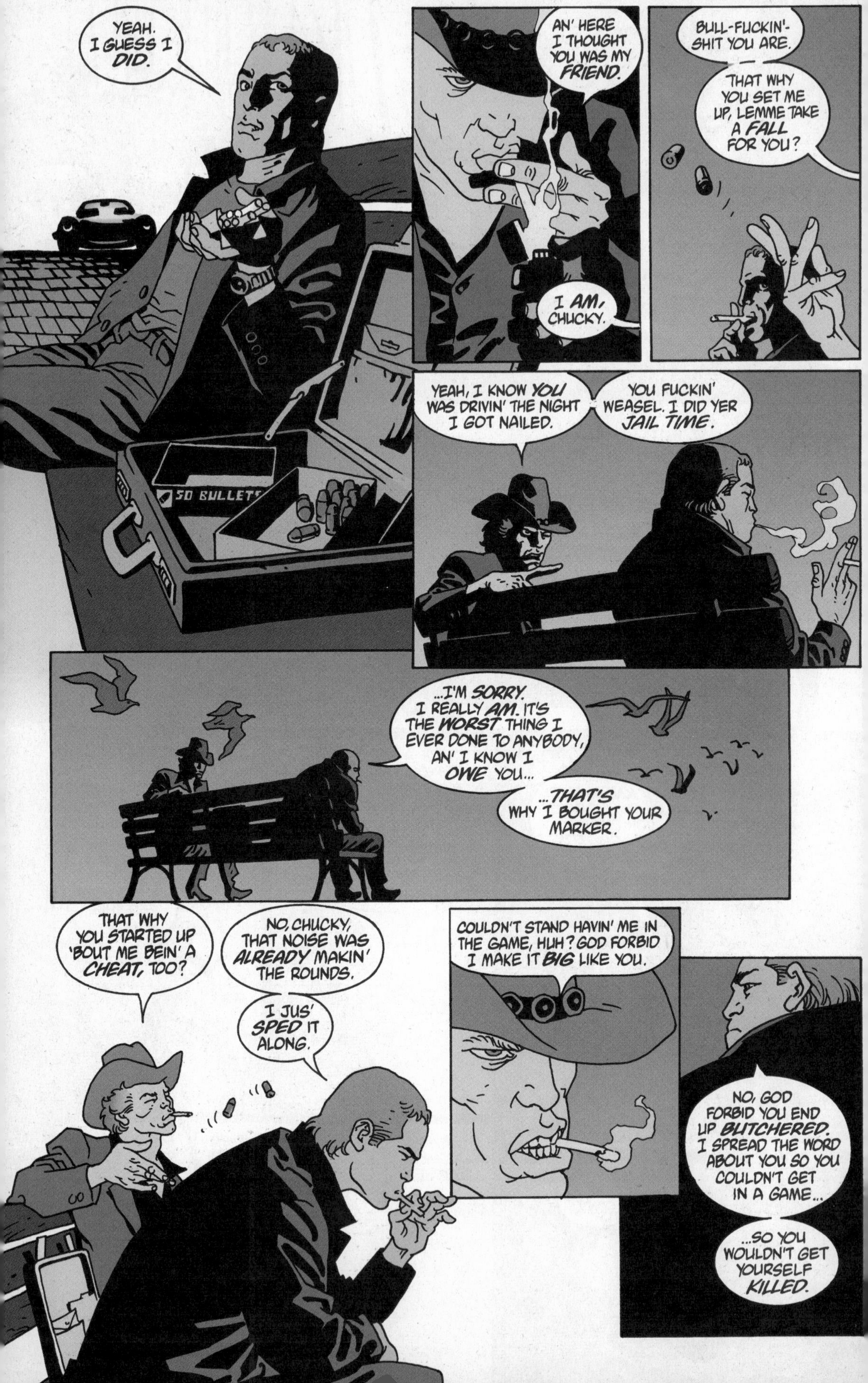
YEAH. I GUESS I DID.
AN' HERE I THOUGHT YOU WAS MY FRIEND.
I AM, CHUCKY.
BULL-FUCKIN'-SHIT YOU ARE.
THAT WHY YOU SET ME UP, LEMME TAKE A FALL FOR YOU?
YEAH, I KNOW YOU WAS DRIVIN' THE NIGHT I GOT NAILED.
YOU FUCKIN' WEASEL. I DID YER JAIL TIME.
50 BULLETS
...I'M SORRY. I REALLY AM. IT'S THE WORST THING I EVER DONE TO ANYBODY, AN' I KNOW I OWE YOU...
...THAT'S WHY I BOUGHT YOUR MARKER.
THAT WHY YOU STARTED UP 'BOUT ME BEIN' A CHEAT, TOO?
NO, CHUCKY, THAT NOISE WAS ALREADY MAKIN' THE ROUNDS.
I JUS' SPED IT ALONG.
COULDN'T STAND HAVIN' ME IN THE GAME, HUH? GOD FORBID I MAKE IT BIG LIKE YOU.
NO, GOD FORBID YOU END UP BUTCHERED. I SPREAD THE WORD ABOUT YOU SO YOU COULDN'T GET IN A GAME...
...SO YOU WOULDN'T GET YOURSELF KILLED.

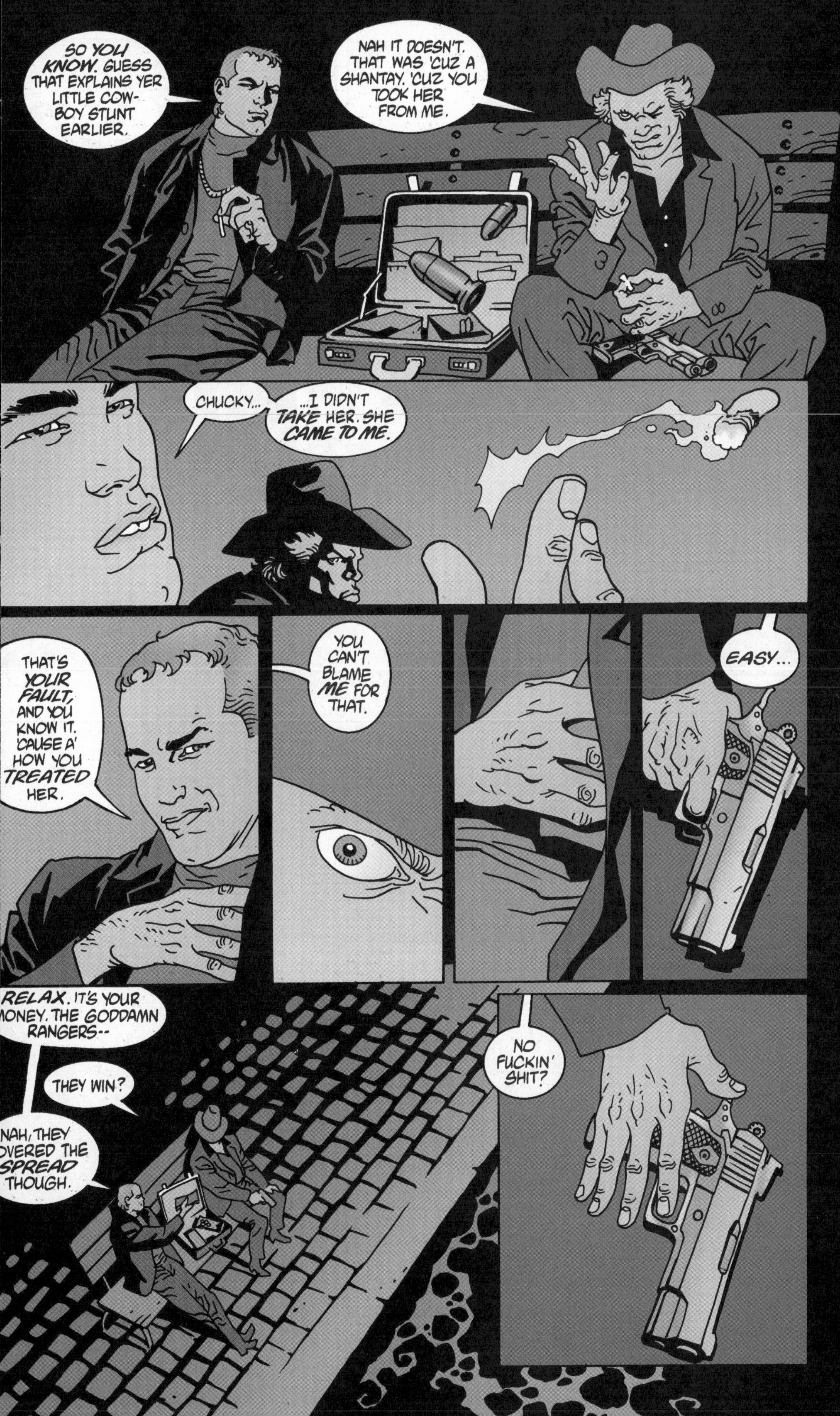
SO YOU KNOW. GUESS THAT EXPLAINS YER LITTLE COW-BOY STUNT EARLIER.
NAH IT DOESN'T. THAT WAS 'CUZ A SHANTAY. 'CUZ YOU TOOK HER FROM ME.
CHUCKY...
...I DIDN'T TAKE HER. SHE CAME TO ME.
THAT'S YOUR FAULT, AND YOU KNOW IT. 'CAUSE A' HOW YOU TREATED HER.
YOU CAN'T BLAME ME FOR THAT.
EASY...
RELAX. IT'S YOUR MONEY. THE GODDAMN RANGERS--
THEY WIN?
NAH, THEY COVERED THE SPREAD THOUGH.
NO FUCKIN' SHIT?

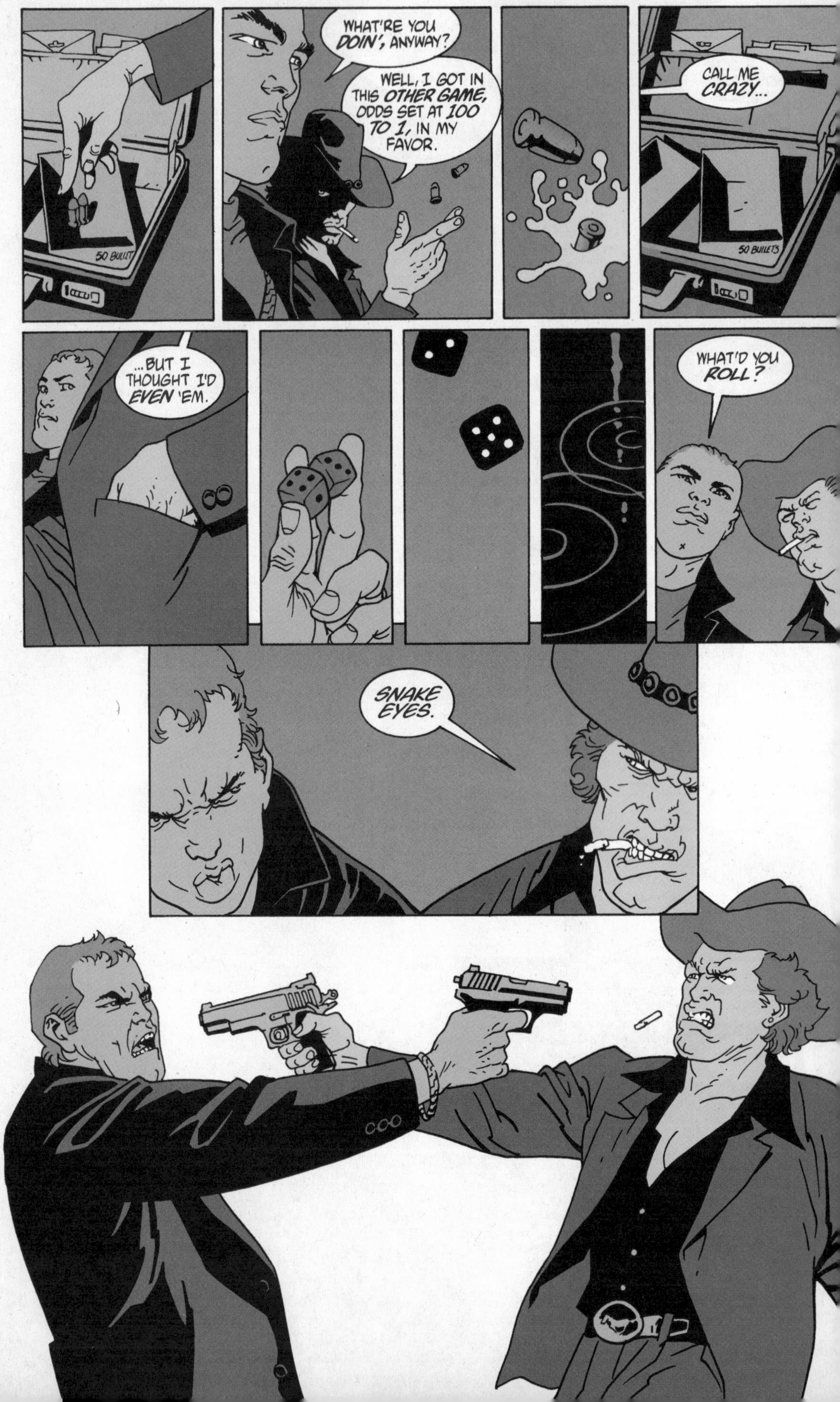
50 BULLET
WHAT'RE YOU DOIN', ANYWAY?
WELL, I GOT IN THIS OTHER GAME, ODDS SET AT 100 TO 1, IN MY FAVOR.
CALL ME CRAZY...
50 BULLETS
...BUT I THOUGHT I'D EVEN 'EM.
WHAT'D YOU ROLL?
SNAKE EYES.

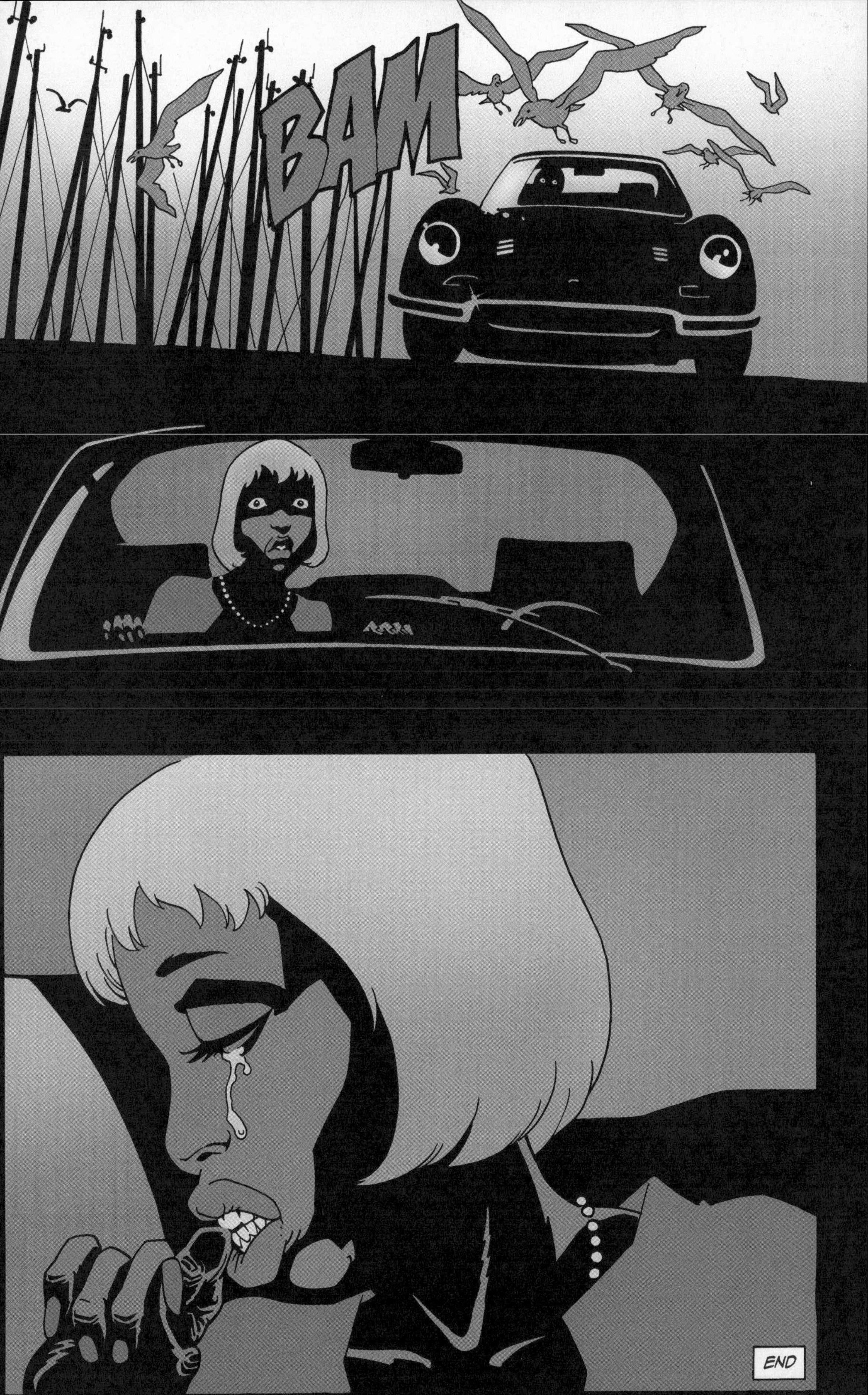
BAM
END

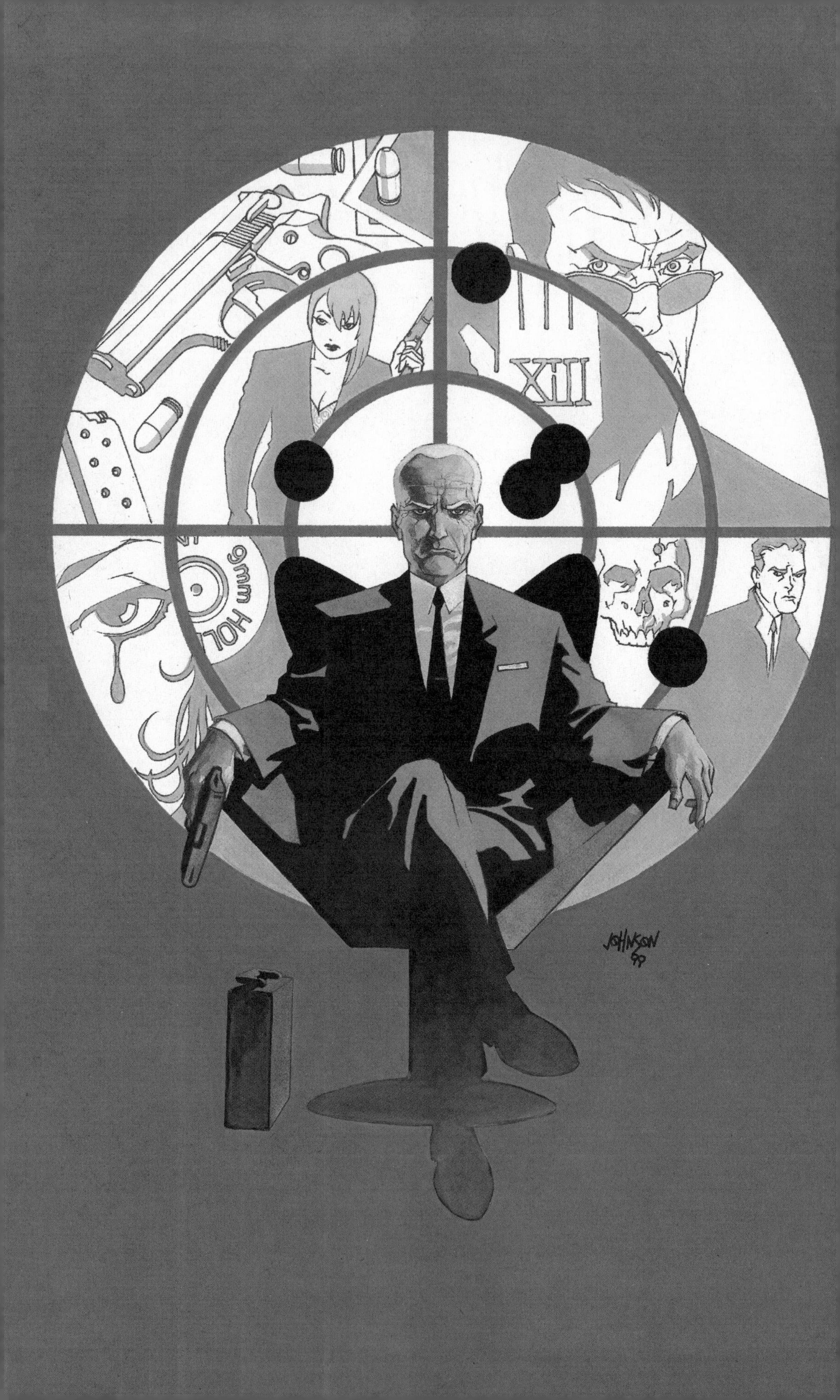
XIII
9mm HOL
JOHNSON
99

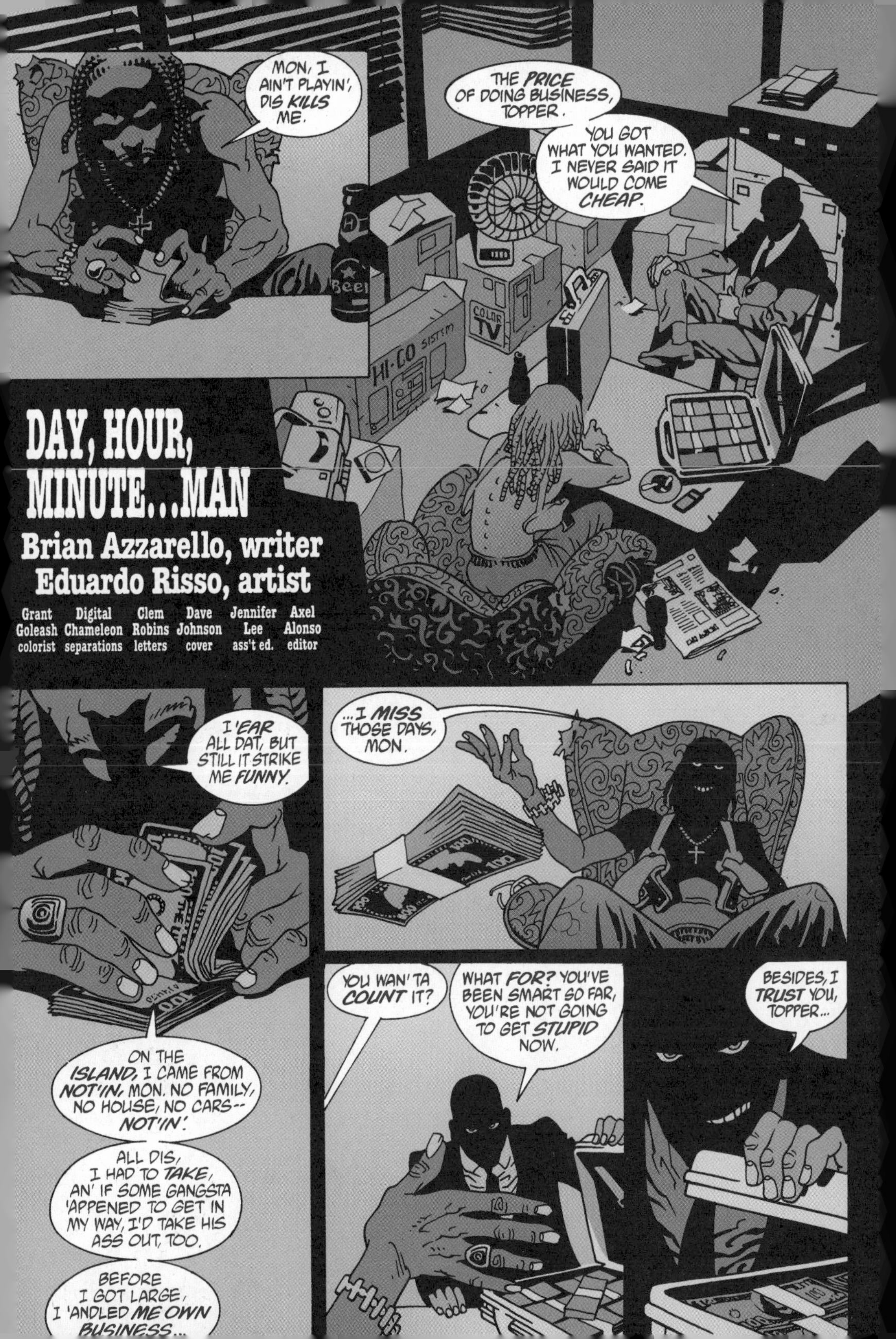
MON, I AIN'T PLAYIN', DIS KILLS ME.
THE PRICE OF DOING BUSINESS, TOPPER.
YOU GOT WHAT YOU WANTED. I NEVER SAID IT WOULD COME CHEAP.
DAY, HOUR, MINUTE...MAN
Brian Azzarello, writer
Eduardo Risso, artist
Grant Goleash colorist
Digital Chameleon separations
Clem Robins letters
Dave Johnson cover
Jennifer Lee ass't ed.
Axel Alonso editor
I'EAR ALL DAT, BUT STILL IT STRIKE ME FUNNY.
ON THE ISLAND, I CAME FROM NOT'IN, MON. NO FAMILY, NO HOUSE, NO CARS-- NOT'IN'.
ALL DIS, I HAD TO TAKE, AN' IF SOME GANGSTA 'APPENED TO GET IN MY WAY, I'D TAKE HIS ASS OUT, TOO.
BEFORE I GOT LARGE, I 'ANDLED ME OWN BUSINESS...
...I MISS THOSE DAYS, MON.
YOU WAN' TA COUNT IT?
WHAT FOR? YOU'VE BEEN SMART SO FAR, YOU'RE NOT GOING TO GET STUPID NOW.
BESIDES, I TRUST YOU, TOPPER...

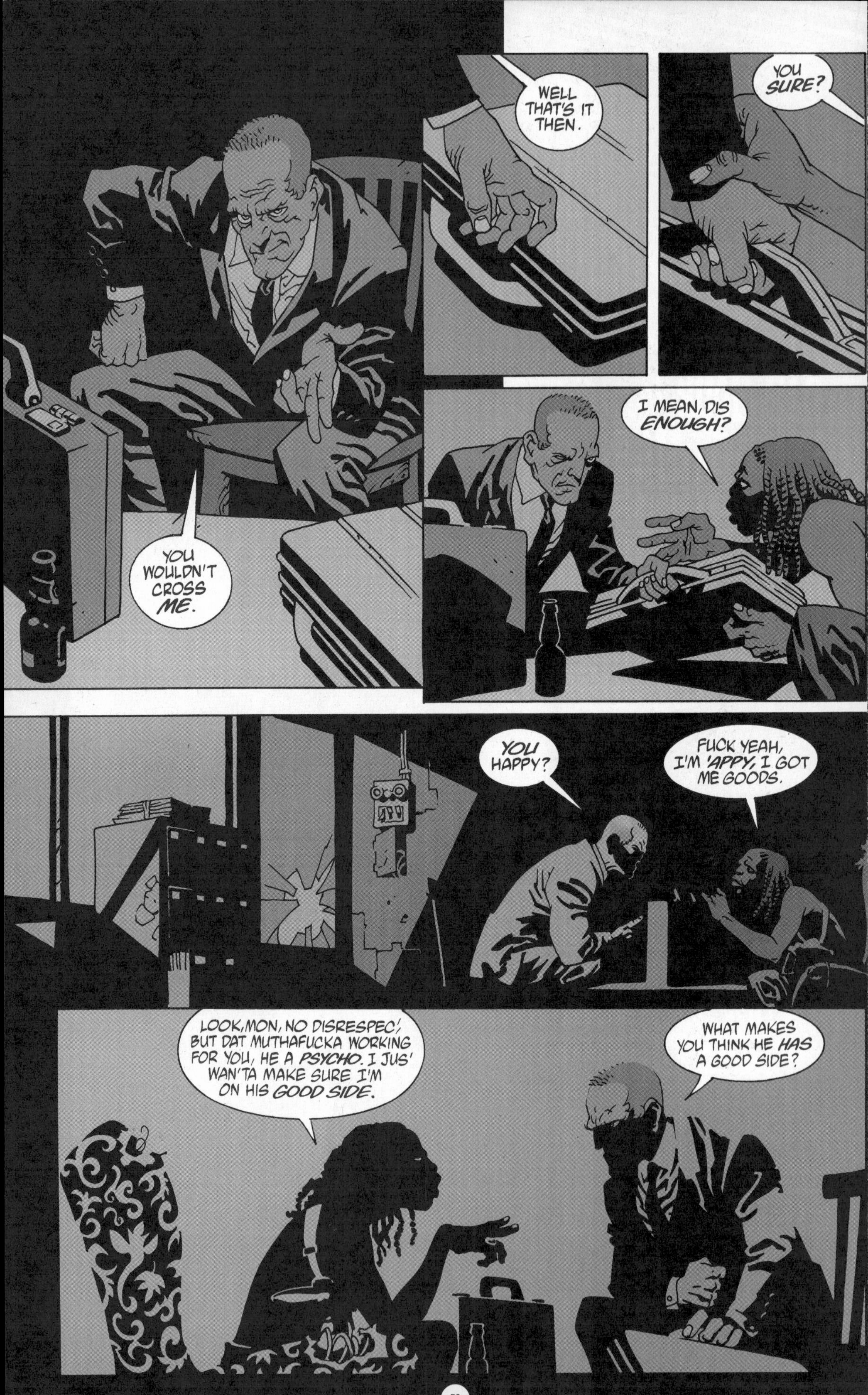
WELL THAT'S IT THEN.
YOU SURE?
YOU WOULDN'T CROSS ME.
I MEAN, DIS ENOUGH?
YOU HAPPY?
FUCK YEAH, I'M 'APPY, I GOT ME GOODS.
LOOK, MON, NO DISRESPEC', BUT DAT MUTHAFUCKA WORKING FOR YOU, HE A PSYCHO. I JUS' WAN'TA MAKE SURE I'M ON HIS GOOD SIDE.
WHAT MAKES YOU THINK HE HAS A GOOD SIDE?

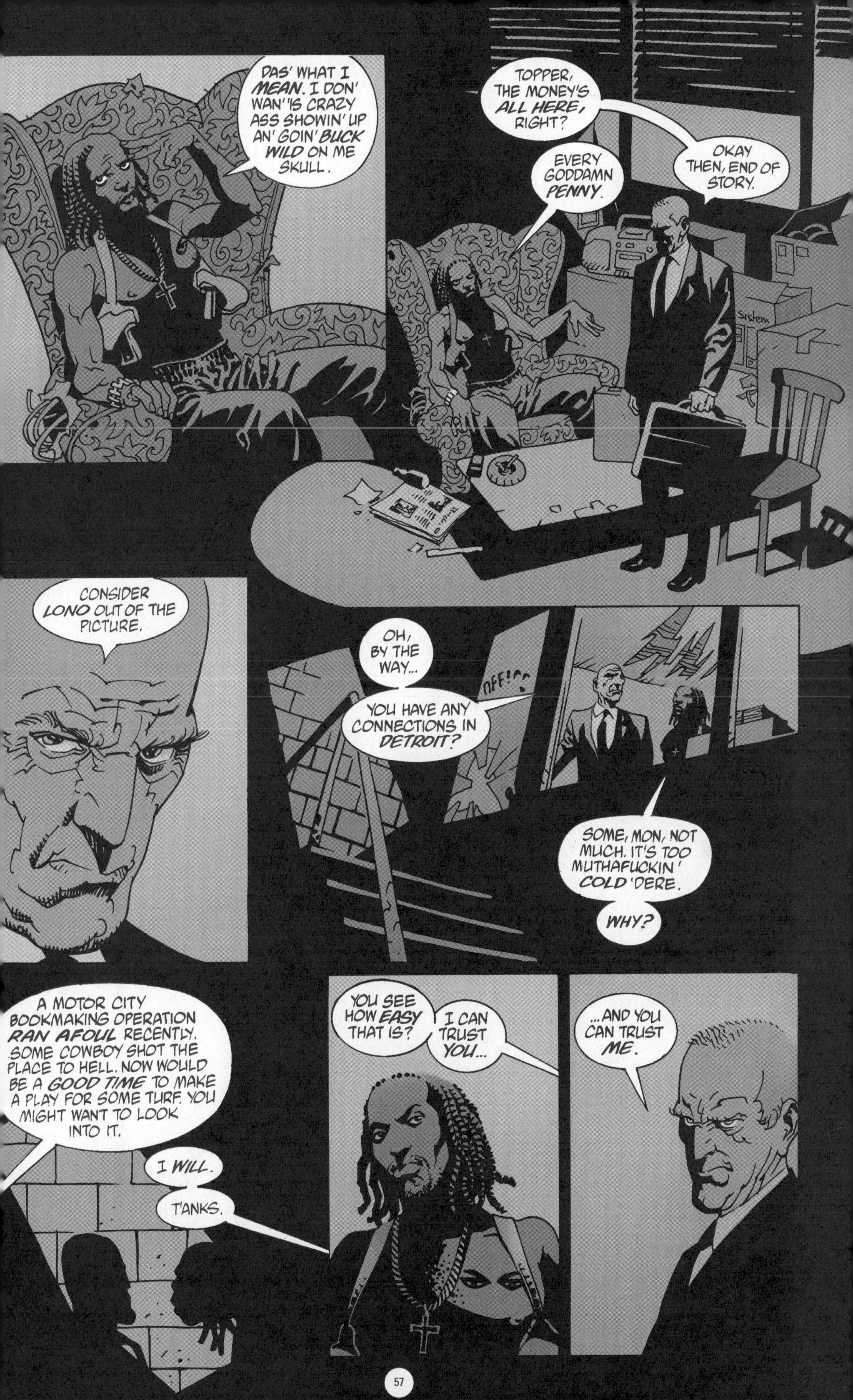

DAS' WHAT I MEAN. I DON' WAN' 'IS CRAZY ASS SHOWIN' UP AN' GOIN' BUCK WILD ON ME SKULL.
TOPPER, THE MONEY'S ALL HERE, RIGHT?
EVERY GODDAMN PENNY.
OKAY THEN, END OF STORY.
System
CONSIDER LONO OUT OF THE PICTURE.
OH, BY THE WAY...
YOU HAVE ANY CONNECTIONS IN DETROIT?
SOME, MON, NOT MUCH. IT'S TOO MUTHAFUCKIN' COLD 'DERE.
WHY?
A MOTOR CITY BOOKMAKING OPERATION RAN AFOUL RECENTLY. SOME COWBOY SHOT THE PLACE TO HELL. NOW WOULD BE A GOOD TIME TO MAKE A PLAY FOR SOME TURF. YOU MIGHT WANT TO LOOK INTO IT.
I WILL.
T'ANKS.
YOU SEE HOW EASY THAT IS?
I CAN TRUST YOU...
...AND YOU CAN TRUST ME.

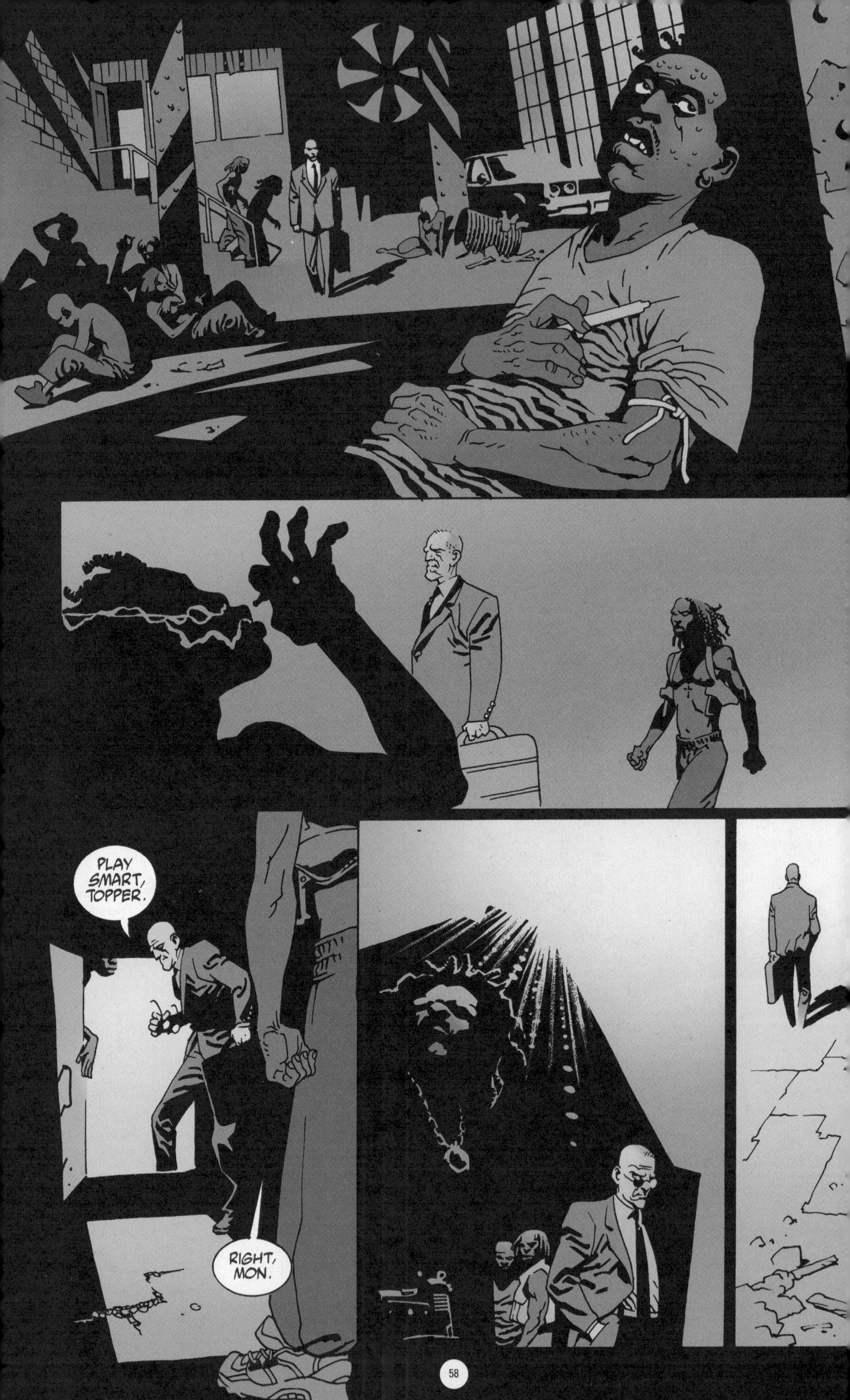
PLAY SMART, TOPPER.
RIGHT, MON.

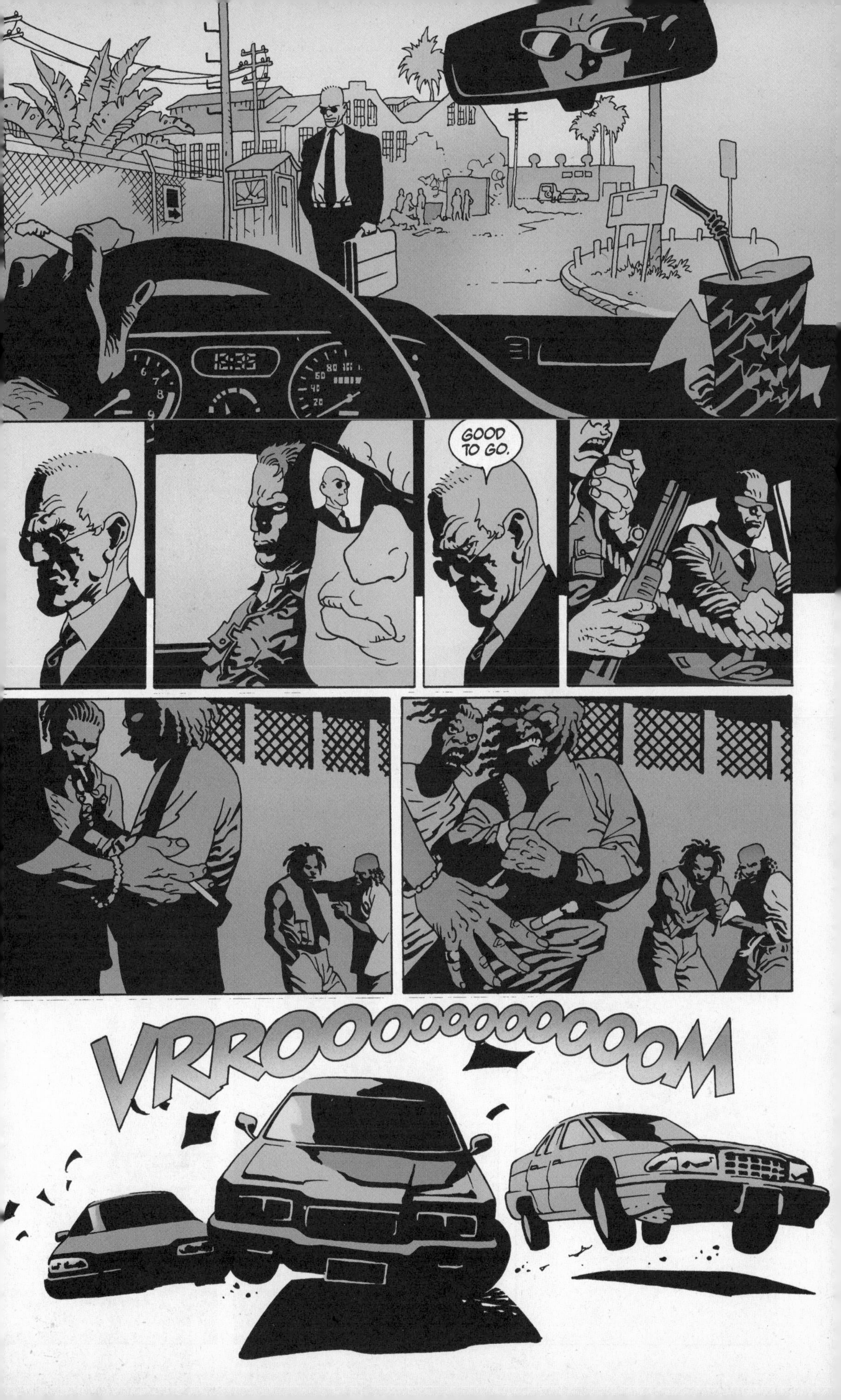
GOOD TO GO.
VRROOOOOOOOOOOM

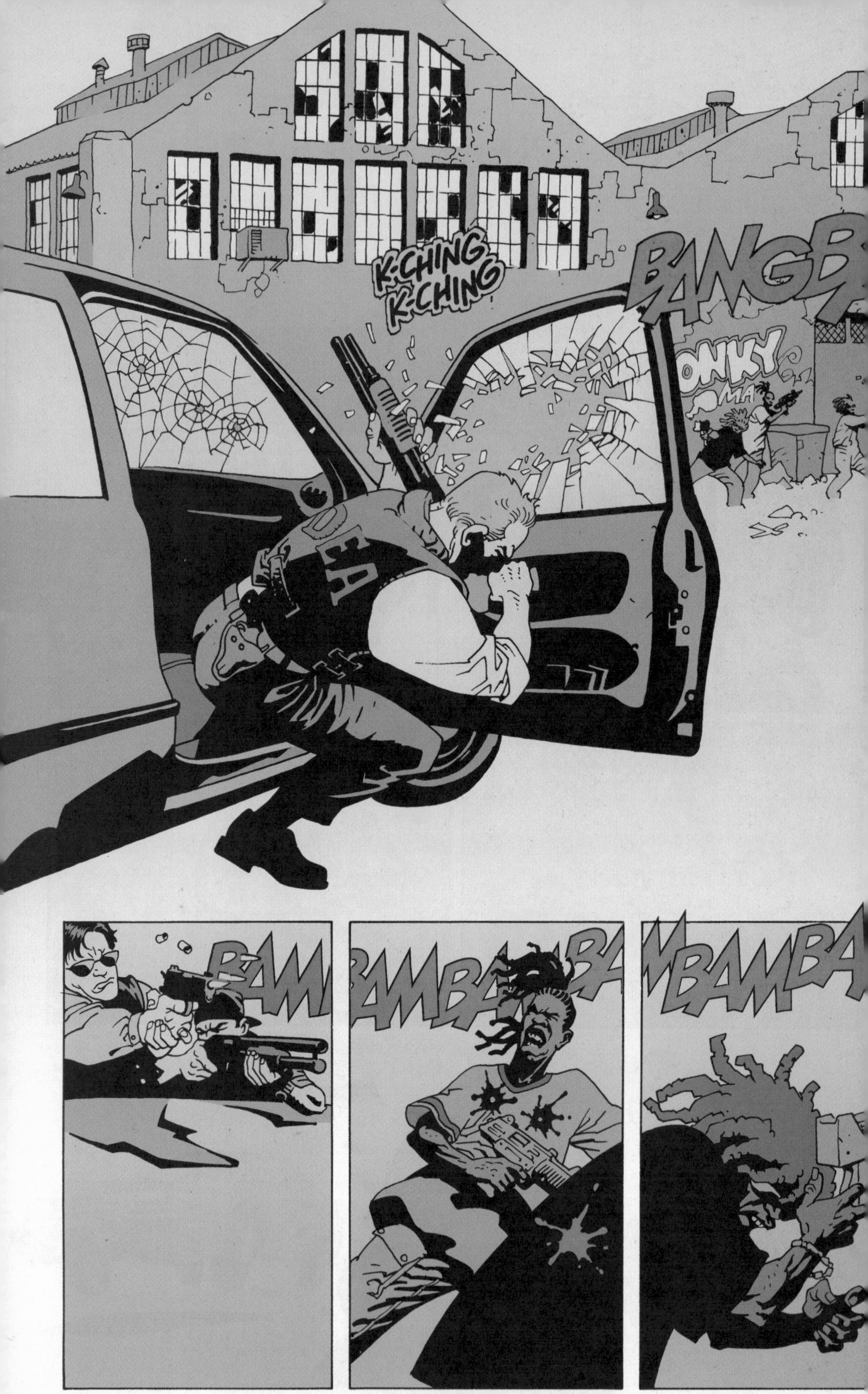
K-CHING
K-CHING
BANGB
DEA
BAM
BAMBA
BAMBA

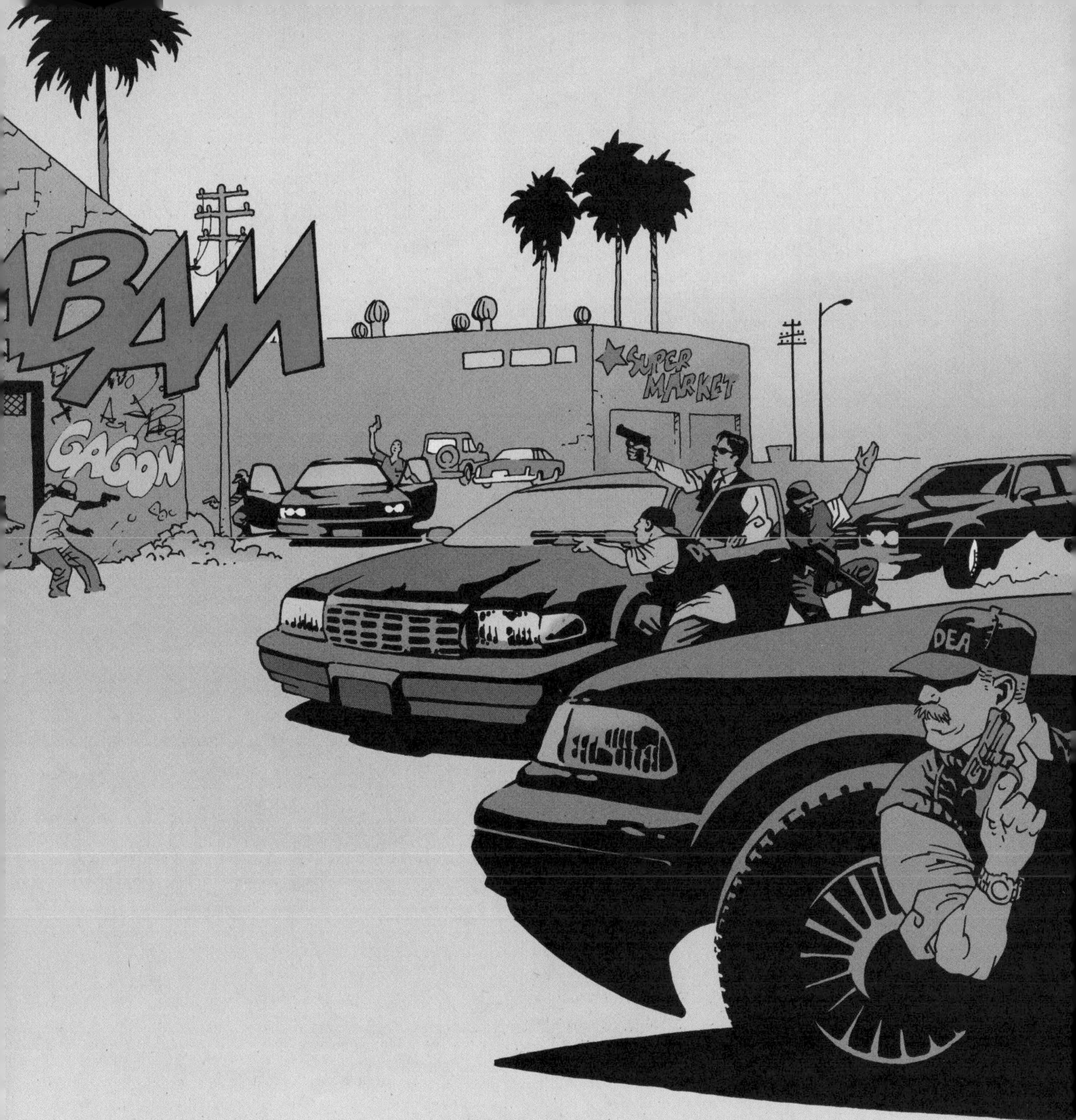
BAM
GAGON
SUPER MARKET
DEA

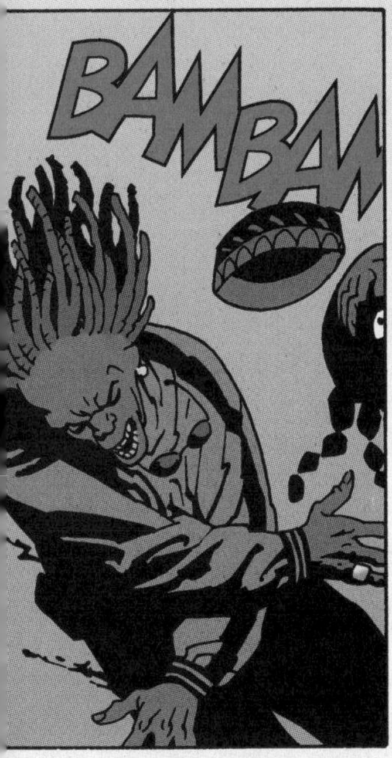
BAMBAM

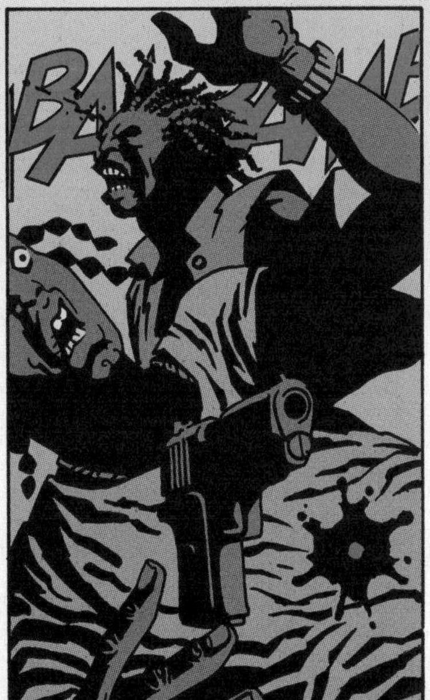

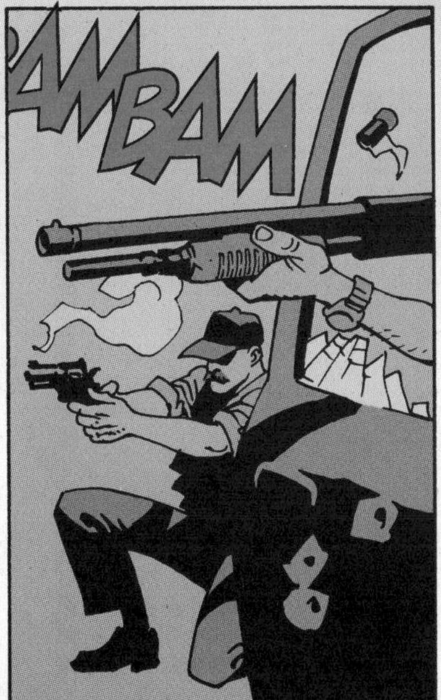
BAMBAM

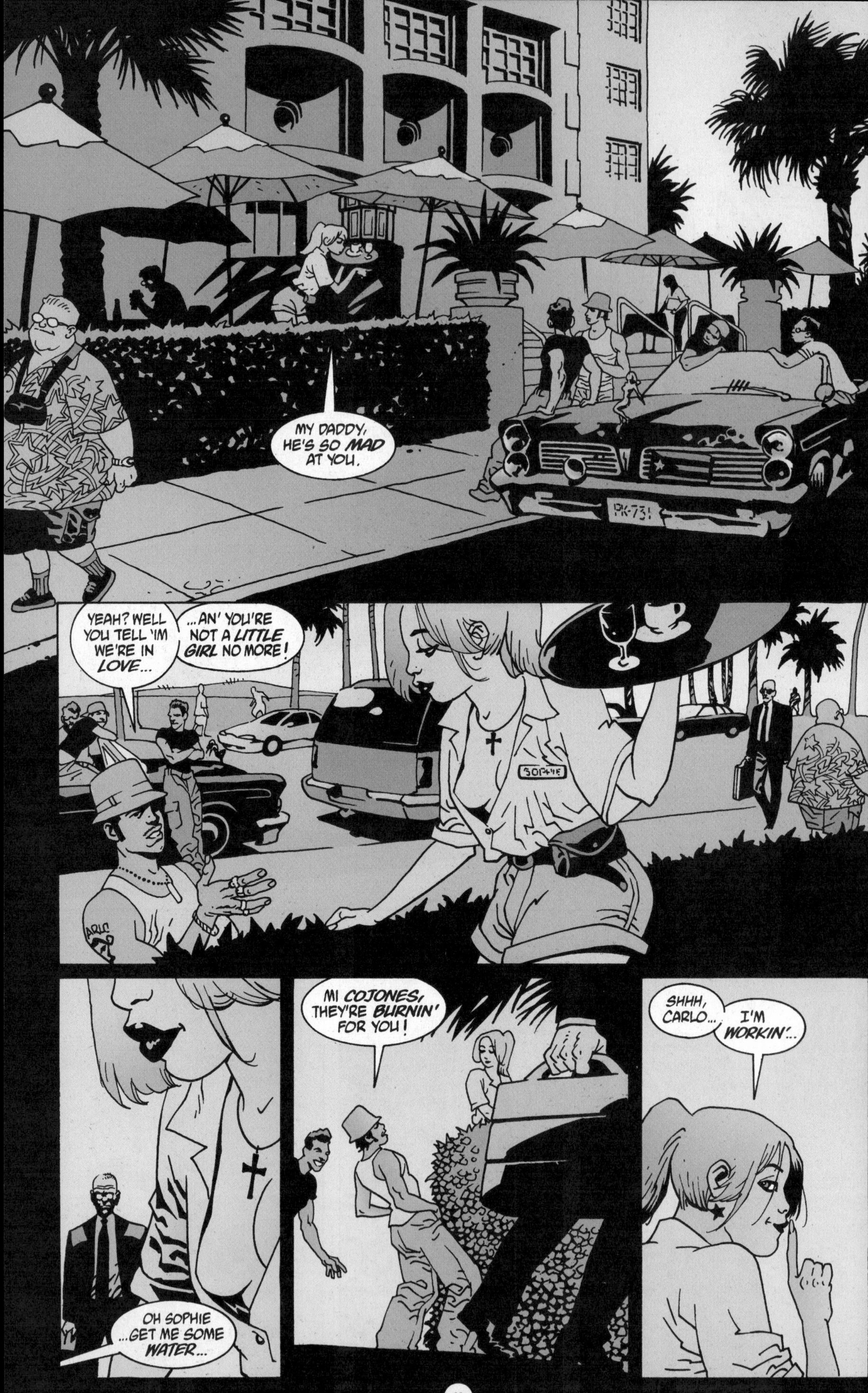
MY DADDY, HE'S SO MAD AT YOU.
YEAH? WELL YOU TELL 'IM WE'RE IN LOVE...
...AN' YOU'RE NOT A LITTLE GIRL NO MORE!
SOPHIE
OH SOPHIE ...GET ME SOME WATER...
MI COJONES, THEY'RE BURNIN' FOR YOU!
SHHH, CARLO...
I'M WORKIN'...

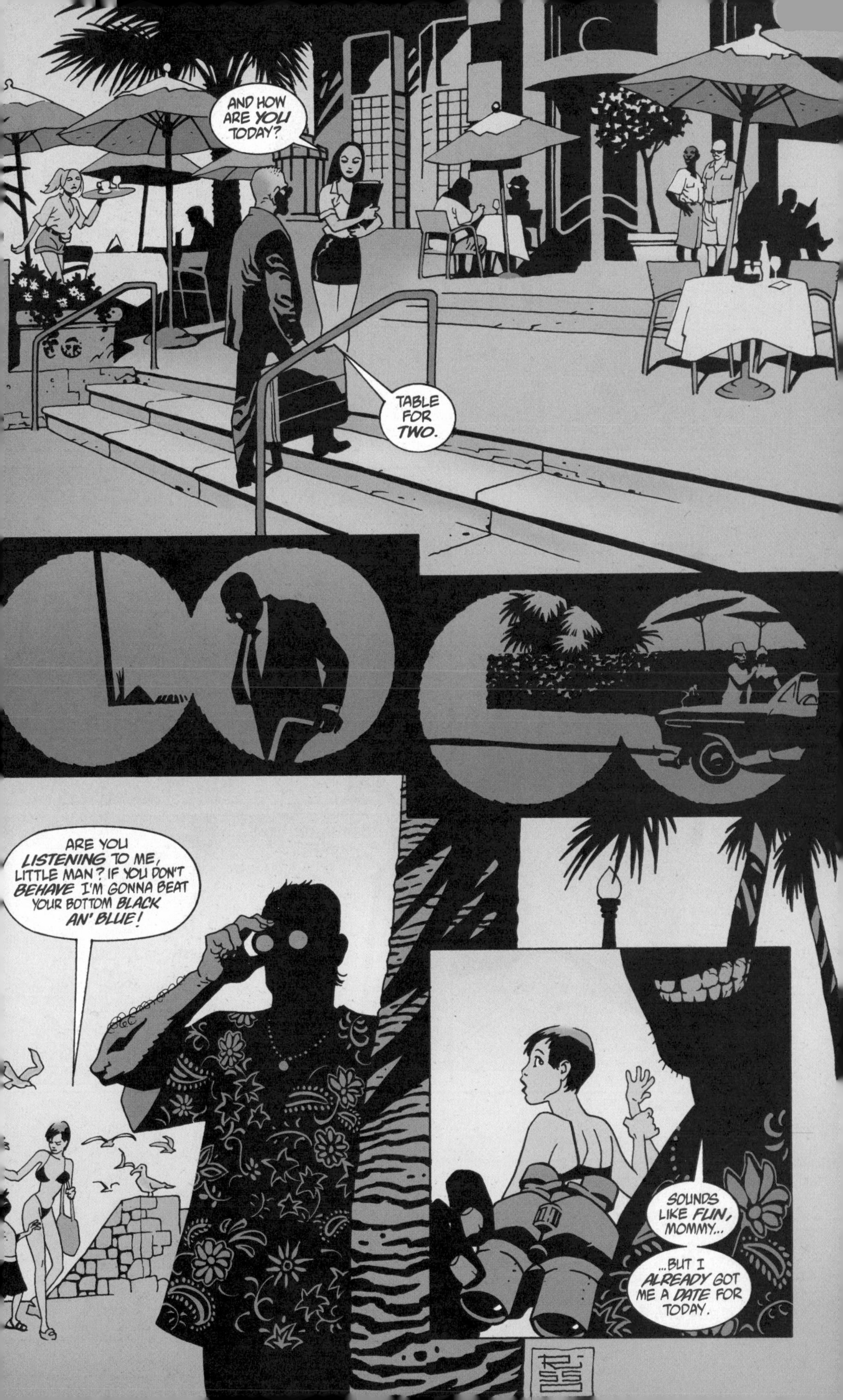
AND HOW ARE YOU TODAY?
TABLE FOR TWO.
ARE YOU LISTENING TO ME, LITTLE MAN? IF YOU DON'T BEHAVE I'M GONNA BEAT YOUR BOTTOM BLACK AN' BLUE!
SOUNDS LIKE FUN, MOMMY...
...BUT I ALREADY GOT ME A DATE FOR TODAY.

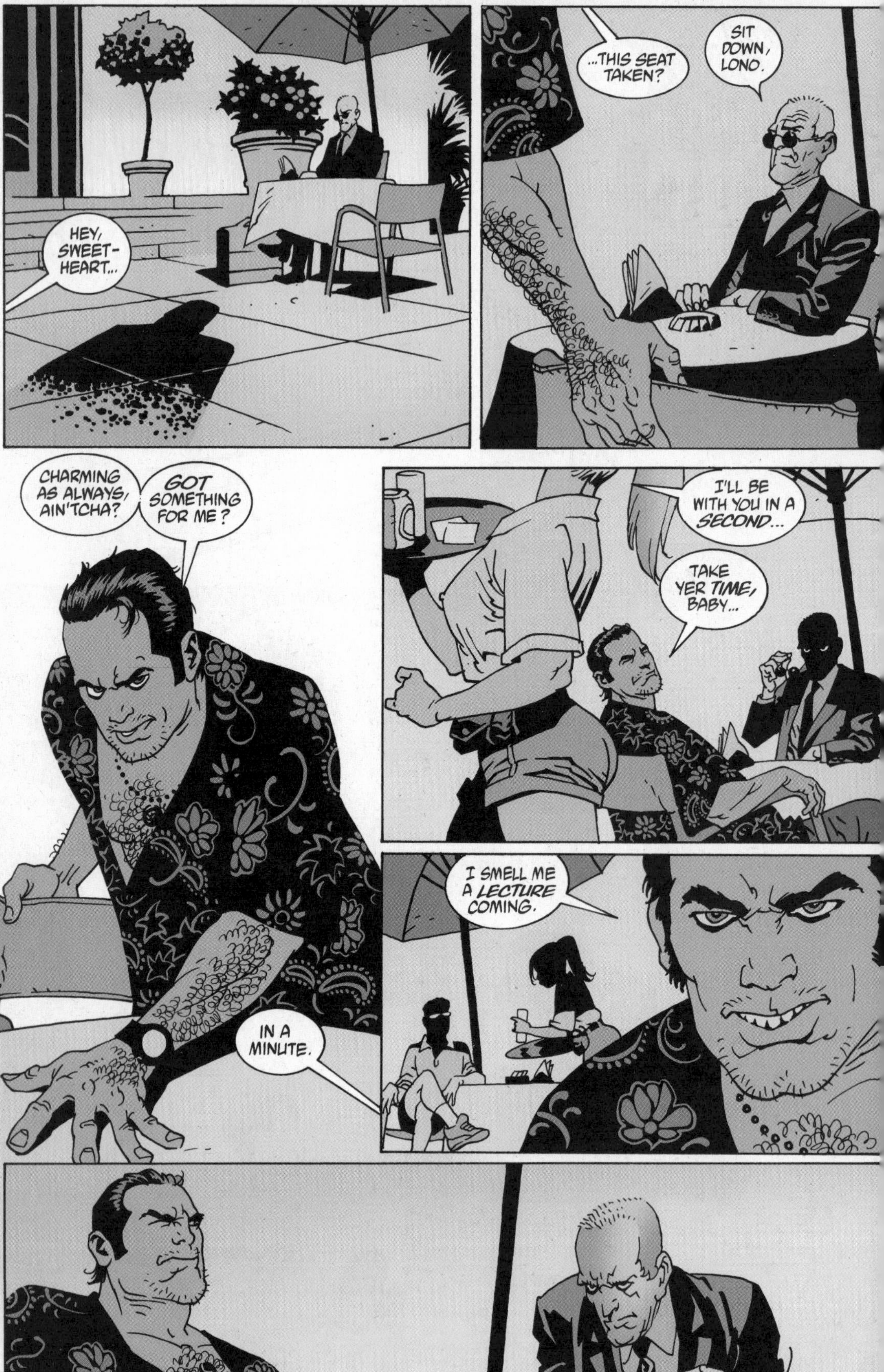
HEY, SWEET-HEART...
...THIS SEAT TAKEN?
SIT DOWN, LONO.
CHARMING AS ALWAYS, AIN'TCHA?
GOT SOMETHING FOR ME?
IN A MINUTE.
I'LL BE WITH YOU IN A SECOND...
TAKE YER TIME, BABY...
I SMELL ME A LECTURE COMING.

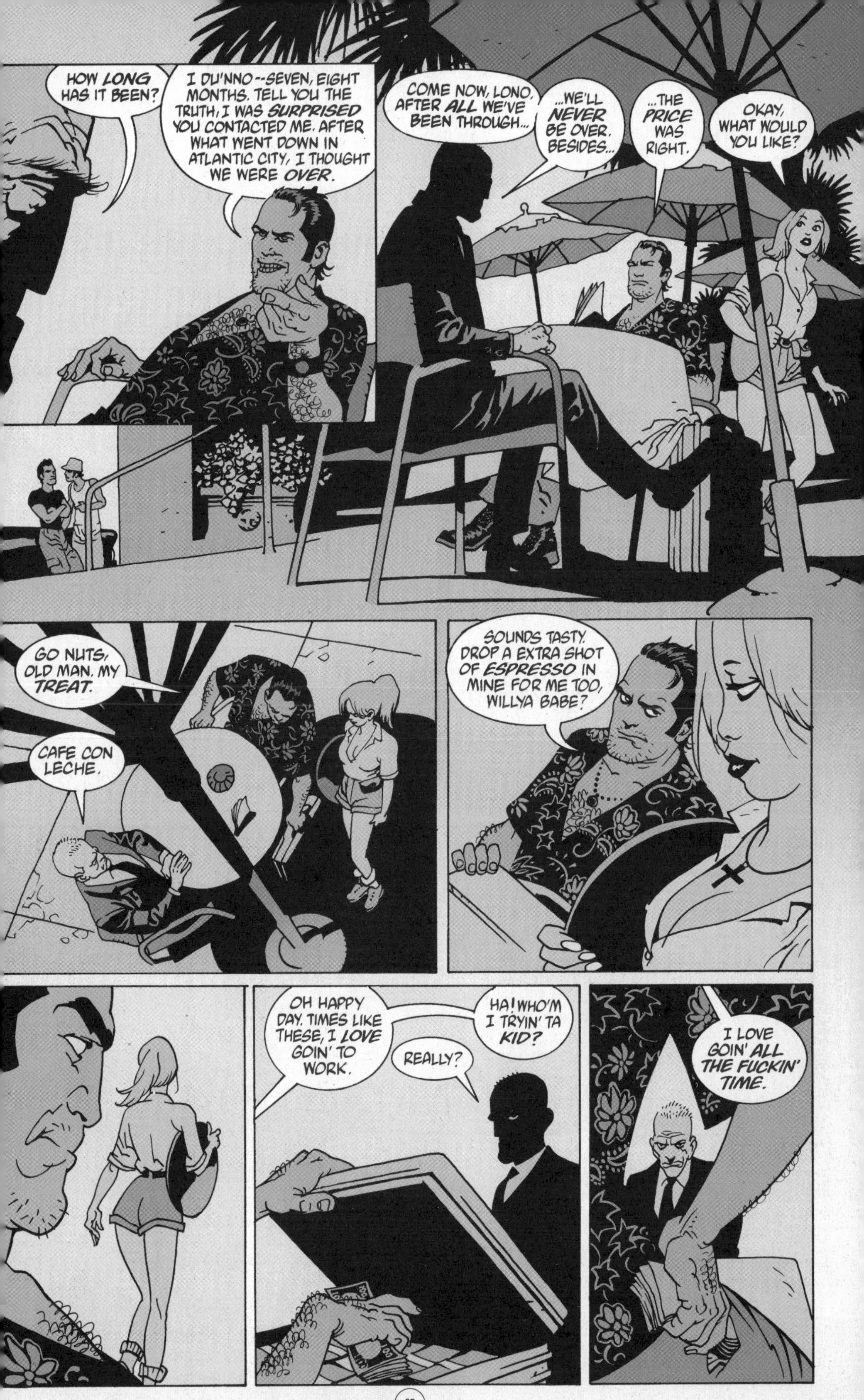
HOW LONG HAS IT BEEN?
I DU'NNO--SEVEN, EIGHT MONTHS. TELL YOU THE TRUTH, I WAS SURPRISED YOU CONTACTED ME. AFTER WHAT WENT DOWN IN ATLANTIC CITY, I THOUGHT WE WERE OVER.
COME NOW, LONO, AFTER ALL WE'VE BEEN THROUGH...
...WE'LL NEVER BE OVER. BESIDES...
...THE PRICE WAS RIGHT.
OKAY, WHAT WOULD YOU LIKE?
GO NUTS, OLD MAN. MY TREAT.
CAFE CON LECHE.
SOUNDS TASTY. DROP A EXTRA SHOT OF ESPRESSO IN MINE FOR ME TOO, WILLYA BABE?
OH HAPPY DAY. TIMES LIKE THESE, I LOVE GOIN' TO WORK.
REALLY?
HA! WHO'M I TRYIN' TA KID?
I LOVE GOIN' ALL THE FUCKIN' TIME.

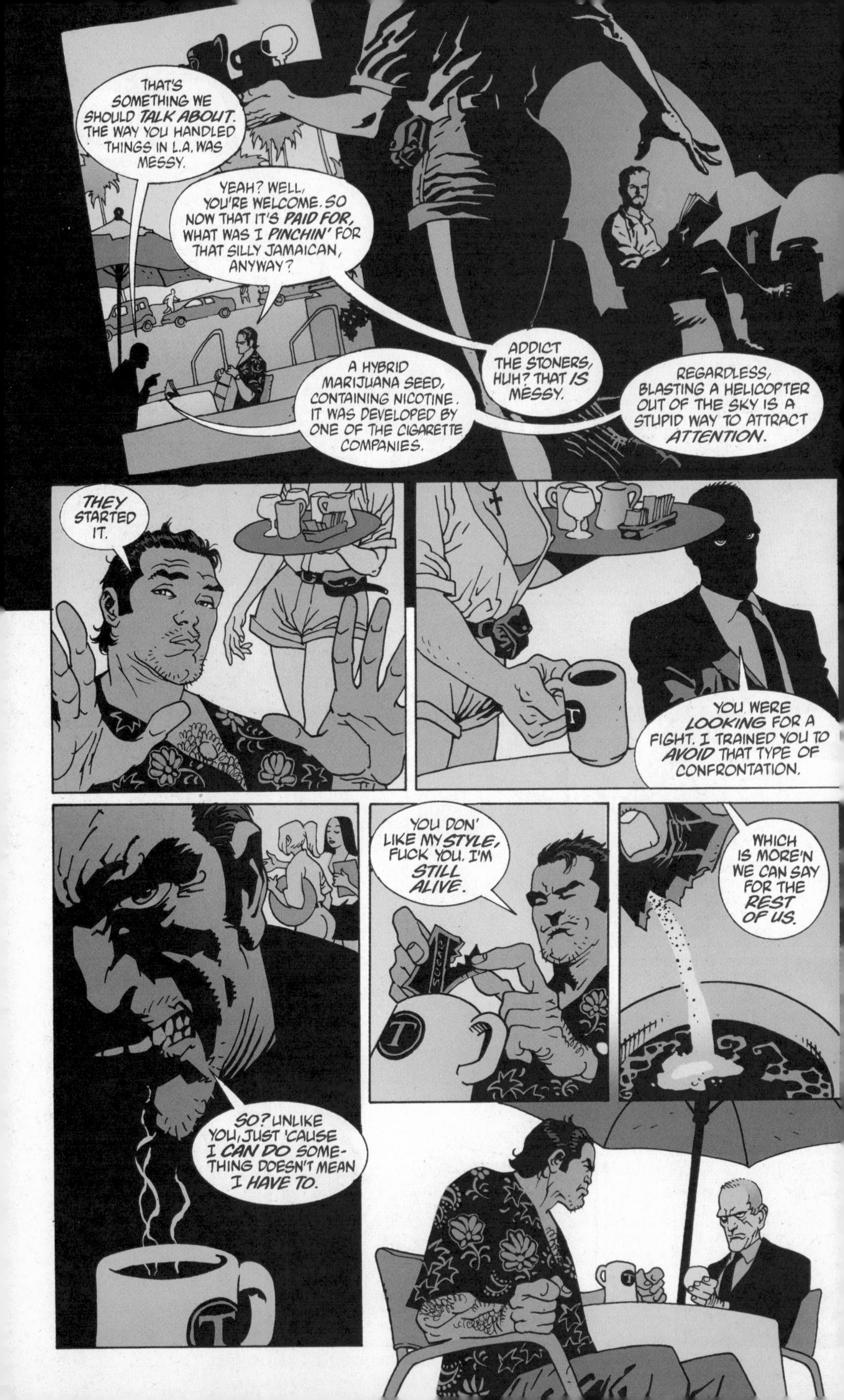
THAT'S SOMETHING WE SHOULD TALK ABOUT. THE WAY YOU HANDLED THINGS IN L.A. WAS MESSY.
YEAH? WELL, YOU'RE WELCOME. SO NOW THAT IT'S PAID FOR, WHAT WAS I PINCHIN' FOR THAT SILLY JAMAICAN, ANYWAY?
A HYBRID MARIJUANA SEED, CONTAINING NICOTINE. IT WAS DEVELOPED BY ONE OF THE CIGARETTE COMPANIES.
ADDICT THE STONERS, HUH? THAT IS MESSY.
REGARDLESS, BLASTING A HELICOPTER OUT OF THE SKY IS A STUPID WAY TO ATTRACT ATTENTION.
THEY STARTED IT.
YOU WERE LOOKING FOR A FIGHT. I TRAINED YOU TO AVOID THAT TYPE OF CONFRONTATION.
SO? UNLIKE YOU, JUST 'CAUSE I CAN DO SOME-THING DOESN'T MEAN I HAVE TO.
YOU DON' LIKE MY STYLE, FUCK YOU. I'M STILL ALIVE.
WHICH IS MORE'N WE CAN SAY FOR THE REST OF US.

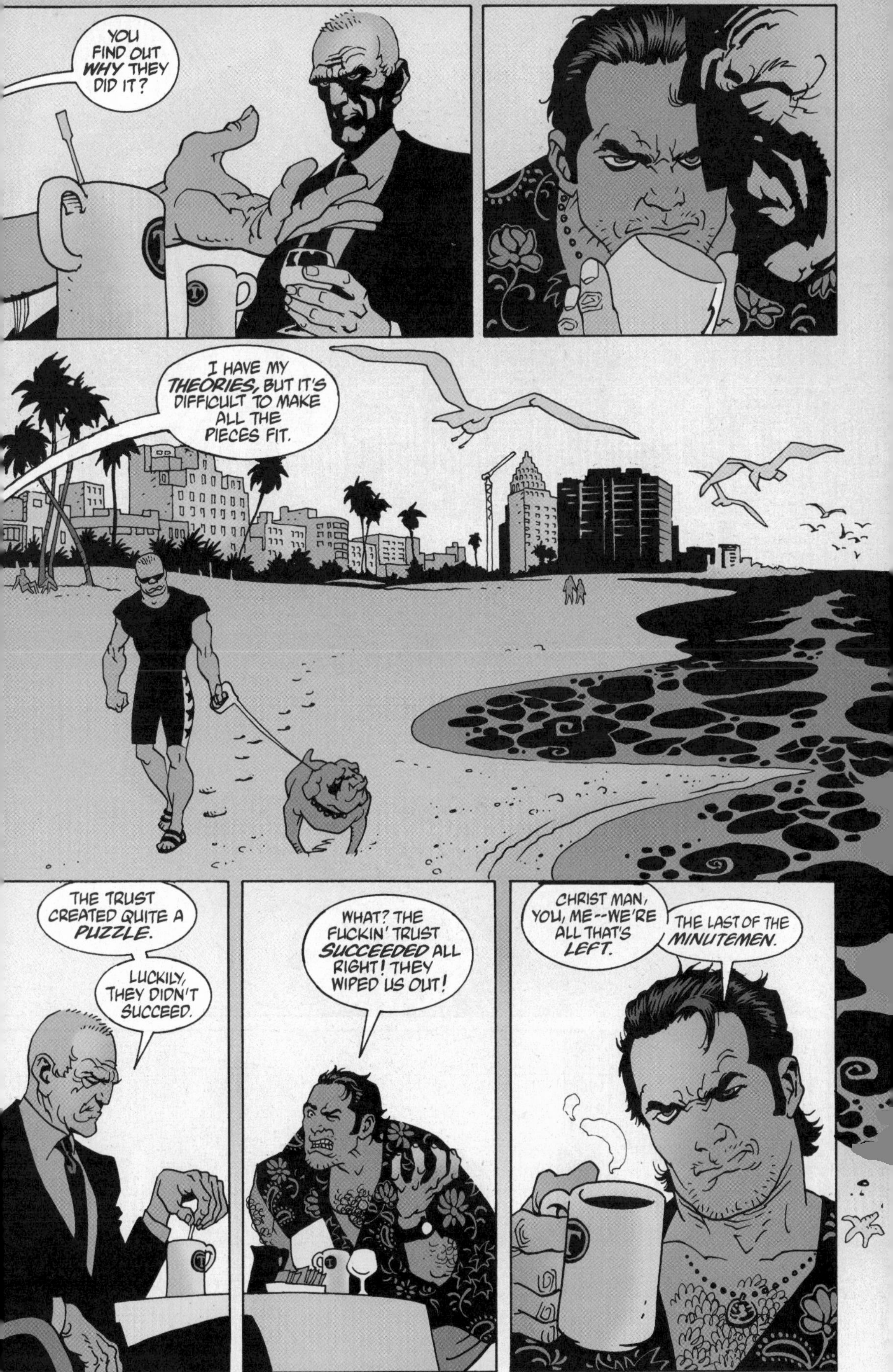
YOU FIND OUT WHY THEY DID IT?
I HAVE MY THEORIES, BUT IT'S DIFFICULT TO MAKE ALL THE PIECES FIT.
THE TRUST CREATED QUITE A PUZZLE.
LUCKILY, THEY DIDN'T SUCCEED.
WHAT? THE FUCKIN' TRUST SUCCEEDED ALL RIGHT! THEY WIPED US OUT!
CHRIST MAN, YOU, ME--WE'RE ALL THAT'S LEFT.
THE LAST OF THE MINUTEMEN.

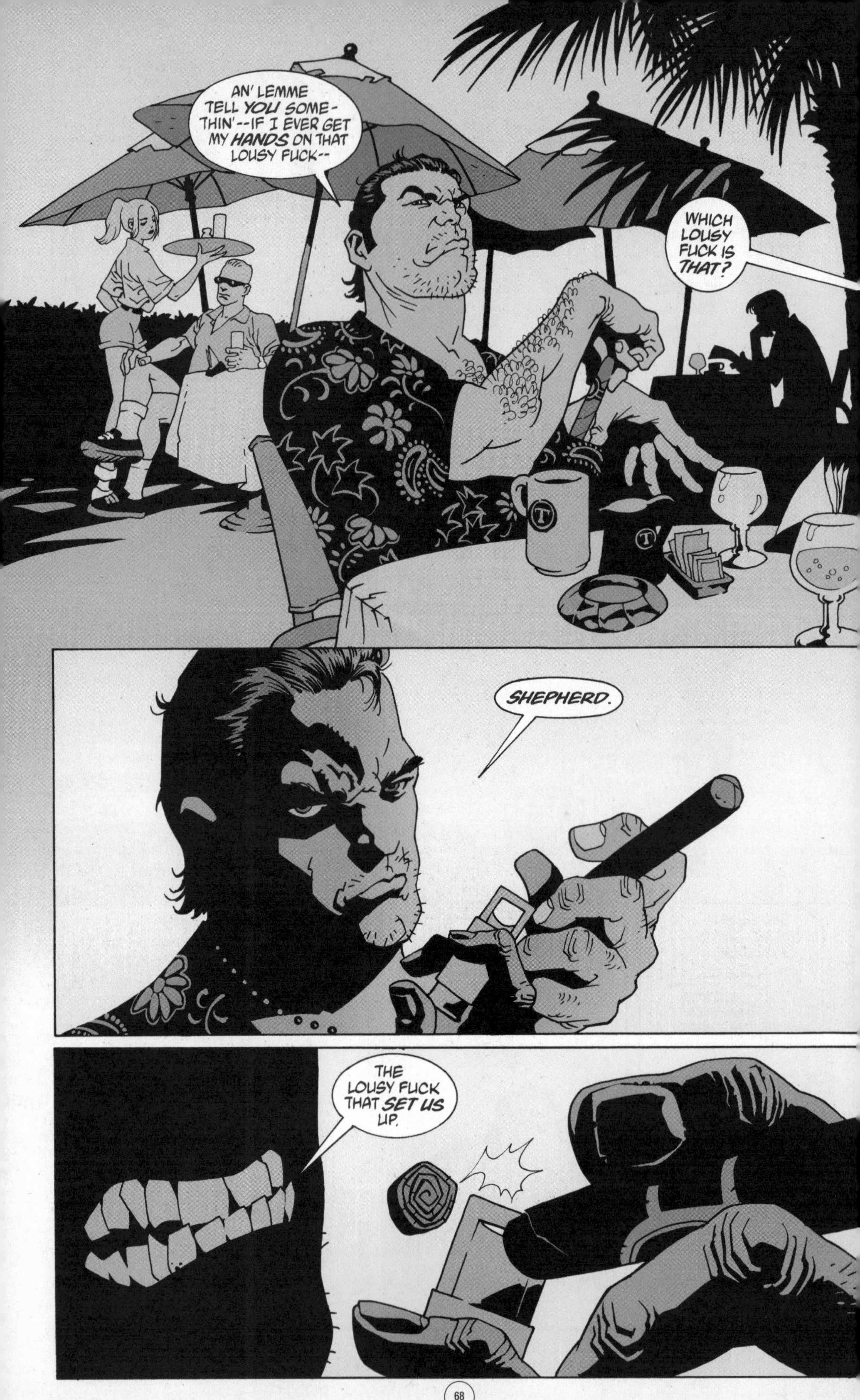
AN' LEMME TELL YOU SOME-THIN'--IF I EVER GET MY HANDS ON THAT LOUSY FUCK--
WHICH LOUSY FUCK IS THAT?
SHEPHERD.
THE LOUSY FUCK THAT SET US UP.

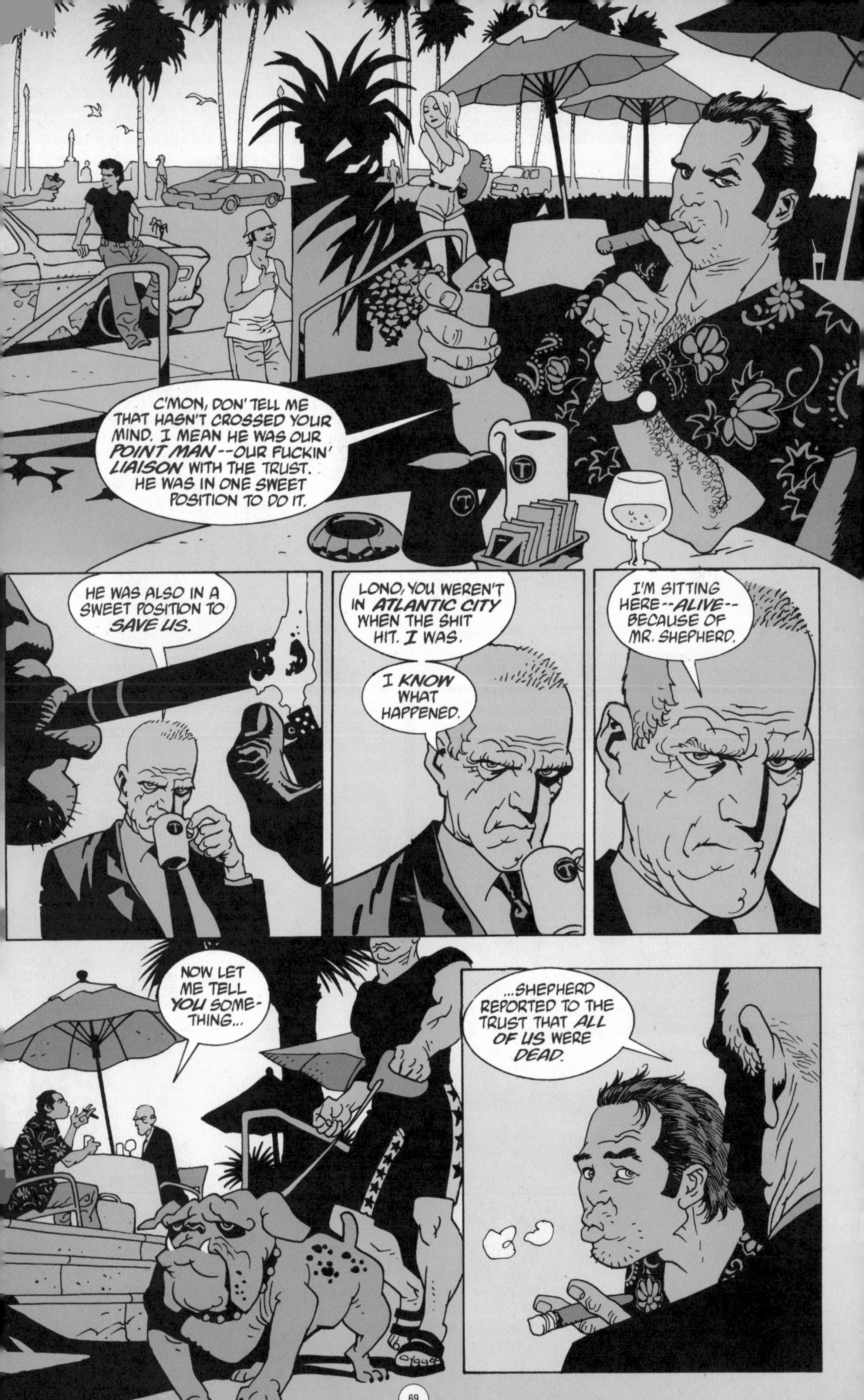
C'MON, DON' TELL ME THAT HASN'T CROSSED YOUR MIND. I MEAN HE WAS OUR POINT MAN--OUR FUCKIN' LIAISON WITH THE TRUST. HE WAS IN ONE SWEET POSITION TO DO IT.
HE WAS ALSO IN A SWEET POSITION TO SAVE US.
LONO, YOU WEREN'T IN ATLANTIC CITY WHEN THE SHIT HIT. I WAS.
I KNOW WHAT HAPPENED.
I'M SITTING HERE--ALIVE--BECAUSE OF MR. SHEPHERD.
NOW LET ME TELL YOU SOME-THING...
...SHEPHERD REPORTED TO THE TRUST THAT ALL OF US WERE DEAD.

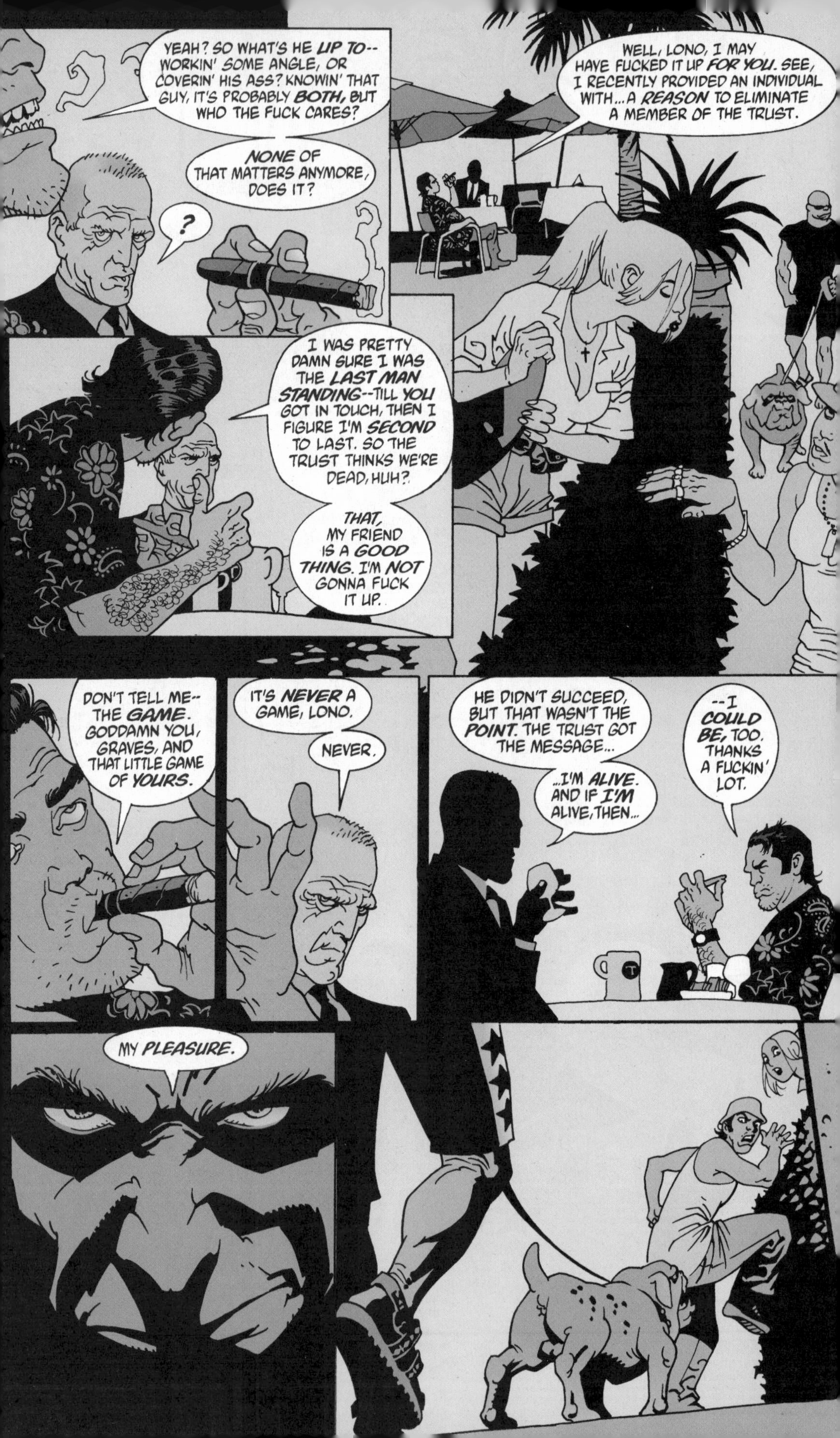

YEAH? SO WHAT'S HE UP TO--WORKIN' SOME ANGLE, OR COVERIN' HIS ASS? KNOWIN' THAT GUY, IT'S PROBABLY BOTH, BUT WHO THE FUCK CARES?
NONE OF THAT MATTERS ANYMORE, DOES IT?
?
WELL, LONO, I MAY HAVE FUCKED IT UP FOR YOU. SEE, I RECENTLY PROVIDED AN INDIVIDUAL WITH...A REASON TO ELIMINATE A MEMBER OF THE TRUST.
I WAS PRETTY DAMN SURE I WAS THE LAST MAN STANDING--TILL YOU GOT IN TOUCH, THEN I FIGURE I'M SECOND TO LAST. SO THE TRUST THINKS WE'RE DEAD, HUH?
THAT, MY FRIEND IS A GOOD THING. I'M NOT GONNA FUCK IT UP.
DON'T TELL ME--THE GAME. GODDAMN YOU, GRAVES, AND THAT LITTLE GAME OF YOURS.
IT'S NEVER A GAME, LONO.
NEVER.
HE DIDN'T SUCCEED, BUT THAT WASN'T THE POINT. THE TRUST GOT THE MESSAGE...
...I'M ALIVE. AND IF I'M ALIVE, THEN...
--I COULD BE, TOO. THANKS A FUCKIN' LOT.
MY PLEASURE.

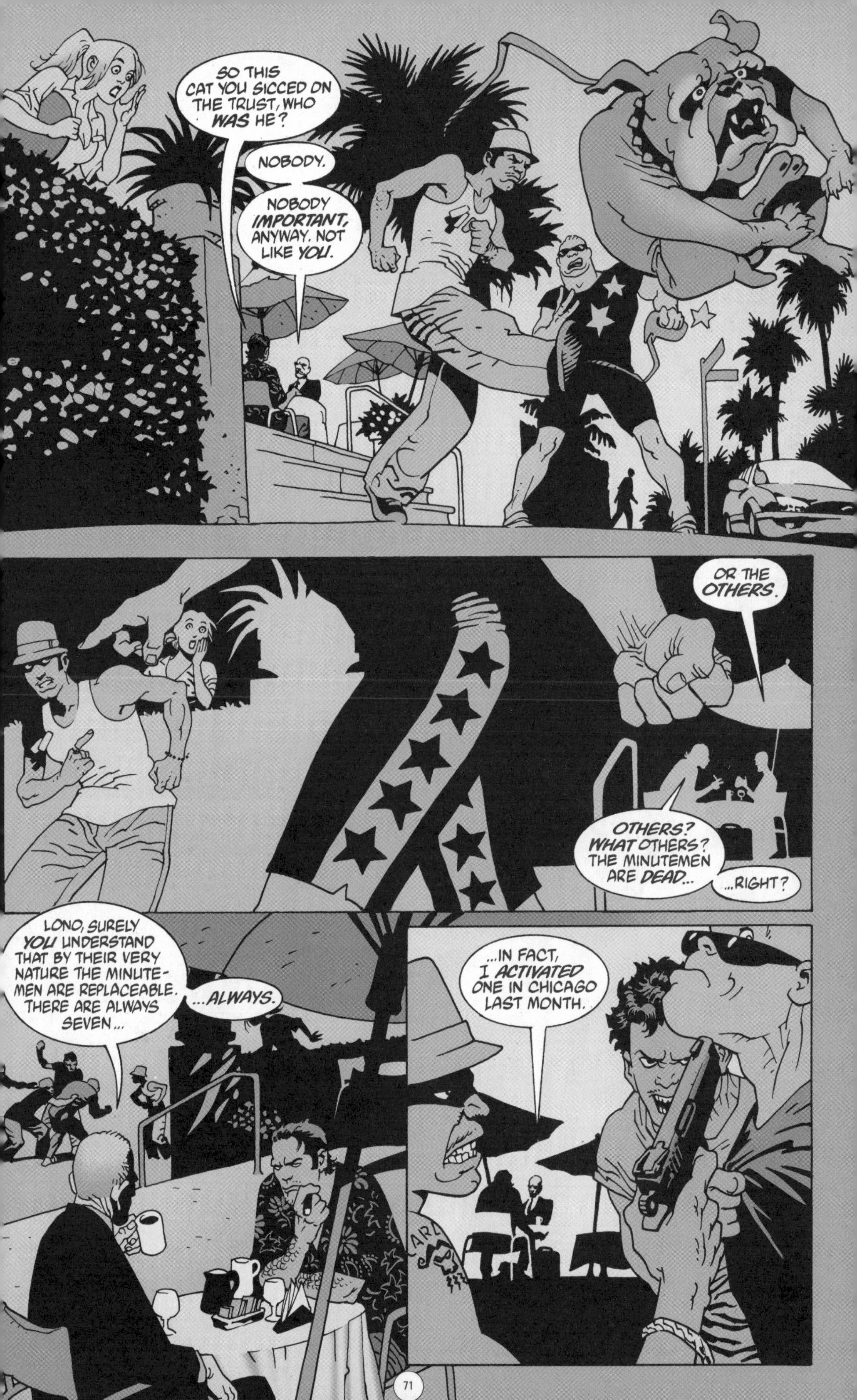

SO THIS CAT YOU SICCED ON THE TRUST, WHO WAS HE?
NOBODY.
NOBODY IMPORTANT, ANYWAY. NOT LIKE YOU.
OR THE OTHERS.
OTHERS? WHAT OTHERS? THE MINUTEMEN ARE DEAD...
...RIGHT?
LONO, SURELY YOU UNDERSTAND THAT BY THEIR VERY NATURE THE MINUTE-MEN ARE REPLACEABLE. THERE ARE ALWAYS SEVEN...
...ALWAYS.
...IN FACT, I ACTIVATED ONE IN CHICAGO LAST MONTH.

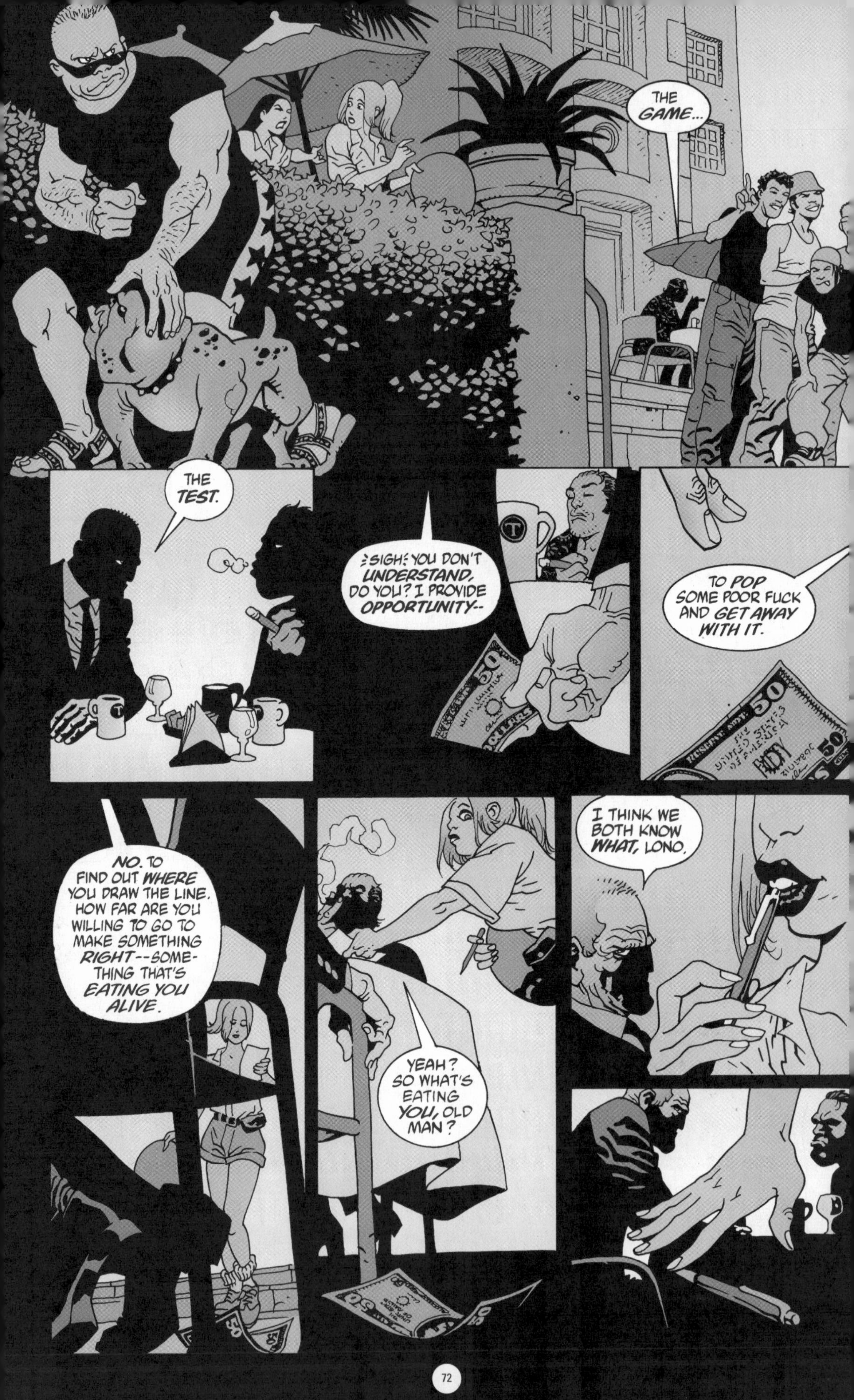
THE GAME...
THE TEST.
:SIGH: YOU DON'T UNDERSTAND, DO YOU? I PROVIDE OPPORTUNITY--
TO POP SOME POOR FUCK AND GET AWAY WITH IT.
NO. TO FIND OUT WHERE YOU DRAW THE LINE. HOW FAR ARE YOU WILLING TO GO TO MAKE SOMETHING RIGHT--SOMETHING THAT'S EATING YOU ALIVE.
YEAH? SO WHAT'S EATING YOU, OLD MAN?
I THINK WE BOTH KNOW WHAT, LONO.

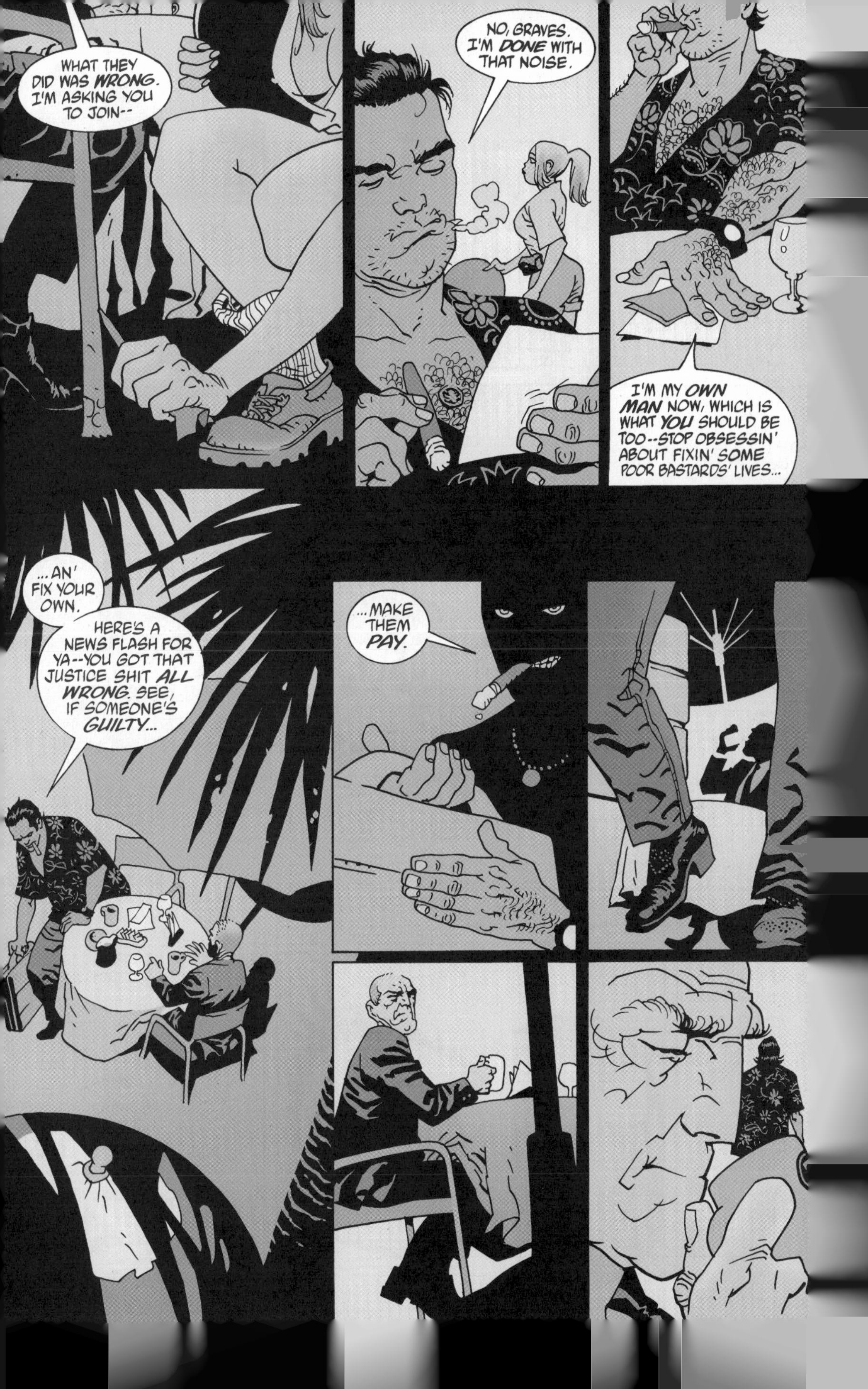
WHAT THEY DID WAS WRONG. I'M ASKING YOU TO JOIN--
NO, GRAVES. I'M DONE WITH THAT NOISE.
I'M MY OWN MAN NOW, WHICH IS WHAT YOU SHOULD BE TOO--STOP OBSESSIN' ABOUT FIXIN' SOME POOR BASTARDS' LIVES...
...AN' FIX YOUR OWN.
HERE'S A NEWS FLASH FOR YA--YOU GOT THAT JUSTICE SHIT ALL WRONG. SEE, IF SOMEONE'S GUILTY...
...MAKE THEM PAY.

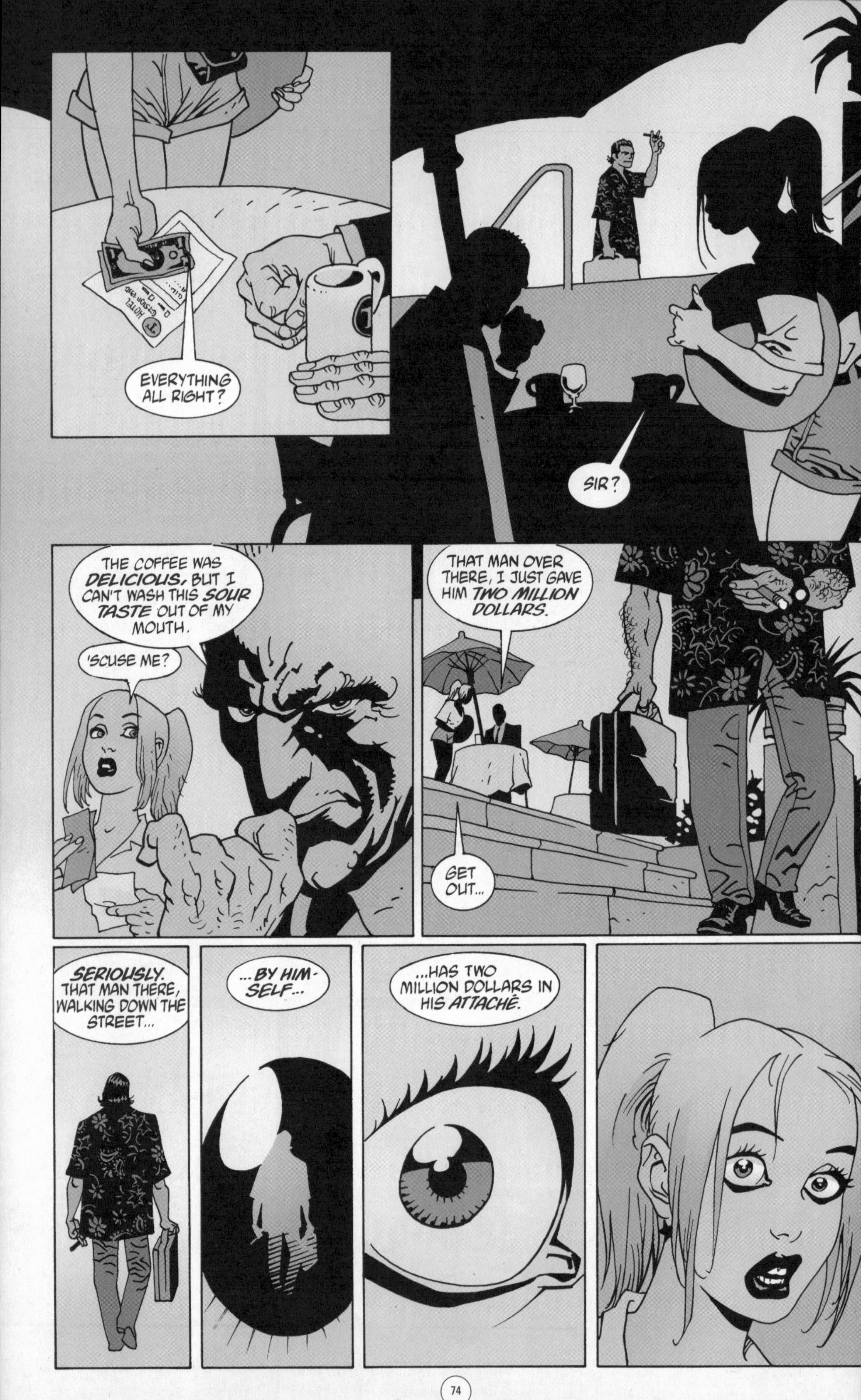
EVERYTHING ALL RIGHT?
SIR?
THE COFFEE WAS DELICIOUS, BUT I CAN'T WASH THIS SOUR TASTE OUT OF MY MOUTH.
'SCUSE ME?
THAT MAN OVER THERE, I JUST GAVE HIM TWO MILLION DOLLARS.
GET OUT...
SERIOUSLY. THAT MAN THERE, WALKING DOWN THE STREET...
...BY HIM-SELF...
...HAS TWO MILLION DOLLARS IN HIS ATTACHÉ.

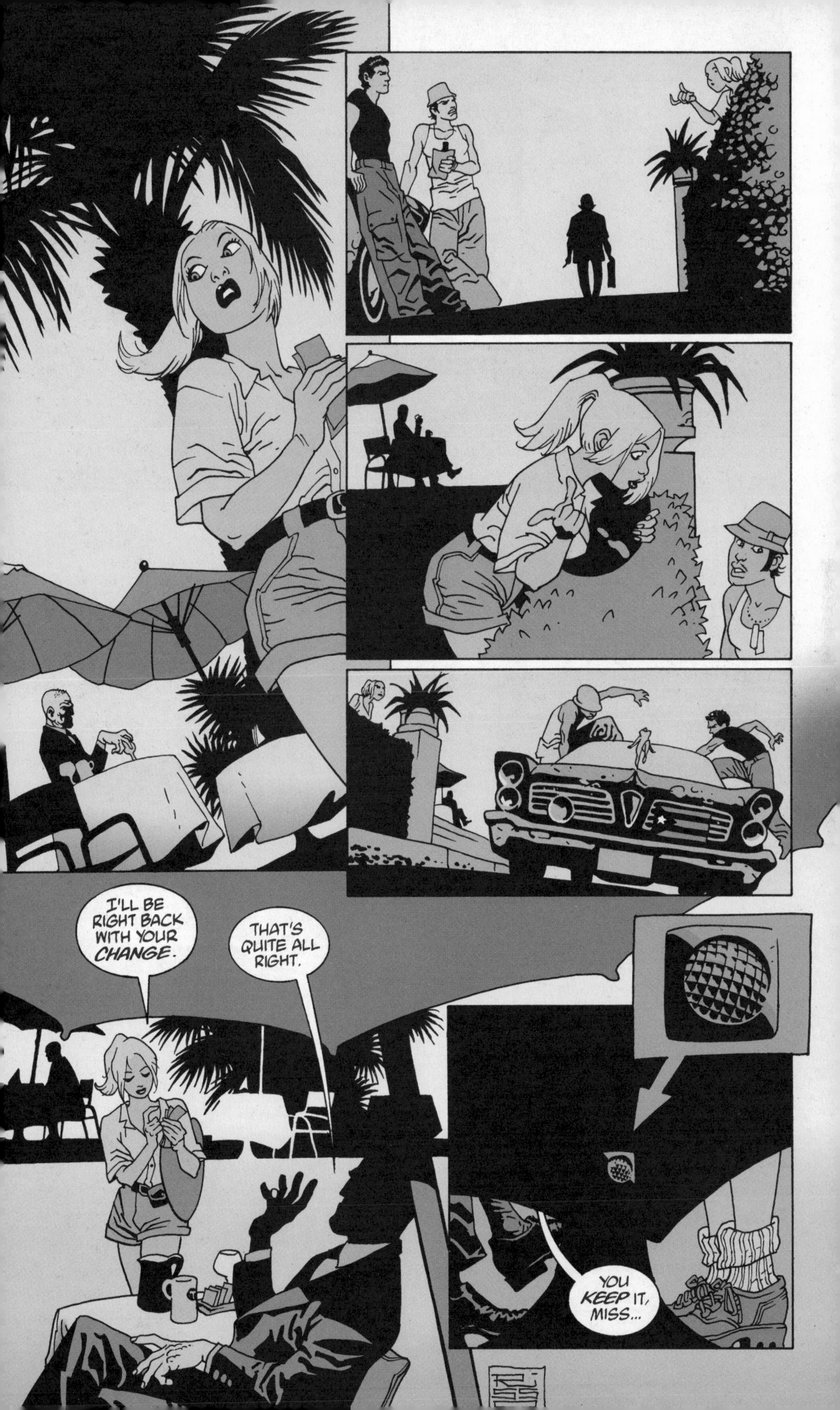
I'LL BE RIGHT BACK WITH YOUR CHANGE.
THAT'S QUITE ALL RIGHT.
YOU KEEP IT, MISS...

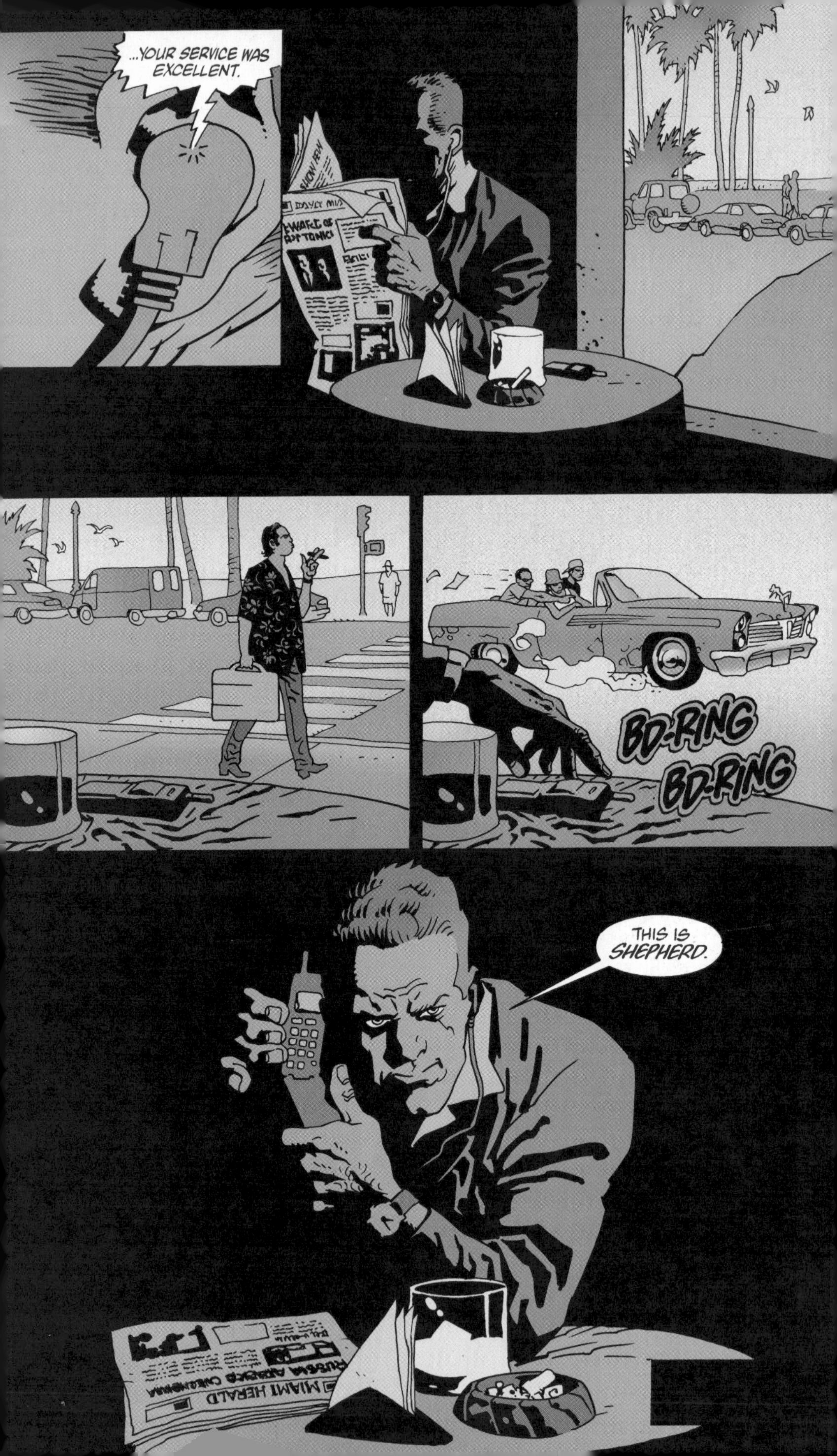
...YOUR SERVICE WAS EXCELLENT.
BD-RING
BD-RING
THIS IS SHEPHERD.
MIAMI HERALD

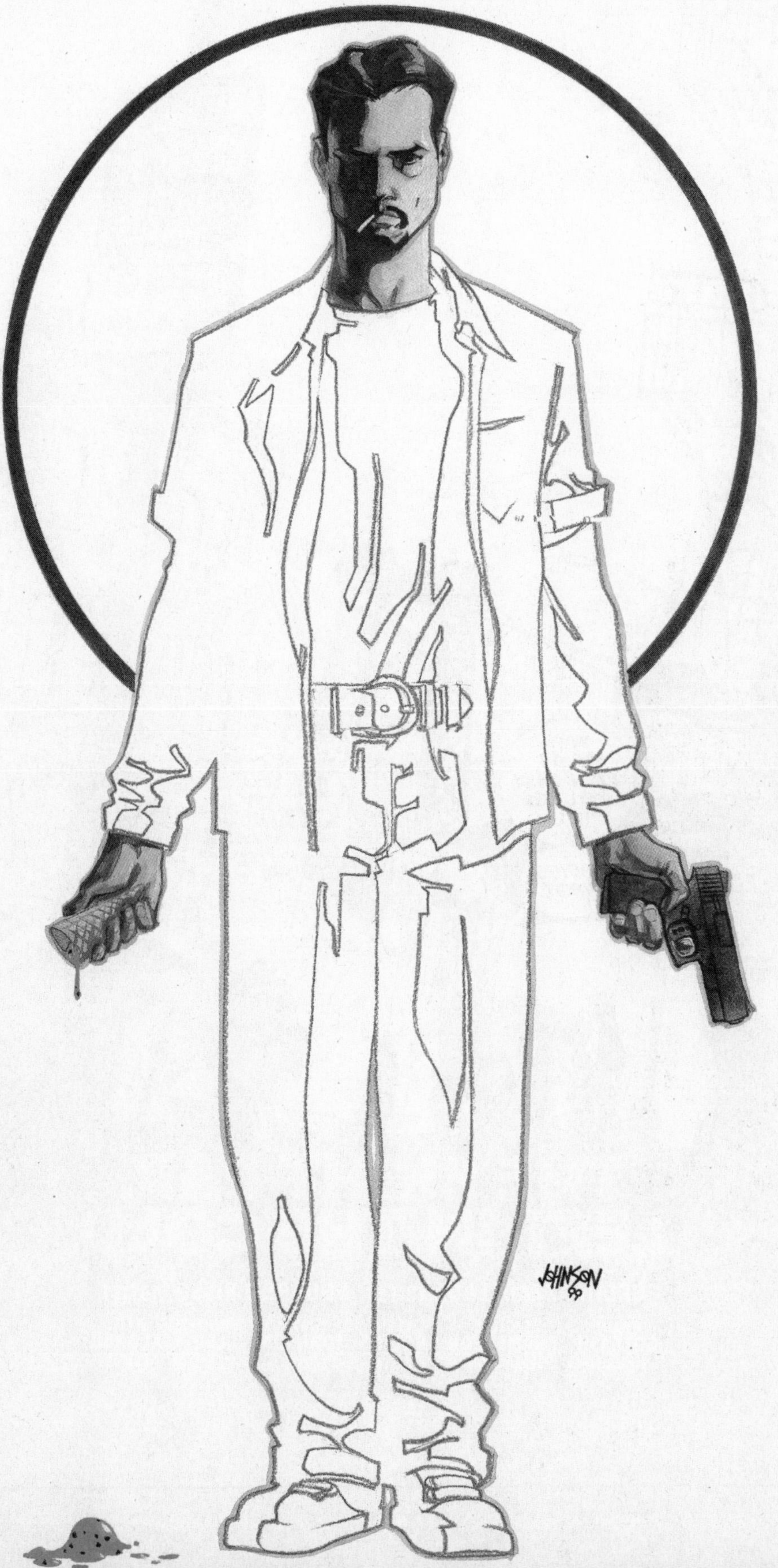
JOHNSON
99

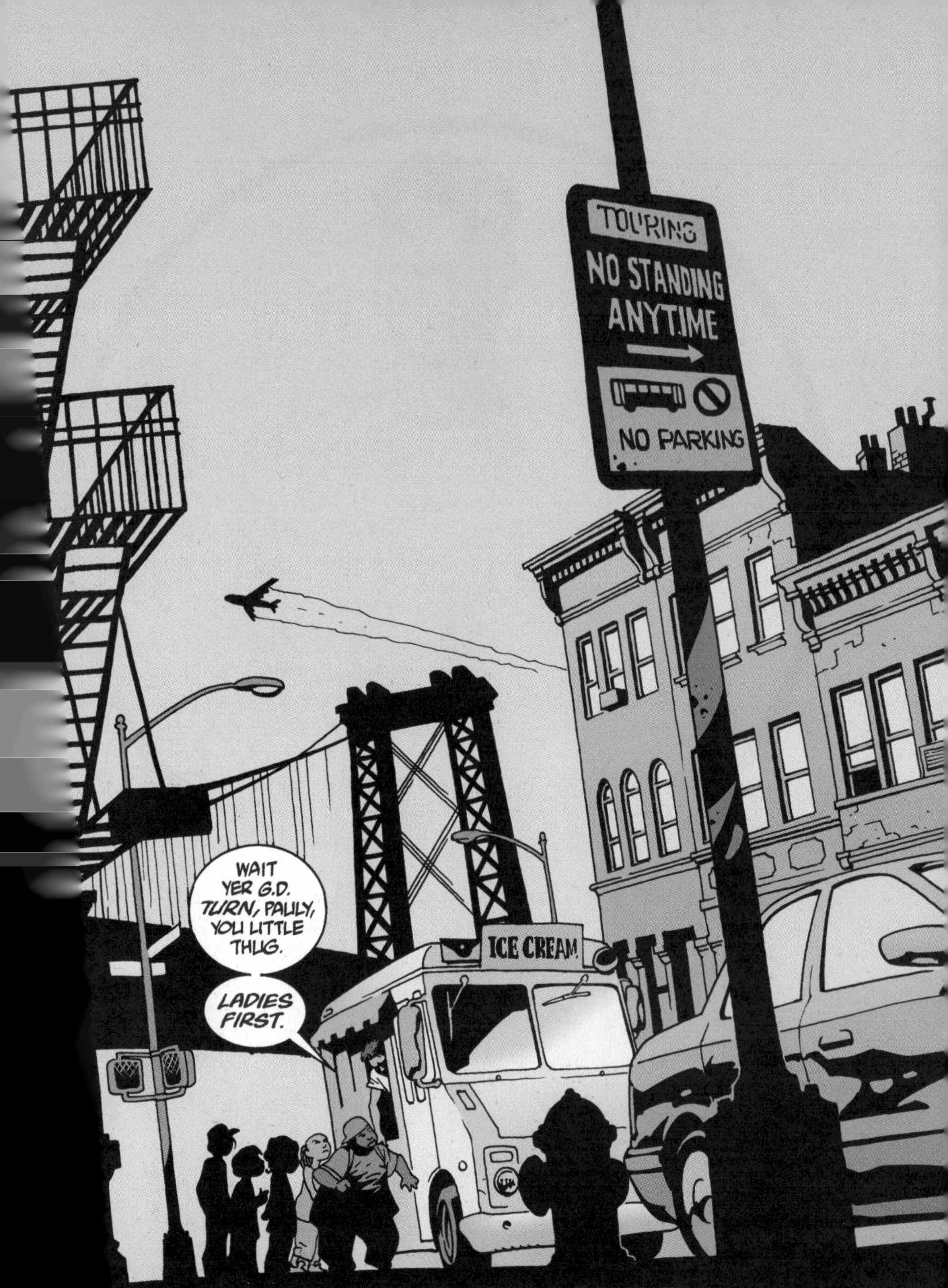
TOURING
NO STANDING ANYTIME
NO PARKING
WAIT YER G.D. TURN, PAULY, YOU LITTLE THUG.
LADIES FIRST.
ICE CREAM

THE RIGHT EAR, LEFT IN THE COLD

BRIAN AZZARELLO, WRITER EDUARDO RISSO, ARTIST

GRANT GOLEASH · DIGITAL CHAMELEON · CLEM ROBINS · DAVE JOHNSON · JENNIFER LEE · AXEL ALONSO

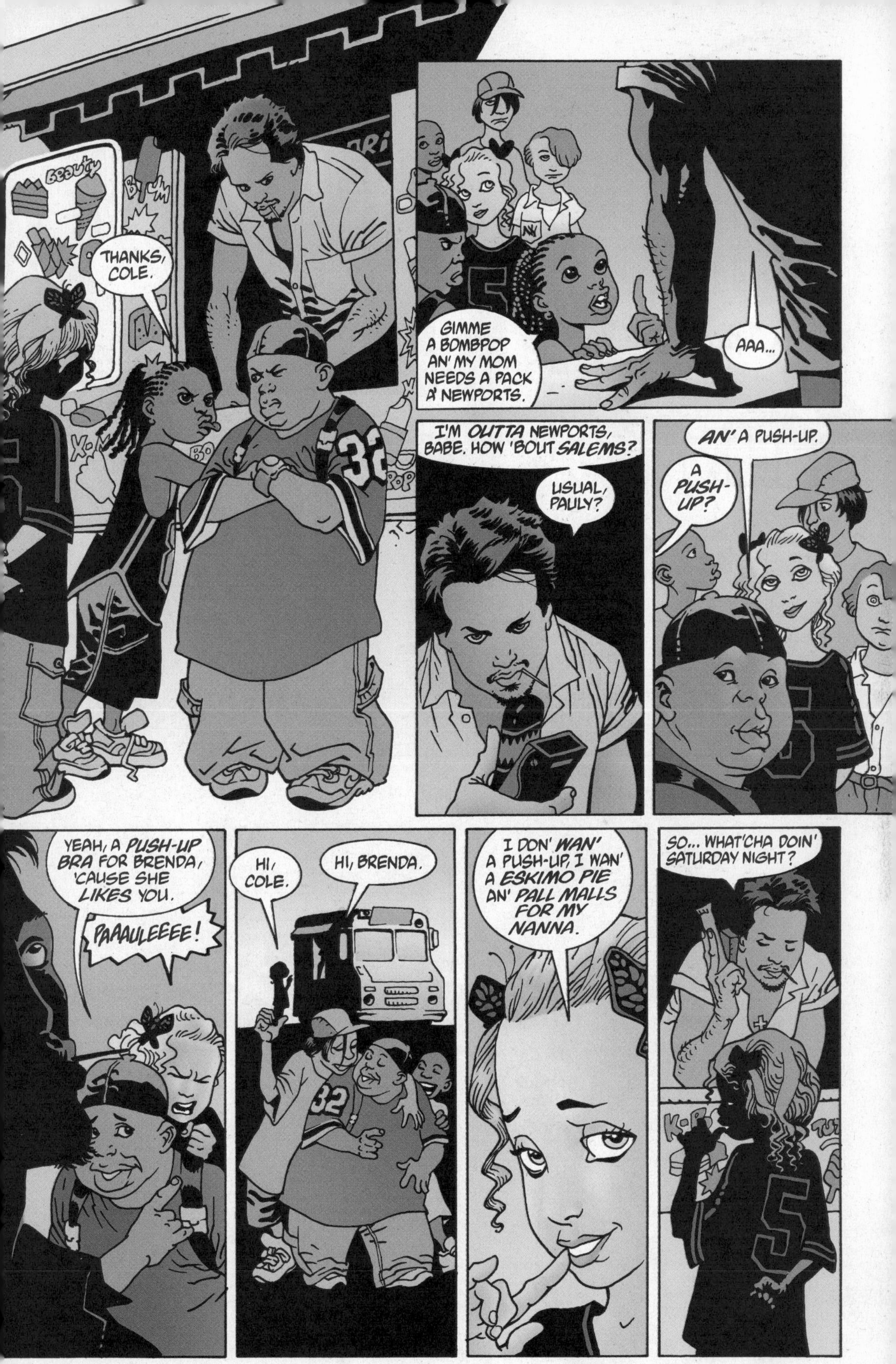
THANKS, COLE.
GIMME A BOMBPOP AN' MY MOM NEEDS A PACK A' NEWPORTS.
AAA...
I'M OUTTA NEWPORTS, BABE. HOW 'BOUT SALEMS?
USUAL, PAULY?
AN' A PUSH-UP.
A PUSH-UP?
YEAH, A PUSH-UP BRA FOR BRENDA, 'CAUSE SHE LIKES YOU.
PAAAULEEEE!
HI, COLE.
HI, BRENDA.
I DON' WAN' A PUSH-UP, I WAN' A ESKIMO PIE AN' PALL MALLS FOR MY NANNA.
SO... WHAT'CHA DOIN' SATURDAY NIGHT?

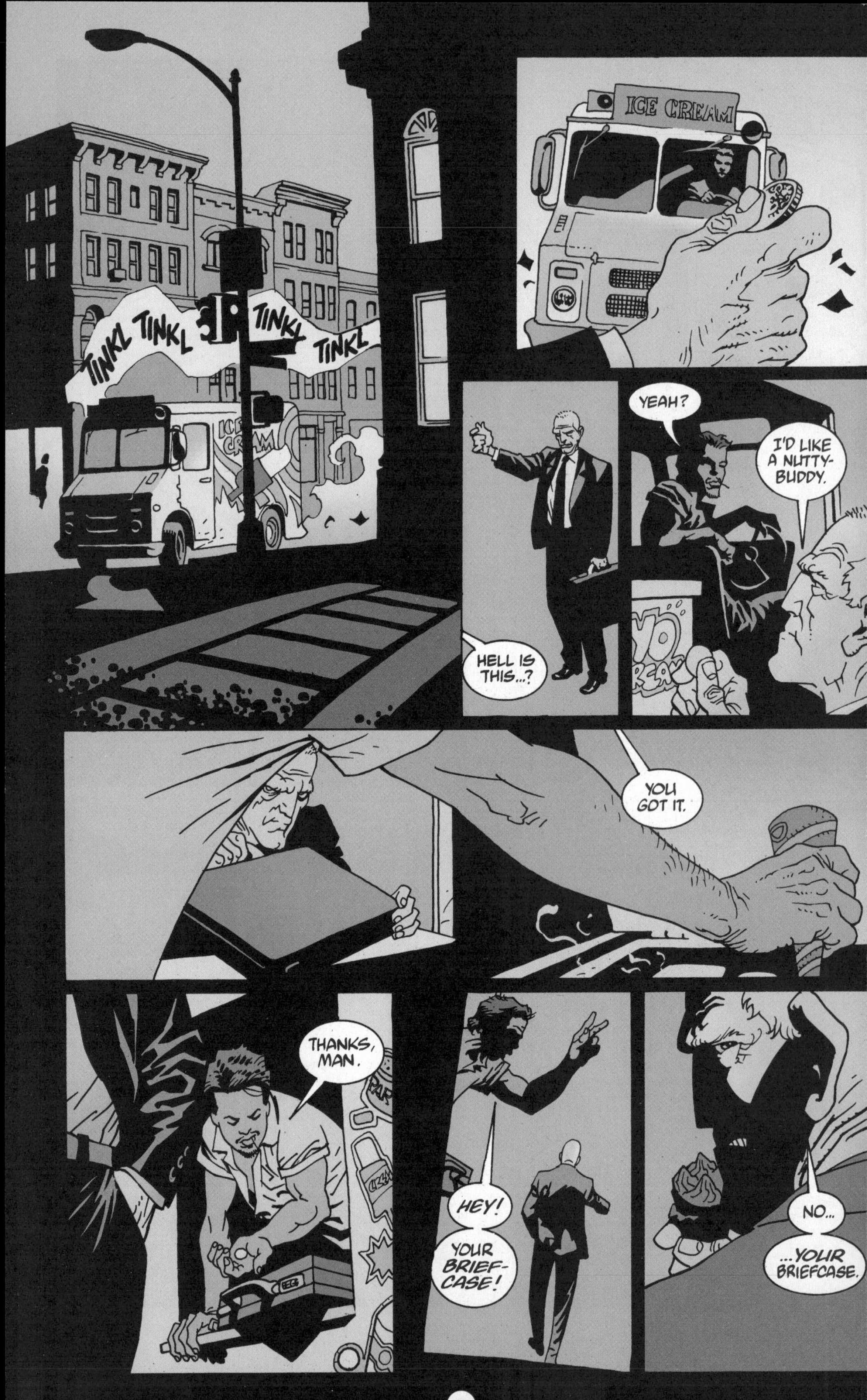
TINKL TINKL
TINKL
TINKL
ICE CREAM
YEAH?
I'D LIKE A NUTTY-BUDDY.
HELL IS THIS...?
YOU GOT IT.
THANKS, MAN.
HEY!
YOUR BRIEF-CASE!
NO...
...YOUR BRIEFCASE.

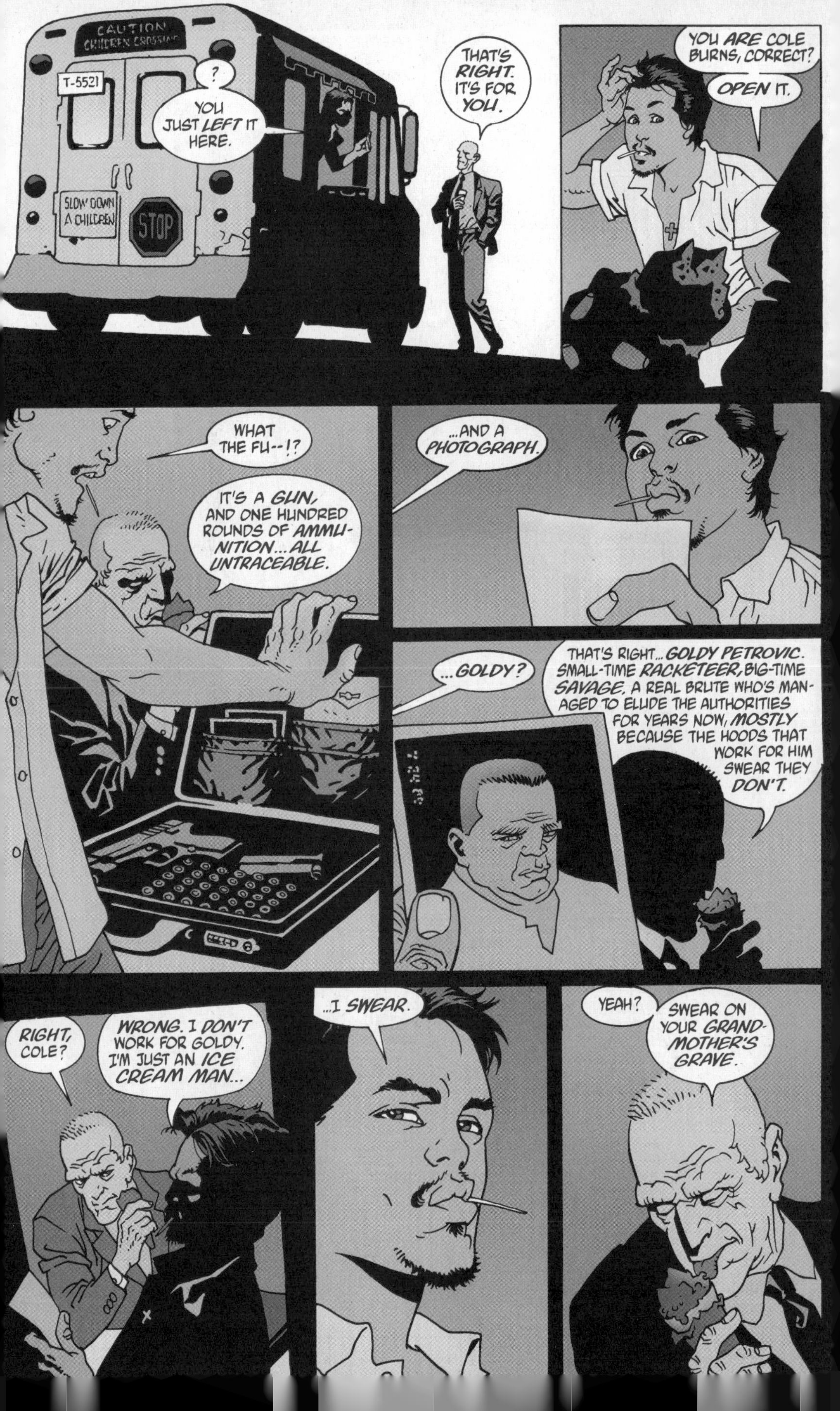
CAUTION
CHILDREN CROSSING
T-5521
SLOW DOWN
CHILDREN
STOP
?
YOU JUST LEFT IT HERE.
THAT'S RIGHT. IT'S FOR YOU.
YOU ARE COLE BURNS, CORRECT?
OPEN IT.
WHAT THE FU--!?
IT'S A GUN, AND ONE HUNDRED ROUNDS OF AMMUNITION... ALL UNTRACEABLE.
...AND A PHOTOGRAPH.
...GOLDY?
THAT'S RIGHT... GOLDY PETROVIC. SMALL-TIME RACKETEER, BIG-TIME SAVAGE, A REAL BRUTE WHO'S MANAGED TO ELUDE THE AUTHORITIES FOR YEARS NOW, MOSTLY BECAUSE THE HOODS THAT WORK FOR HIM SWEAR THEY DON'T.
RIGHT, COLE?
WRONG. I DON'T WORK FOR GOLDY. I'M JUST AN ICE CREAM MAN...
...I SWEAR.
YEAH?
SWEAR ON YOUR GRANDMOTHER'S GRAVE.

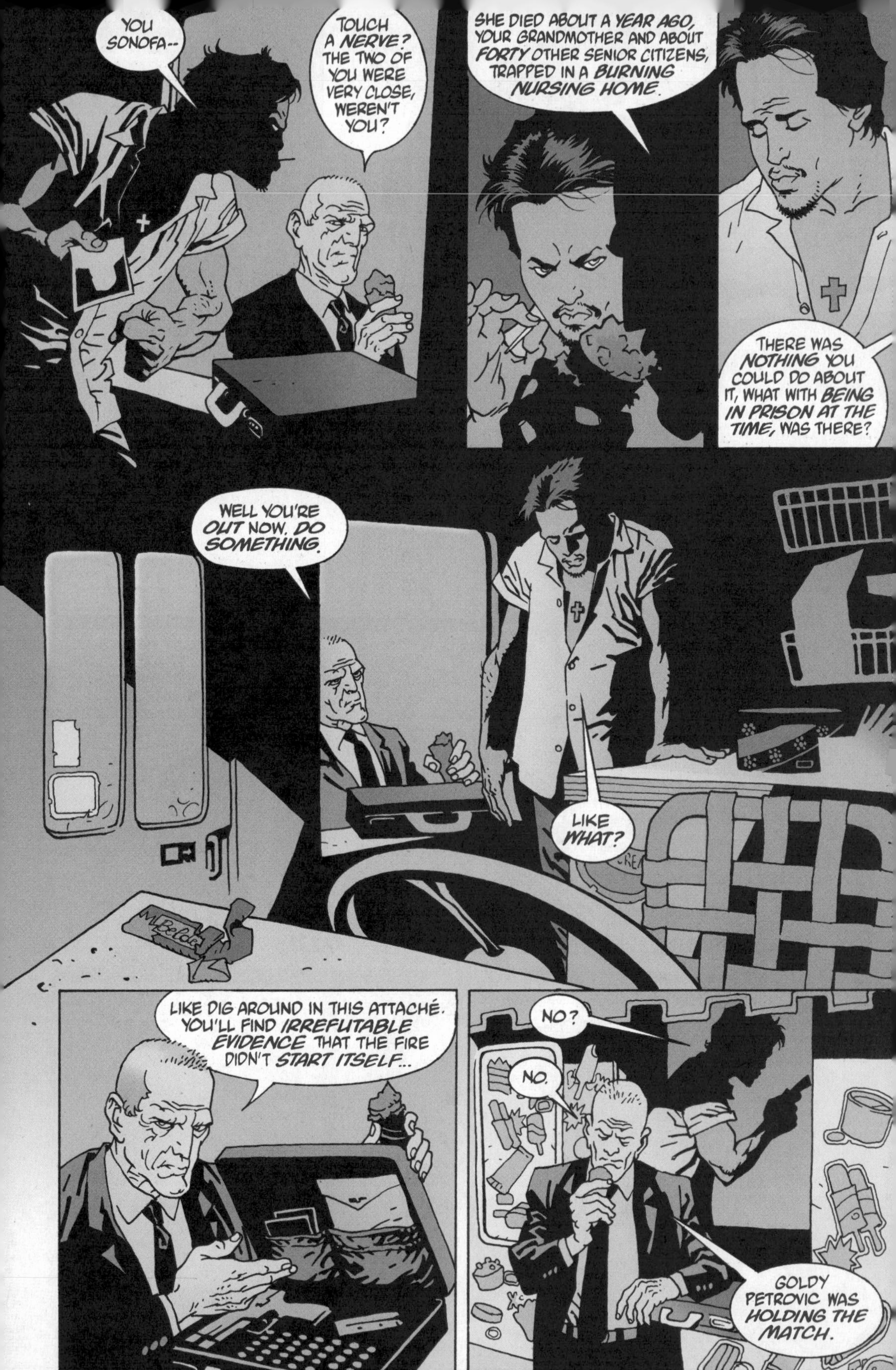

YOU SONOFA--
TOUCH A NERVE? THE TWO OF YOU WERE VERY CLOSE, WEREN'T YOU?
SHE DIED ABOUT A YEAR AGO, YOUR GRANDMOTHER AND ABOUT FORTY OTHER SENIOR CITIZENS, TRAPPED IN A BURNING NURSING HOME.
THERE WAS NOTHING YOU COULD DO ABOUT IT, WHAT WITH BEING IN PRISON AT THE TIME, WAS THERE?
WELL YOU'RE OUT NOW. DO SOMETHING.
LIKE WHAT?
LIKE DIG AROUND IN THIS ATTACHÉ. YOU'LL FIND IRREFUTABLE EVIDENCE THAT THE FIRE DIDN'T START ITSELF...
NO?
NO.
GOLDY PETROVIC WAS HOLDING THE MATCH.

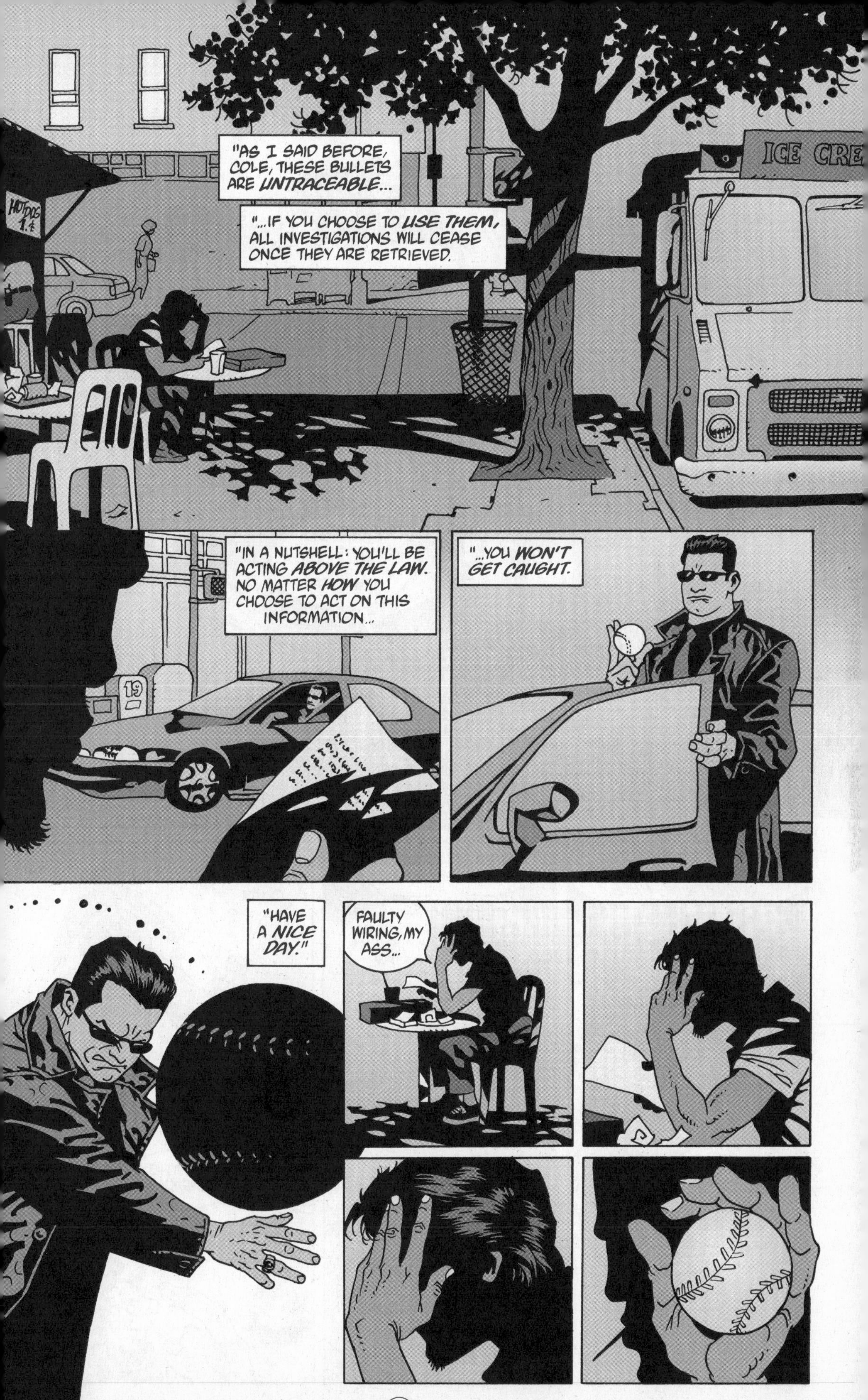
HOT DOG 1.¢
"AS I SAID BEFORE, COLE, THESE BULLETS ARE UNTRACEABLE...
"...IF YOU CHOOSE TO USE THEM, ALL INVESTIGATIONS WILL CEASE ONCE THEY ARE RETRIEVED.
ICE CRE
"IN A NUTSHELL: YOU'LL BE ACTING ABOVE THE LAW. NO MATTER HOW YOU CHOOSE TO ACT ON THIS INFORMATION...
19
"...YOU WON'T GET CAUGHT.
"HAVE A NICE DAY."
FAULTY WIRING, MY ASS...

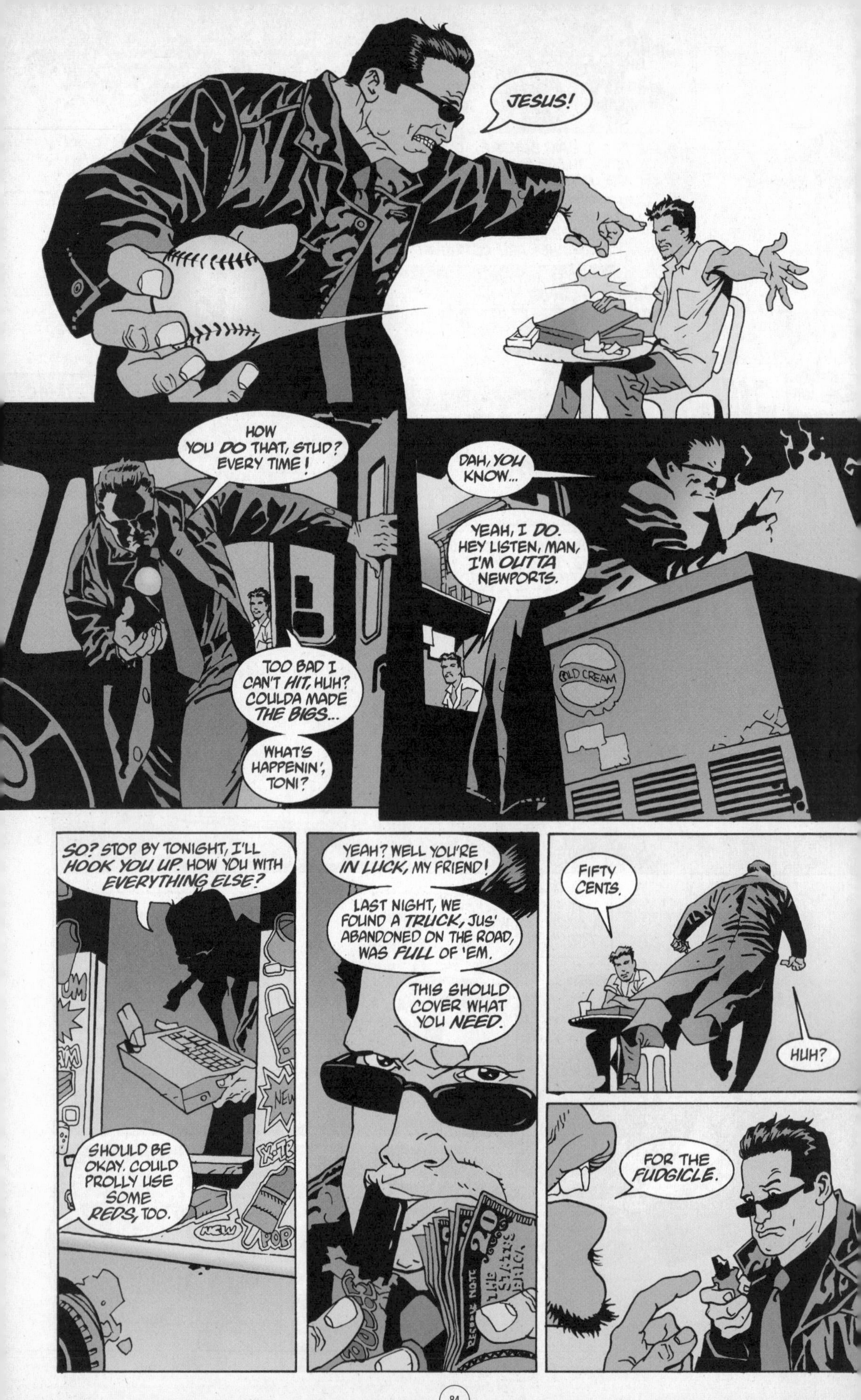
JESUS!
HOW YOU DO THAT, STUD? EVERY TIME!
TOO BAD I CAN'T HIT, HUH? COULDA MADE THE BIGS...
WHAT'S HAPPENIN', TONI?
DAH, YOU KNOW...
YEAH, I DO. HEY LISTEN, MAN, I'M OUTTA NEWPORTS.
OLD CREAM
SO? STOP BY TONIGHT, I'LL HOOK YOU UP. HOW YOU WITH EVERYTHING ELSE?
SHOULD BE OKAY. COULD PROLLY USE SOME REDS, TOO.
YEAH? WELL YOU'RE IN LUCK, MY FRIEND!
LAST NIGHT, WE FOUND A TRUCK, JUS' ABANDONED ON THE ROAD, WAS FULL OF 'EM.
THIS SHOULD COVER WHAT YOU NEED.
FIFTY CENTS.
HUH?
FOR THE FUDGICLE.

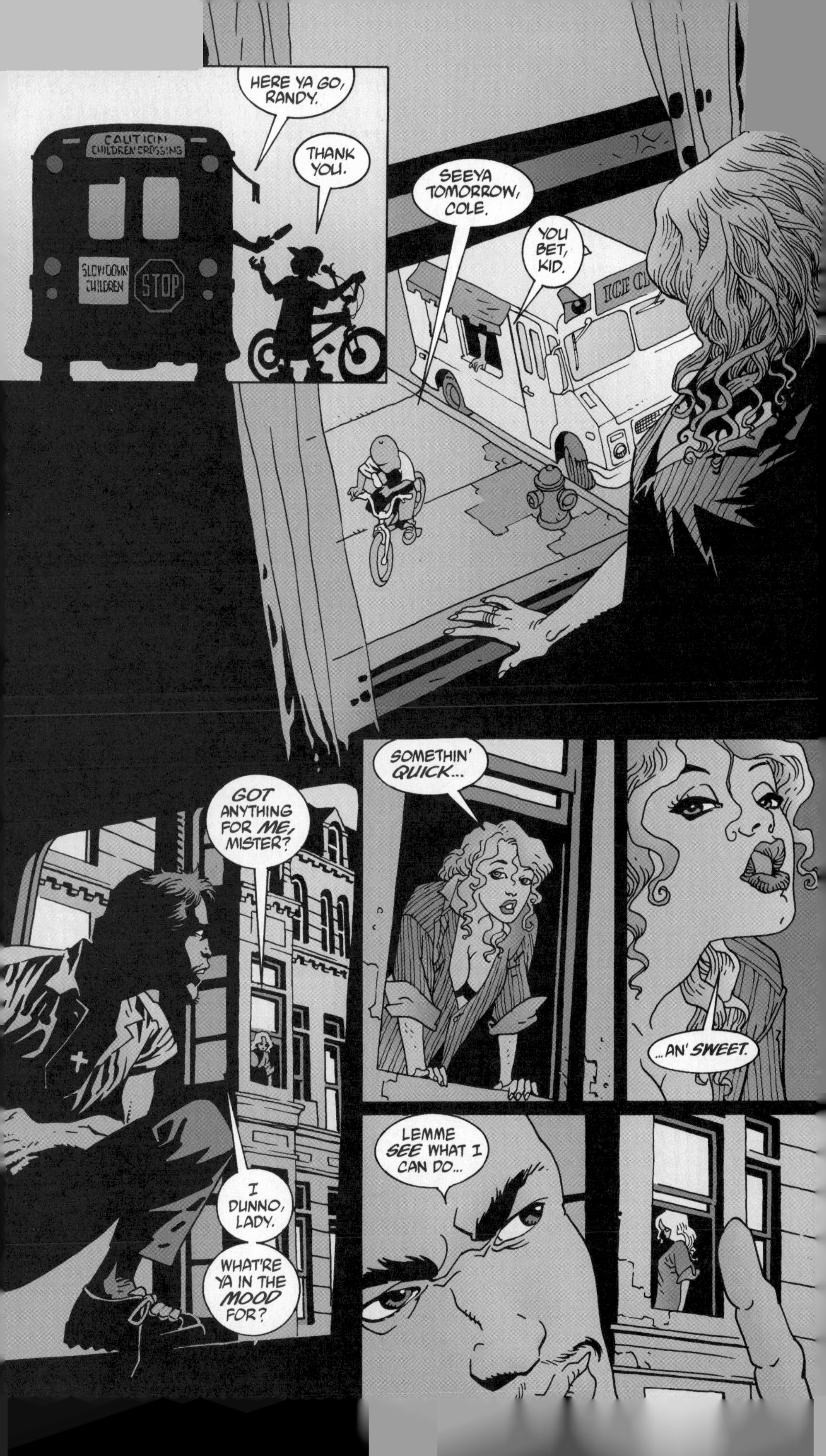
CAUTION
CHILDREN CROSSING
SLOW DOWN
CHILDREN
STOP
HERE YA GO, RANDY.
THANK YOU.
SEEYA TOMORROW, COLE.
YOU BET, KID.
GOT ANYTHING FOR ME, MISTER?
SOMETHIN' QUICK...
...AN' SWEET.
I DUNNO, LADY.
WHAT'RE YA IN THE MOOD FOR?
LEMME SEE WHAT I CAN DO...

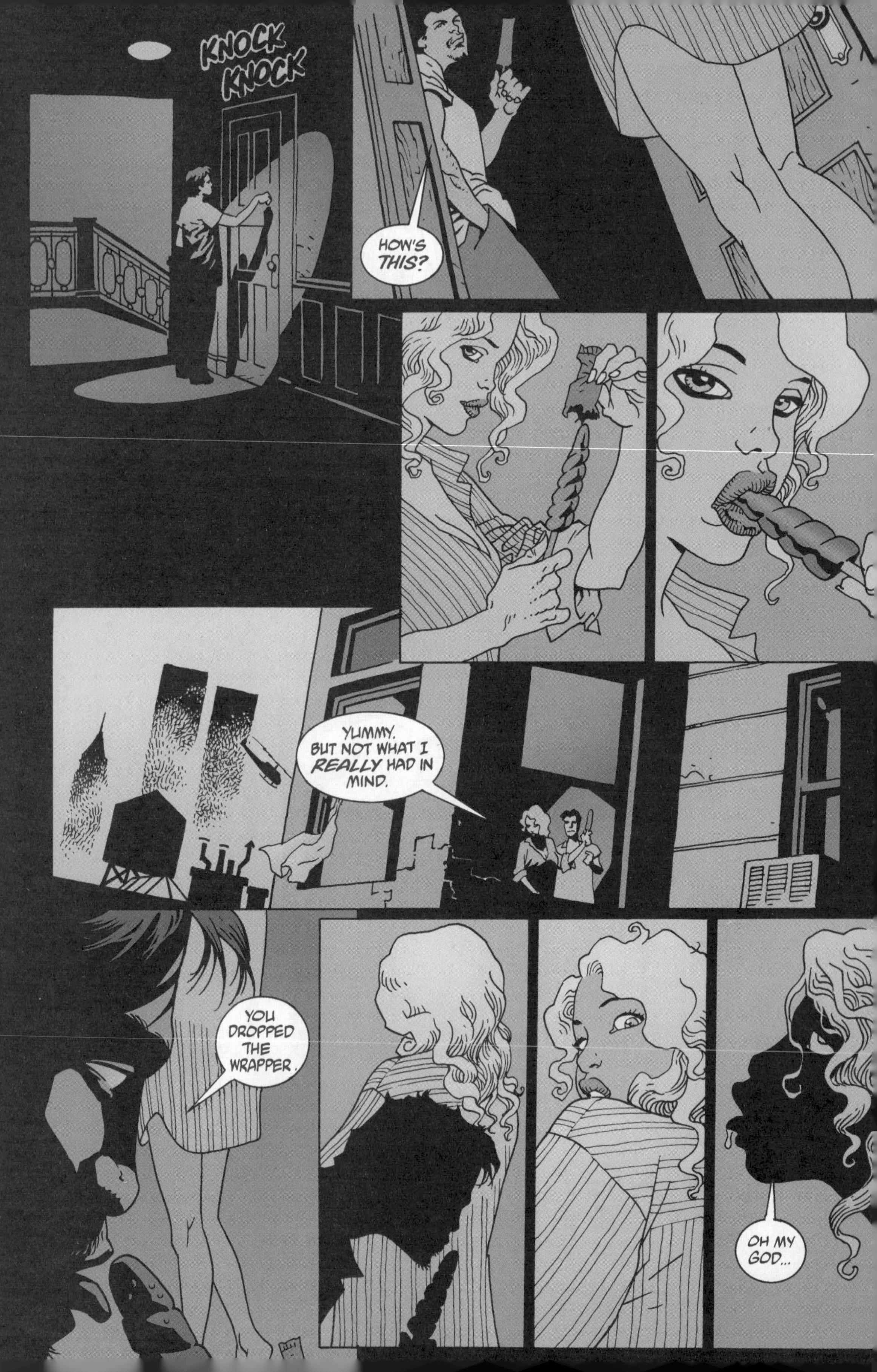
KNOCK KNOCK
HOW'S THIS?
YUMMY. BUT NOT WHAT I REALLY HAD IN MIND.
YOU DROPPED THE WRAPPER.
OH MY GOD...

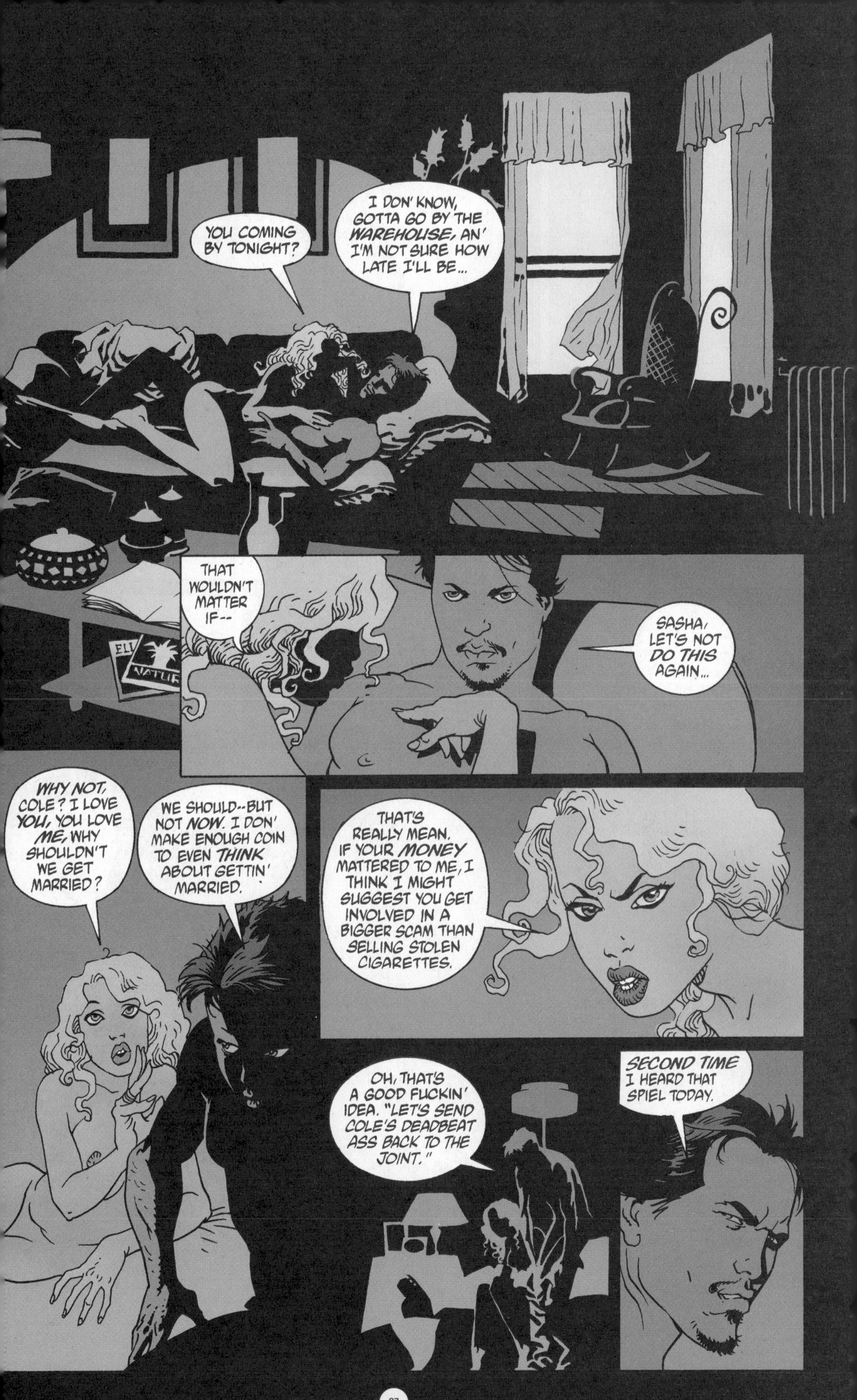
YOU COMING BY TONIGHT?
I DON' KNOW, GOTTA GO BY THE WAREHOUSE, AN' I'M NOT SURE HOW LATE I'LL BE...
THAT WOULDN'T MATTER IF--
SASHA, LET'S NOT DO THIS AGAIN...
WHY NOT, COLE? I LOVE YOU, YOU LOVE ME, WHY SHOULDN'T WE GET MARRIED?
WE SHOULD--BUT NOT NOW. I DON' MAKE ENOUGH COIN TO EVEN THINK ABOUT GETTIN' MARRIED.
THAT'S REALLY MEAN. IF YOUR MONEY MATTERED TO ME, I THINK I MIGHT SUGGEST YOU GET INVOLVED IN A BIGGER SCAM THAN SELLING STOLEN CIGARETTES.
OH, THAT'S A GOOD FUCKIN' IDEA. "LET'S SEND COLE'S DEADBEAT ASS BACK TO THE JOINT."
SECOND TIME I HEARD THAT SPIEL TODAY.

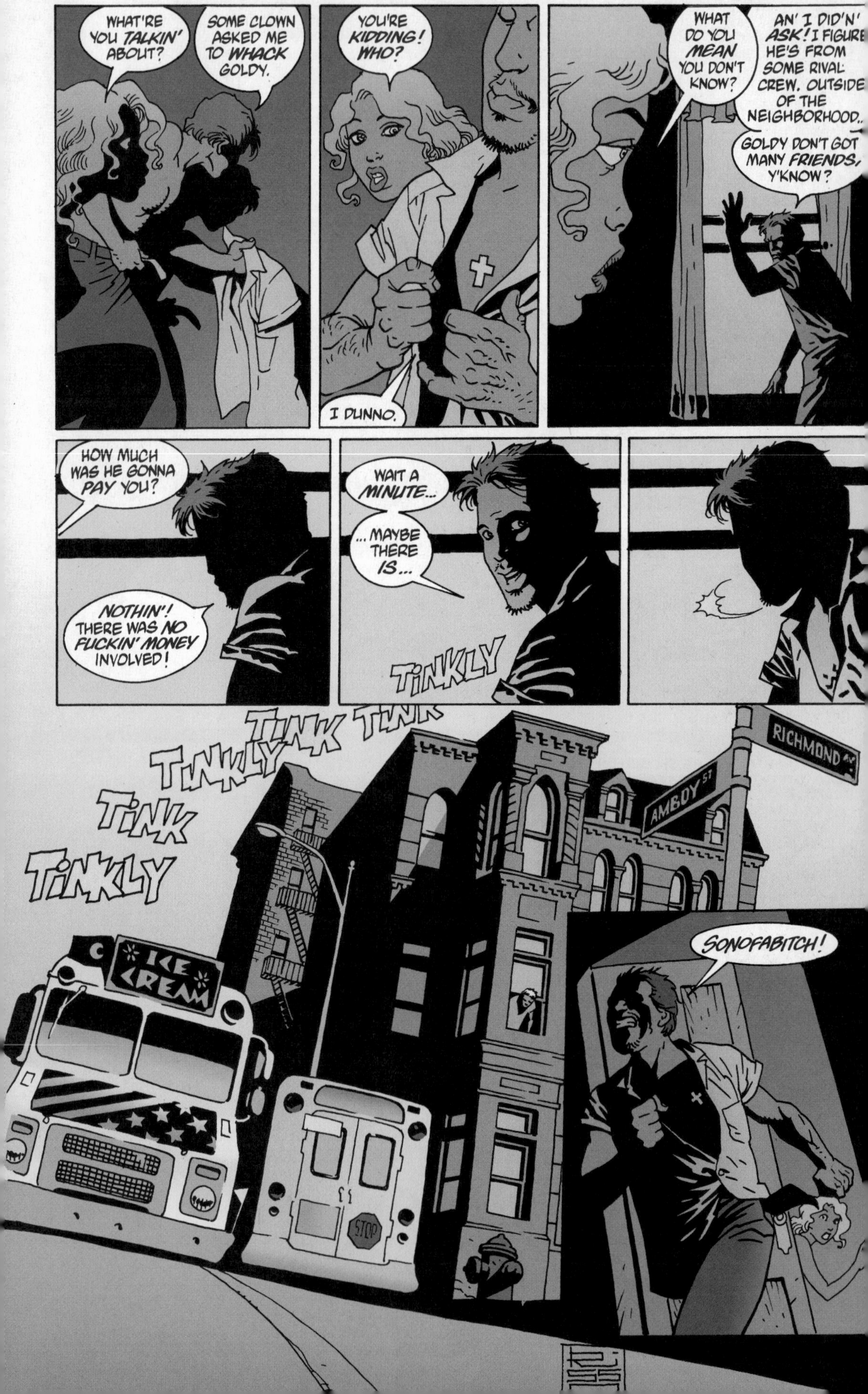
WHAT'RE YOU TALKIN' ABOUT?
SOME CLOWN ASKED ME TO WHACK GOLDY.
YOU'RE KIDDING! WHO?
I DUNNO.
WHAT DO YOU MEAN YOU DON'T KNOW?
AN' I DID'N' ASK! I FIGURE HE'S FROM SOME RIVAL CREW. OUTSIDE OF THE NEIGHBORHOOD..
GOLDY DON'T GOT MANY FRIENDS, Y'KNOW?
HOW MUCH WAS HE GONNA PAY YOU?
NOTHIN'! THERE WAS NO FUCKIN' MONEY INVOLVED!
WAIT A MINUTE...
...MAYBE THERE IS...
TINKLY
TINK TINK
TINKLY
TINK
TINKLY
RICHMOND AV
AMBOY ST
ICE CREAM
STOP
SONOFABITCH!

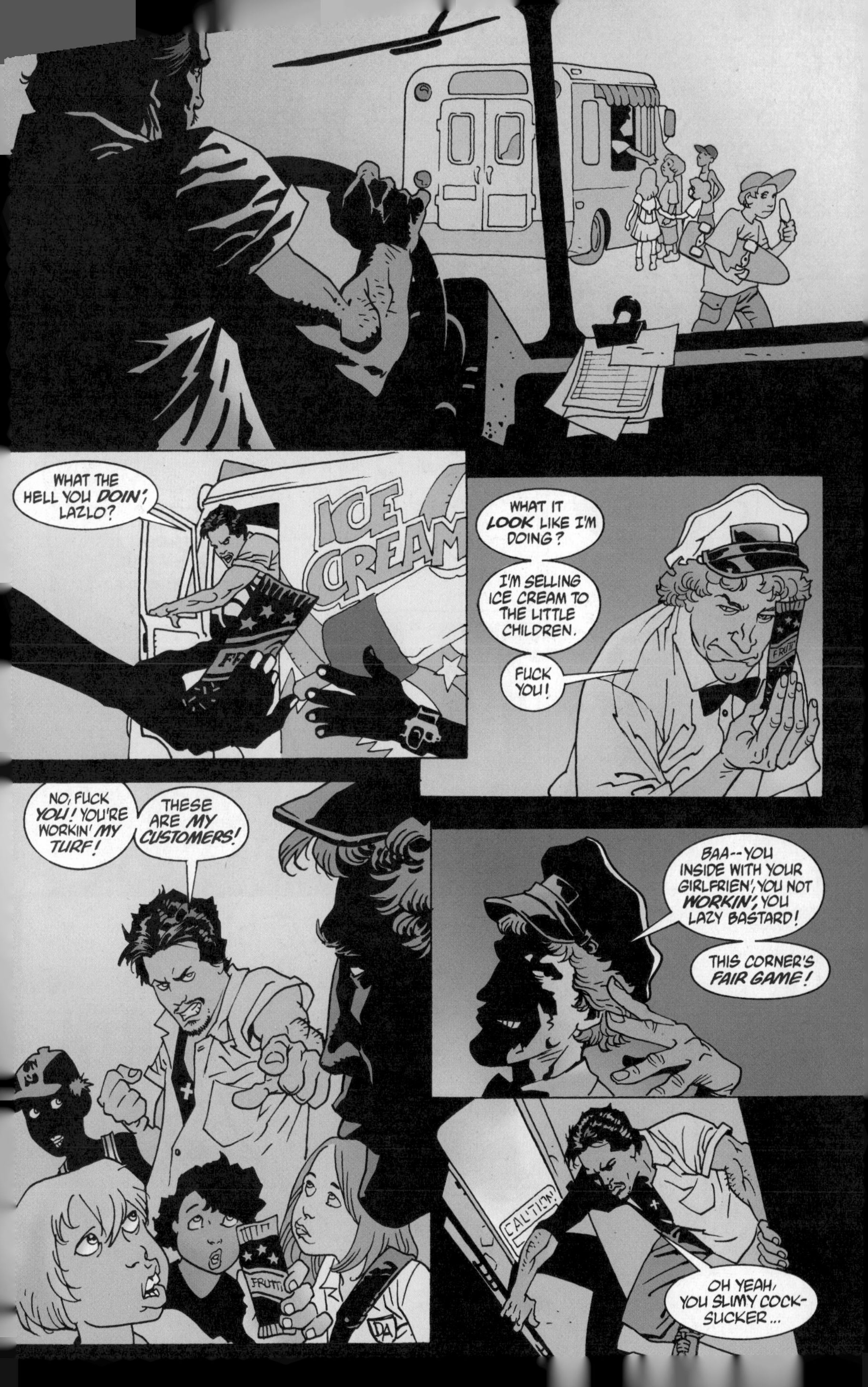

WHAT THE HELL YOU DOIN', LAZLO?
ICE CREAM
WHAT IT LOOK LIKE I'M DOING?
I'M SELLING ICE CREAM TO THE LITTLE CHILDREN.
FUCK YOU!
NO, FUCK YOU! YOU'RE WORKIN' MY TURF!
THESE ARE MY CUSTOMERS!
BAA--YOU INSIDE WITH YOUR GIRLFRIEN', YOU NOT WORKIN', YOU LAZY BASTARD!
THIS CORNER'S FAIR GAME!
FRUTTI
CAUTION
OH YEAH, YOU SLIMY COCK-SUCKER...

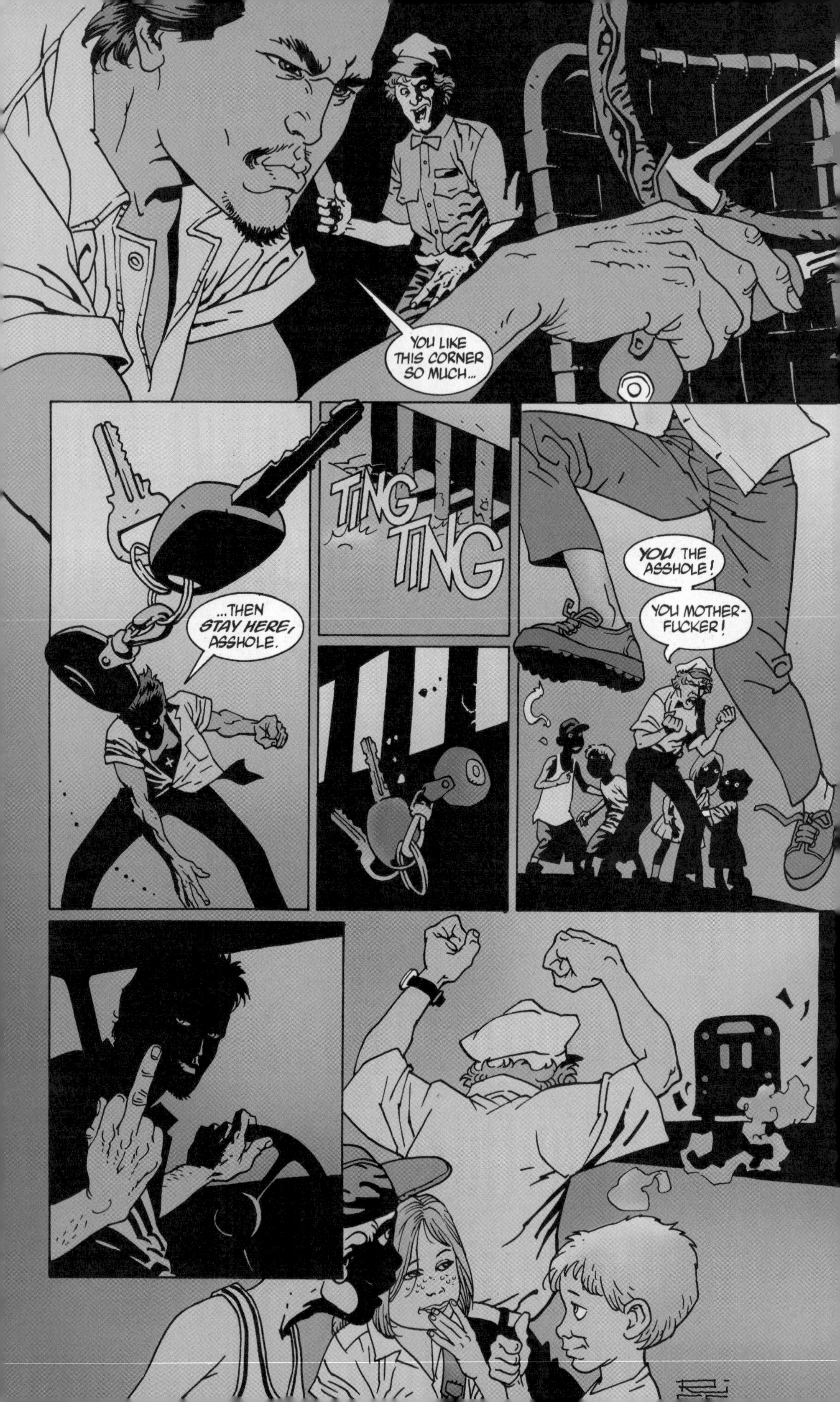
YOU LIKE THIS CORNER SO MUCH...
...THEN STAY HERE, ASSHOLE.
TING
TING
YOU THE ASSHOLE!
YOU MOTHER-FUCKER!

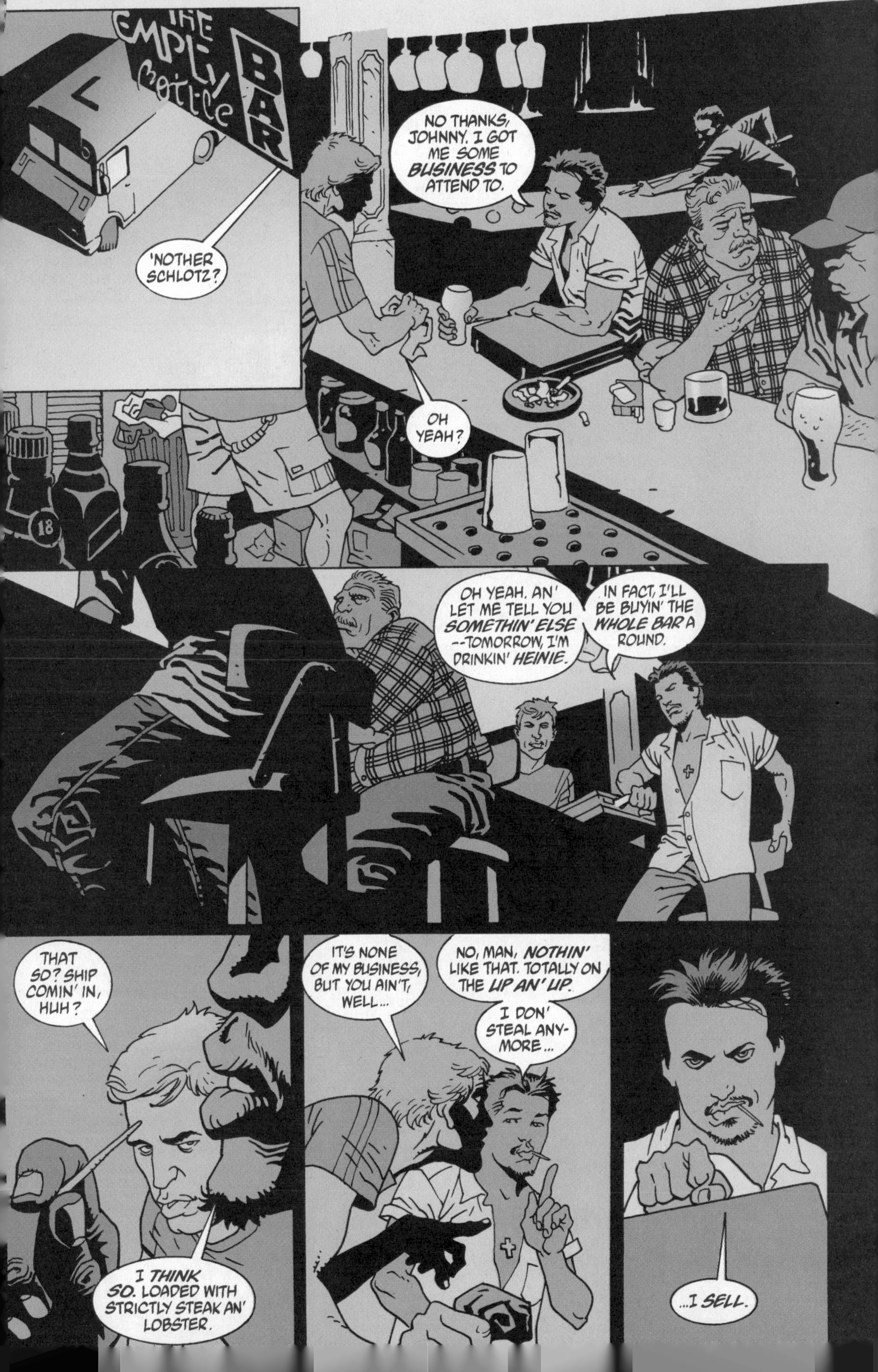
THE EMPTY BOTTLE
BAR
'NOTHER SCHLOTZ?
NO THANKS, JOHNNY. I GOT ME SOME BUSINESS TO ATTEND TO.
OH YEAH?
18
OH YEAH. AN' LET ME TELL YOU SOMETHIN' ELSE --TOMORROW, I'M DRINKIN' HEINIE.
IN FACT, I'LL BE BUYIN' THE WHOLE BAR A ROUND.
THAT SO? SHIP COMIN' IN, HUH?
I THINK SO. LOADED WITH STRICTLY STEAK AN' LOBSTER.
IT'S NONE OF MY BUSINESS, BUT YOU AIN'T, WELL...
NO, MAN, NOTHIN' LIKE THAT. TOTALLY ON THE UP AN' UP.
I DON' STEAL ANY-MORE...
...I SELL.

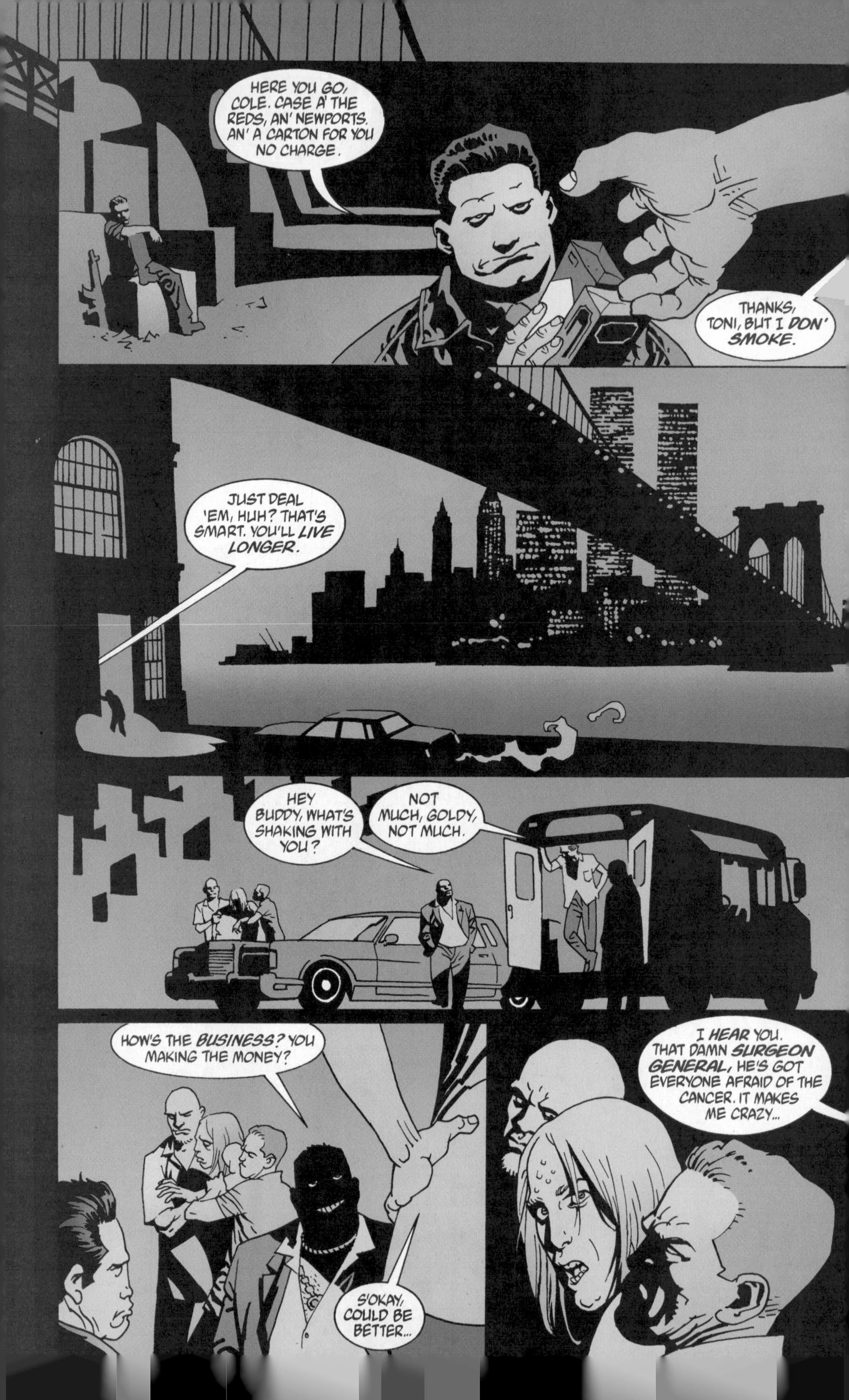
HERE YOU GO, COLE. CASE A' THE REDS, AN' NEWPORTS. AN' A CARTON FOR YOU NO CHARGE.
THANKS, TONI, BUT I DON' SMOKE.
JUST DEAL 'EM, HUH? THAT'S SMART. YOU'LL LIVE LONGER.
HEY BUDDY, WHAT'S SHAKING WITH YOU?
NOT MUCH, GOLDY, NOT MUCH.
HOW'S THE BUSINESS? YOU MAKING THE MONEY?
S'OKAY, COULD BE BETTER...
I HEAR YOU. THAT DAMN SURGEON GENERAL, HE'S GOT EVERYONE AFRAID OF THE CANCER. IT MAKES ME CRAZY...

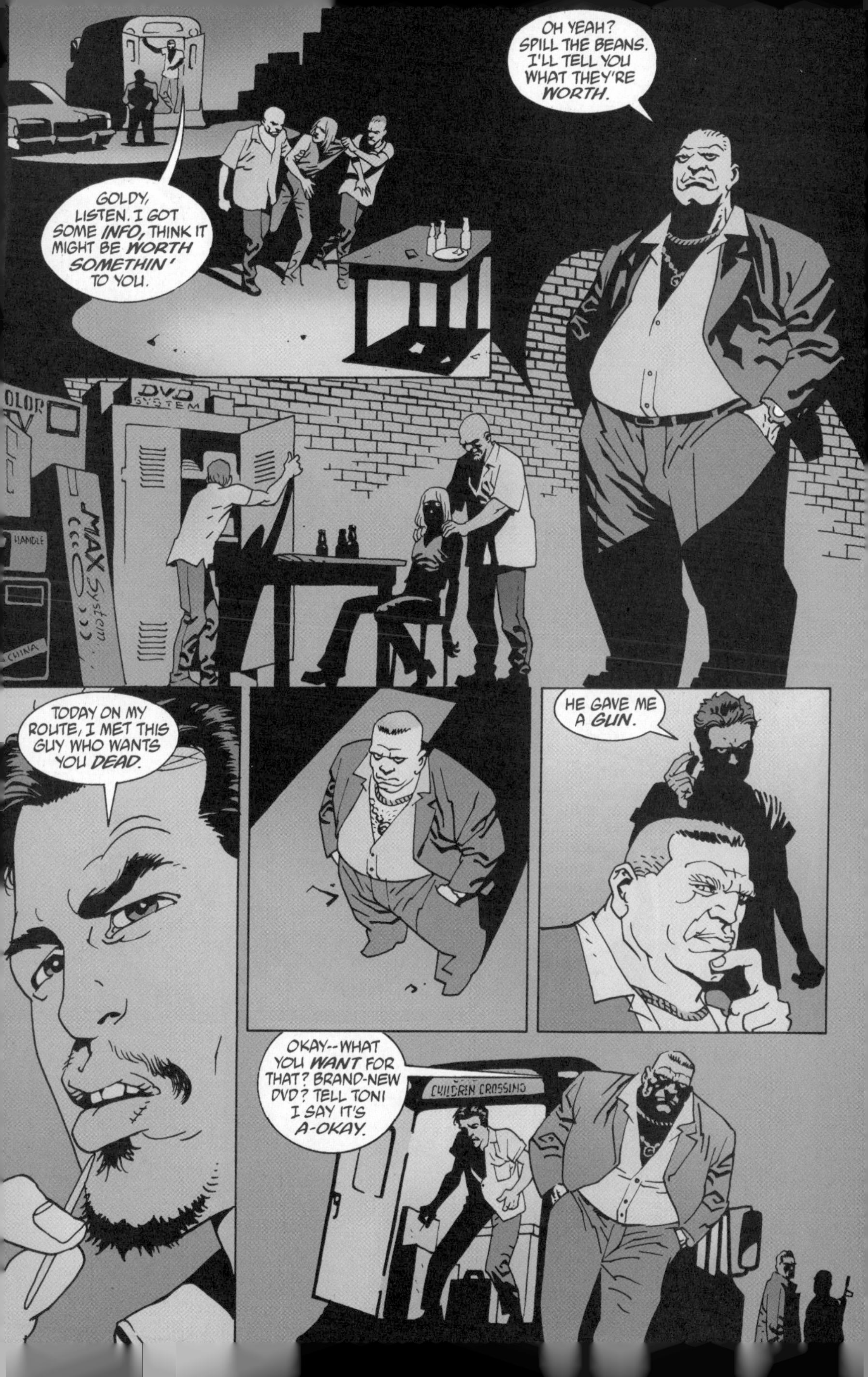
GOLDY, LISTEN. I GOT SOME INFO, THINK IT MIGHT BE WORTH SOMETHIN' TO YOU.
OH YEAH? SPILL THE BEANS. I'LL TELL YOU WHAT THEY'RE WORTH.
DVD SYSTEM
OLOR TV
MAX System
HANDLE
CHINA
TODAY ON MY ROUTE, I MET THIS GUY WHO WANTS YOU DEAD.
HE GAVE ME A GUN.
OKAY--WHAT YOU WANT FOR THAT? BRAND-NEW DVD? TELL TONI I SAY IT'S A-OKAY.
CHILDREN CROSSING

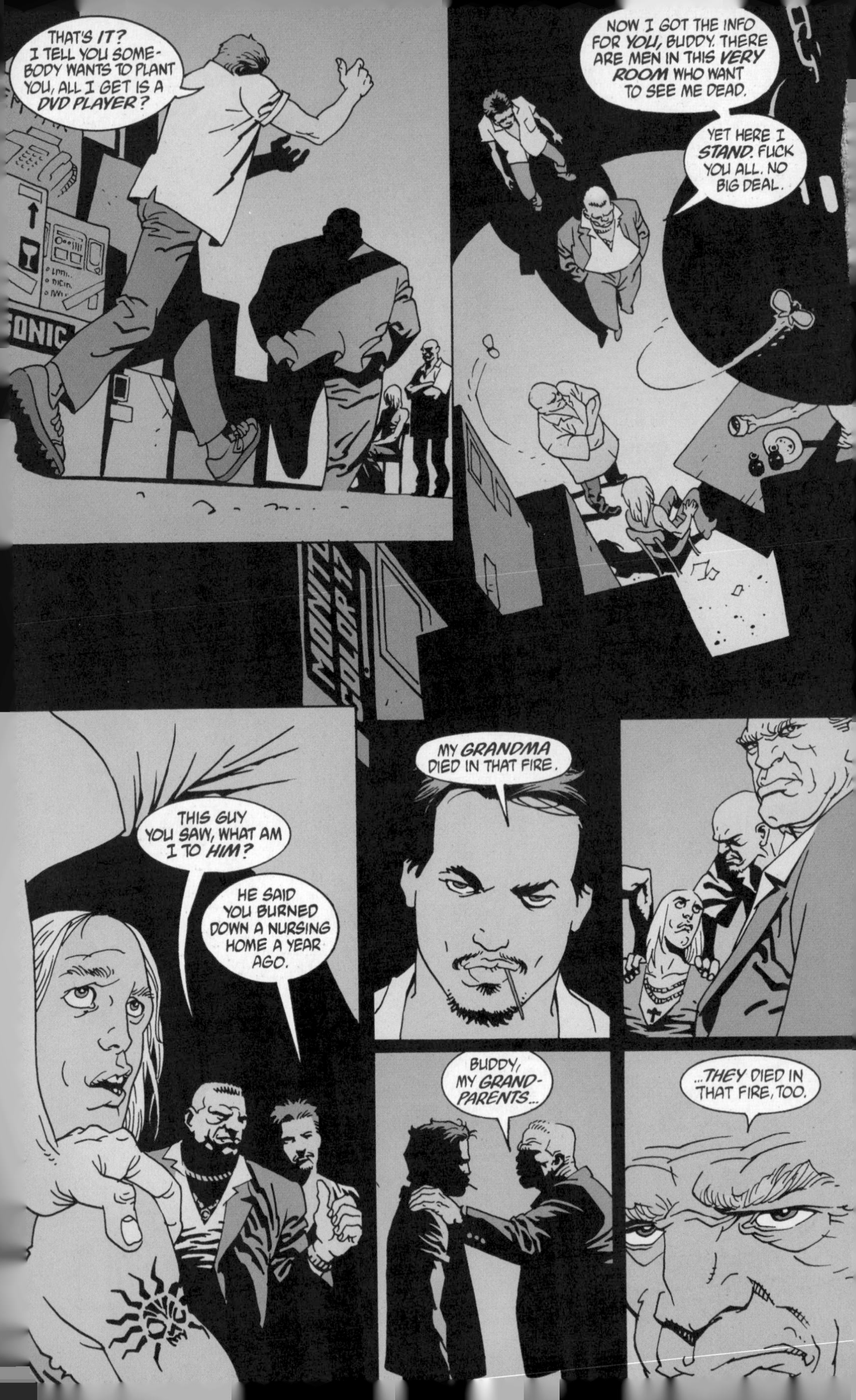
THAT'S IT? I TELL YOU SOMEBODY WANTS TO PLANT YOU, ALL I GET IS A DVD PLAYER?
NOW I GOT THE INFO FOR YOU, BUDDY. THERE ARE MEN IN THIS VERY ROOM WHO WANT TO SEE ME DEAD.
YET HERE I STAND. FUCK YOU ALL. NO BIG DEAL.
THIS GUY YOU SAW, WHAT AM I TO HIM?
HE SAID YOU BURNED DOWN A NURSING HOME A YEAR AGO.
MY GRANDMA DIED IN THAT FIRE.
BUDDY, MY GRANDPARENTS...
...THEY DIED IN THAT FIRE, TOO.

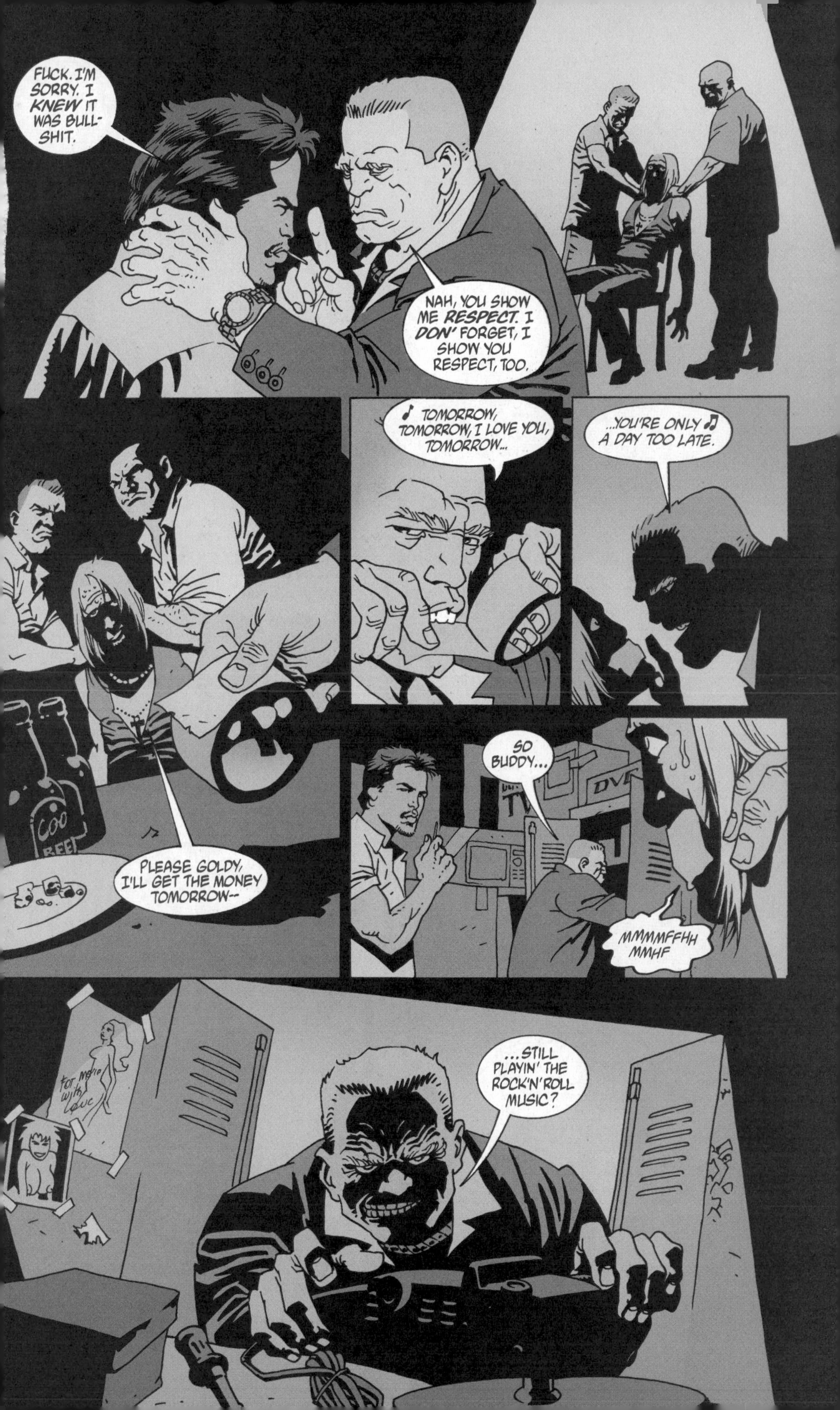
FUCK. I'M SORRY. I KNEW IT WAS BULL-SHIT.
NAH, YOU SHOW ME RESPECT. I DON' FORGET, I SHOW YOU RESPECT, TOO.
PLEASE GOLDY, I'LL GET THE MONEY TOMORROW--
♪ TOMORROW, TOMORROW, I LOVE YOU, TOMORROW...
...YOU'RE ONLY ♫ A DAY TOO LATE.
SO BUDDY...
DVD
MMMMFFHH MMHF
...STILL PLAYIN' THE ROCK'N'ROLL MUSIC?

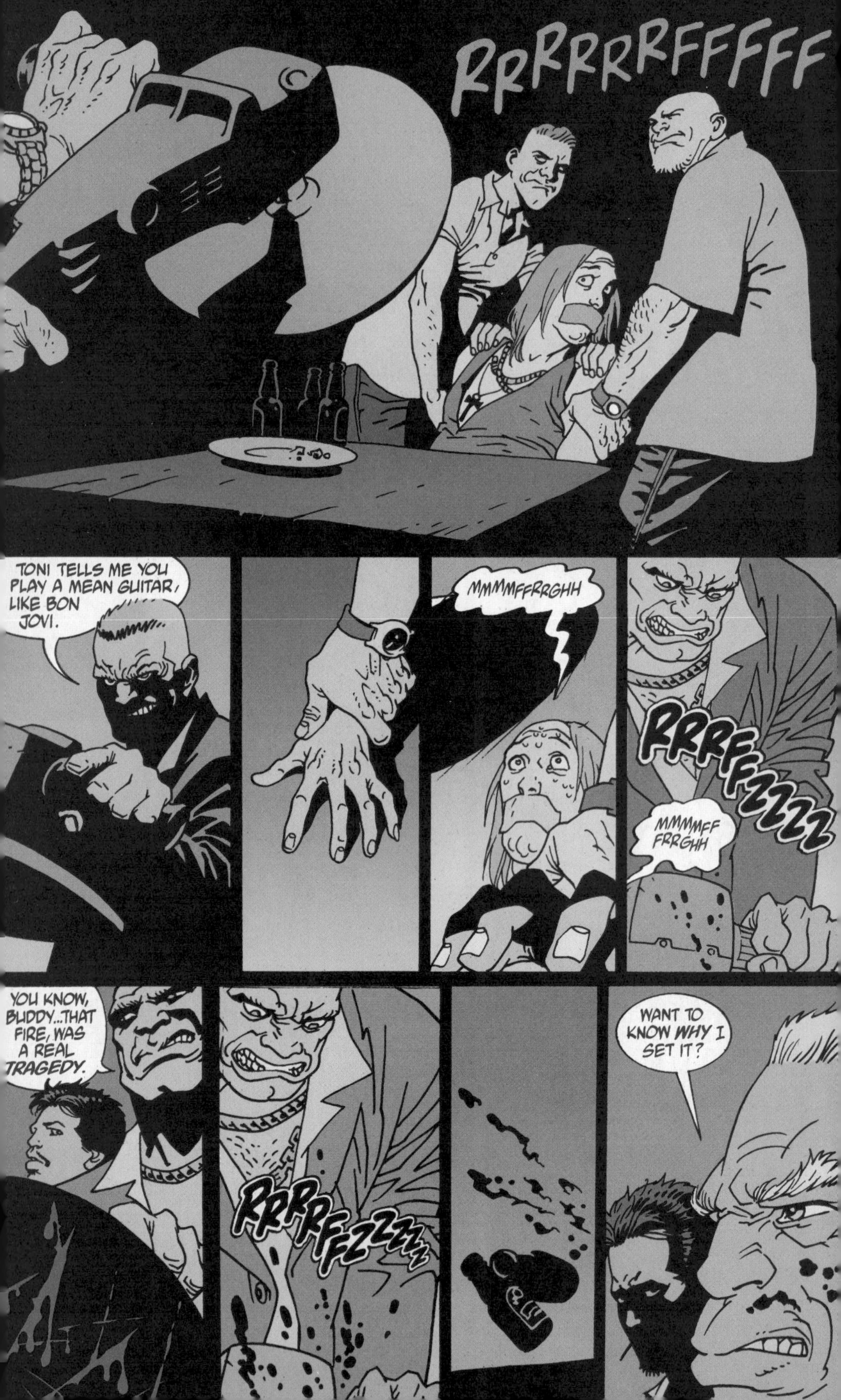
RRRRRRFFFFF
TONI TELLS ME YOU PLAY A MEAN GUITAR, LIKE BON JOVI.
MMMMFFRRGHH
RRRFFZZZZZ
MMMMFF FRRGHH
YOU KNOW, BUDDY...THAT FIRE, WAS A REAL TRAGEDY.
RRRRFFZZZZZ
WANT TO KNOW WHY I SET IT?

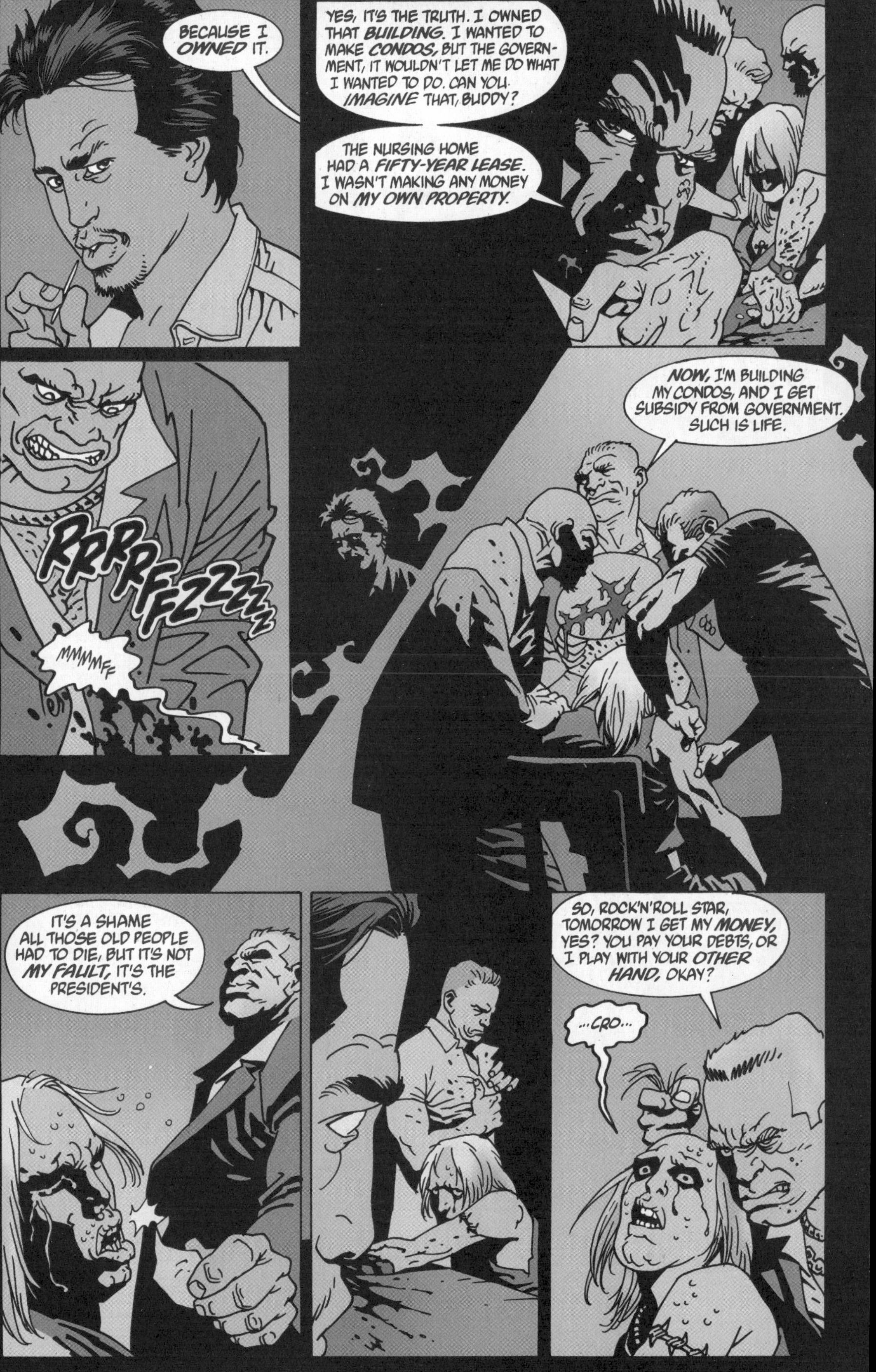
BECAUSE I OWNED IT.
YES, IT'S THE TRUTH. I OWNED THAT BUILDING. I WANTED TO MAKE CONDOS, BUT THE GOVERNMENT, IT WOULDN'T LET ME DO WHAT I WANTED TO DO. CAN YOU IMAGINE THAT, BUDDY?
THE NURSING HOME HAD A FIFTY-YEAR LEASE. I WASN'T MAKING ANY MONEY ON MY OWN PROPERTY.
RRRRFFZZZZZZ
MMMMFF
NOW, I'M BUILDING MY CONDOS, AND I GET SUBSIDY FROM GOVERNMENT. SUCH IS LIFE.
IT'S A SHAME ALL THOSE OLD PEOPLE HAD TO DIE, BUT IT'S NOT MY FAULT, IT'S THE PRESIDENT'S.
SO, ROCK'N'ROLL STAR, TOMORROW I GET MY MONEY, YES? YOU PAY YOUR DEBTS, OR I PLAY WITH YOUR OTHER HAND, OKAY?
...CRO...

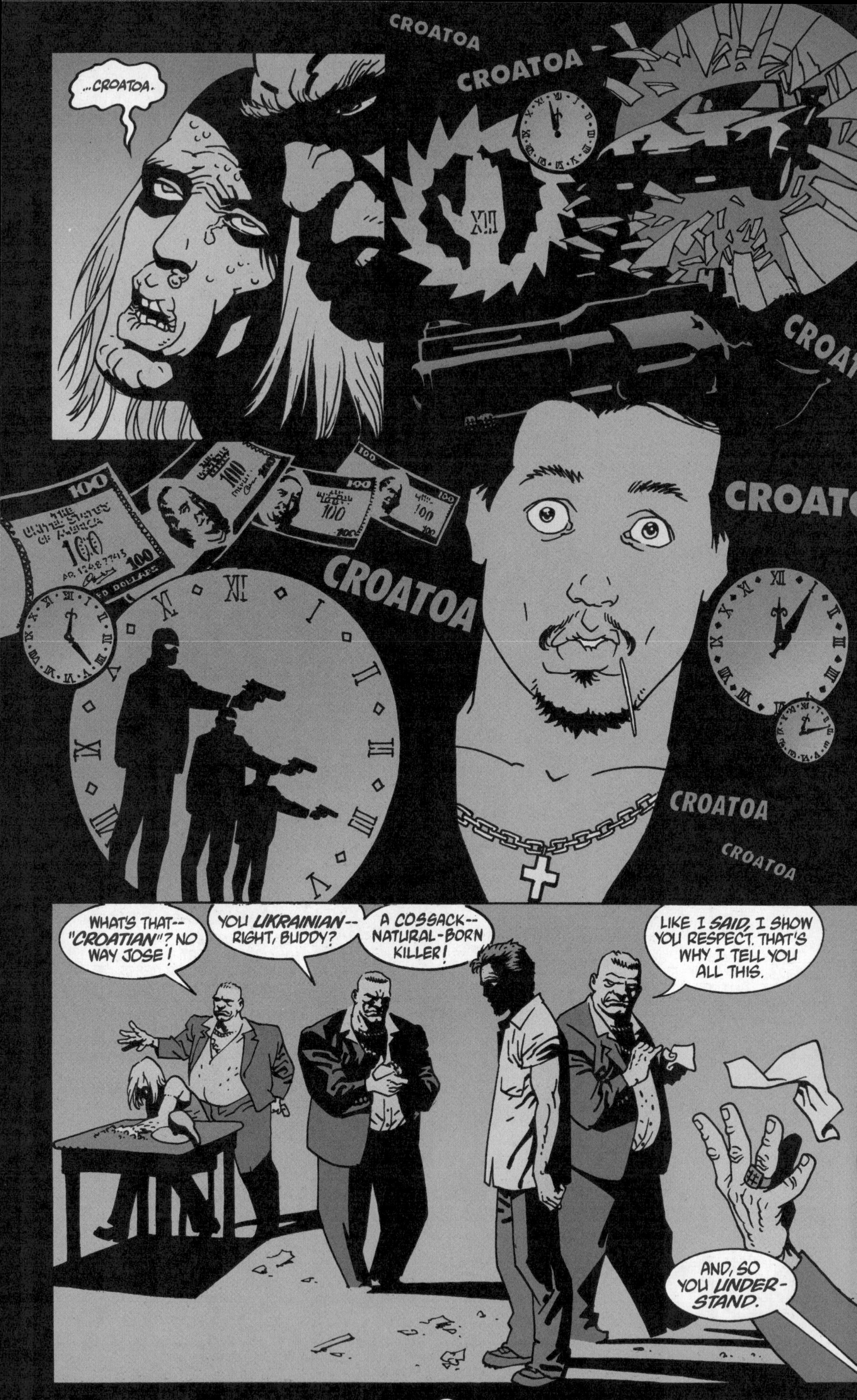

...CROATOA.
CROATOA
CROATOA
CROATOA
CROATOA
CROATOA
CROATOA
CROATOA
WHAT'S THAT-- "CROATIAN"? NO WAY JOSE!
YOU UKRAINIAN-- RIGHT, BUDDY?
A COSSACK-- NATURAL-BORN KILLER!
LIKE I SAID, I SHOW YOU RESPECT. THAT'S WHY I TELL YOU ALL THIS.
AND, SO YOU UNDER-STAND.

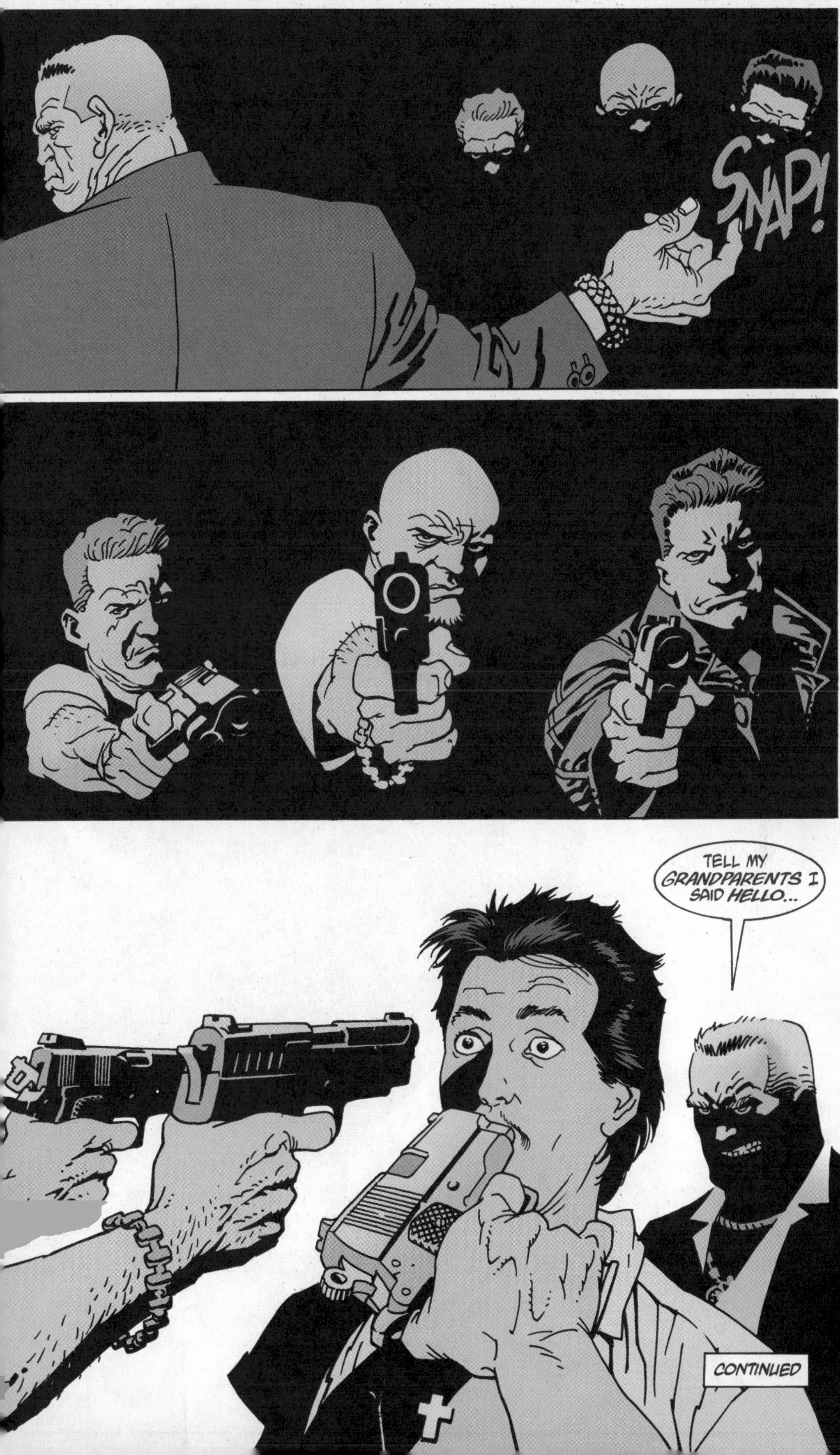
SNAP!
TELL MY GRANDPARENTS I SAID HELLO...
CONTINUED

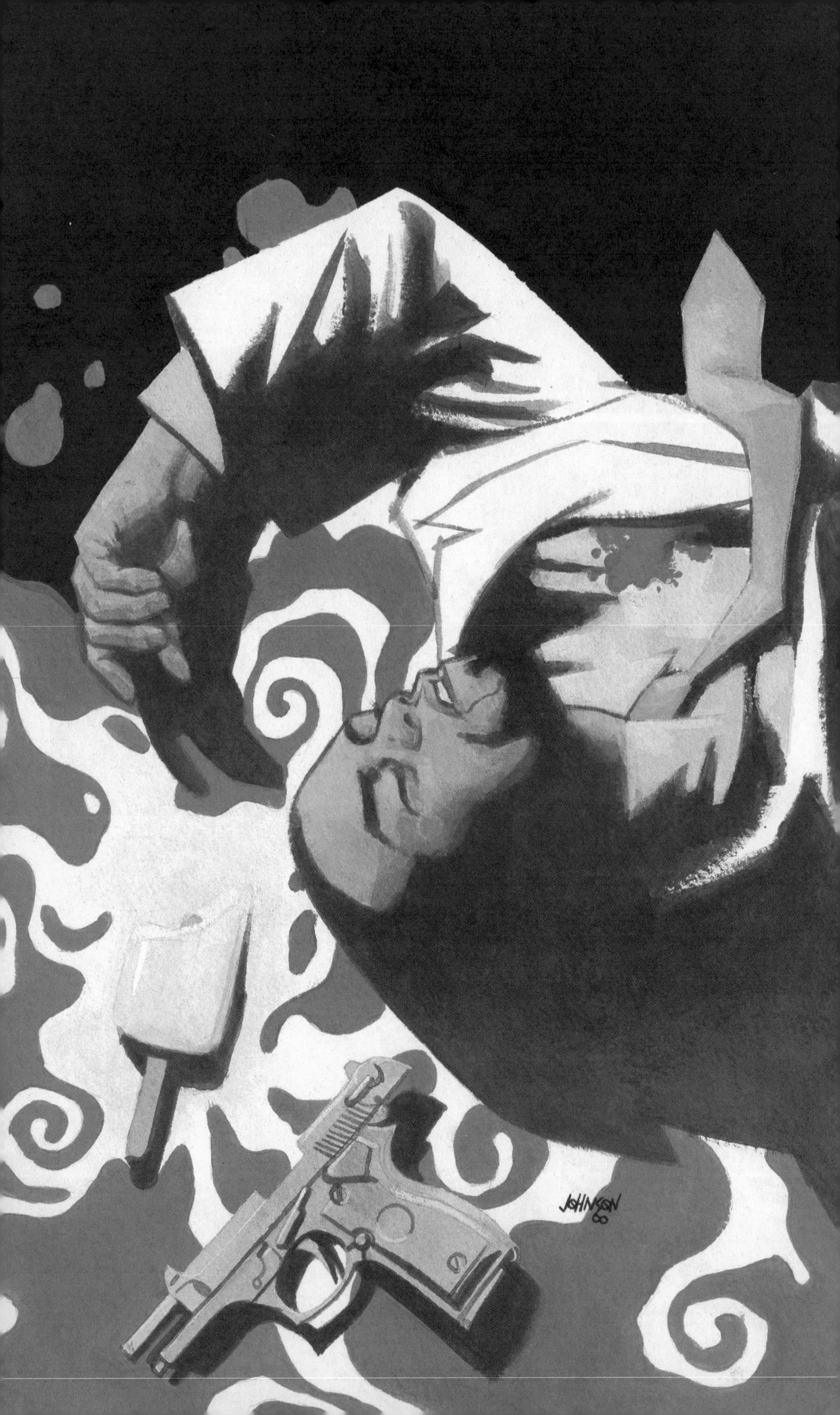
JOHNSON
60

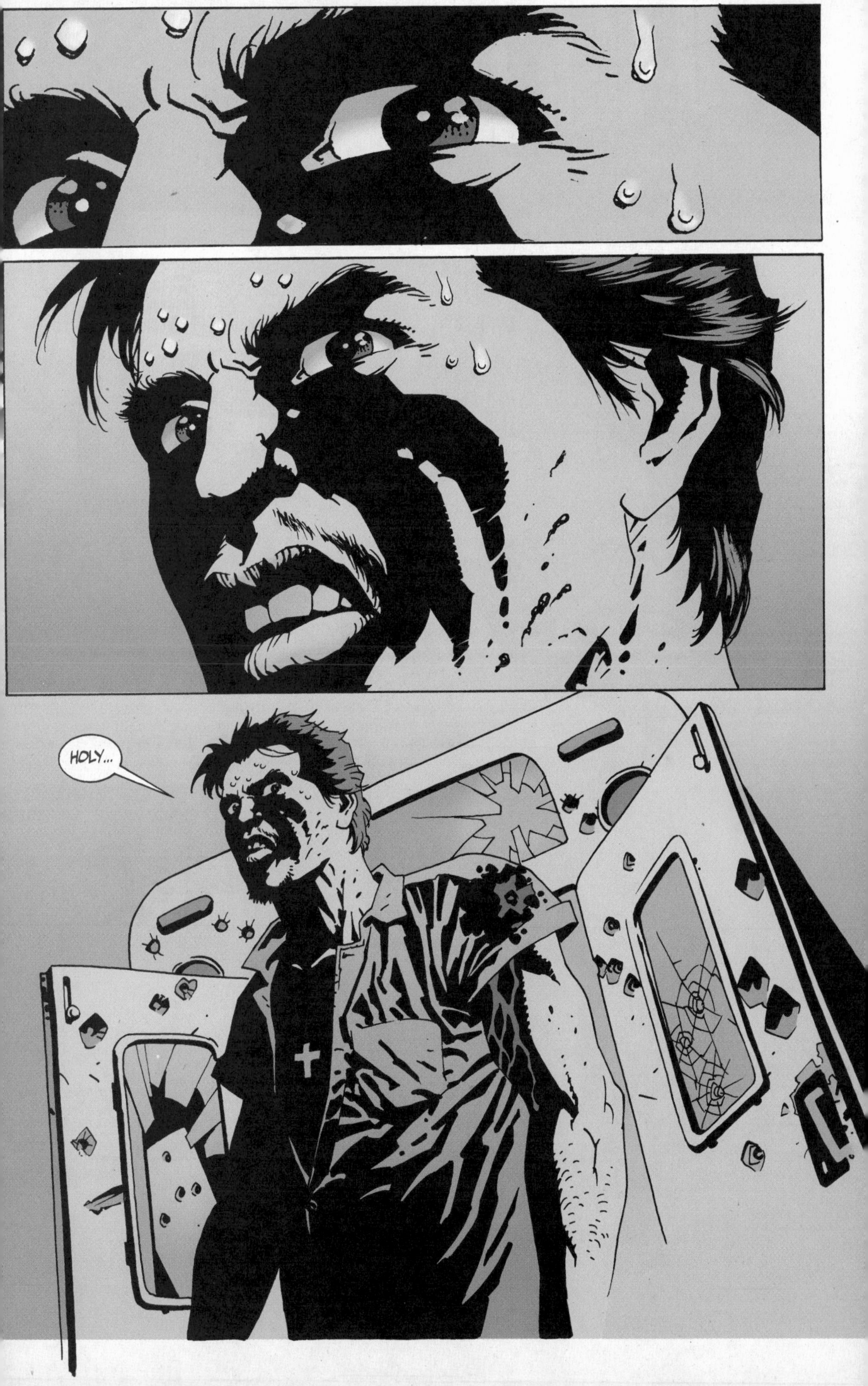
HOLY...

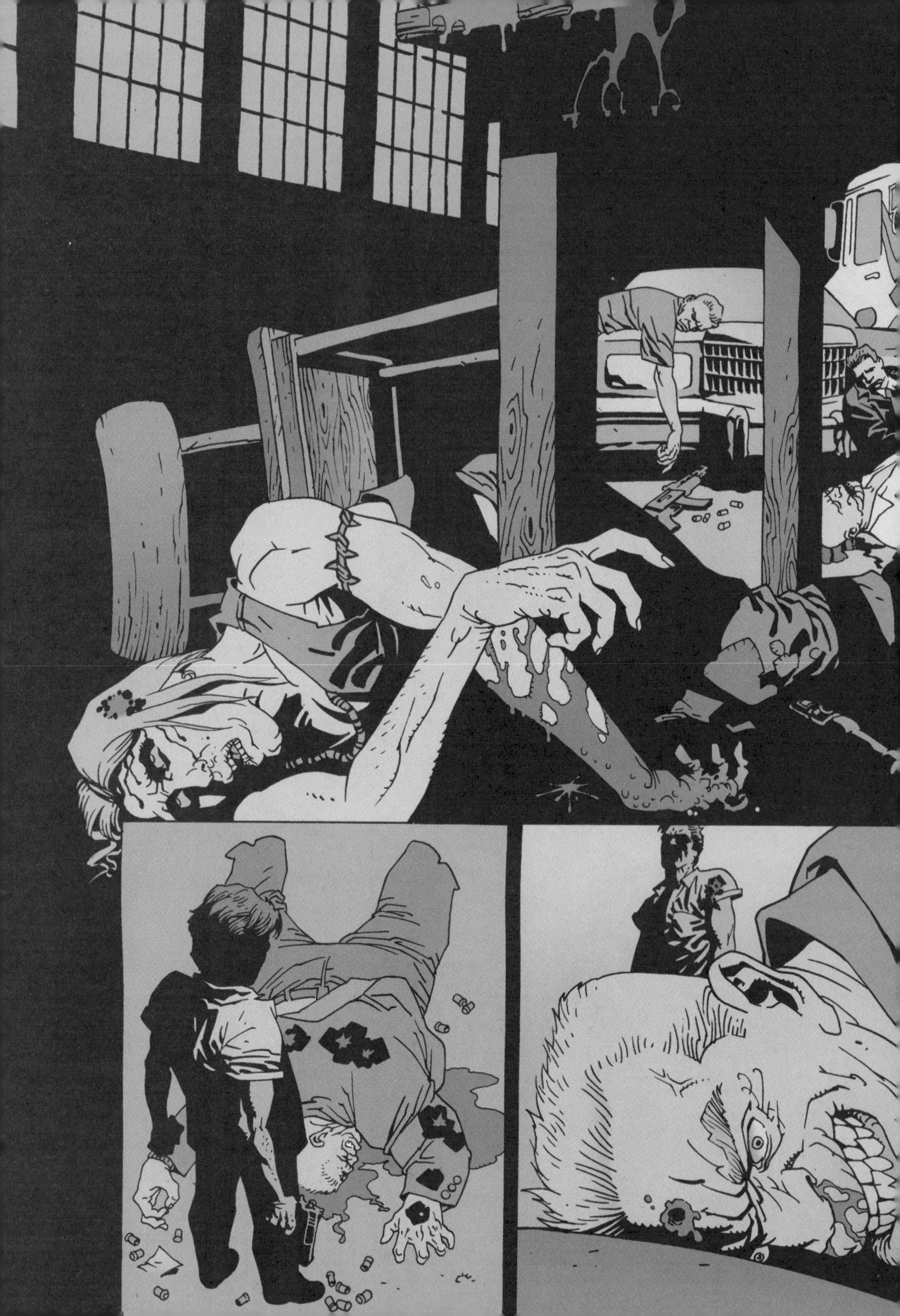

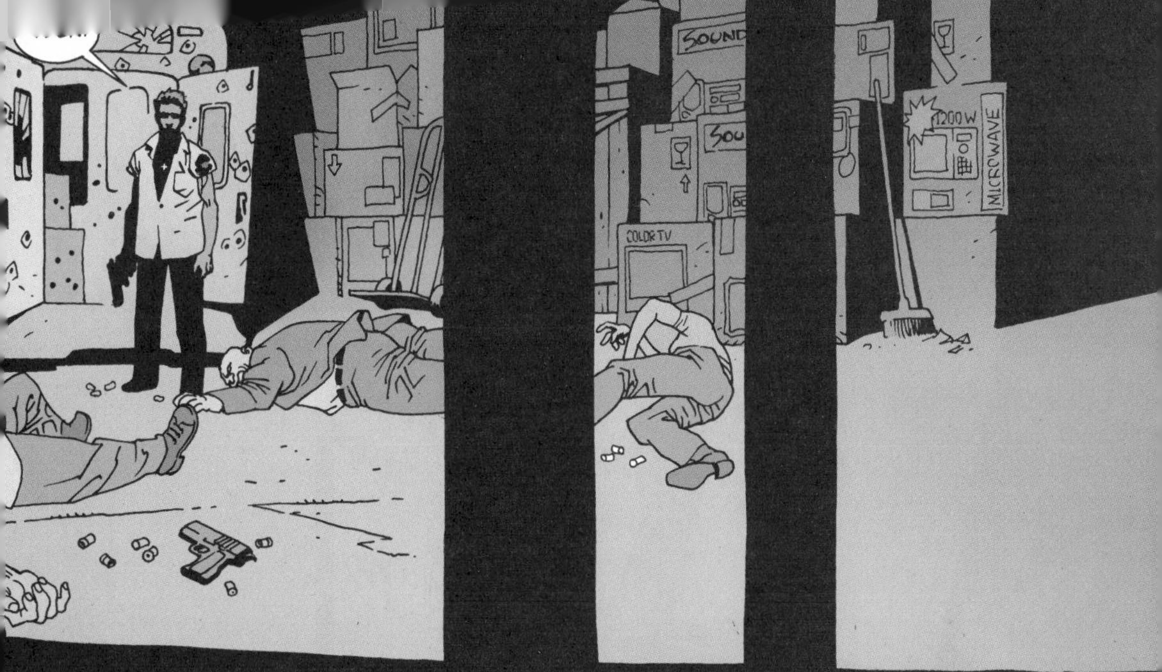
SOUND
SOU
COLOR TV
1200 W
MICROWAVE

THE RIGHT EAR, LEFT IN THE COLD

PART TWO

BRIAN AZZARELLO, WRITER
EDUARDO RISSO, ARTIST

GRANT **GOLEASH** COLORIST
DIGITAL **CHAMELEON** SEPARATIONS
CLEM **ROBINS** LETTERS
DAVE **JOHNSON** COVER
JENNIFER **LEE** ASS'T EDITOR
AXEL **ALONSO** EDITOR

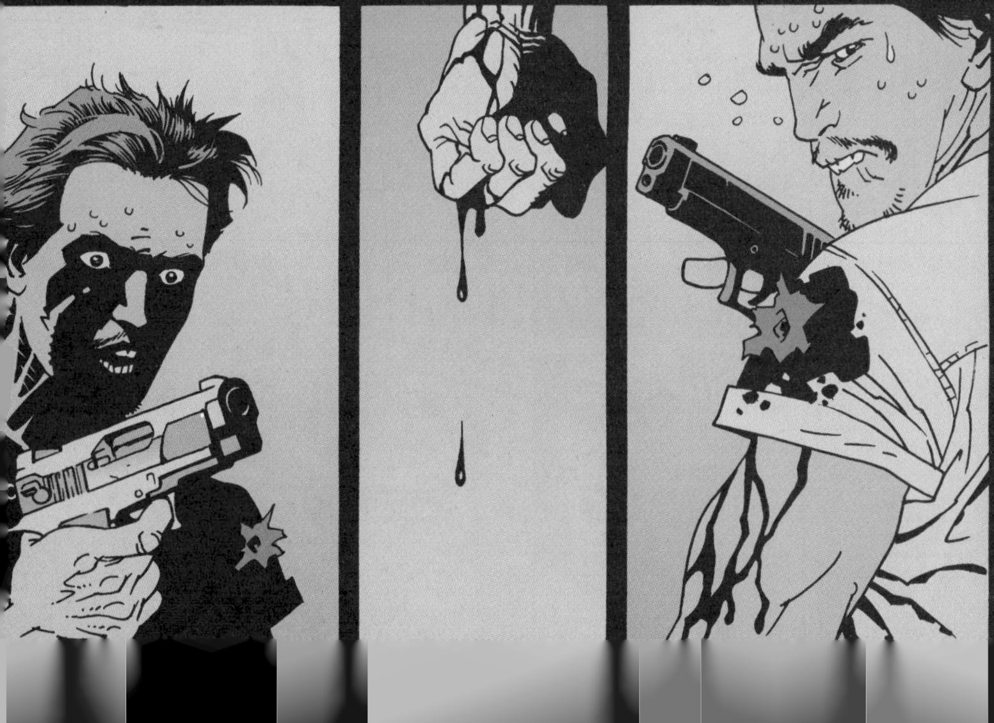

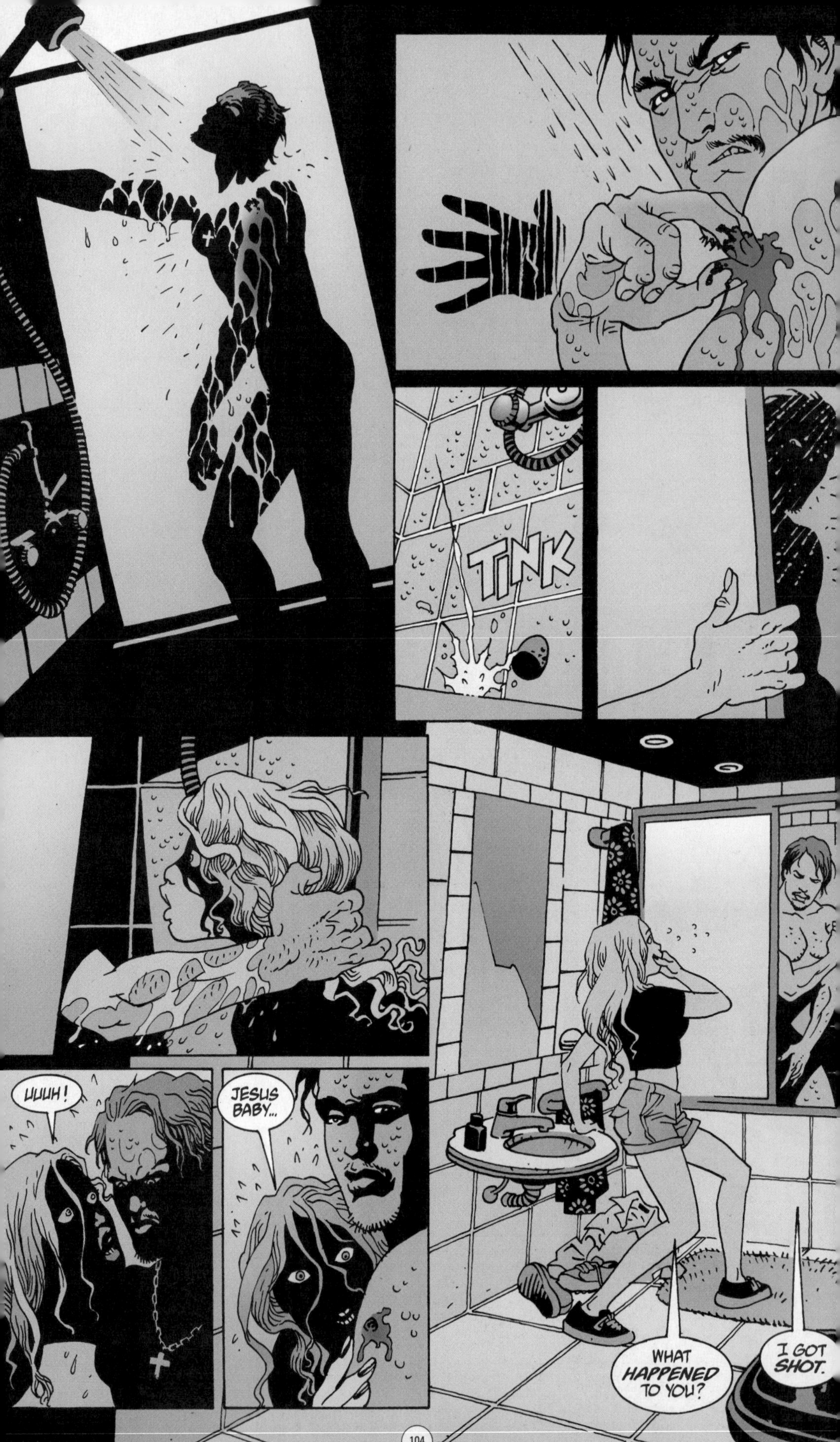
TINK
UUUH!
JESUS BABY...
WHAT HAPPENED TO YOU?
I GOT SHOT.

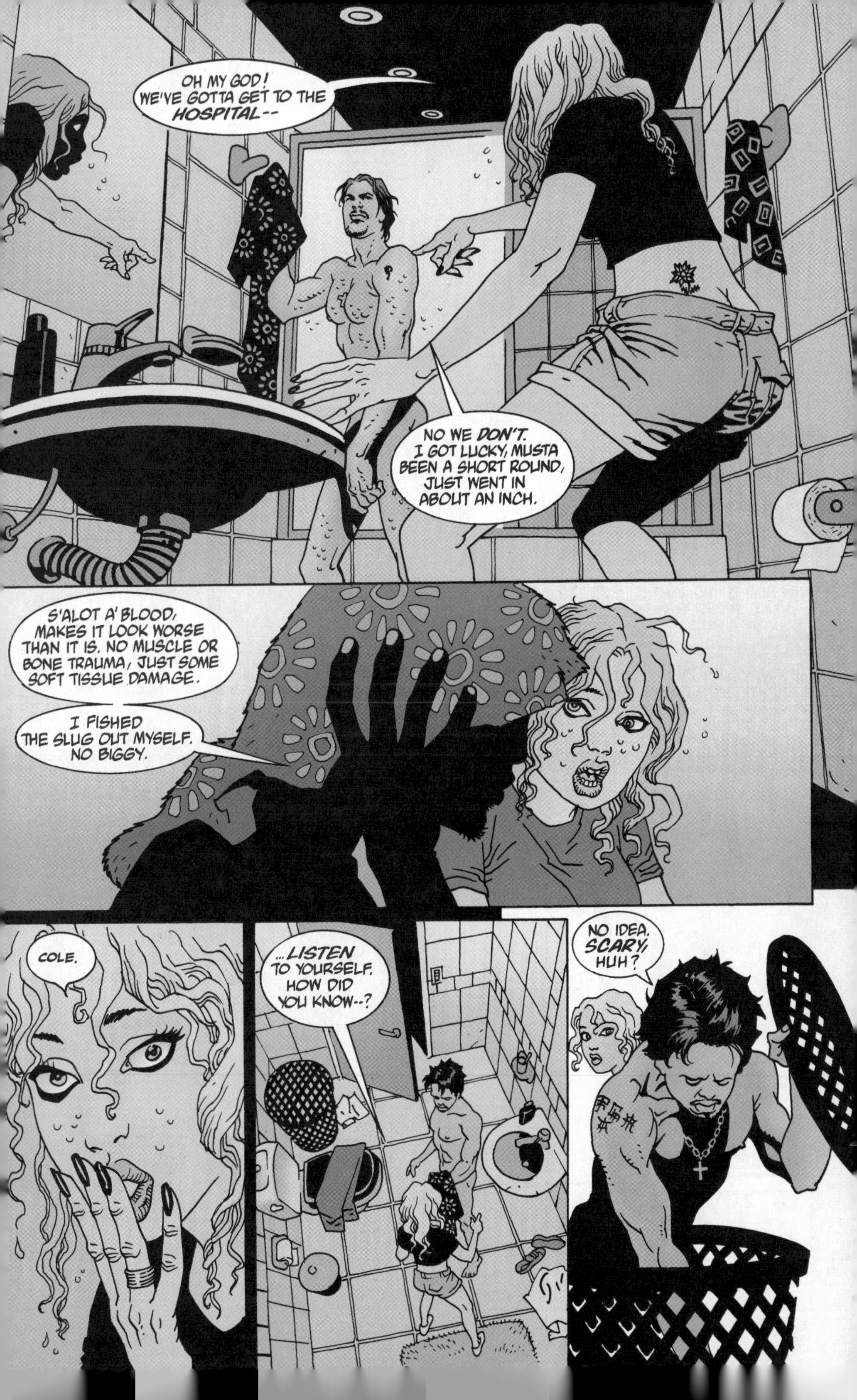
OH MY GOD! WE'VE GOTTA GET TO THE HOSPITAL--
NO WE DON'T. I GOT LUCKY, MUSTA BEEN A SHORT ROUND, JUST WENT IN ABOUT AN INCH.
S'ALOT A' BLOOD, MAKES IT LOOK WORSE THAN IT IS. NO MUSCLE OR BONE TRAUMA, JUST SOME SOFT TISSUE DAMAGE.
I FISHED THE SLUG OUT MYSELF. NO BIGGY.
COLE.
...LISTEN TO YOURSELF. HOW DID YOU KNOW--?
NO IDEA. SCARY, HUH?

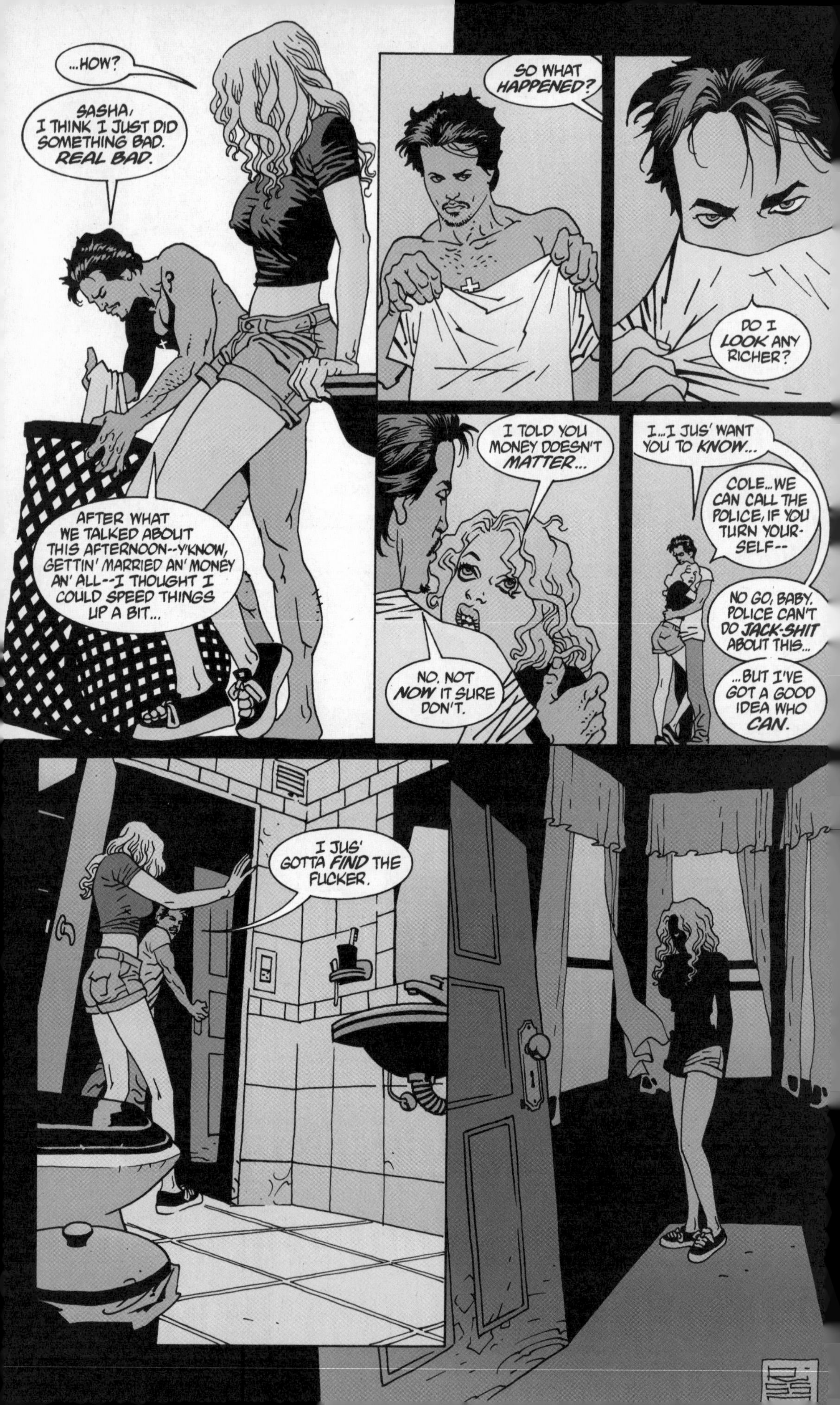

...HOW?
SASHA, I THINK I JUST DID SOMETHING BAD. REAL BAD.
AFTER WHAT WE TALKED ABOUT THIS AFTERNOON--Y'KNOW, GETTIN' MARRIED AN' MONEY AN' ALL--I THOUGHT I COULD SPEED THINGS UP A BIT...
SO WHAT HAPPENED?
DO I LOOK ANY RICHER?
I TOLD YOU MONEY DOESN'T MATTER...
NO. NOT NOW IT SURE DON'T.
I...I JUS' WANT YOU TO KNOW...
COLE...WE CAN CALL THE POLICE, IF YOU TURN YOUR-SELF--
NO GO, BABY. POLICE CAN'T DO JACK-SHIT ABOUT THIS...
...BUT I'VE GOT A GOOD IDEA WHO CAN.
I JUS' GOTTA FIND THE FUCKER.

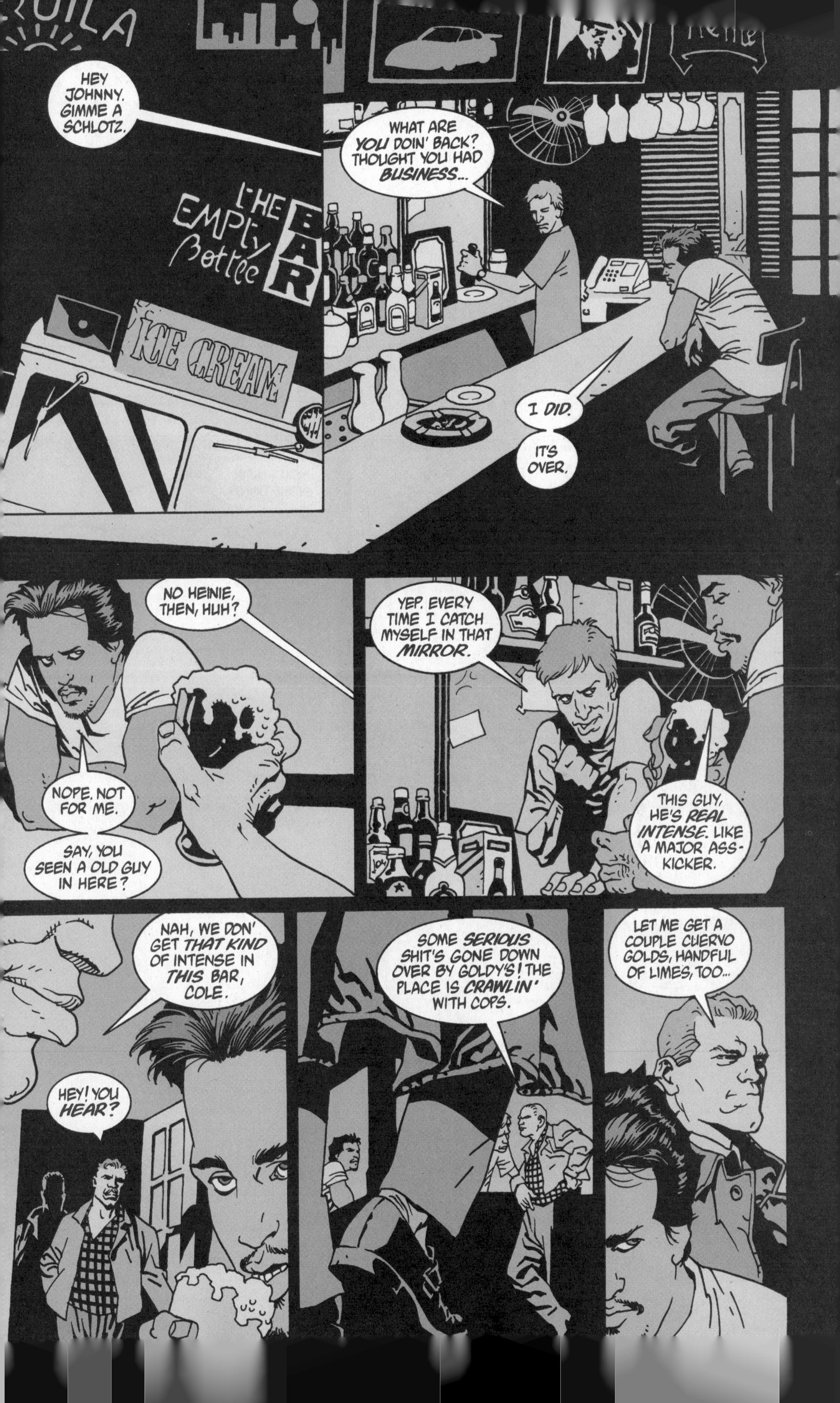

HEY JOHNNY. GIMME A SCHLOTZ.
WHAT ARE YOU DOIN' BACK? THOUGHT YOU HAD BUSINESS...
THE EMPTy Bottle
BAR
ICE CREAM
I DID.
IT'S OVER.
NO HEINIE, THEN, HUH?
NOPE. NOT FOR ME.
SAY, YOU SEEN A OLD GUY IN HERE?
YEP. EVERY TIME I CATCH MYSELF IN THAT MIRROR.
THIS GUY, HE'S REAL INTENSE. LIKE A MAJOR ASS-KICKER.
NAH, WE DON' GET THAT KIND OF INTENSE IN THIS BAR, COLE.
HEY! YOU HEAR?
SOME SERIOUS SHIT'S GONE DOWN OVER BY GOLDY'S! THE PLACE IS CRAWLIN' WITH COPS.
LET ME GET A COUPLE CUERVO GOLDS, HANDFUL OF LIMES, TOO...

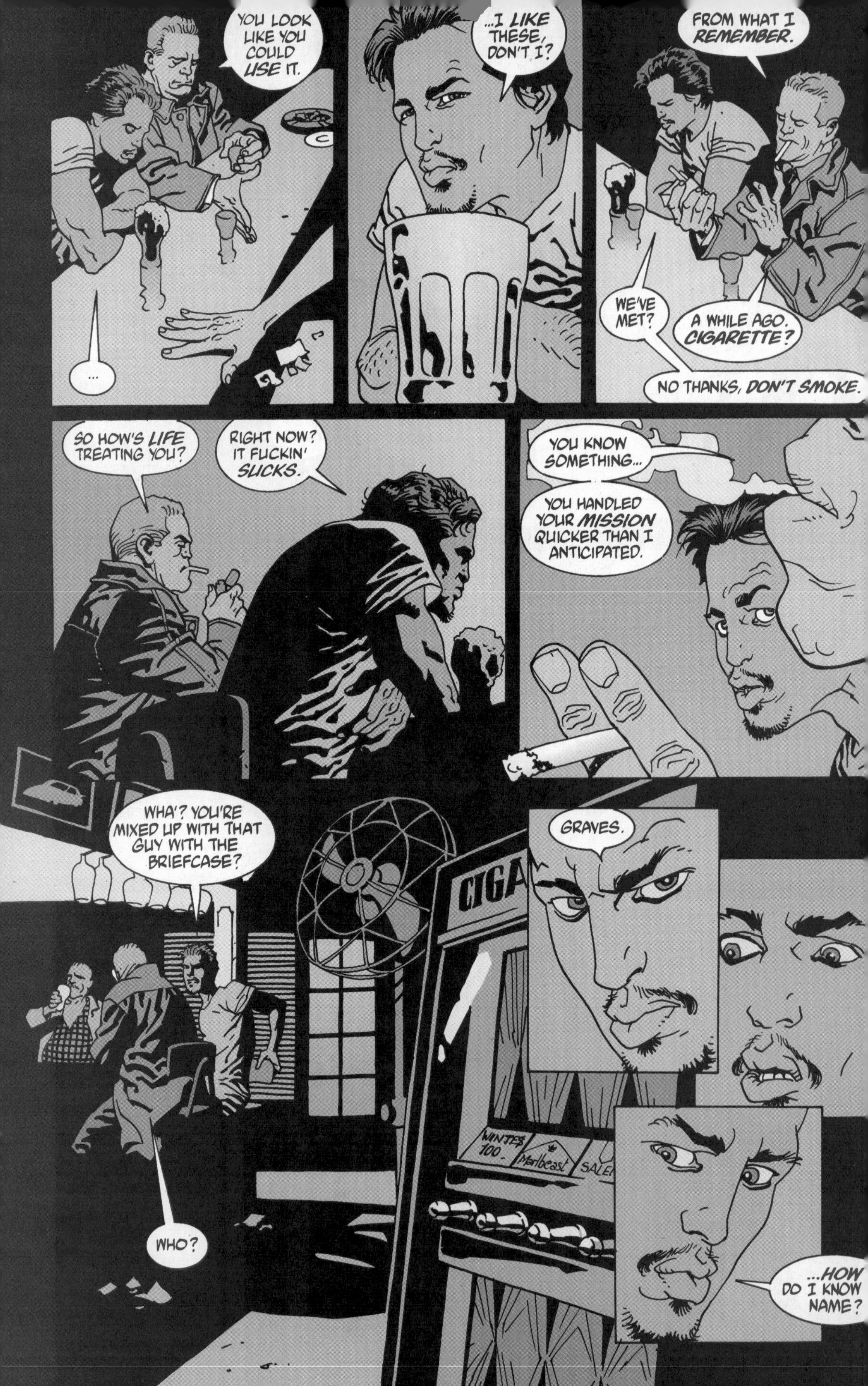

YOU LOOK LIKE YOU COULD USE IT.
...
...I LIKE THESE, DON'T I?
FROM WHAT I REMEMBER.
WE'VE MET?
A WHILE AGO. CIGARETTE?
NO THANKS, DON'T SMOKE.
SO HOW'S LIFE TREATING YOU?
RIGHT NOW? IT FUCKIN' SUCKS.
YOU KNOW SOMETHING...
YOU HANDLED YOUR MISSION QUICKER THAN I ANTICIPATED.
WHA'? YOU'RE MIXED UP WITH THAT GUY WITH THE BRIEFCASE?
WHO?
CIGA
GRAVES.
WINTE$ 100.
Marlbeast
SALE
...HOW DO I KNOW NAME?

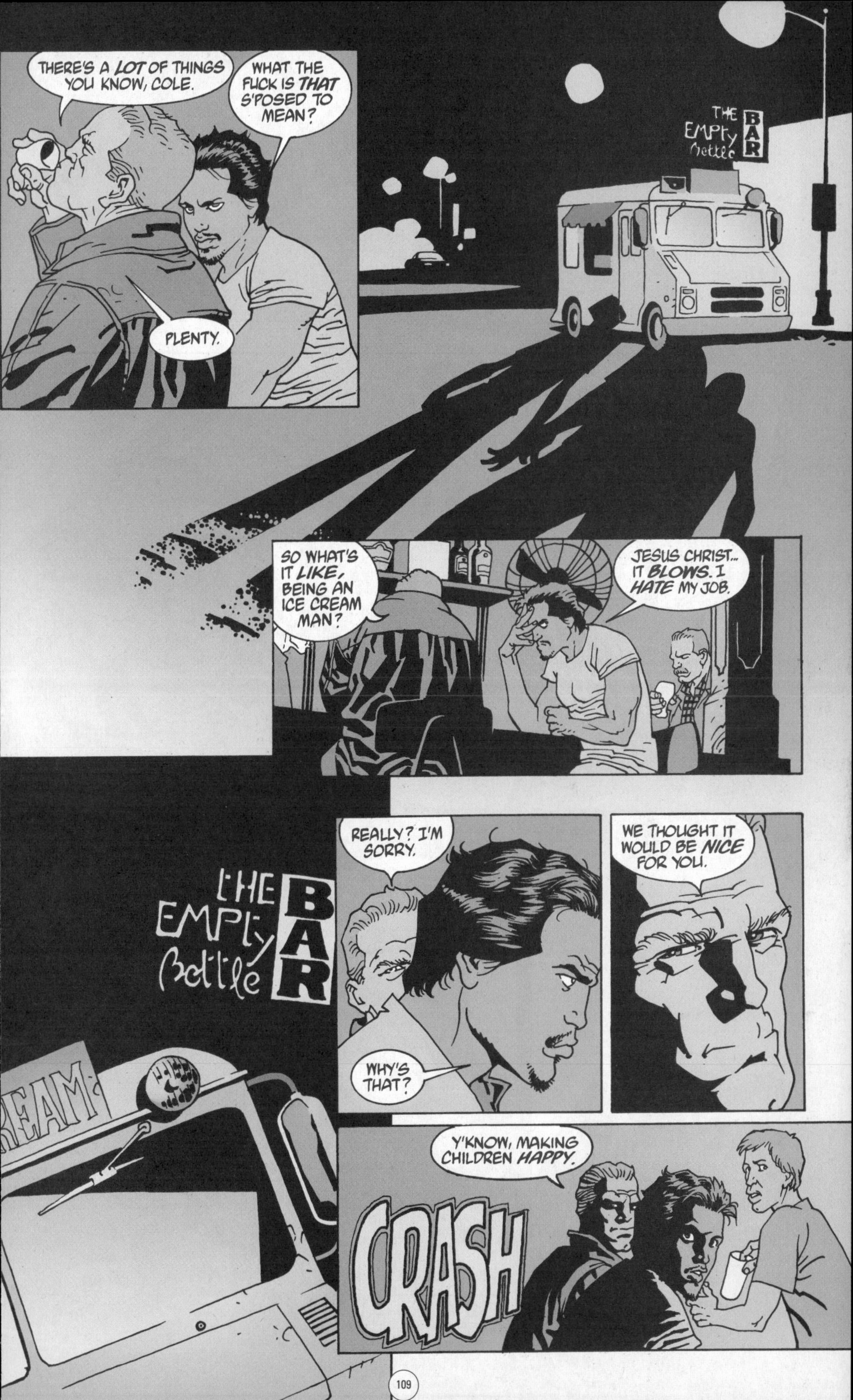
THERE'S A LOT OF THINGS YOU KNOW, COLE.
WHAT THE FUCK IS THAT S'POSED TO MEAN?
PLENTY.
THE EMPTY Bottle BAR
SO WHAT'S IT LIKE, BEING AN ICE CREAM MAN?
JESUS CHRIST... IT BLOWS. I HATE MY JOB.
THE EMPTY Bottle BAR
REALLY? I'M SORRY.
WHY'S THAT?
WE THOUGHT IT WOULD BE NICE FOR YOU.
REAM
Y'KNOW, MAKING CHILDREN HAPPY.
CRASH

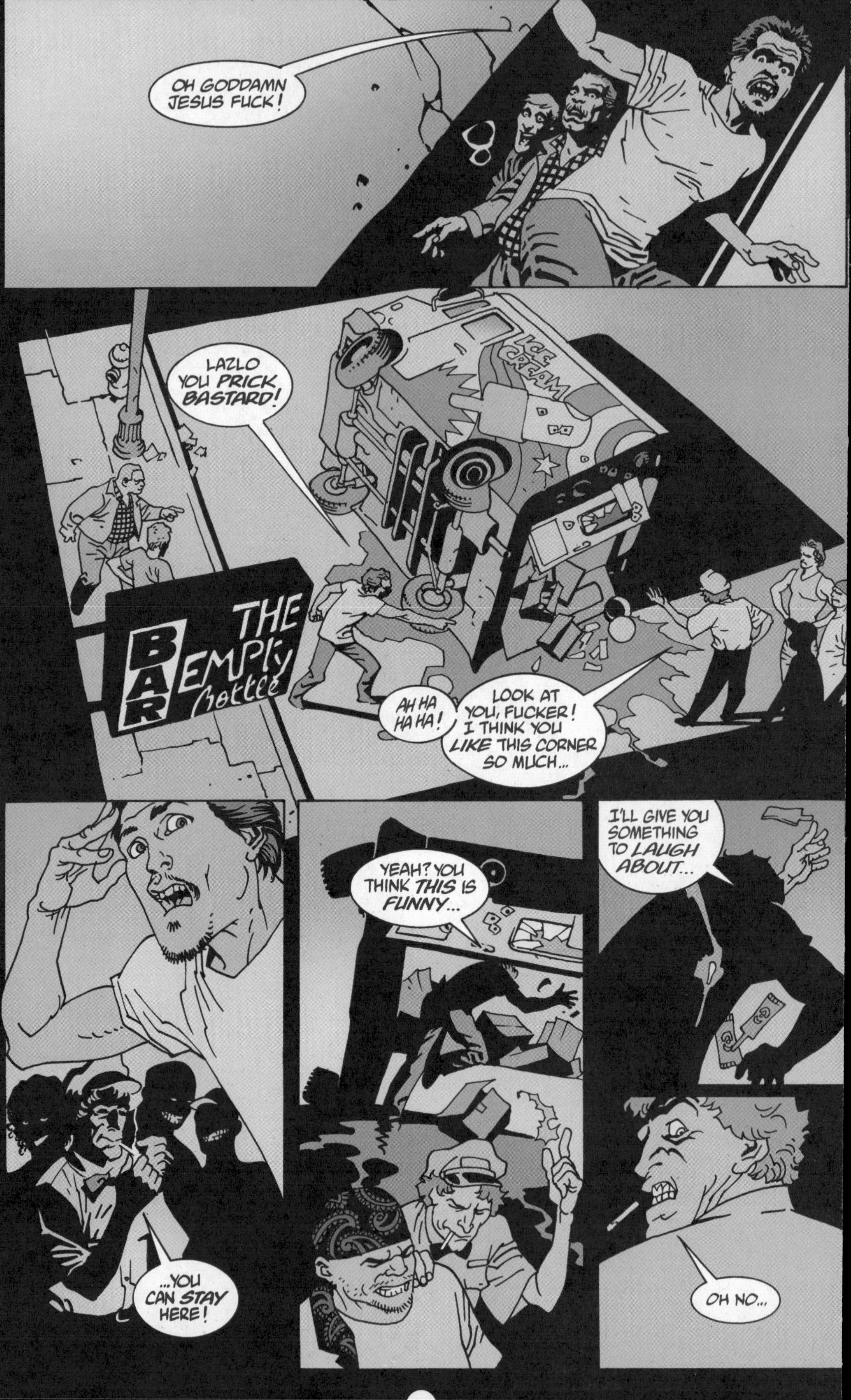
OH GODDAMN JESUS FUCK!
LAZLO YOU PRICK BASTARD!
ICE CREAM
THE EMPTY BOTTLE BAR
AH HA HA HA!
LOOK AT YOU, FUCKER! I THINK YOU LIKE THIS CORNER SO MUCH...
...YOU CAN STAY HERE!
YEAH? YOU THINK THIS IS FUNNY...
I'LL GIVE YOU SOMETHING TO LAUGH ABOUT...
OH NO...

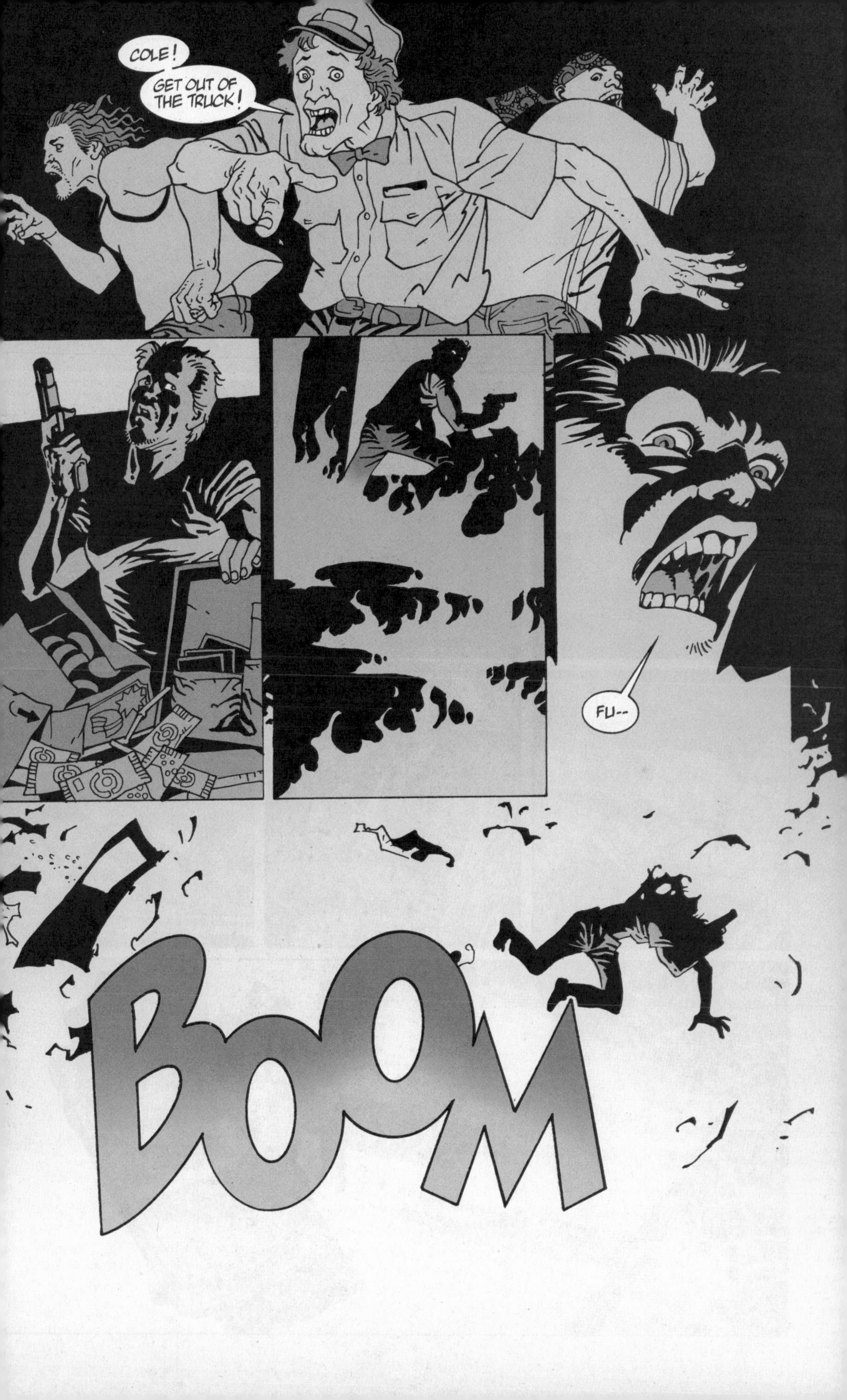
COLE!
GET OUT OF THE TRUCK!
FU--
BOOM

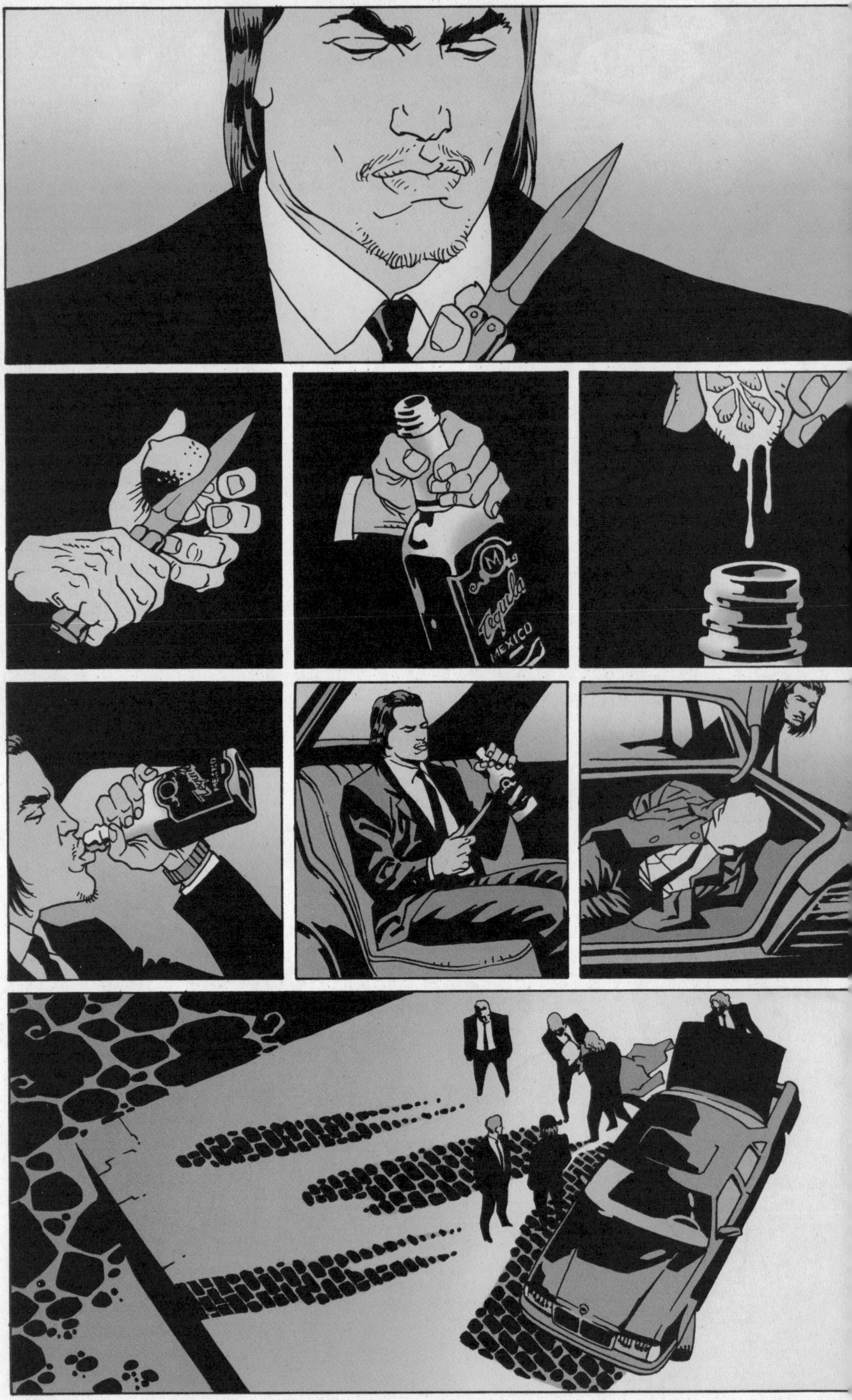
M
Tequila
MEXICO

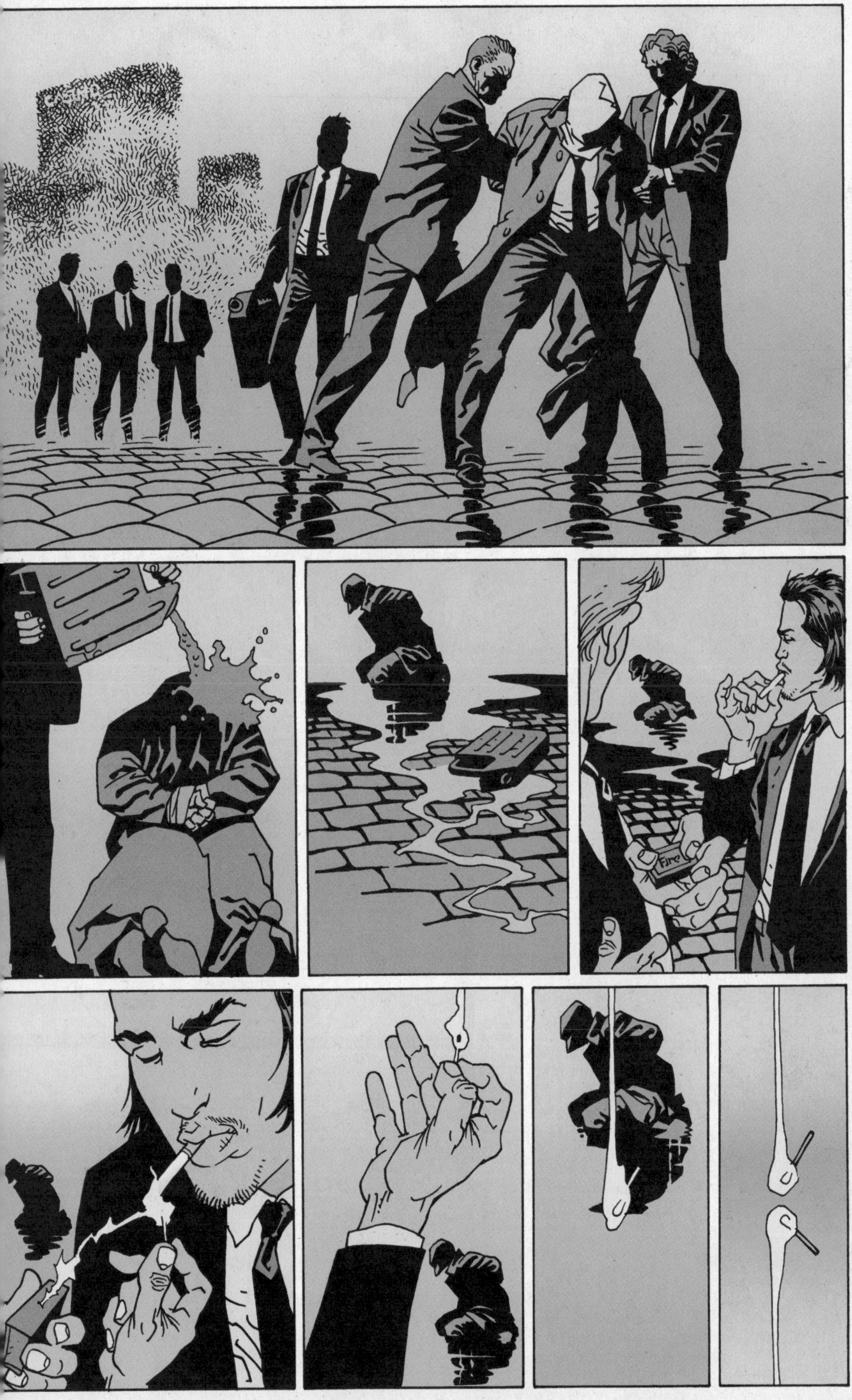
Fire

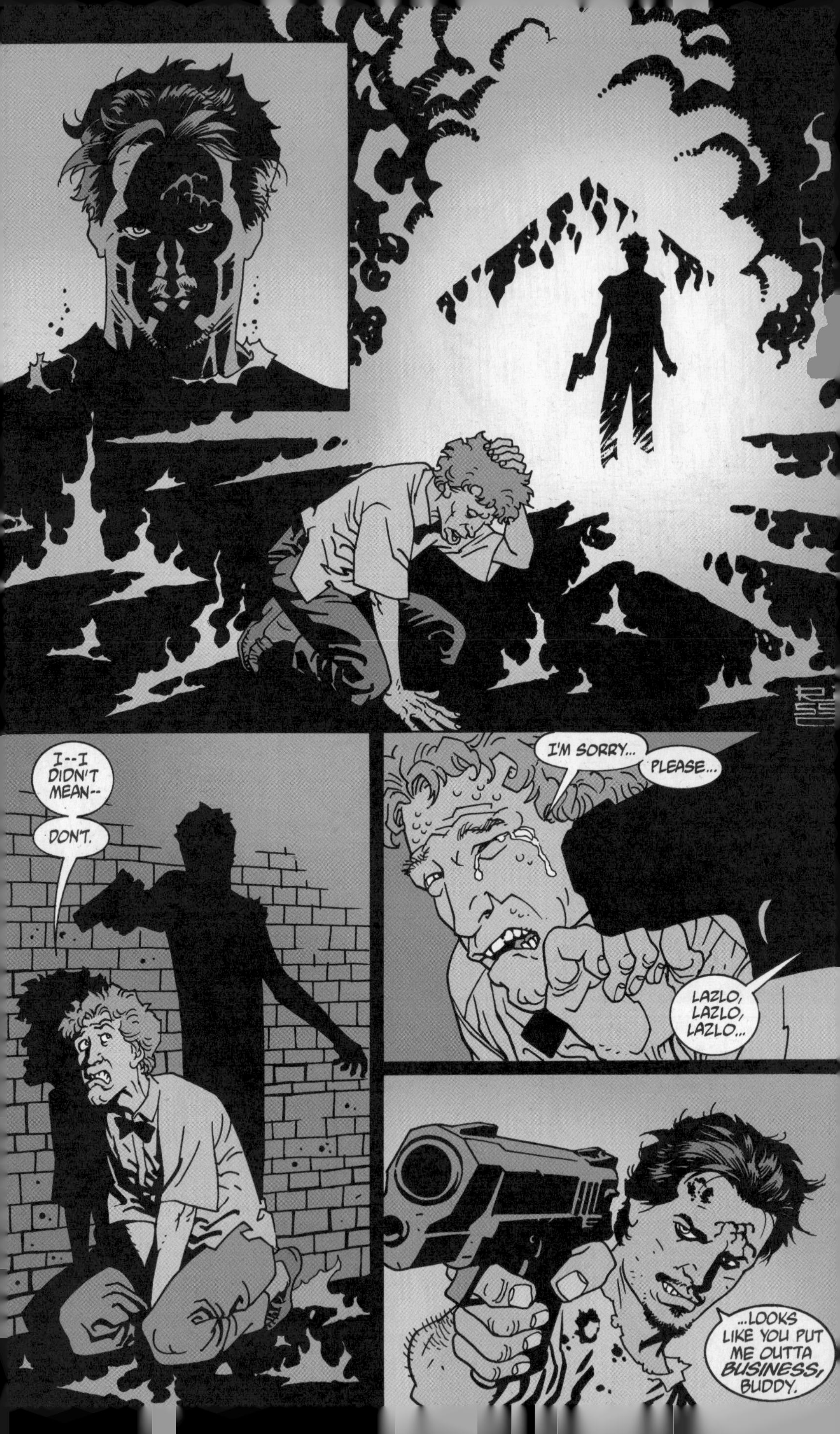
I--I DIDN'T MEAN--
DON'T.
I'M SORRY...
PLEASE...
LAZLO, LAZLO, LAZLO...
...LOOKS LIKE YOU PUT ME OUTTA BUSINESS, BUDDY.

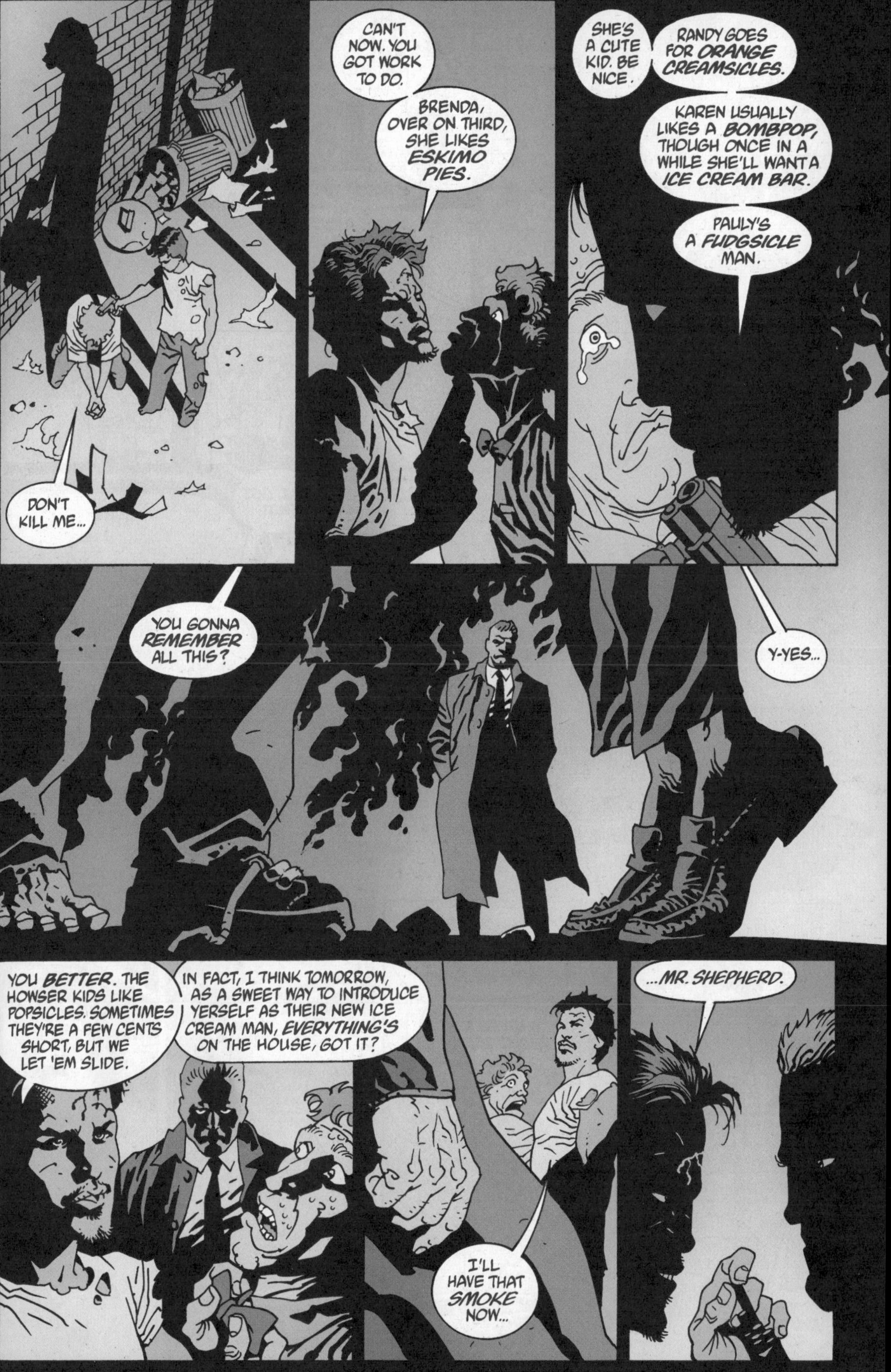
DON'T KILL ME...
CAN'T NOW. YOU GOT WORK TO DO.
BRENDA, OVER ON THIRD, SHE LIKES *ESKIMO PIES*.
SHE'S A CUTE KID. BE NICE.
RANDY GOES FOR *ORANGE CREAMSICLES*.
KAREN USUALLY LIKES A *BOMBPOP*, THOUGH ONCE IN A WHILE SHE'LL WANT A *ICE CREAM BAR*.
PAULY'S A *FUDGSICLE* MAN.
YOU GONNA *REMEMBER* ALL THIS?
Y-YES...
YOU *BETTER*. THE HOWSER KIDS LIKE POPSICLES. SOMETIMES THEY'RE A FEW CENTS SHORT, BUT WE LET 'EM SLIDE.
IN FACT, I THINK TOMORROW, AS A SWEET WAY TO INTRODUCE YERSELF AS THEIR NEW ICE CREAM MAN, *EVERYTHING'S* ON THE HOUSE, GOT IT?
I'LL HAVE THAT *SMOKE* NOW...
...*MR. SHEPHERD*.

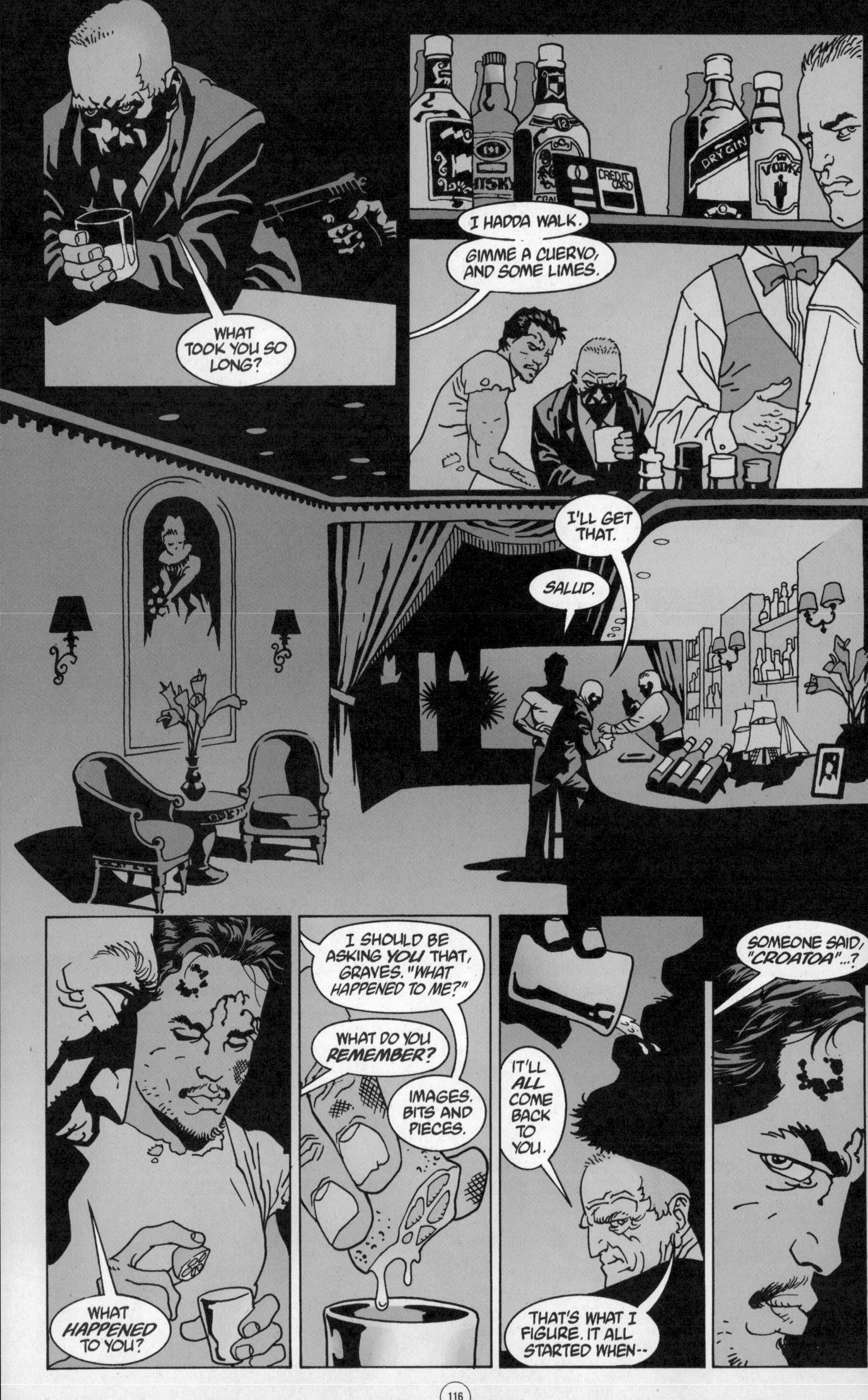

WHAT TOOK YOU SO LONG?
I HADDA WALK.
GIMME A CUERVO, AND SOME LIMES.
DRY GIN
VODKA
CREDIT CARD
I'LL GET THAT.
SALUD.
WHAT HAPPENED TO YOU?
I SHOULD BE ASKING YOU THAT, GRAVES. "WHAT HAPPENED TO ME?"
WHAT DO YOU REMEMBER?
IMAGES. BITS AND PIECES.
IT'LL ALL COME BACK TO YOU.
THAT'S WHAT I FIGURE. IT ALL STARTED WHEN--
SOMEONE SAID, "CROATOA"...?

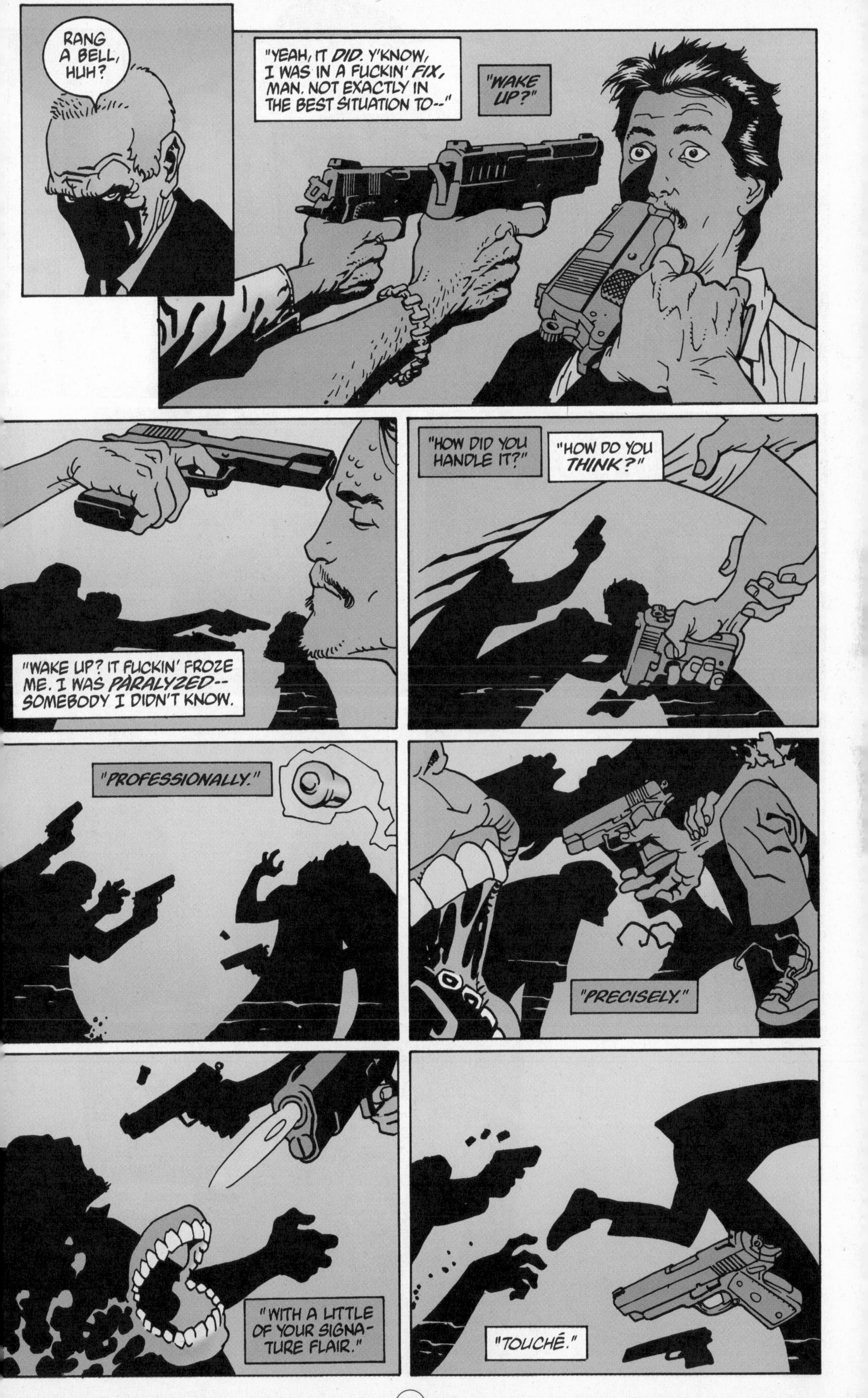
RANG A BELL, HUH?
"YEAH, IT DID. Y'KNOW, I WAS IN A FUCKIN' FIX, MAN. NOT EXACTLY IN THE BEST SITUATION TO--"
"WAKE UP?"
"WAKE UP? IT FUCKIN' FROZE ME. I WAS PARALYZED-- SOMEBODY I DIDN'T KNOW.
"HOW DID YOU HANDLE IT?"
"HOW DO YOU THINK?"
"PROFESSIONALLY."
"PRECISELY."
"WITH A LITTLE OF YOUR SIGNATURE FLAIR."
"TOUCHÉ."

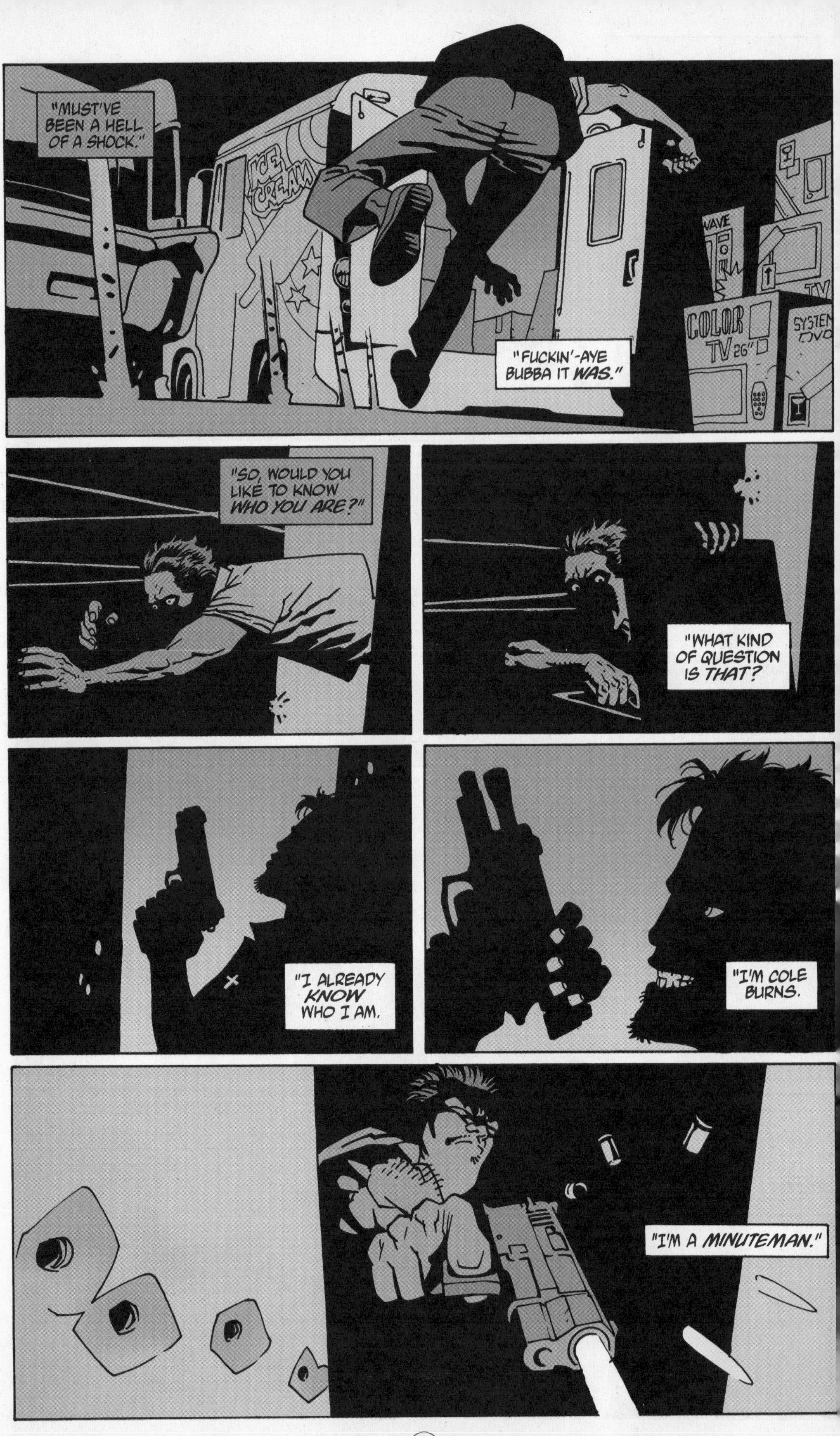
"MUST'VE BEEN A HELL OF A SHOCK."
ICE CREAM
"FUCKIN'-AYE BUBBA IT WAS."
COLOR TV 26"
"SO, WOULD YOU LIKE TO KNOW WHO YOU ARE?"
"WHAT KIND OF QUESTION IS THAT?
"I ALREADY KNOW WHO I AM.
"I'M COLE BURNS.
"I'M A MINUTEMAN."

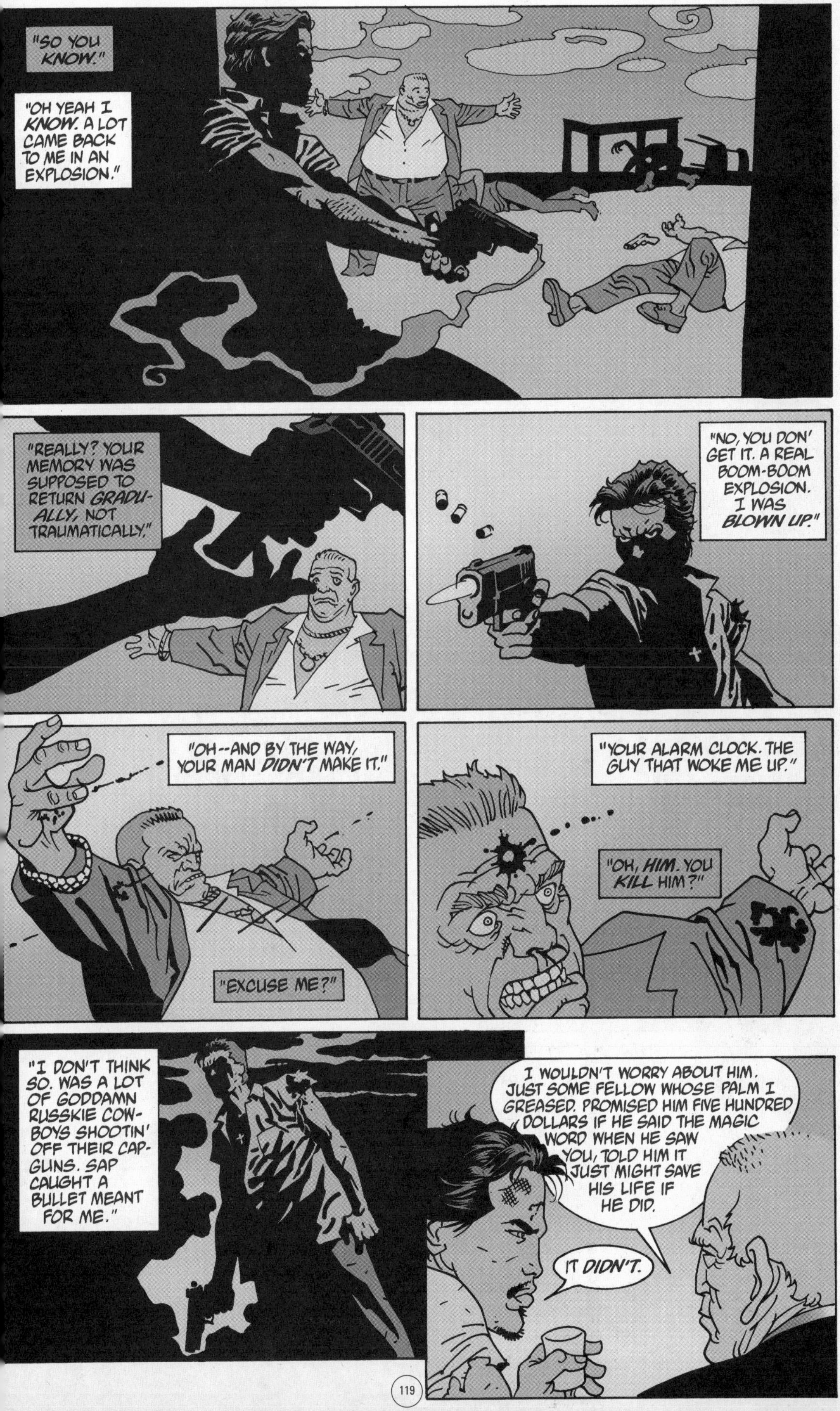

"SO YOU KNOW."
"OH YEAH I KNOW. A LOT CAME BACK TO ME IN AN EXPLOSION."
"REALLY? YOUR MEMORY WAS SUPPOSED TO RETURN GRADUALLY, NOT TRAUMATICALLY."
"NO, YOU DON' GET IT. A REAL BOOM-BOOM EXPLOSION. I WAS BLOWN UP."
"OH--AND BY THE WAY, YOUR MAN DIDN'T MAKE IT."
"EXCUSE ME?"
"YOUR ALARM CLOCK. THE GUY THAT WOKE ME UP."
"OH, HIM. YOU KILL HIM?"
"I DON'T THINK SO. WAS A LOT OF GODDAMN RUSSKIE COWBOYS SHOOTIN' OFF THEIR CAP-GUNS. SAP CAUGHT A BULLET MEANT FOR ME."
I WOULDN'T WORRY ABOUT HIM. JUST SOME FELLOW WHOSE PALM I GREASED. PROMISED HIM FIVE HUNDRED DOLLARS IF HE SAID THE MAGIC WORD WHEN HE SAW YOU, TOLD HIM IT JUST MIGHT SAVE HIS LIFE IF HE DID.
IT DIDN'T.

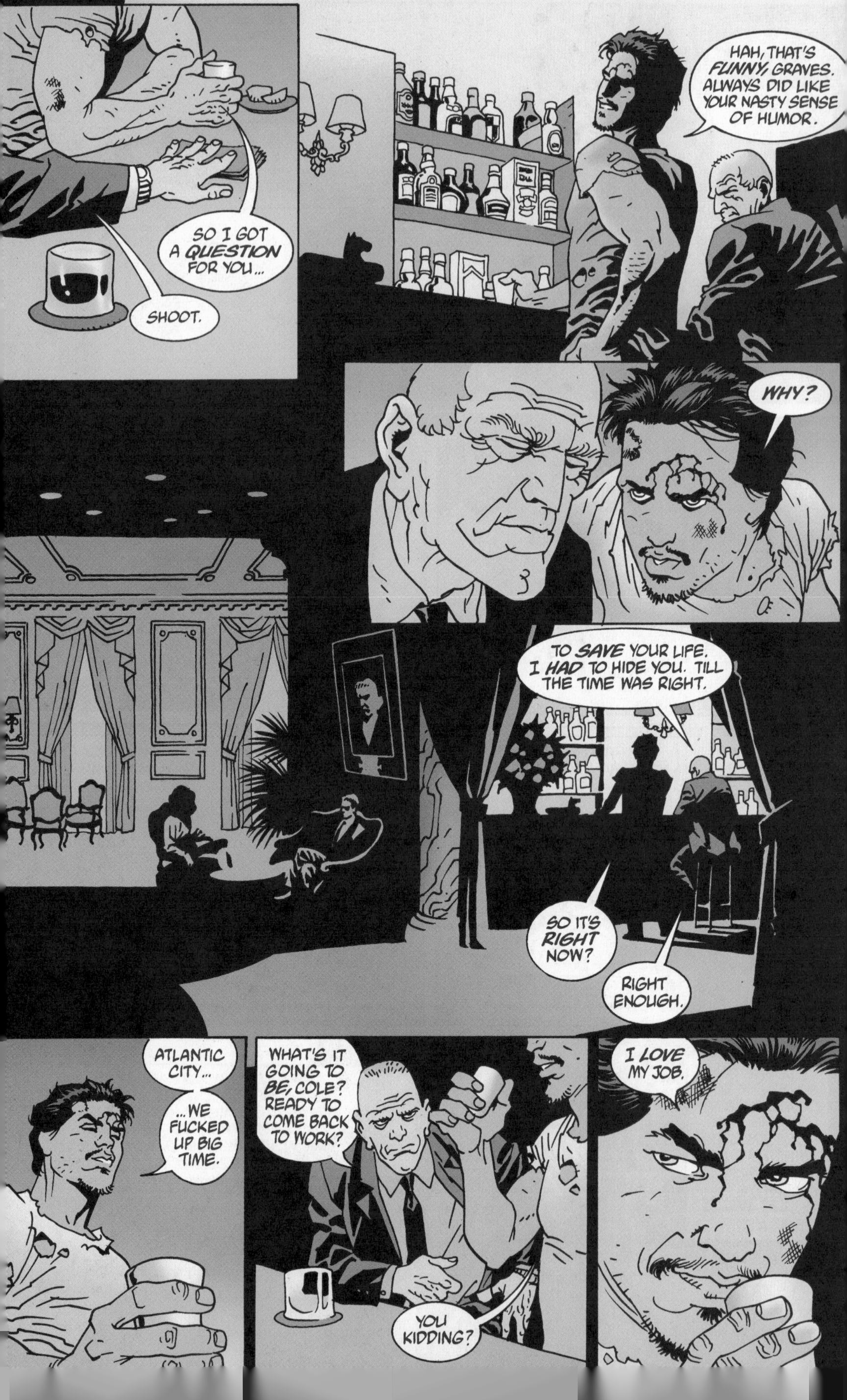
SO I GOT A QUESTION FOR YOU...
SHOOT.
HAH, THAT'S FUNNY, GRAVES. ALWAYS DID LIKE YOUR NASTY SENSE OF HUMOR.
WHY?
TO SAVE YOUR LIFE. I HAD TO HIDE YOU. TILL THE TIME WAS RIGHT.
SO IT'S RIGHT NOW?
RIGHT ENOUGH.
ATLANTIC CITY...
...WE FUCKED UP BIG TIME.
WHAT'S IT GOING TO BE, COLE? READY TO COME BACK TO WORK?
YOU KIDDING?
I LOVE MY JOB.

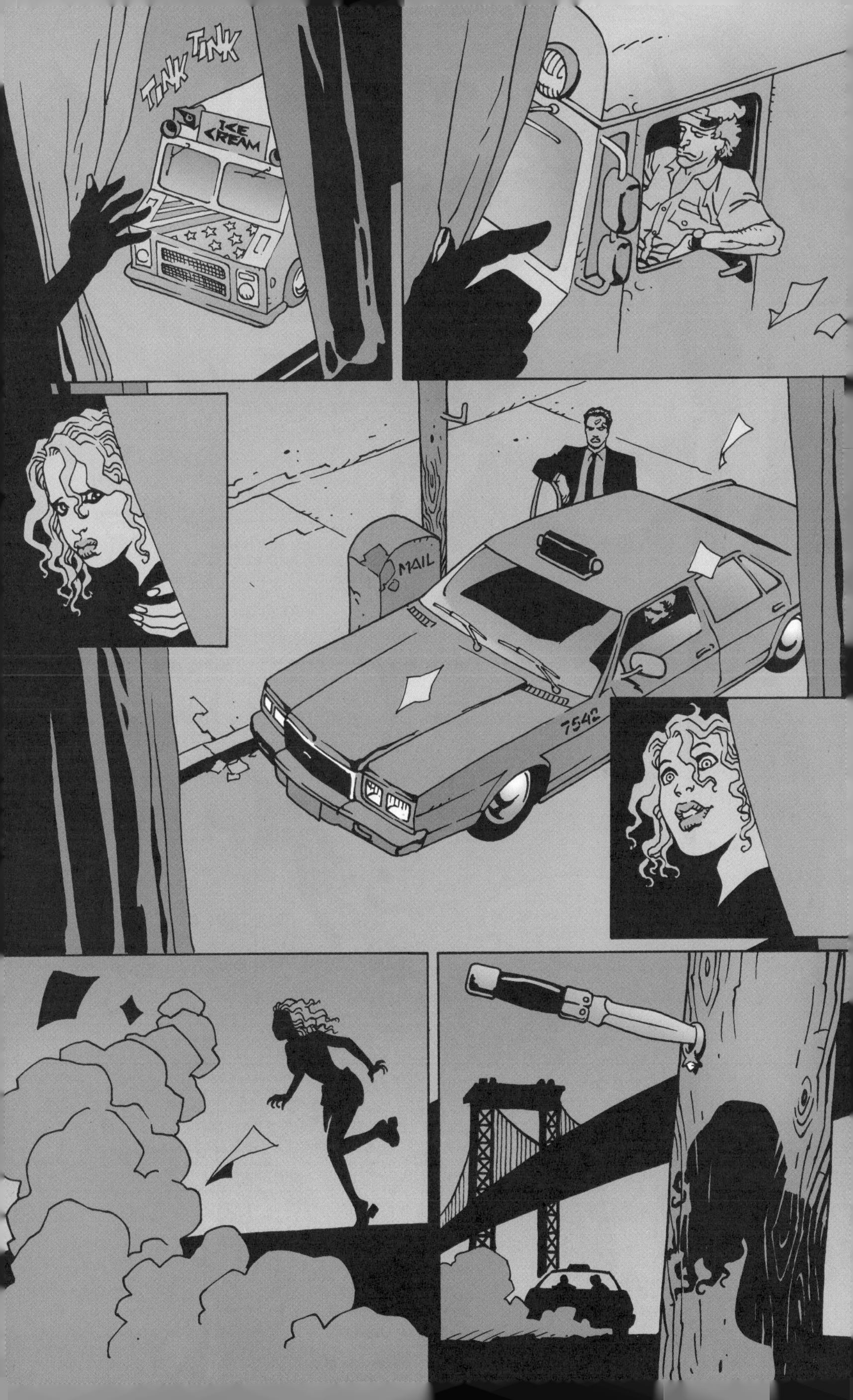
TINK TINK
ICE CREAM
MAIL
7542

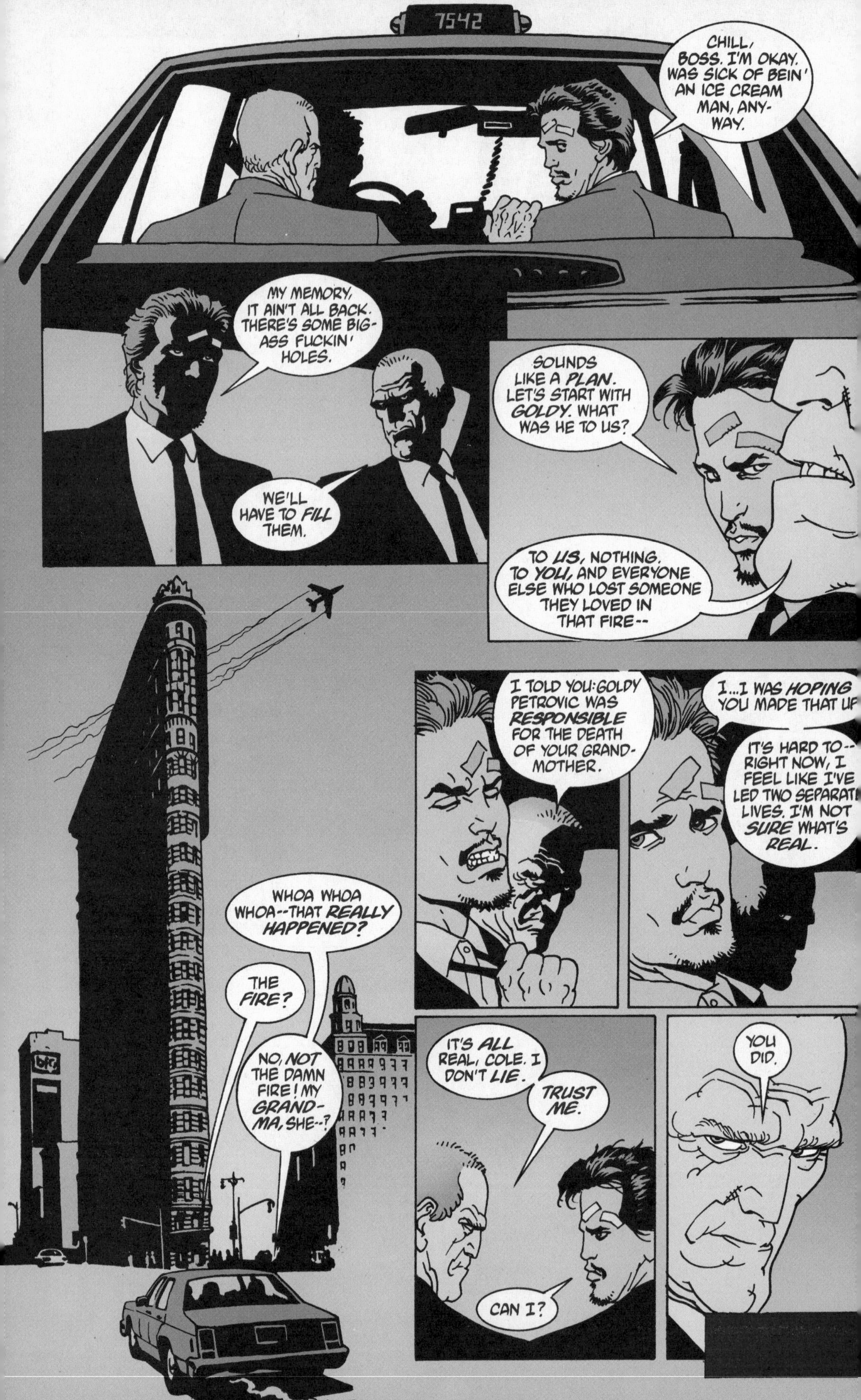

7542
CHILL, BOSS. I'M OKAY. WAS SICK OF BEIN' AN ICE CREAM MAN, ANY-WAY.
MY MEMORY, IT AIN'T ALL BACK. THERE'S SOME BIG-ASS FUCKIN' HOLES.
WE'LL HAVE TO FILL THEM.
SOUNDS LIKE A PLAN. LET'S START WITH GOLDY. WHAT WAS HE TO US?
TO US, NOTHING. TO YOU, AND EVERYONE ELSE WHO LOST SOMEONE THEY LOVED IN THAT FIRE--
WHOA WHOA WHOA--THAT REALLY HAPPENED?
THE FIRE?
NO, NOT THE DAMN FIRE! MY GRAND-MA, SHE--?
I TOLD YOU: GOLDY PETROVIC WAS RESPONSIBLE FOR THE DEATH OF YOUR GRAND-MOTHER.
I...I WAS HOPING YOU MADE THAT UP
IT'S HARD TO-- RIGHT NOW, I FEEL LIKE I'VE LED TWO SEPARAT LIVES. I'M NOT SURE WHAT'S REAL.
IT'S ALL REAL, COLE. I DON'T LIE.
TRUST ME.
CAN I?
YOU DID.

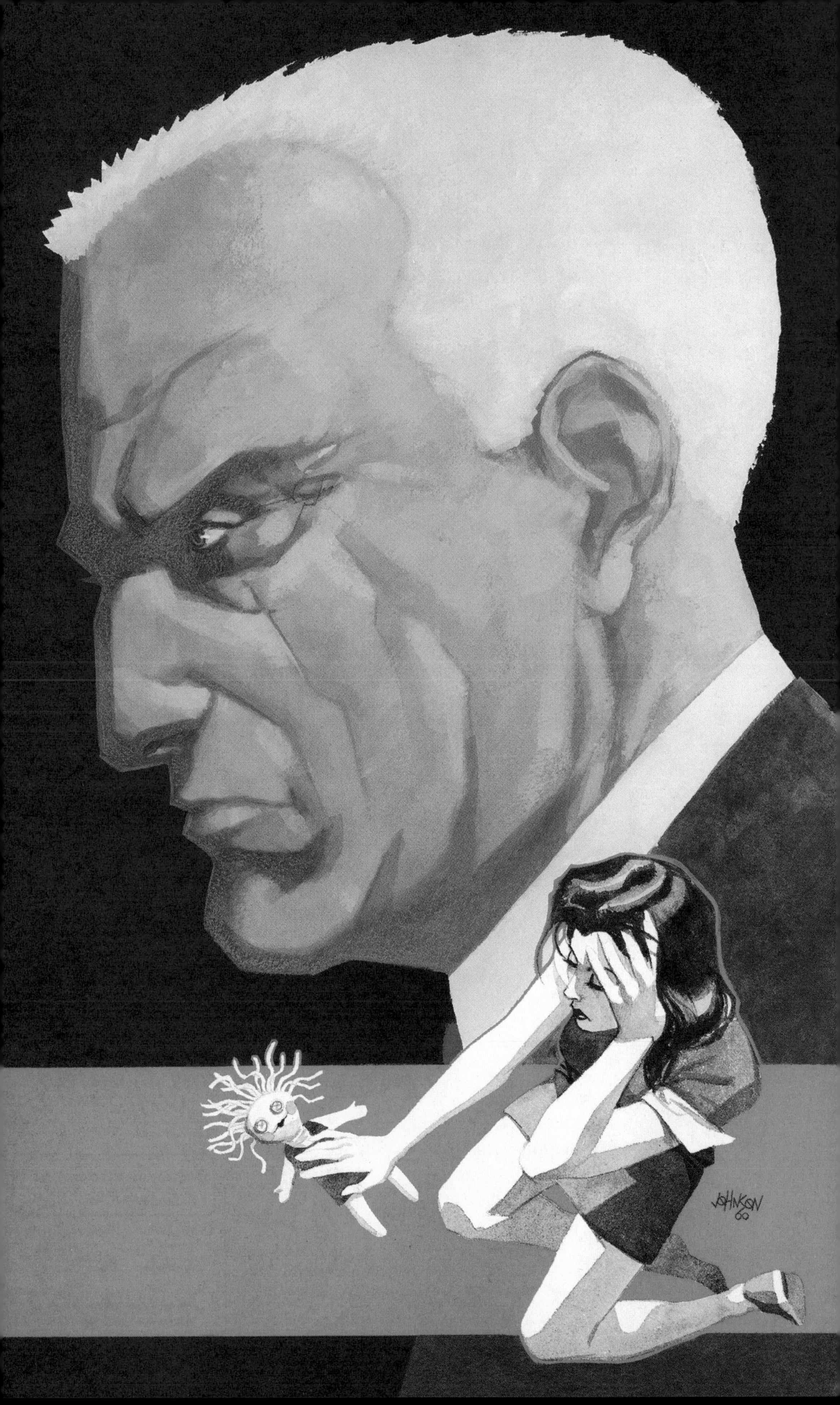
JOHNSON
60

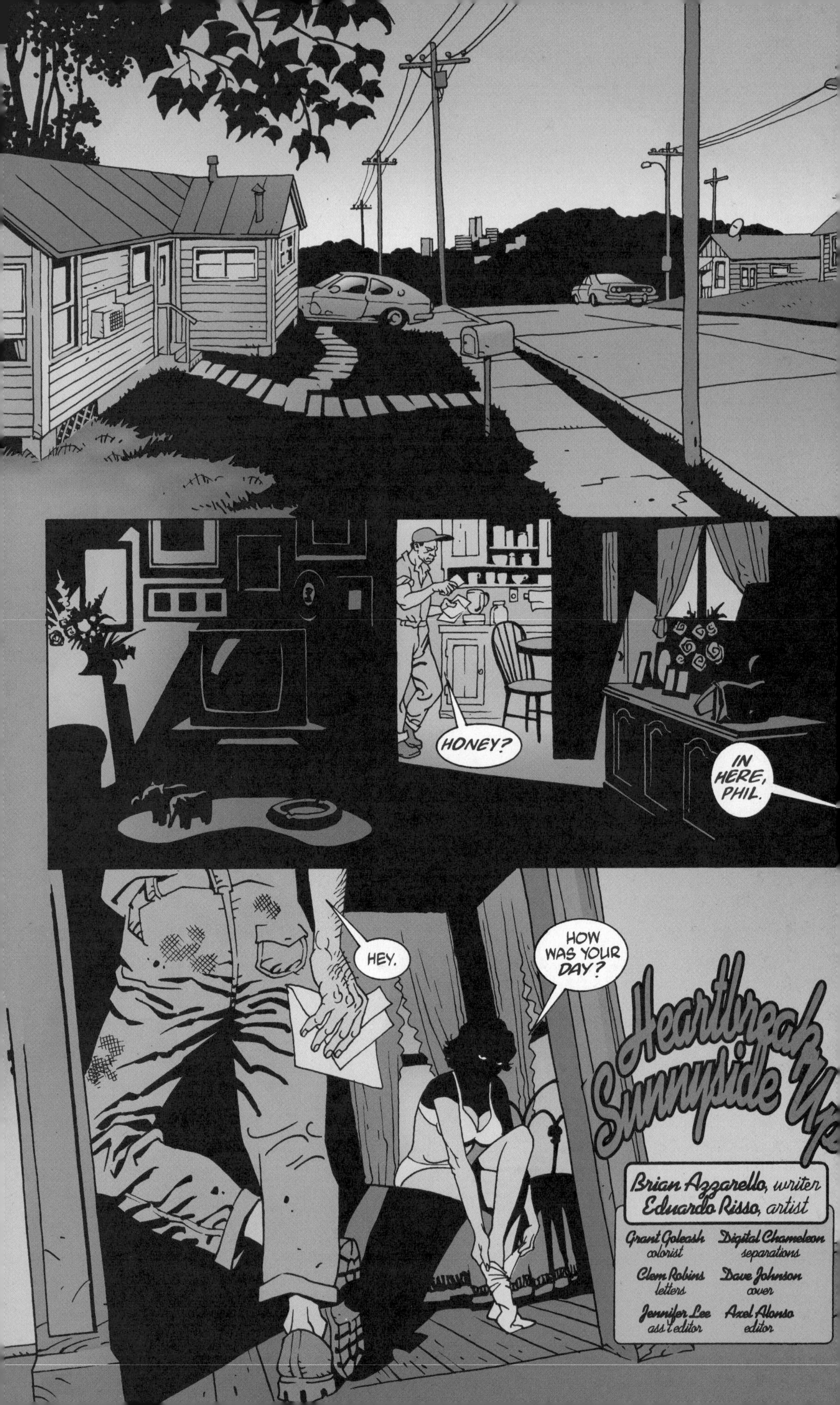
HONEY?
IN HERE, PHIL.
HEY.
HOW WAS YOUR DAY?
Heartbreak Sunnyside Up
Brian Azzarello, writer
Eduardo Risso, artist
Grant Goleash colorist
Digital Chameleon separations
Clem Robins letters
Dave Johnson cover
Jennifer Lee ass't editor
Axel Alonso editor

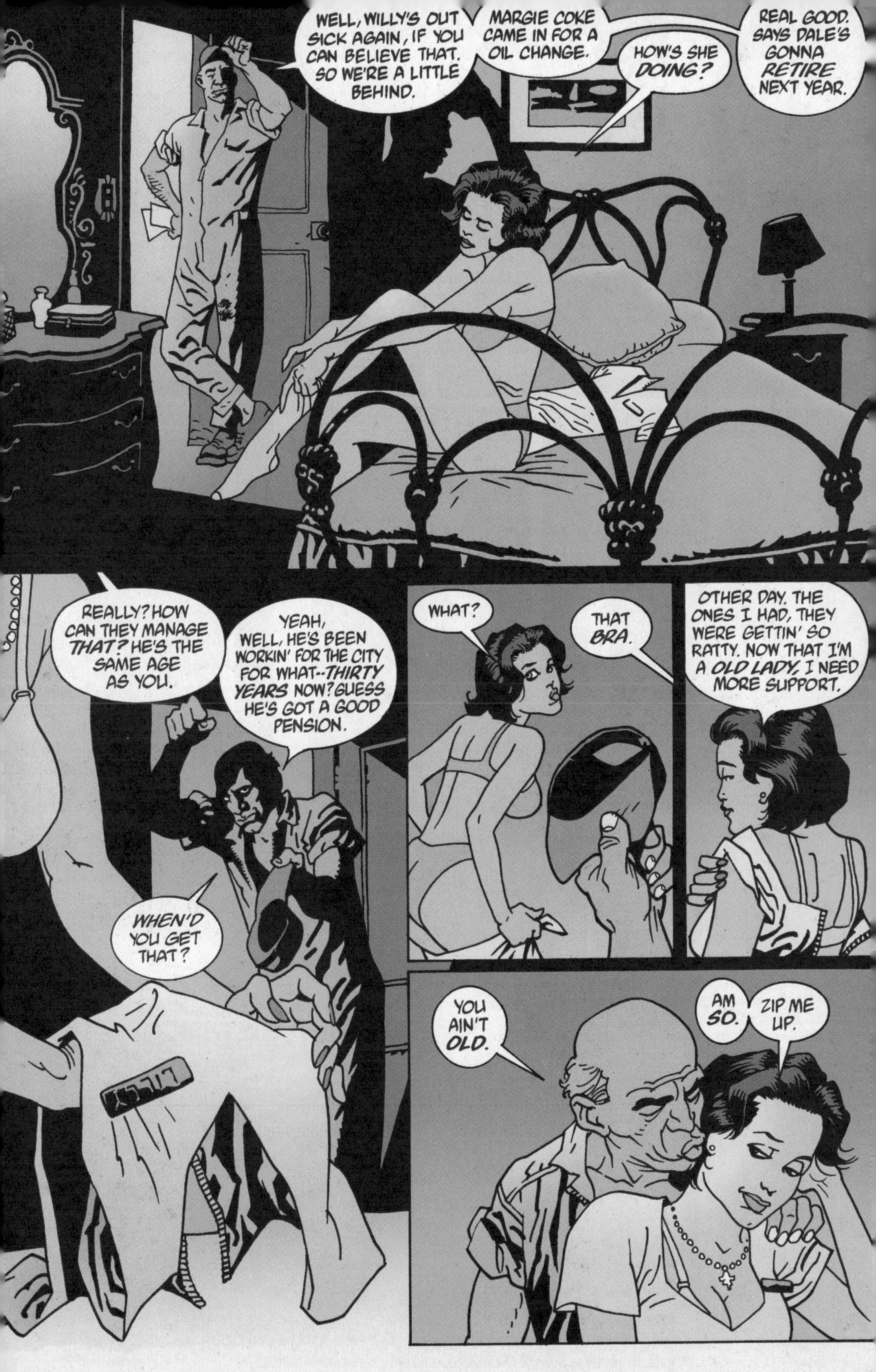
WELL, WILLY'S OUT SICK AGAIN, IF YOU CAN BELIEVE THAT. SO WE'RE A LITTLE BEHIND.
MARGIE COKE CAME IN FOR A OIL CHANGE.
HOW'S SHE DOING?
REAL GOOD. SAYS DALE'S GONNA RETIRE NEXT YEAR.
REALLY? HOW CAN THEY MANAGE THAT? HE'S THE SAME AGE AS YOU.
YEAH, WELL, HE'S BEEN WORKIN' FOR THE CITY FOR WHAT--THIRTY YEARS NOW? GUESS HE'S GOT A GOOD PENSION.
WHEN'D YOU GET THAT?
WHAT?
THAT BRA.
OTHER DAY. THE ONES I HAD, THEY WERE GETTIN' SO RATTY. NOW THAT I'M A OLD LADY, I NEED MORE SUPPORT.
YOU AIN'T OLD.
AM SO.
ZIP ME UP.

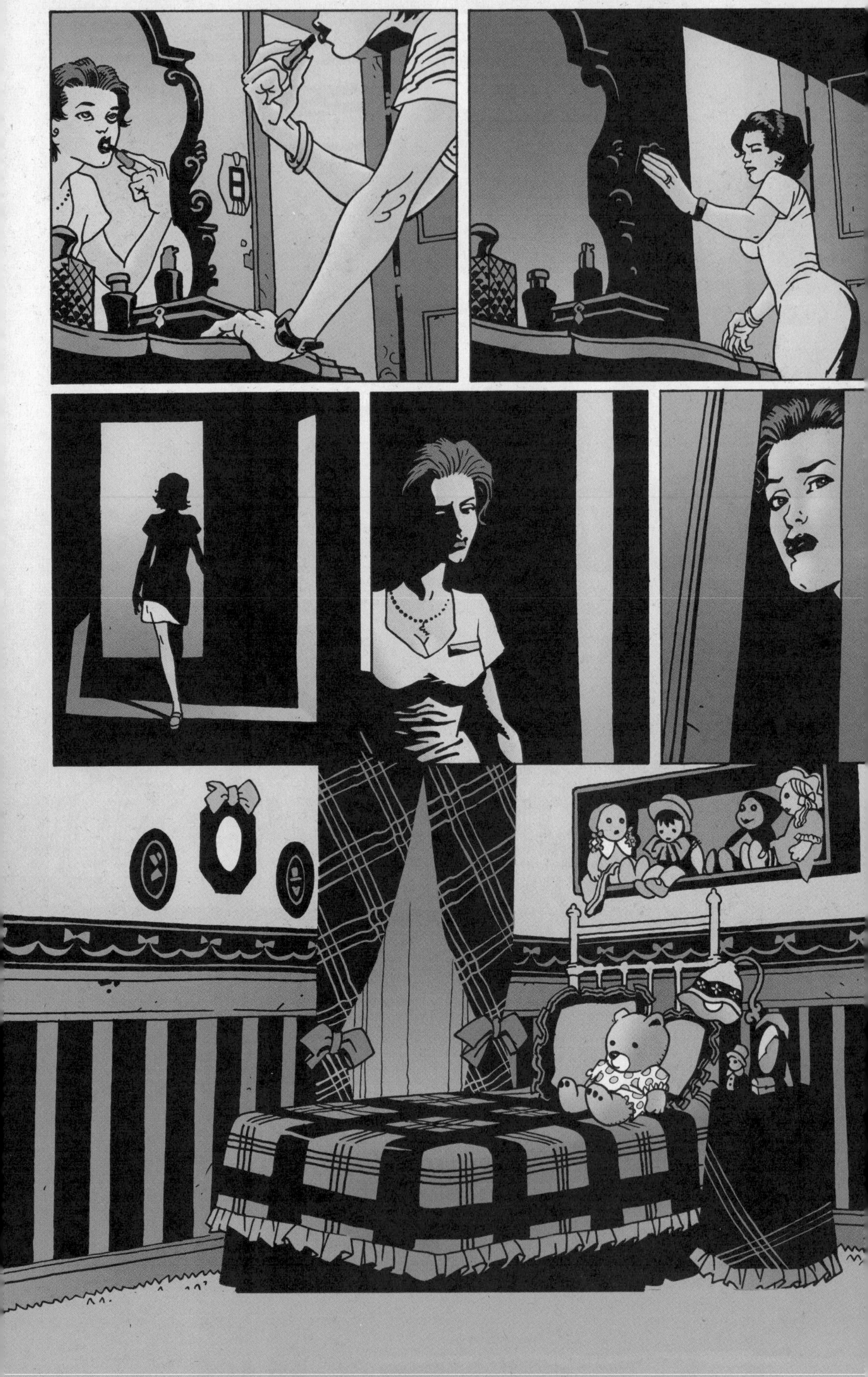

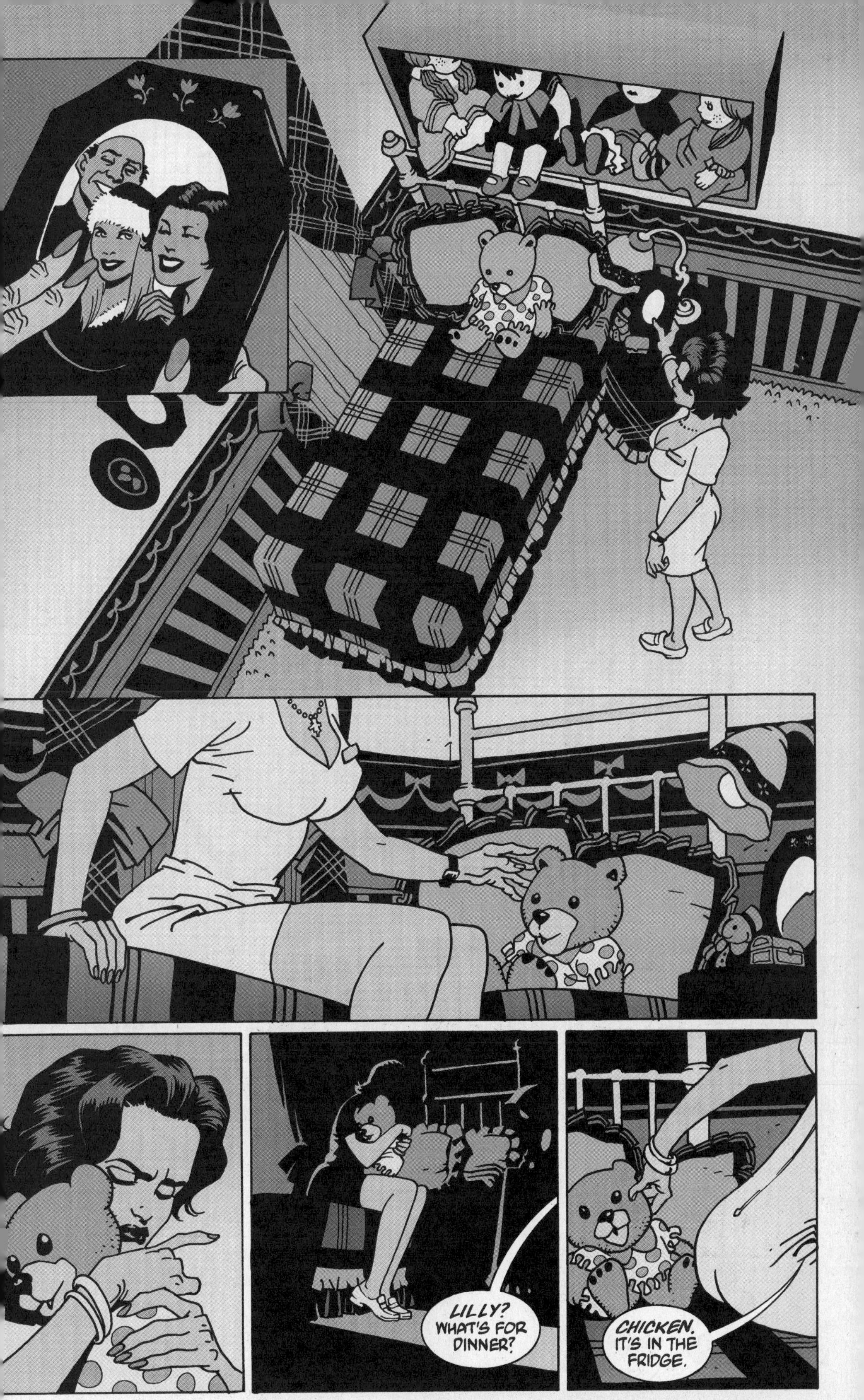
LILLY? WHAT'S FOR DINNER?
CHICKEN. IT'S IN THE FRIDGE.

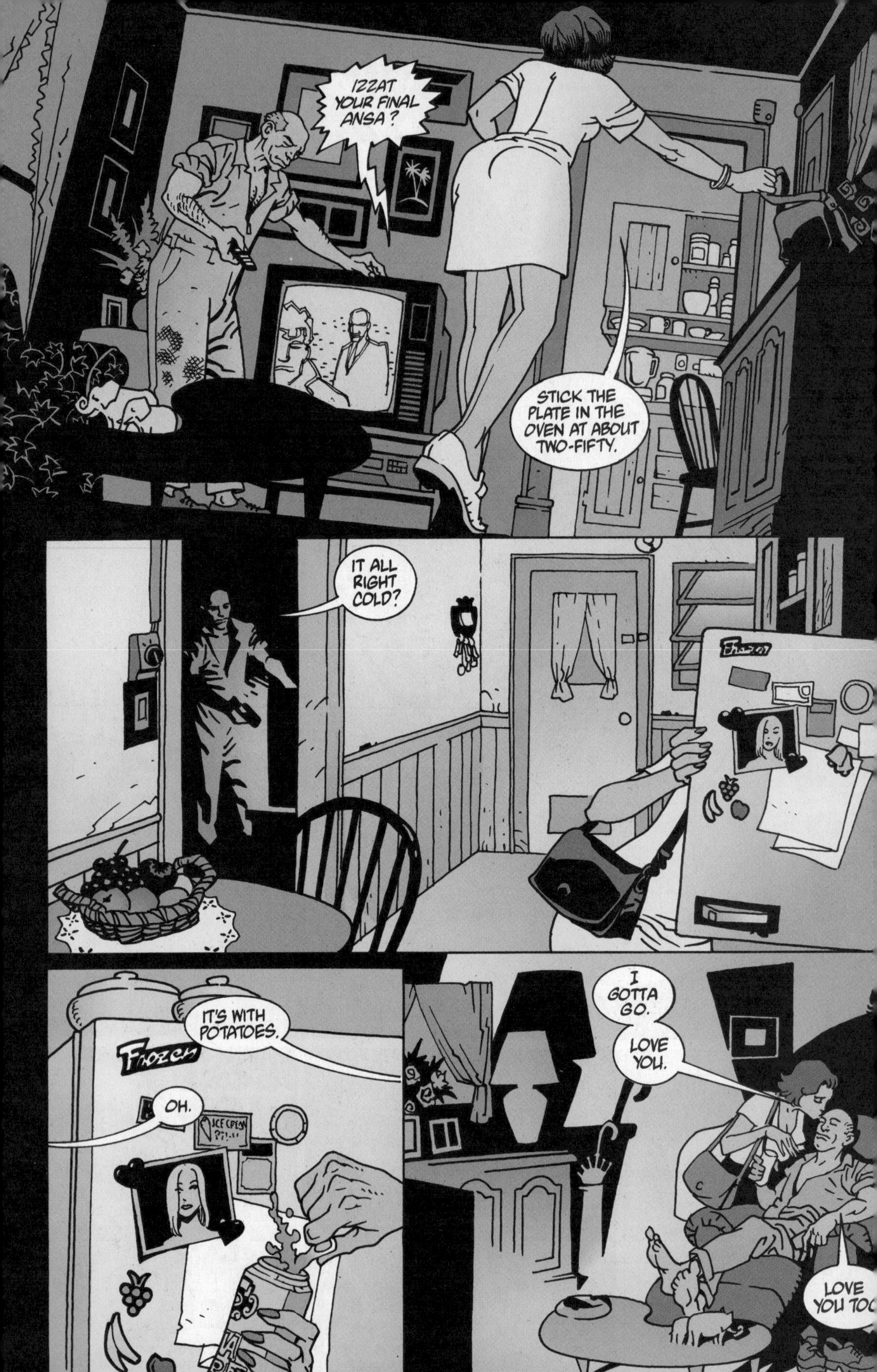
IZZAT YOUR FINAL ANSA?
STICK THE PLATE IN THE OVEN AT ABOUT TWO-FIFTY.
IT ALL RIGHT COLD?
IT'S WITH POTATOES.
OH.
I GOTTA GO.
LOVE YOU.
LOVE YOU TOO

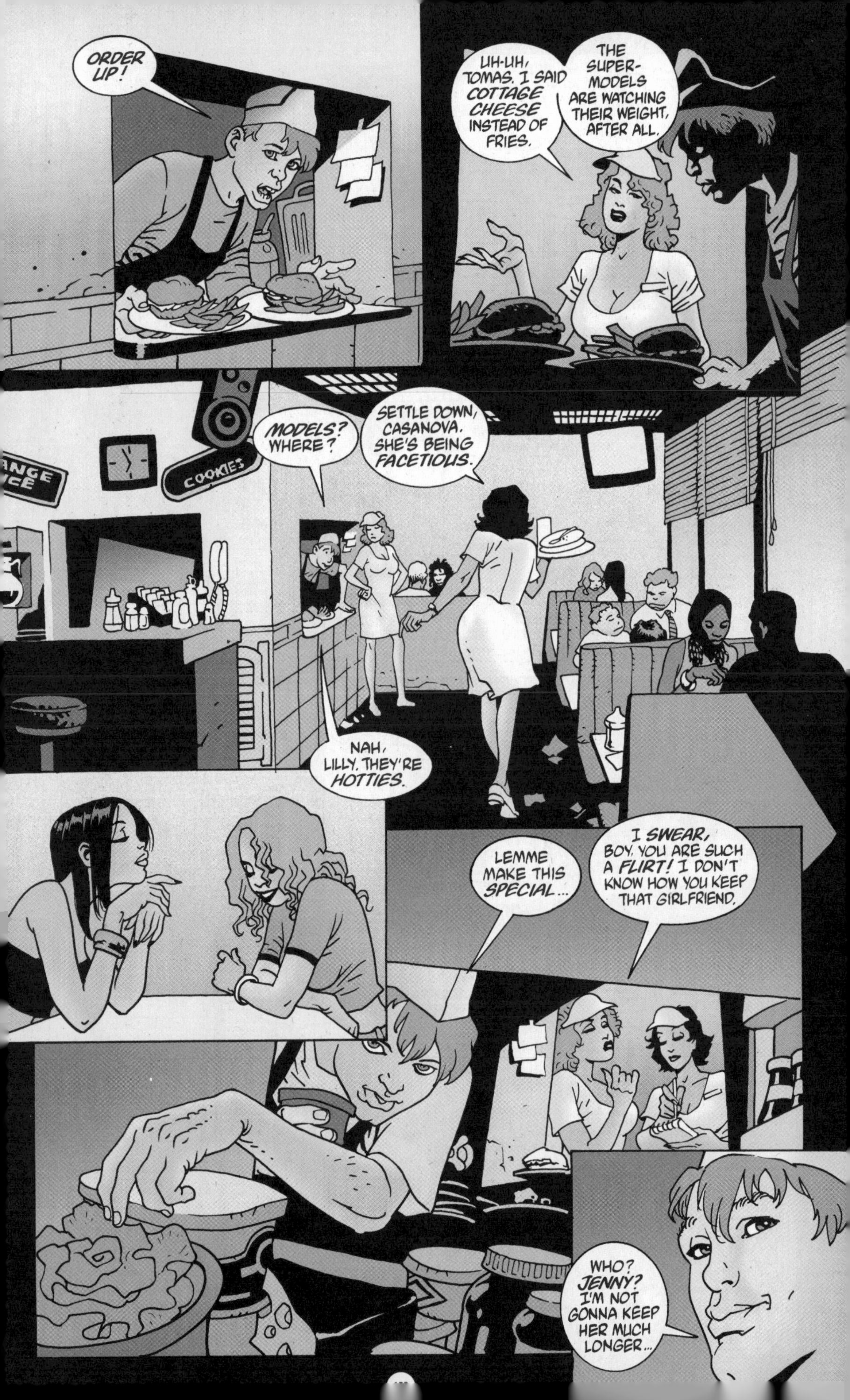
ORDER UP!
UH-UH, TOMAS. I SAID COTTAGE CHEESE INSTEAD OF FRIES.
THE SUPER-MODELS ARE WATCHING THEIR WEIGHT, AFTER ALL.
MODELS? WHERE?
SETTLE DOWN, CASANOVA. SHE'S BEING FACETIOUS.
COOKIES
NAH, LILLY. THEY'RE HOTTIES.
LEMME MAKE THIS SPECIAL...
I SWEAR, BOY, YOU ARE SUCH A FLIRT! I DON'T KNOW HOW YOU KEEP THAT GIRLFRIEND.
WHO? JENNY? I'M NOT GONNA KEEP HER MUCH LONGER...

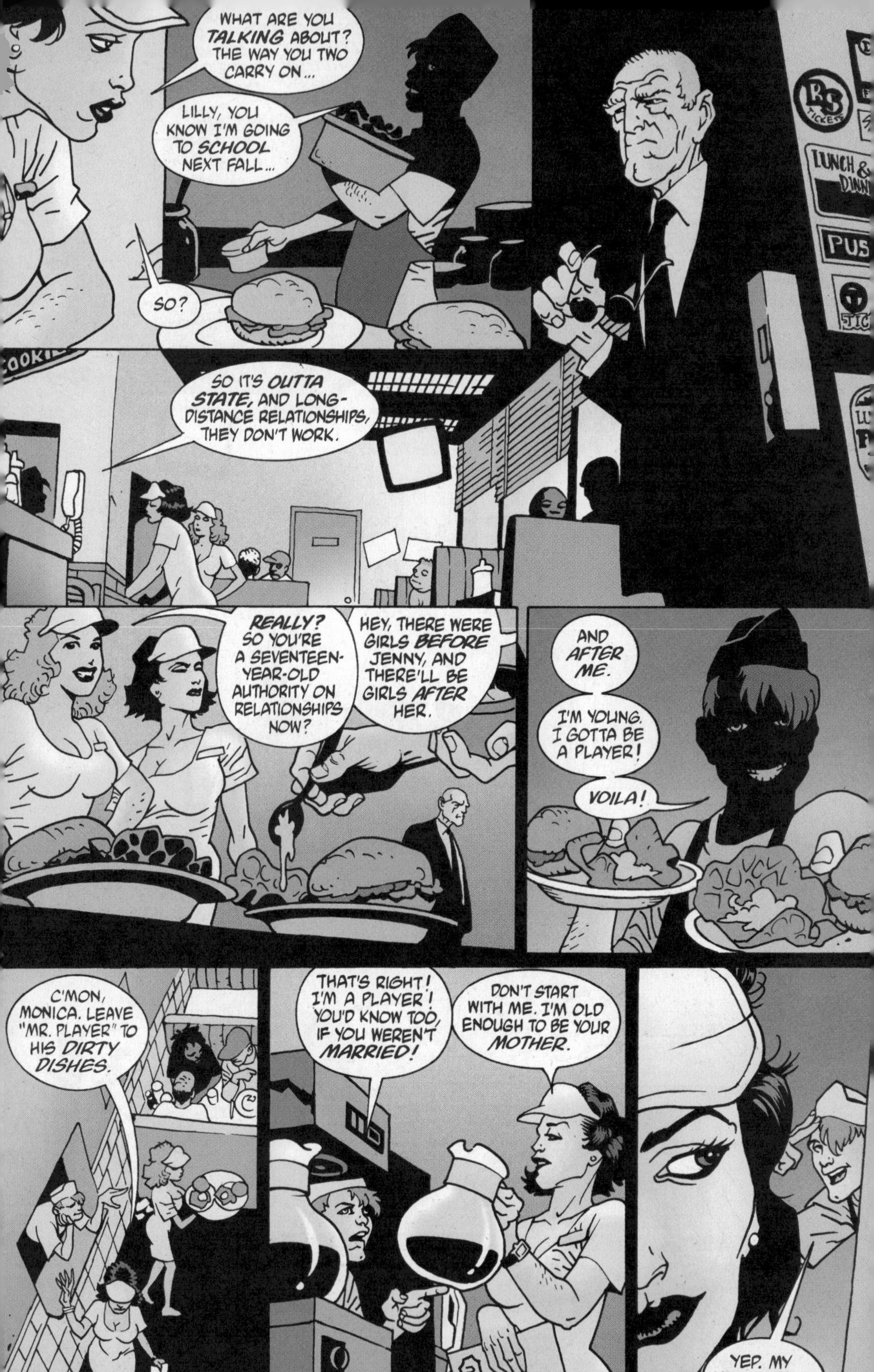
WHAT ARE YOU TALKING ABOUT? THE WAY YOU TWO CARRY ON...
LILLY, YOU KNOW I'M GOING TO SCHOOL NEXT FALL...
SO?
SO IT'S OUTTA STATE, AND LONG-DISTANCE RELATIONSHIPS, THEY DON'T WORK.
REALLY? SO YOU'RE A SEVENTEEN-YEAR-OLD AUTHORITY ON RELATIONSHIPS NOW?
HEY, THERE WERE GIRLS BEFORE JENNY, AND THERE'LL BE GIRLS AFTER HER.
AND AFTER ME.
I'M YOUNG. I GOTTA BE A PLAYER!
VOILA!
C'MON, MONICA. LEAVE "MR. PLAYER" TO HIS DIRTY DISHES.
THAT'S RIGHT! I'M A PLAYER! YOU'D KNOW TOO, IF YOU WEREN'T MARRIED!
DON'T START WITH ME. I'M OLD ENOUGH TO BE YOUR MOTHER.
YEP. MY YOUNG, SEXY MOTHER.
MENU
LUNCH & DINN
PUS

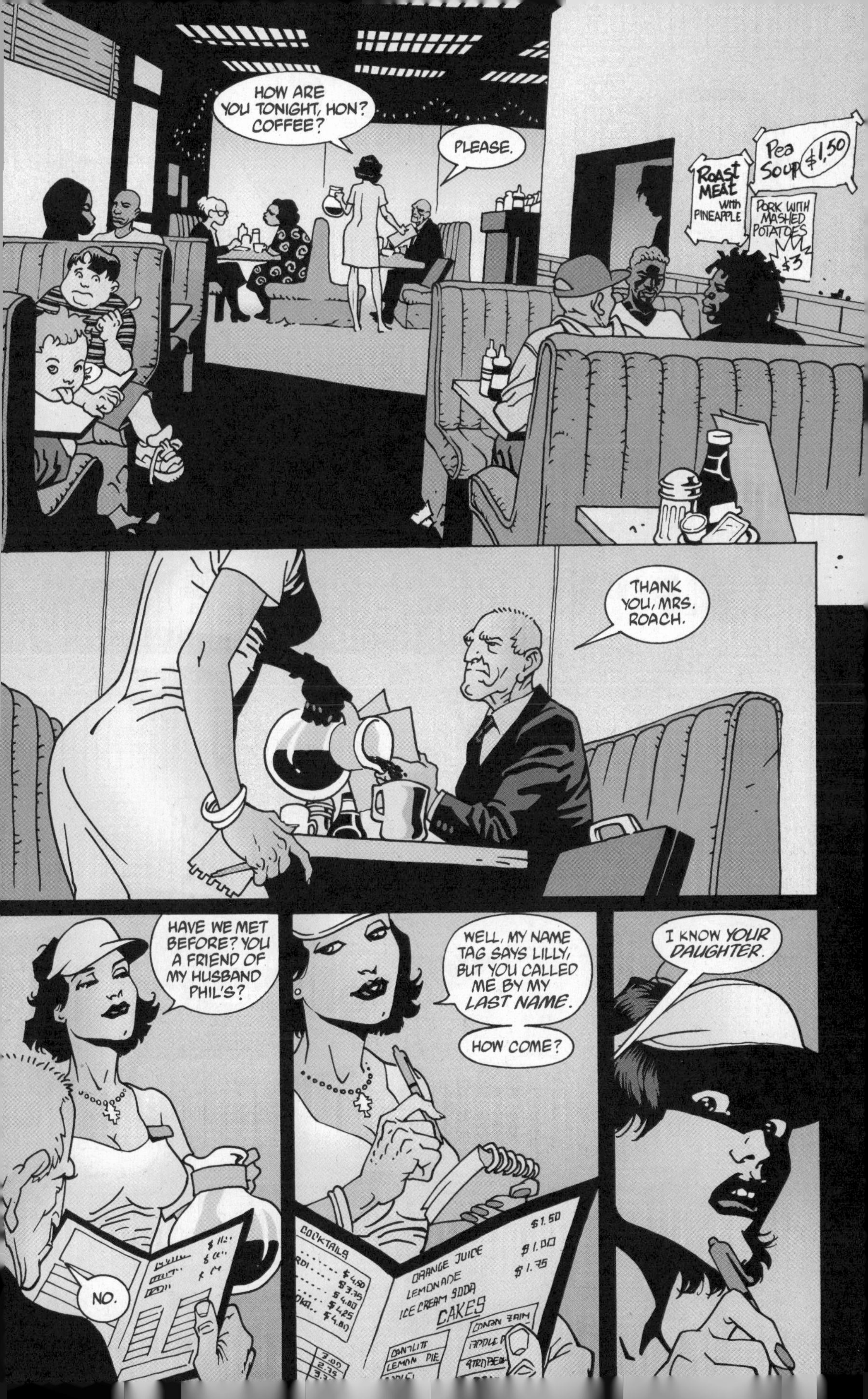

HOW ARE YOU TONIGHT, HON? COFFEE?
PLEASE.
Roast MEAT with PINEAPPLE
Pea Soup $1.50
PORK WITH MASHED POTATOES $3
THANK YOU, MRS. ROACH.
HAVE WE MET BEFORE? YOU A FRIEND OF MY HUSBAND PHIL'S?
NO.
WELL, MY NAME TAG SAYS LILLY, BUT YOU CALLED ME BY MY LAST NAME.
HOW COME?
COCKTAILS
ORANGE JUICE $1.50
LEMONADE $1.00
ICE CREAM SODA $1.75
CAKES
LEMON PIE
I KNOW YOUR DAUGHTER.

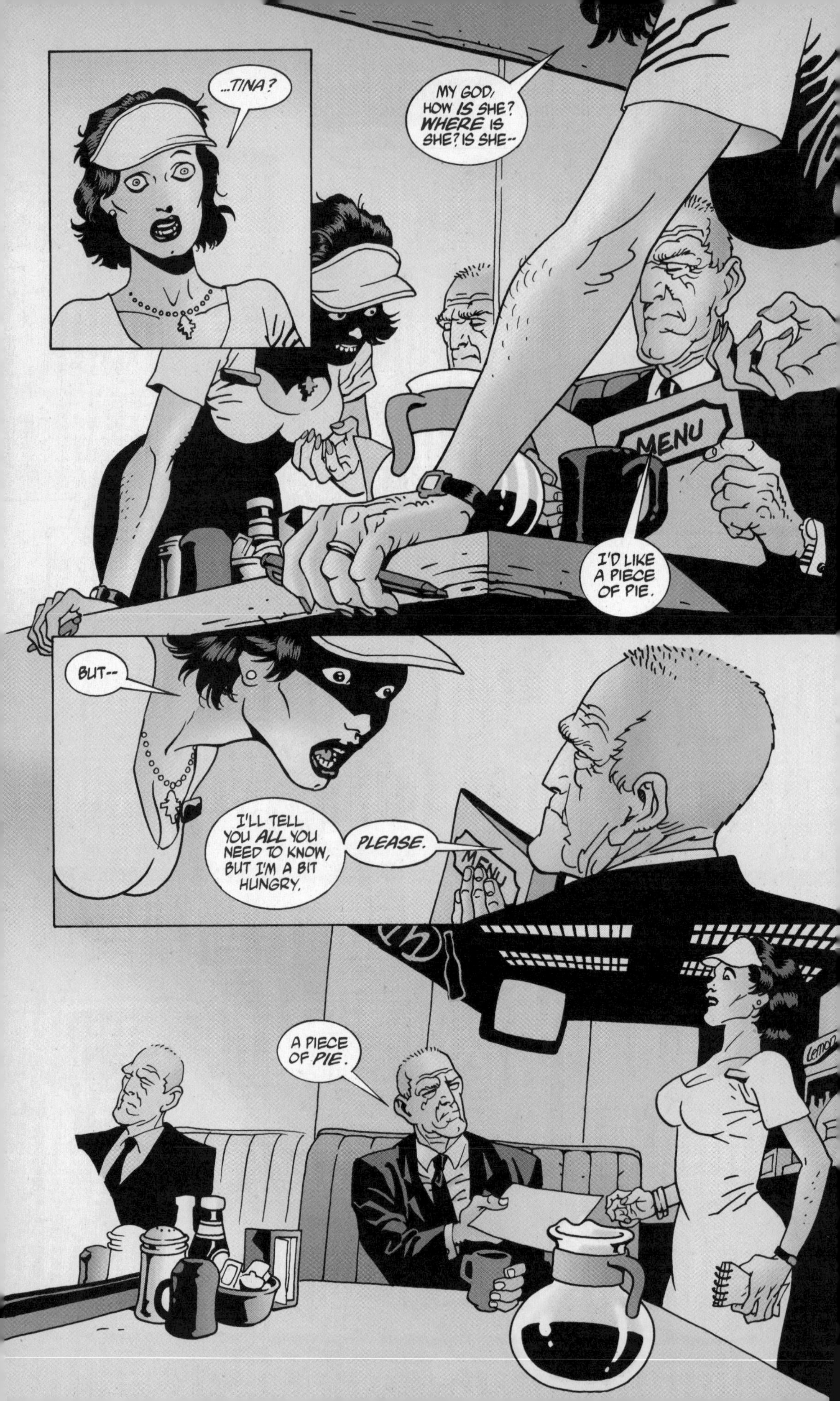
...TINA?
MY GOD, HOW IS SHE? WHERE IS SHE? IS SHE--
I'D LIKE A PIECE OF PIE.
MENU
BUT--
PLEASE.
I'LL TELL YOU ALL YOU NEED TO KNOW, BUT I'M A BIT HUNGRY.
MENU
A PIECE OF PIE.
Lemon

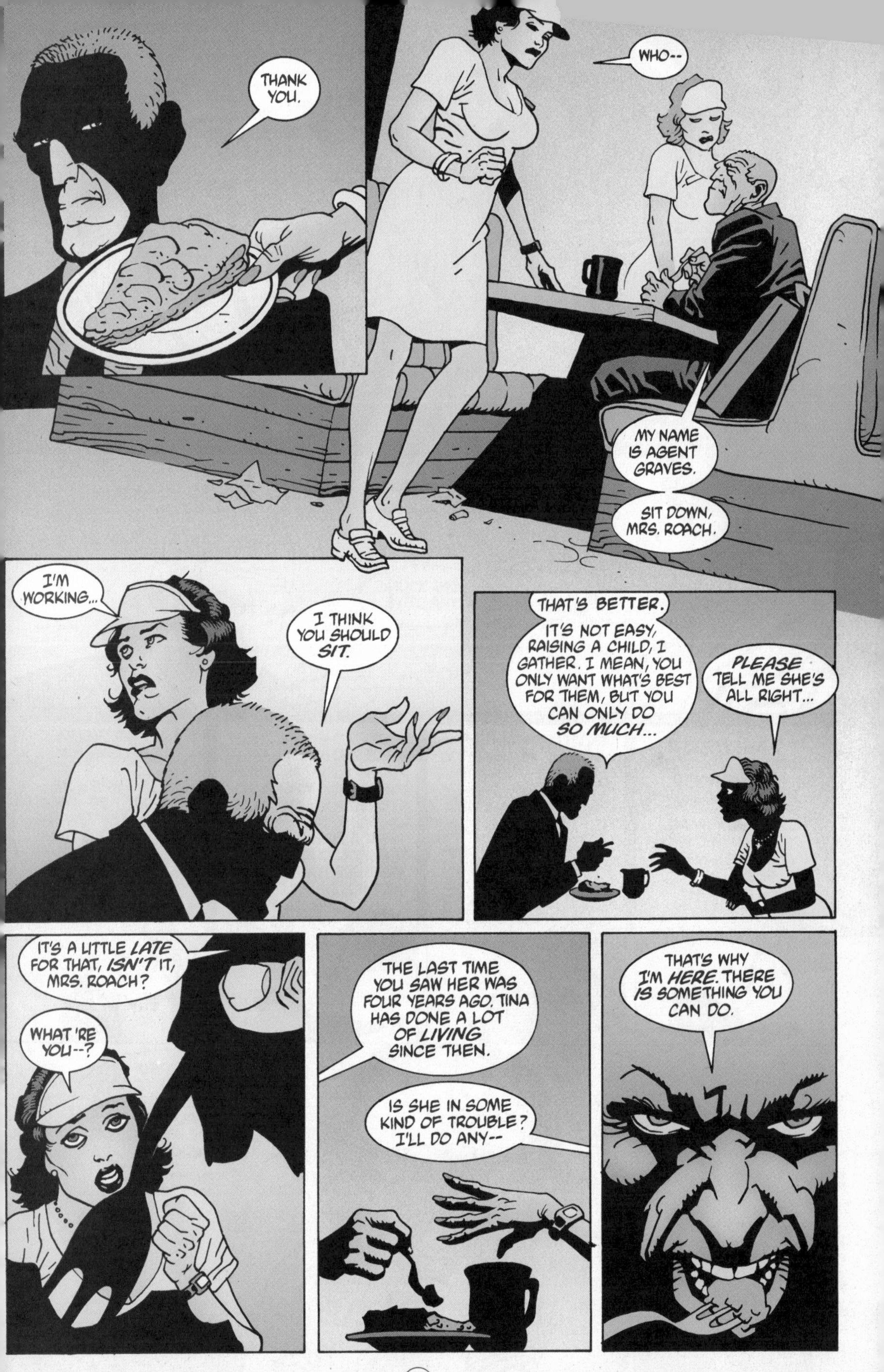
THANK YOU.
WHO--
MY NAME IS AGENT GRAVES.
SIT DOWN, MRS. ROACH.
I'M WORKING...
I THINK YOU SHOULD SIT.
THAT'S BETTER.
IT'S NOT EASY, RAISING A CHILD, I GATHER. I MEAN, YOU ONLY WANT WHAT'S BEST FOR THEM, BUT YOU CAN ONLY DO SO MUCH...
PLEASE TELL ME SHE'S ALL RIGHT...
IT'S A LITTLE LATE FOR THAT, ISN'T IT, MRS. ROACH?
WHAT 'RE YOU--?
THE LAST TIME YOU SAW HER WAS FOUR YEARS AGO. TINA HAS DONE A LOT OF LIVING SINCE THEN.
IS SHE IN SOME KIND OF TROUBLE? I'LL DO ANY--
THAT'S WHY I'M HERE. THERE IS SOMETHING YOU CAN DO.

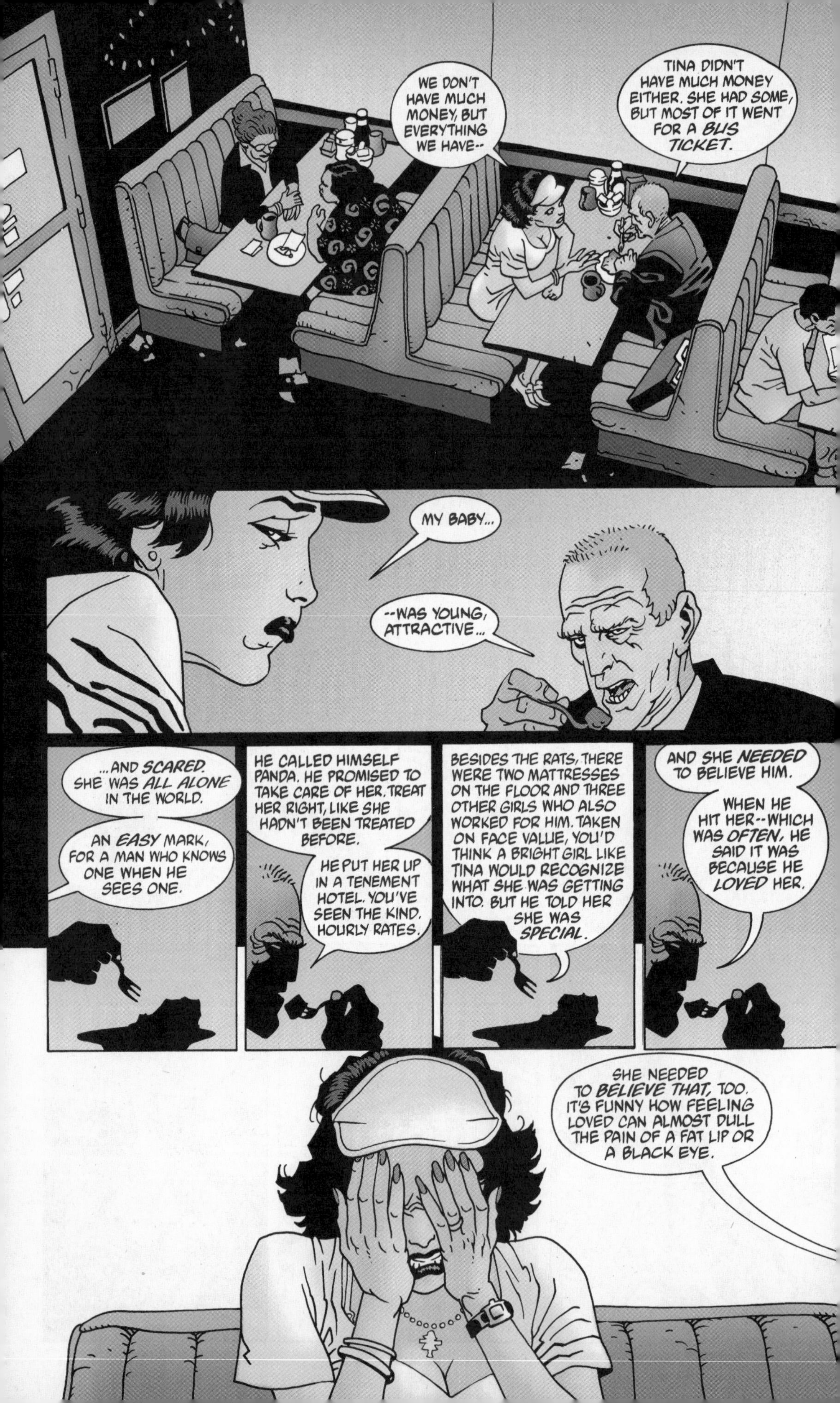
WE DON'T HAVE MUCH MONEY, BUT EVERYTHING WE HAVE--
TINA DIDN'T HAVE MUCH MONEY EITHER. SHE HAD SOME, BUT MOST OF IT WENT FOR A BUS TICKET.
MY BABY...
--WAS YOUNG, ATTRACTIVE...
...AND SCARED. SHE WAS ALL ALONE IN THE WORLD.
AN EASY MARK, FOR A MAN WHO KNOWS ONE WHEN HE SEES ONE.
HE CALLED HIMSELF PANDA. HE PROMISED TO TAKE CARE OF HER, TREAT HER RIGHT, LIKE SHE HADN'T BEEN TREATED BEFORE.
HE PUT HER UP IN A TENEMENT HOTEL. YOU'VE SEEN THE KIND. HOURLY RATES.
BESIDES THE RATS, THERE WERE TWO MATTRESSES ON THE FLOOR AND THREE OTHER GIRLS WHO ALSO WORKED FOR HIM. TAKEN ON FACE VALUE, YOU'D THINK A BRIGHT GIRL LIKE TINA WOULD RECOGNIZE WHAT SHE WAS GETTING INTO. BUT HE TOLD HER SHE WAS SPECIAL.
AND SHE NEEDED TO BELIEVE HIM.
WHEN HE HIT HER--WHICH WAS OFTEN, HE SAID IT WAS BECAUSE HE LOVED HER.
SHE NEEDED TO BELIEVE THAT, TOO. IT'S FUNNY HOW FEELING LOVED CAN ALMOST DULL THE PAIN OF A FAT LIP OR A BLACK EYE.

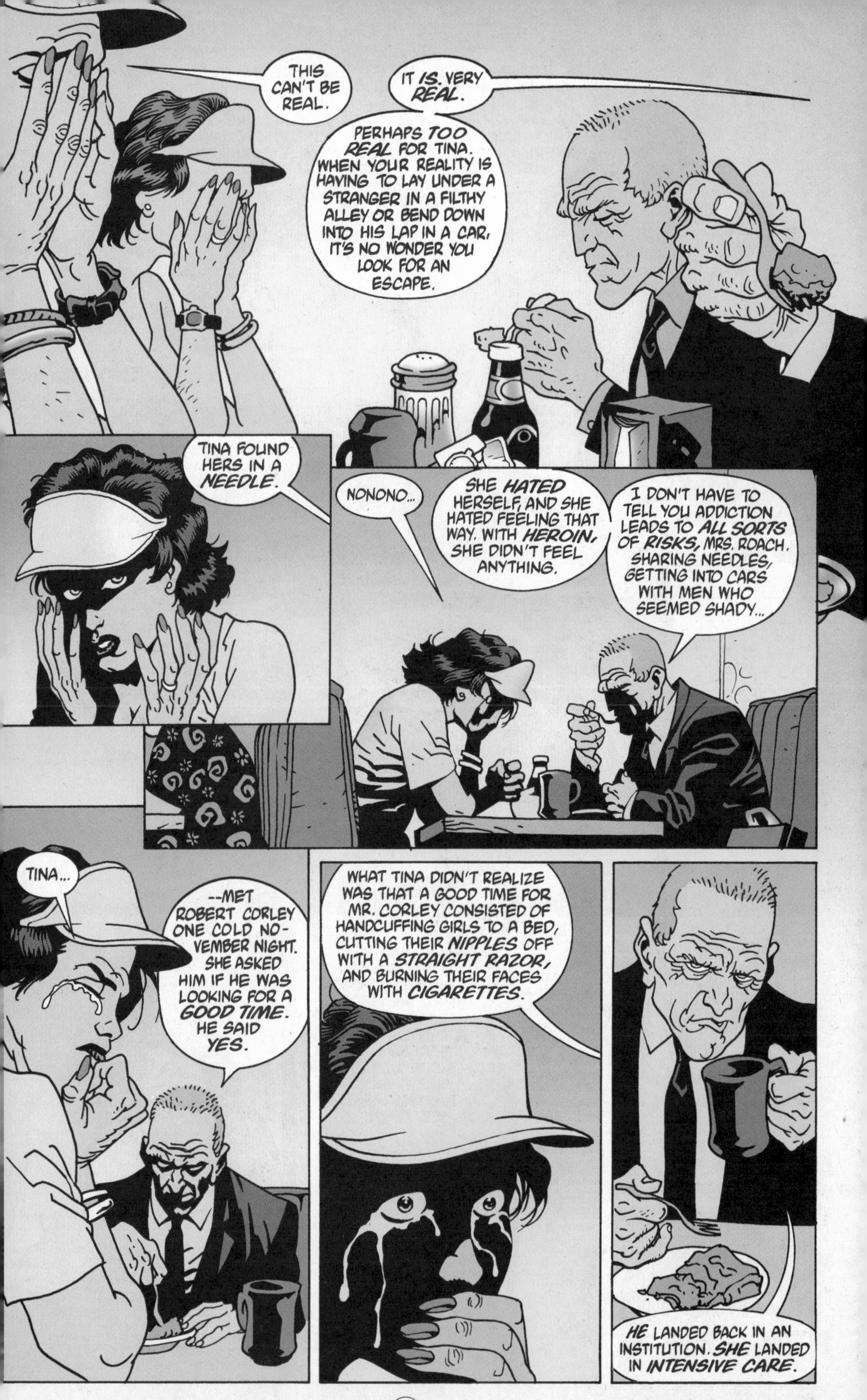
THIS CAN'T BE REAL.
IT IS. VERY REAL.
PERHAPS TOO REAL FOR TINA. WHEN YOUR REALITY IS HAVING TO LAY UNDER A STRANGER IN A FILTHY ALLEY OR BEND DOWN INTO HIS LAP IN A CAR, IT'S NO WONDER YOU LOOK FOR AN ESCAPE.
TINA FOUND HERS IN A NEEDLE.
NONONO...
SHE HATED HERSELF, AND SHE HATED FEELING THAT WAY. WITH HEROIN, SHE DIDN'T FEEL ANYTHING.
I DON'T HAVE TO TELL YOU ADDICTION LEADS TO ALL SORTS OF RISKS, MRS. ROACH. SHARING NEEDLES, GETTING INTO CARS WITH MEN WHO SEEMED SHADY...
TINA...
--MET ROBERT CORLEY ONE COLD NO-VEMBER NIGHT. SHE ASKED HIM IF HE WAS LOOKING FOR A GOOD TIME. HE SAID YES.
WHAT TINA DIDN'T REALIZE WAS THAT A GOOD TIME FOR MR. CORLEY CONSISTED OF HANDCUFFING GIRLS TO A BED, CUTTING THEIR NIPPLES OFF WITH A STRAIGHT RAZOR, AND BURNING THEIR FACES WITH CIGARETTES.
HE LANDED BACK IN AN INSTITUTION. SHE LANDED IN INTENSIVE CARE.

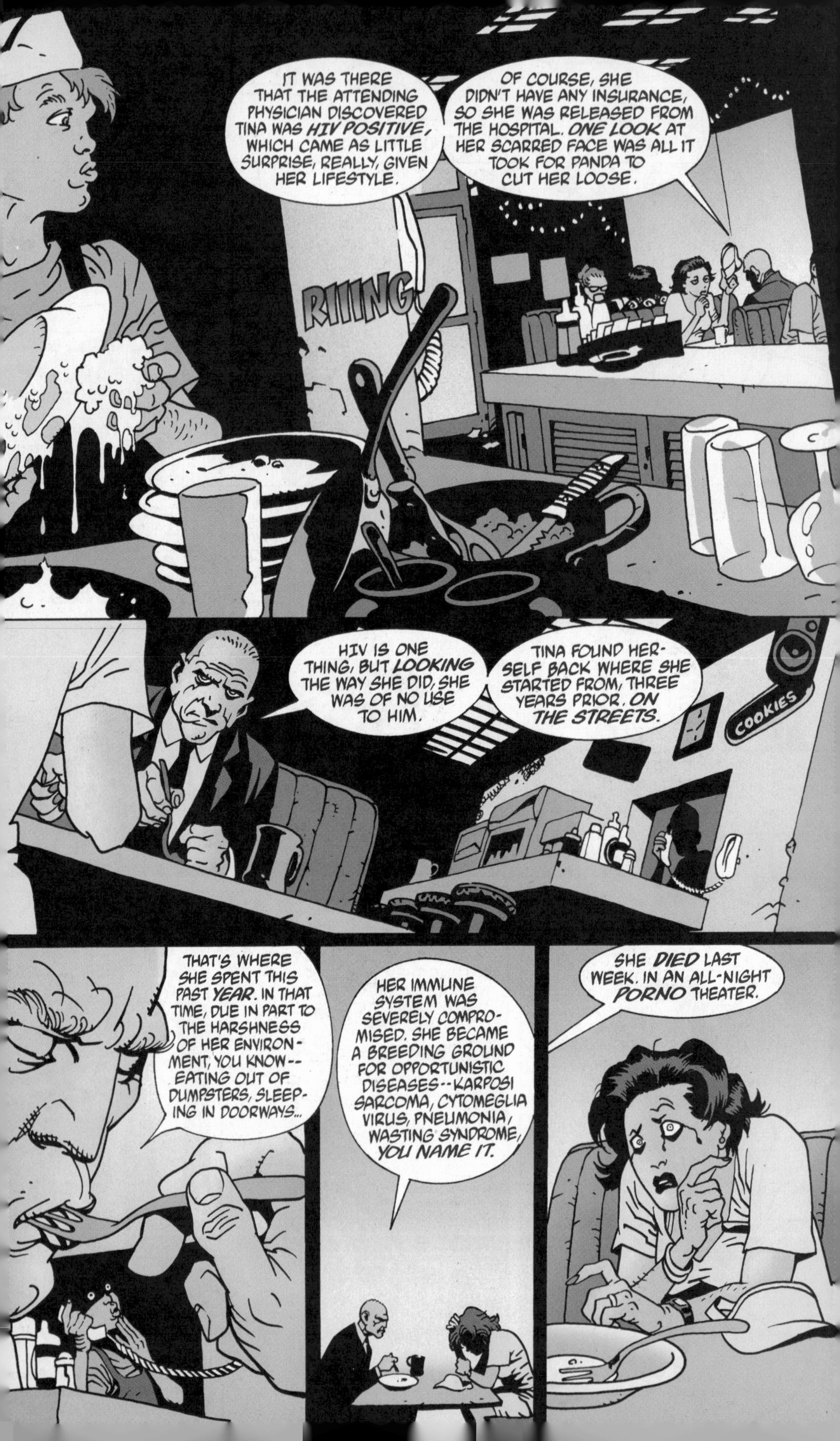

IT WAS THERE THAT THE ATTENDING PHYSICIAN DISCOVERED TINA WAS HIV POSITIVE, WHICH CAME AS LITTLE SURPRISE, REALLY, GIVEN HER LIFESTYLE.
OF COURSE, SHE DIDN'T HAVE ANY INSURANCE, SO SHE WAS RELEASED FROM THE HOSPITAL. ONE LOOK AT HER SCARRED FACE WAS ALL IT TOOK FOR PANDA TO CUT HER LOOSE.
RIIING
HIV IS ONE THING, BUT LOOKING THE WAY SHE DID, SHE WAS OF NO USE TO HIM.
TINA FOUND HERSELF BACK WHERE SHE STARTED FROM, THREE YEARS PRIOR. ON THE STREETS.
COOKIES
THAT'S WHERE SHE SPENT THIS PAST YEAR. IN THAT TIME, DUE IN PART TO THE HARSHNESS OF HER ENVIRONMENT, YOU KNOW-- EATING OUT OF DUMPSTERS, SLEEPING IN DOORWAYS...
HER IMMUNE SYSTEM WAS SEVERELY COMPROMISED. SHE BECAME A BREEDING GROUND FOR OPPORTUNISTIC DISEASES--KARPOSI SARCOMA, CYTOMEGLIA VIRUS, PNEUMONIA, WASTING SYNDROME, YOU NAME IT.
SHE DIED LAST WEEK. IN AN ALL-NIGHT PORNO THEATER.

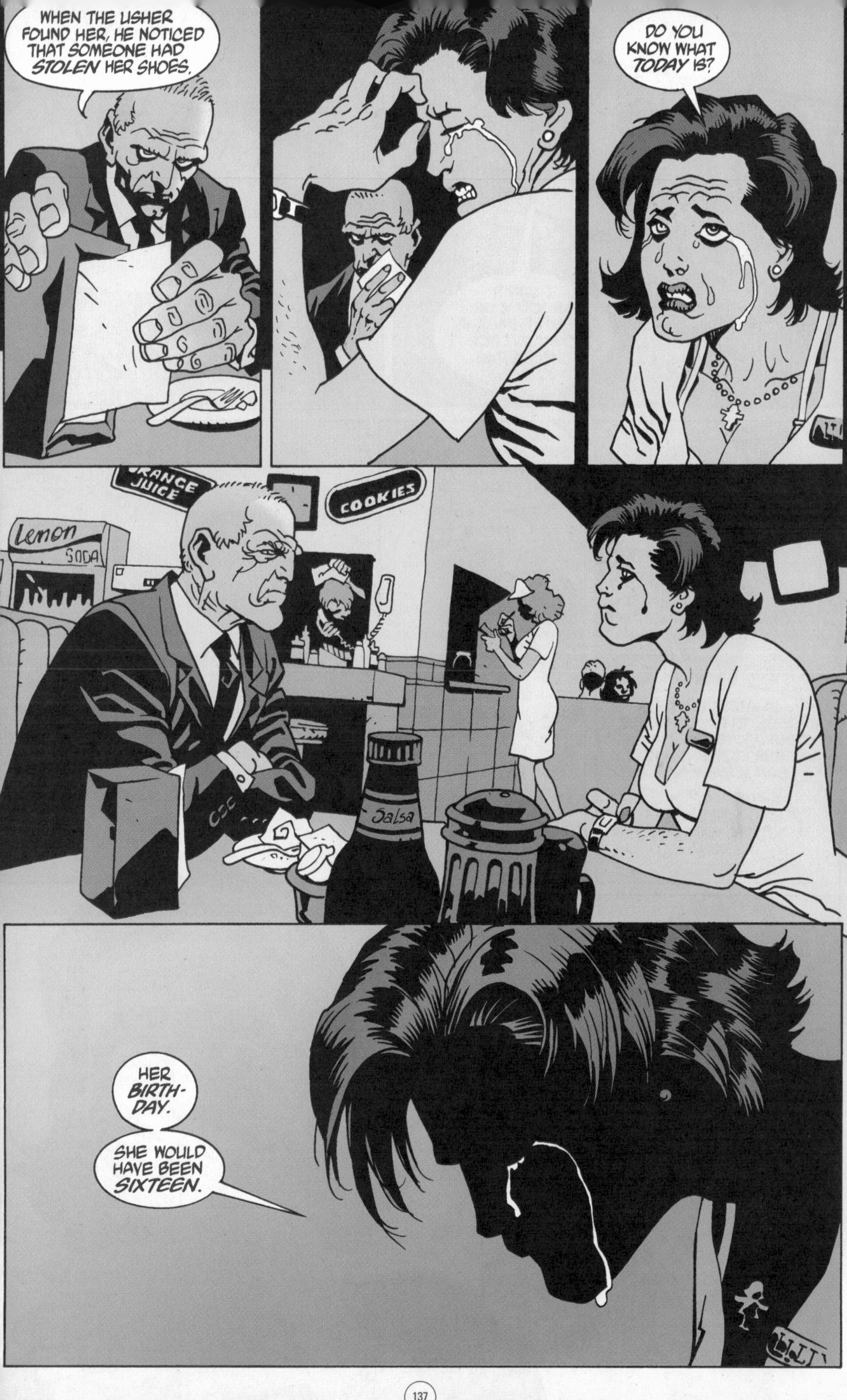
WHEN THE USHER FOUND HER, HE NOTICED THAT SOMEONE HAD STOLEN HER SHOES.
DO YOU KNOW WHAT TODAY IS?
ORANGE JUICE
COOKIES
Lemon SODA
Salsa
HER BIRTH-DAY.
SHE WOULD HAVE BEEN SIXTEEN.

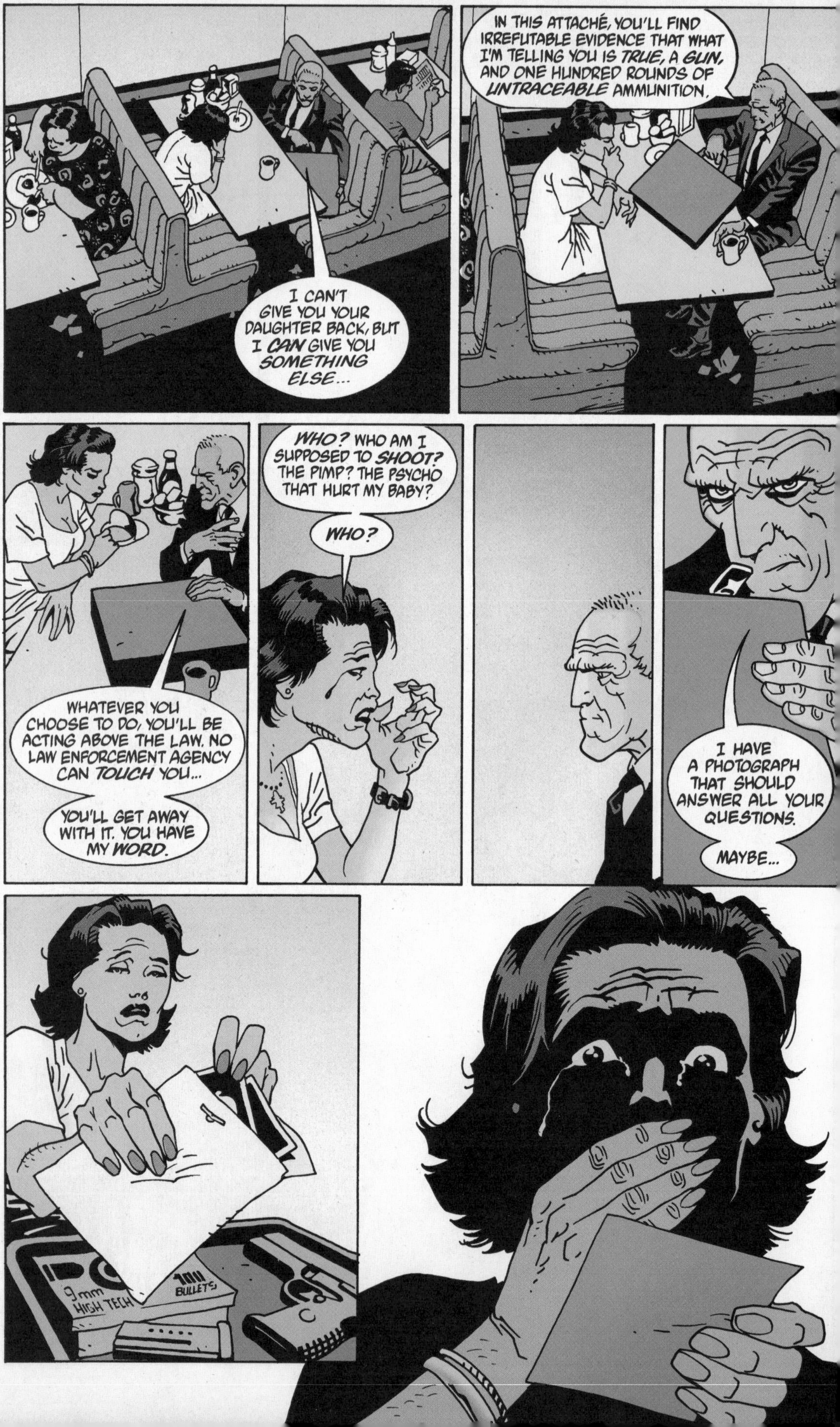
I CAN'T GIVE YOU YOUR DAUGHTER BACK, BUT I CAN GIVE YOU SOMETHING ELSE...
IN THIS ATTACHÉ, YOU'LL FIND IRREFUTABLE EVIDENCE THAT WHAT I'M TELLING YOU IS TRUE, A GUN, AND ONE HUNDRED ROUNDS OF UNTRACEABLE AMMUNITION.
WHATEVER YOU CHOOSE TO DO, YOU'LL BE ACTING ABOVE THE LAW. NO LAW ENFORCEMENT AGENCY CAN TOUCH YOU...
YOU'LL GET AWAY WITH IT. YOU HAVE MY WORD.
WHO? WHO AM I SUPPOSED TO SHOOT? THE PIMP? THE PSYCHO THAT HURT MY BABY?
WHO?
I HAVE A PHOTOGRAPH THAT SHOULD ANSWER ALL YOUR QUESTIONS.
MAYBE...
9mm HIGH TECH
100 BULLETS

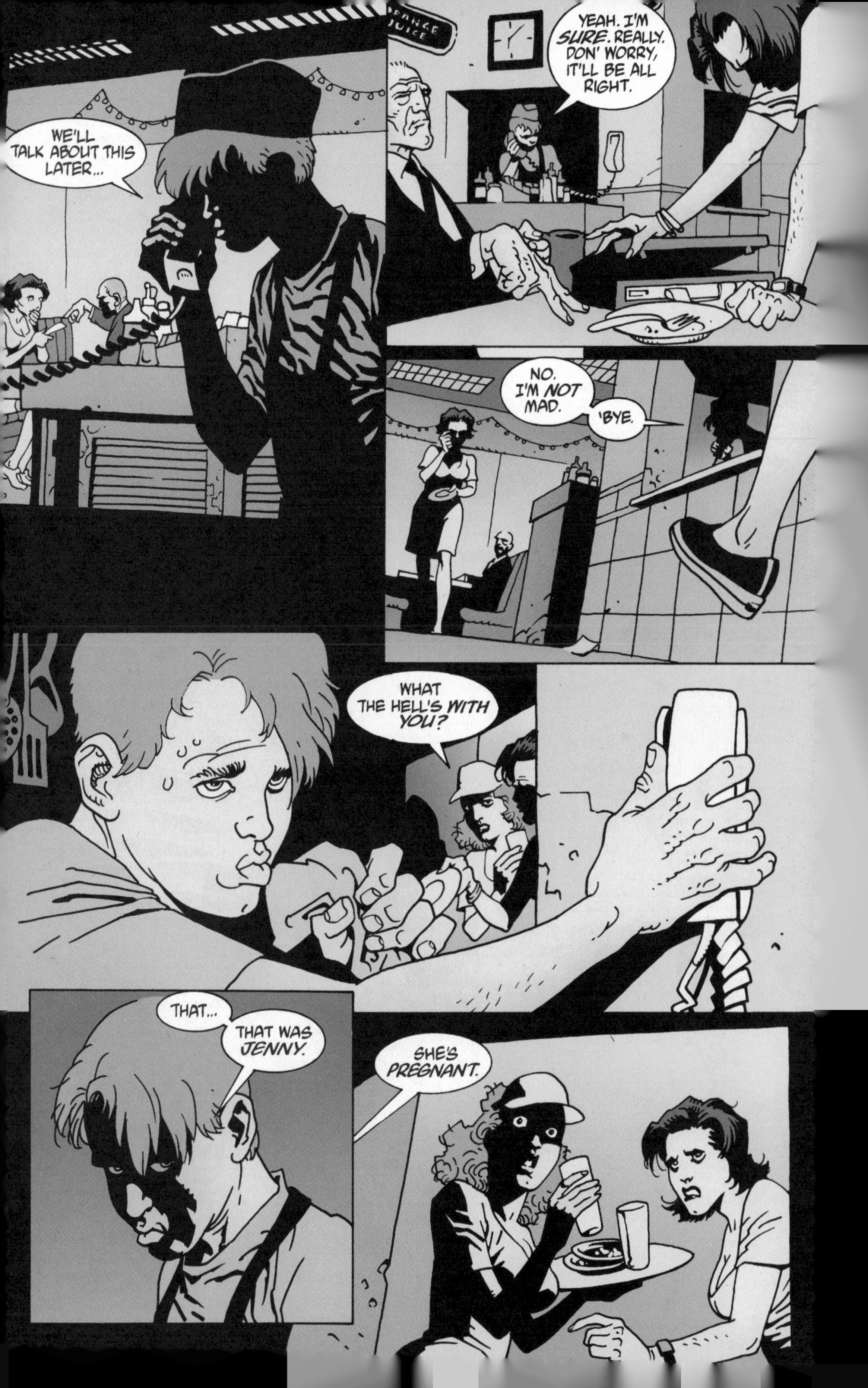
ORANGE JUICE
WE'LL TALK ABOUT THIS LATER...
YEAH. I'M SURE. REALLY. DON' WORRY, IT'LL BE ALL RIGHT.
NO. I'M NOT MAD.
'BYE.
WHAT THE HELL'S WITH YOU?
THAT...
THAT WAS JENNY.
SHE'S PREGNANT.

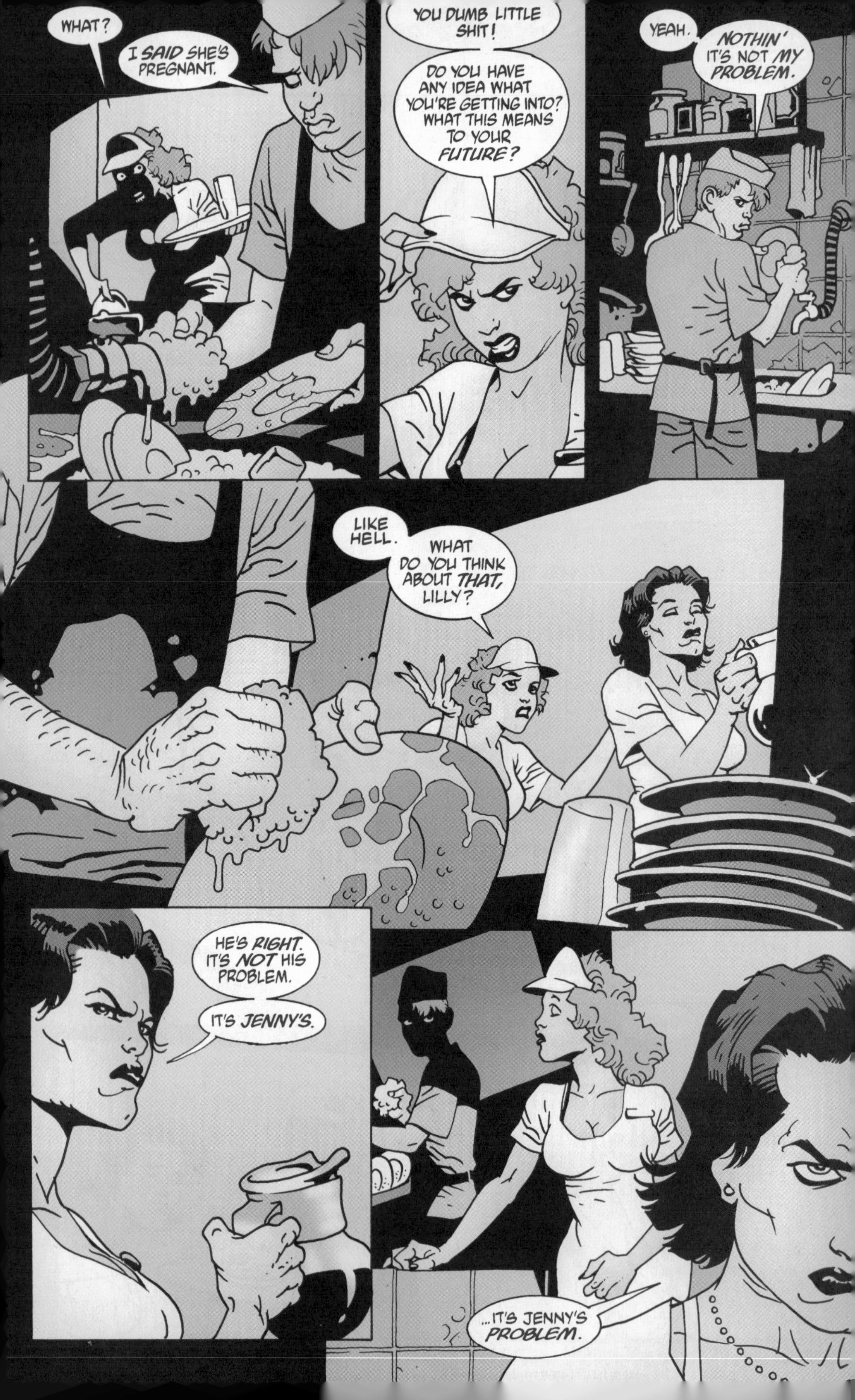
WHAT?
I SAID SHE'S PREGNANT.
YOU DUMB LITTLE SHIT!
DO YOU HAVE ANY IDEA WHAT YOU'RE GETTING INTO? WHAT THIS MEANS TO YOUR FUTURE?
YEAH.
NOTHIN' IT'S NOT MY PROBLEM.
LIKE HELL.
WHAT DO YOU THINK ABOUT THAT, LILLY?
HE'S RIGHT. IT'S NOT HIS PROBLEM.
IT'S JENNY'S.
...IT'S JENNY'S PROBLEM.

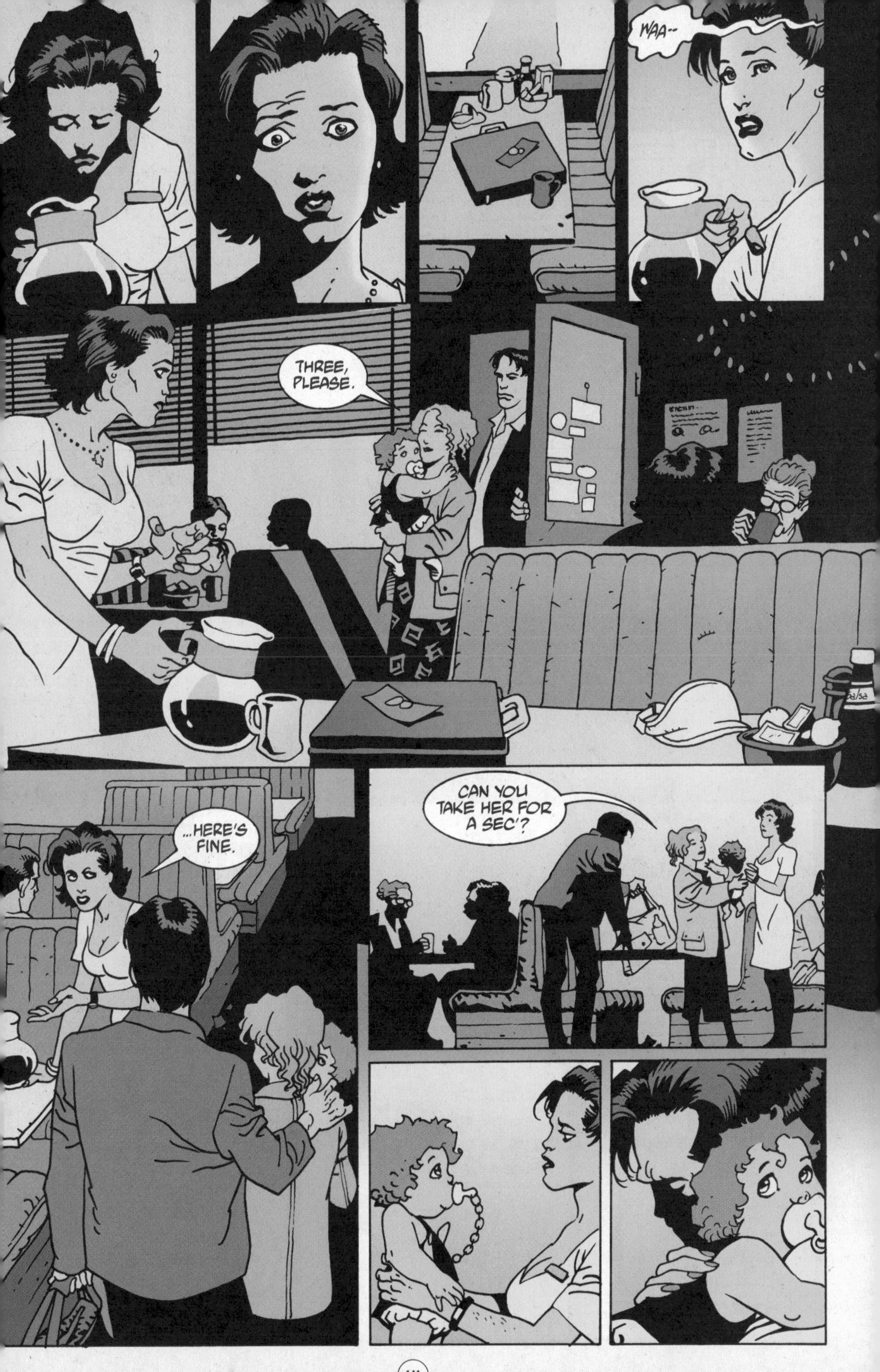
WAA--
THREE, PLEASE.
...HERE'S FINE.
CAN YOU TAKE HER FOR A SEC'?
Salsa

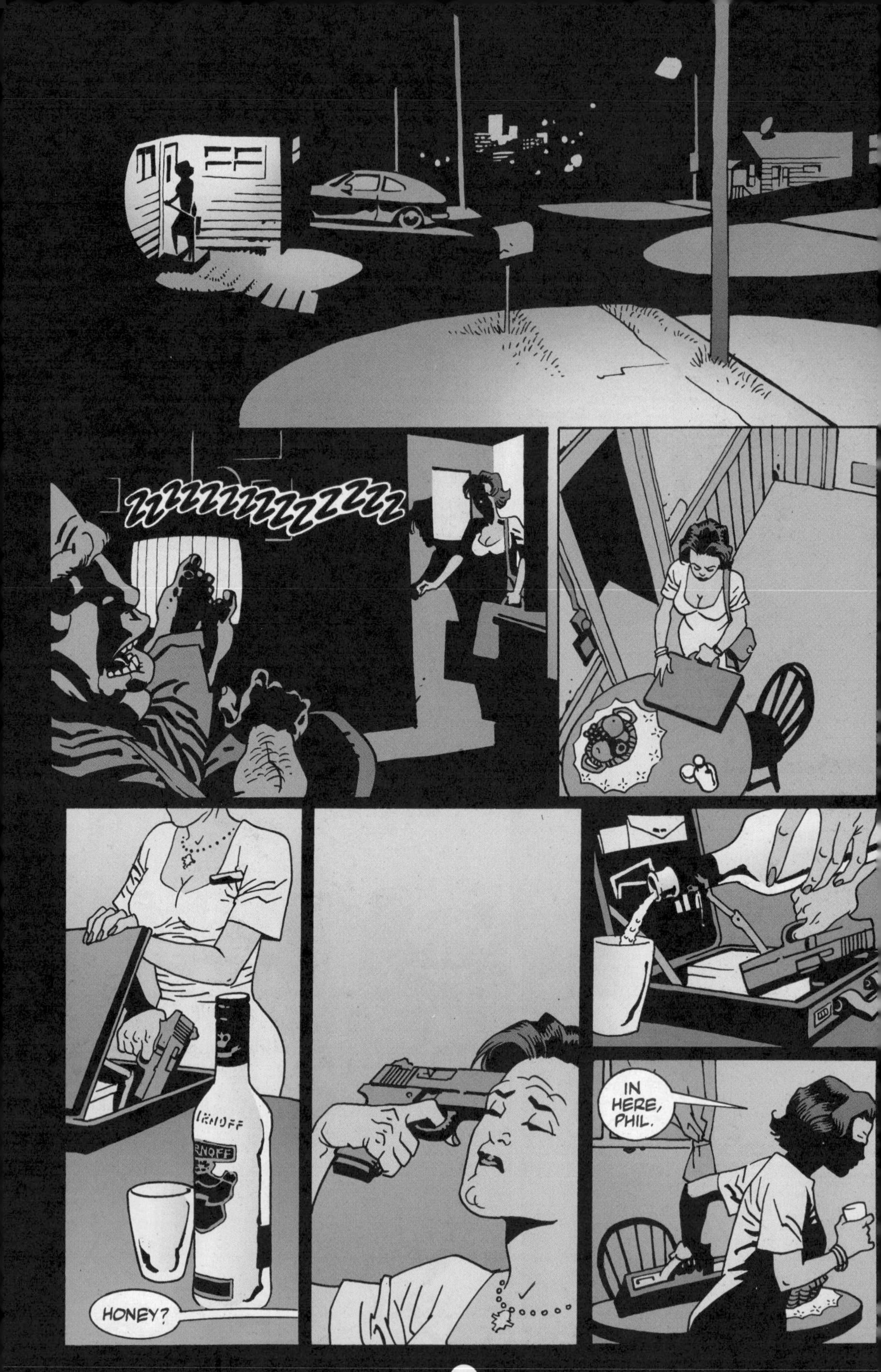
ZZZZZZZZZZZZZZZZZ
HONEY?
IN HERE, PHIL.

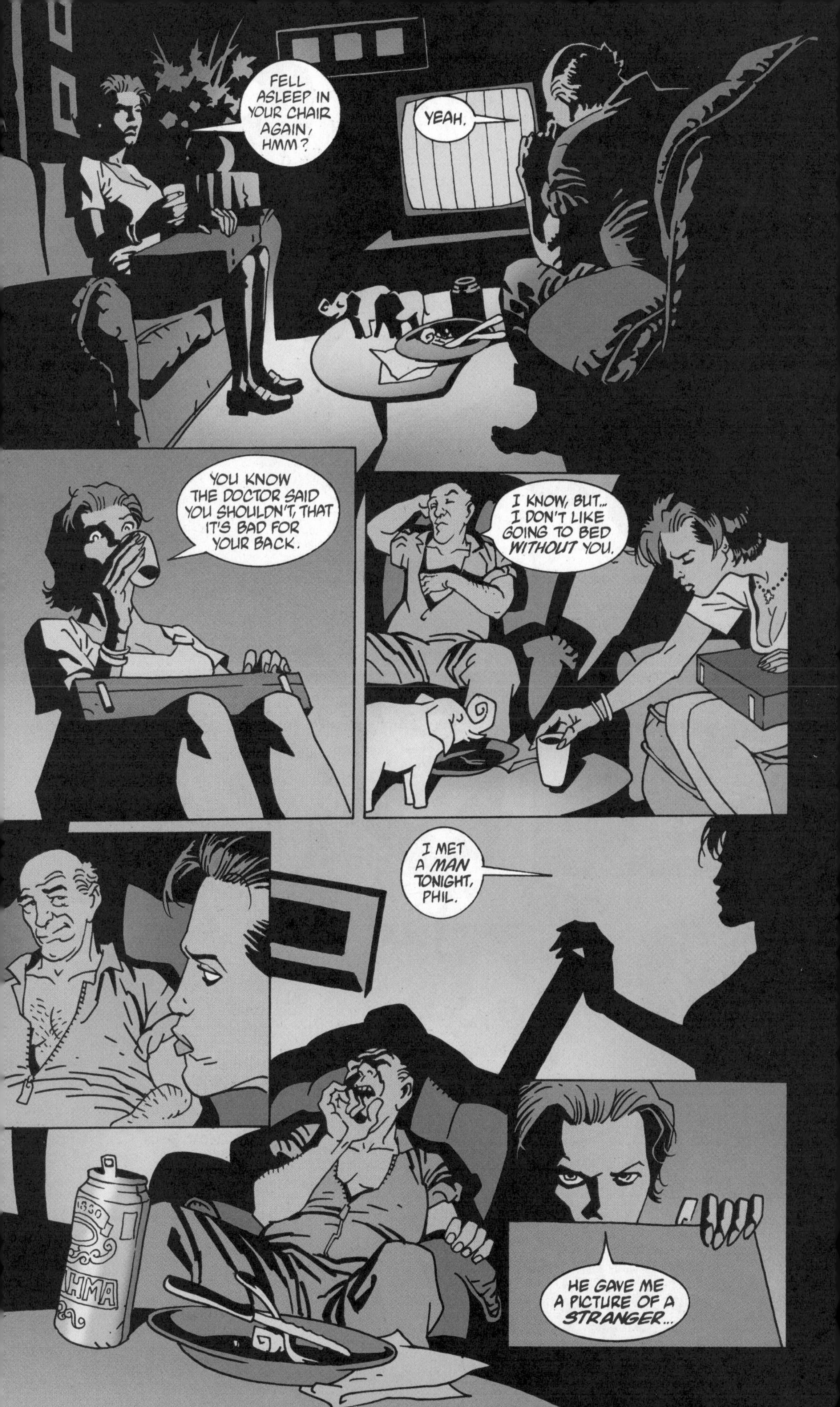
FELL ASLEEP IN YOUR CHAIR AGAIN, HMM?
YEAH.
YOU KNOW THE DOCTOR SAID YOU SHOULDN'T, THAT IT'S BAD FOR YOUR BACK.
I KNOW, BUT... I DON'T LIKE GOING TO BED WITHOUT YOU.
I MET A MAN TONIGHT, PHIL.
HE GAVE ME A PICTURE OF A STRANGER...

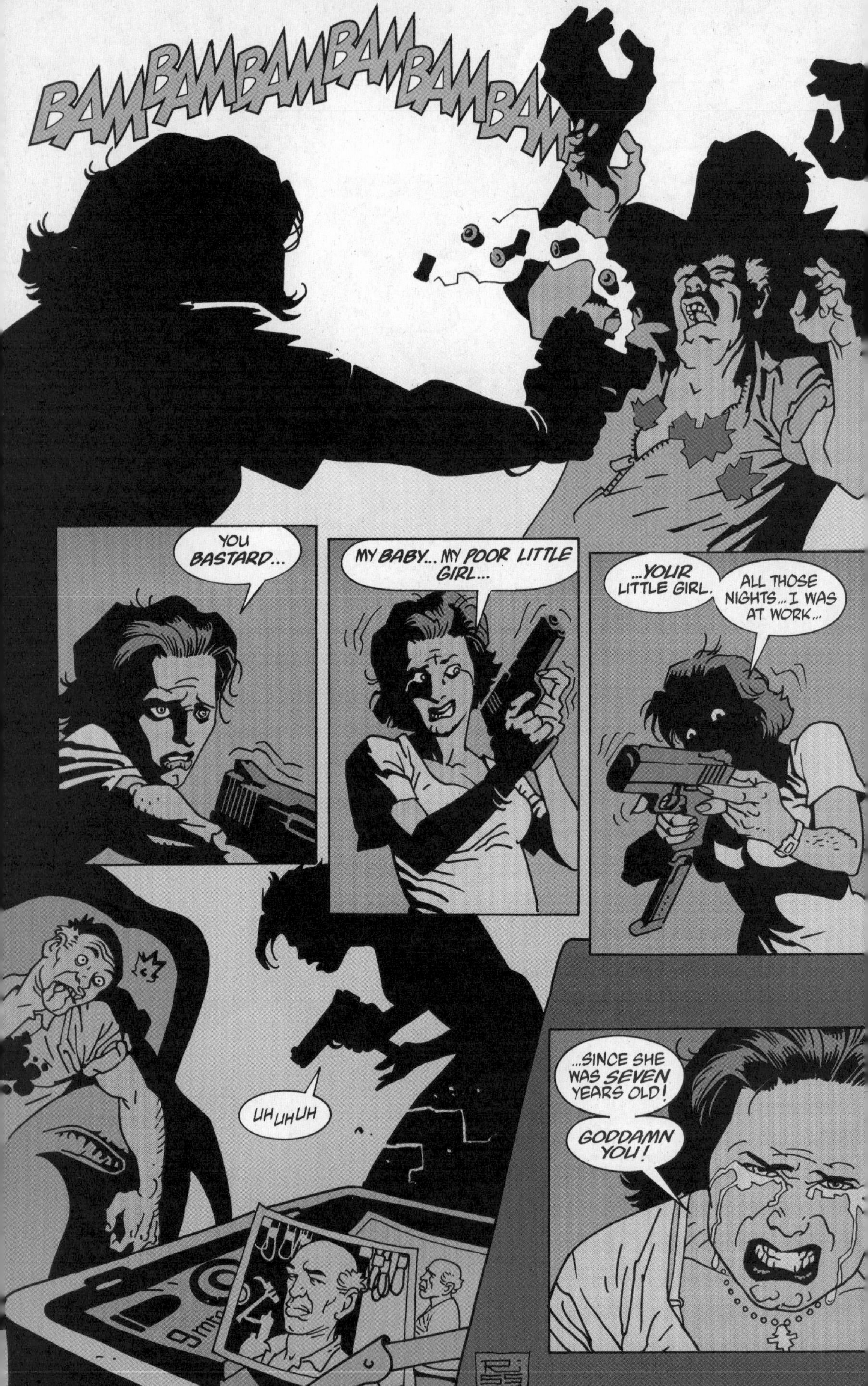
BAMBAMBAMBAMBAMBAM
YOU BASTARD...
MY BABY... MY POOR LITTLE GIRL...
...YOUR LITTLE GIRL.
ALL THOSE NIGHTS... I WAS AT WORK...
UHUHUH
...SINCE SHE WAS SEVEN YEARS OLD!
GODDAMN YOU!

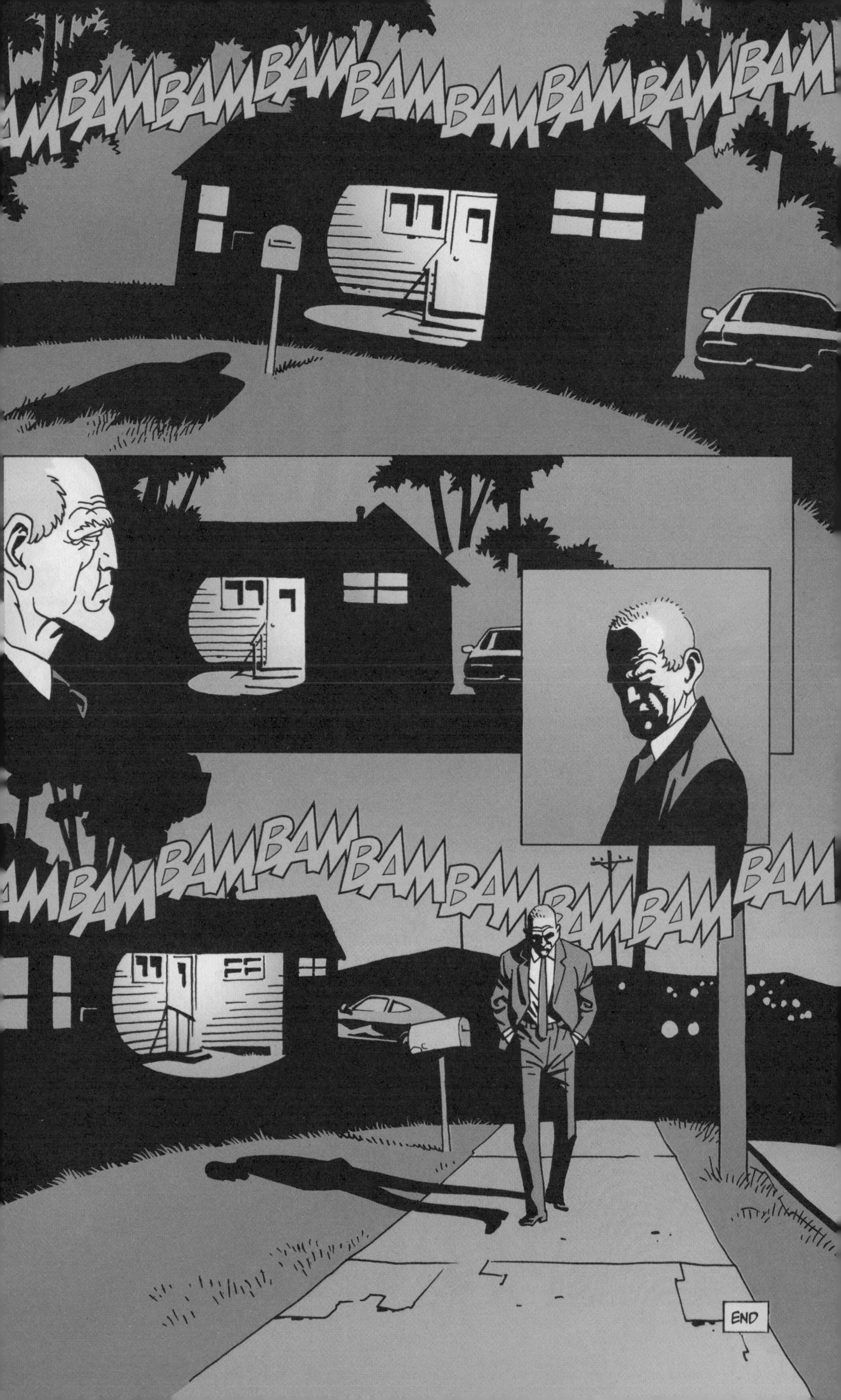

AMBAMBAMBAMBAMBAMBAMBAMBAM
AMBAMBAMBAMBAMBAMBAMBAMBAM
END

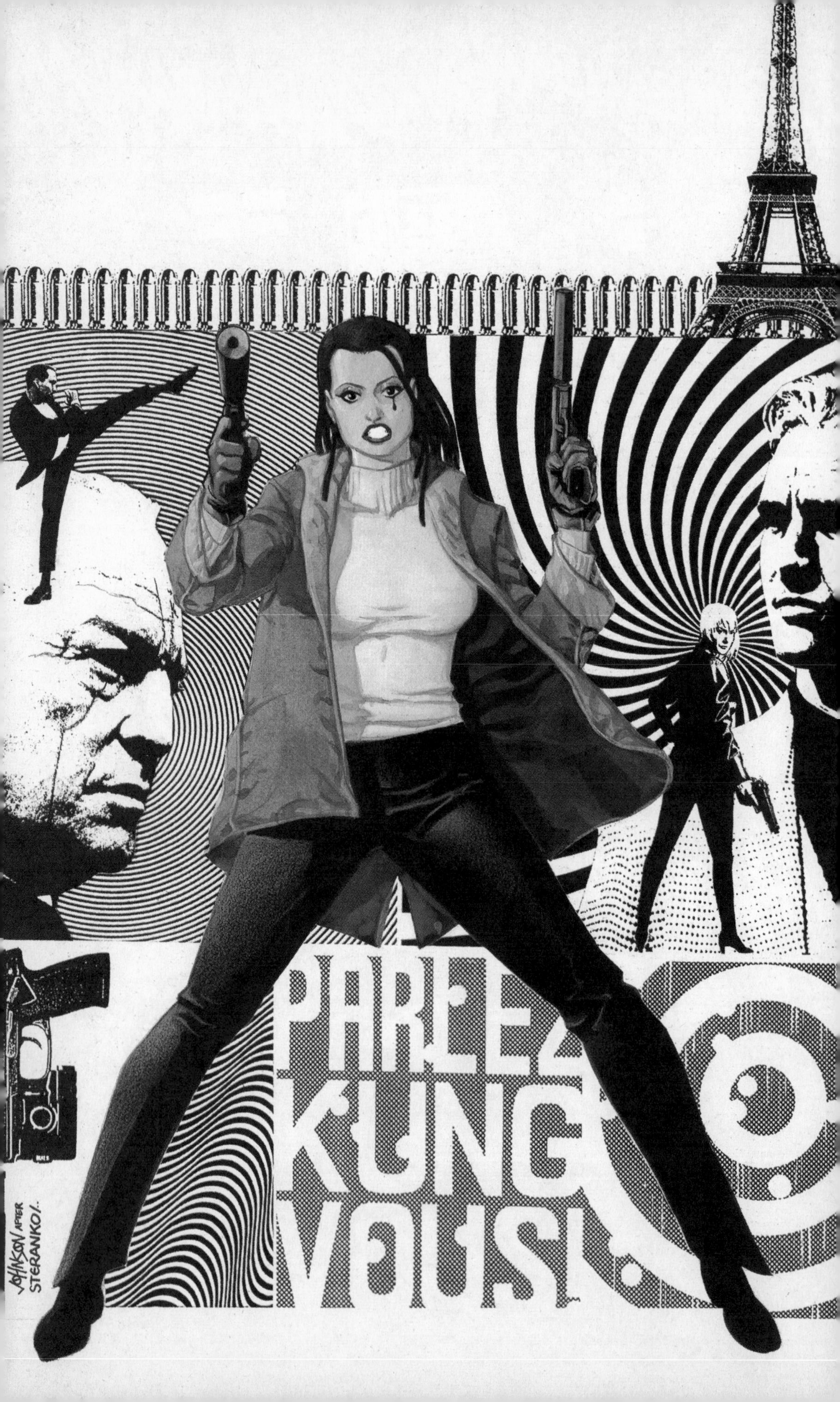

PARLEZ KUNG VOUS!
JOHNSON AFTER STERANKO!.

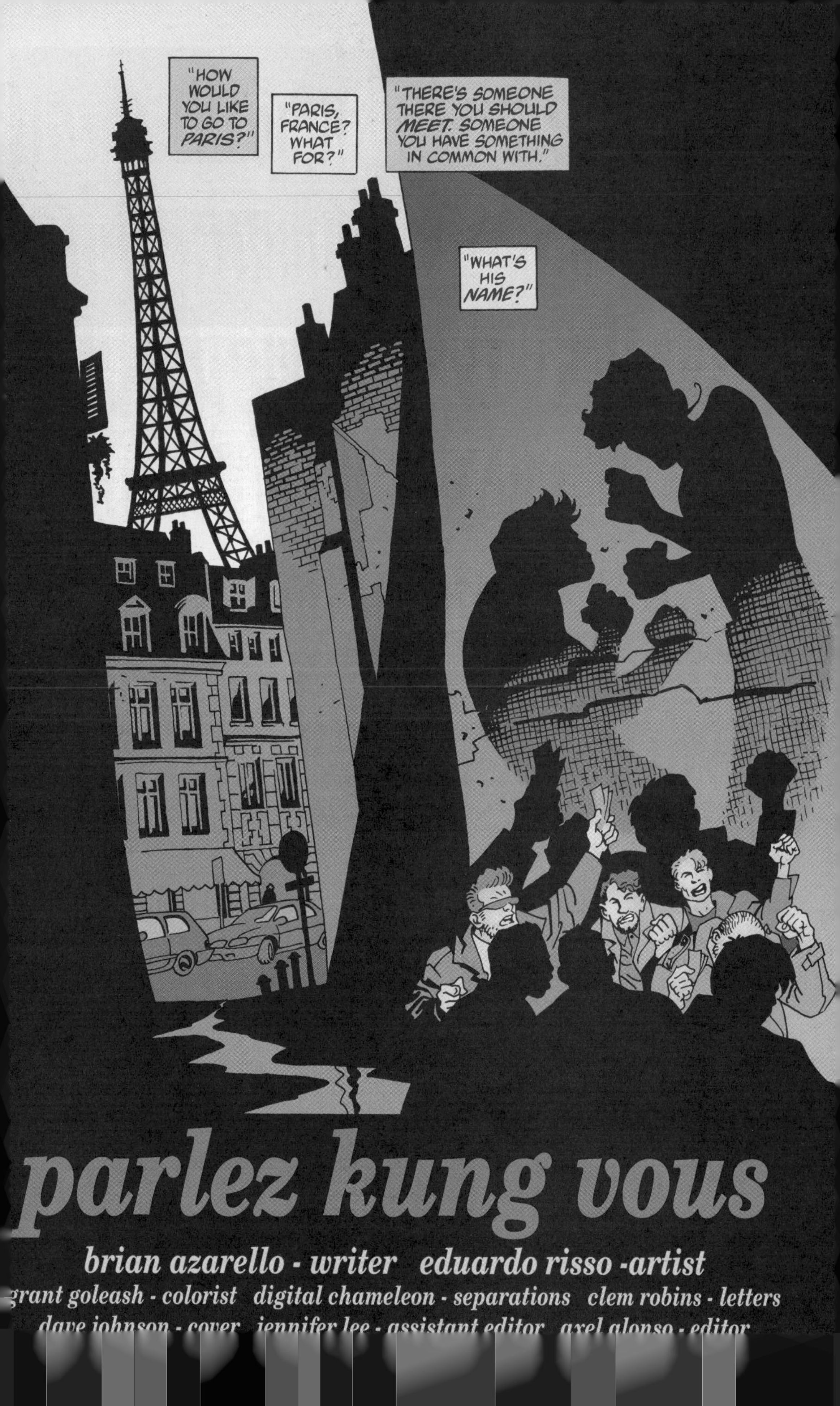

"HOW WOULD YOU LIKE TO GO TO PARIS?"
"PARIS, FRANCE? WHAT FOR?"
"THERE'S SOMEONE THERE YOU SHOULD MEET. SOMEONE YOU HAVE SOMETHING IN COMMON WITH."
"WHAT'S HIS NAME?"

parlez kung vous

brian azarello - writer eduardo risso -artist

grant goleash - colorist digital chameleon - separations clem robins - letters

dave johnson - cover jennifer lee - assistant editor axel alonso - editor

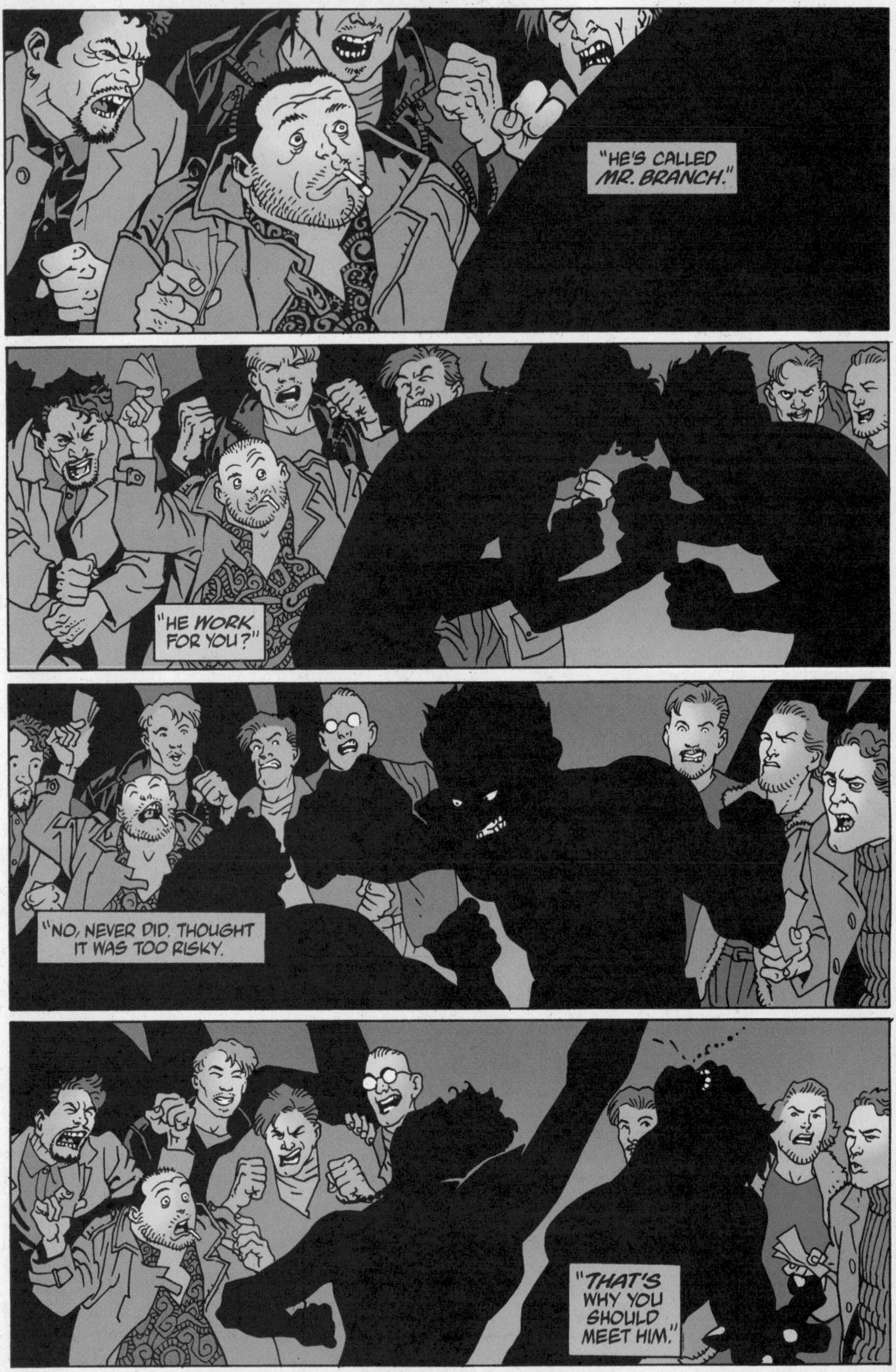
"HE'S CALLED MR. BRANCH."
"HE WORK FOR YOU?"
"NO, NEVER DID. THOUGHT IT WAS TOO RISKY.
"THAT'S WHY YOU SHOULD MEET HIM."

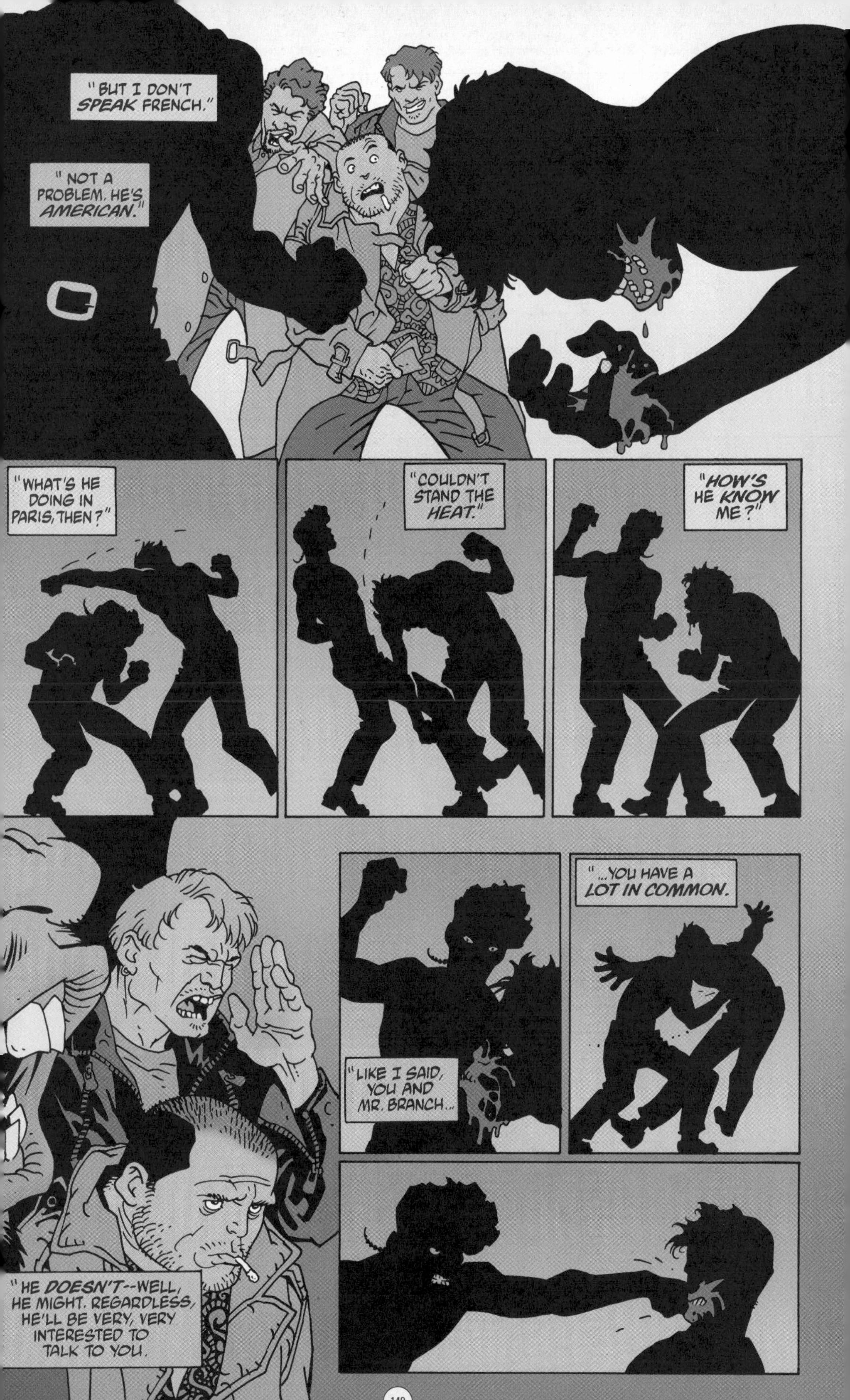

"BUT I DON'T SPEAK FRENCH."
"NOT A PROBLEM. HE'S AMERICAN."
"WHAT'S HE DOING IN PARIS, THEN?"
"COULDN'T STAND THE HEAT."
"HOW'S HE KNOW ME?"
"HE DOESN'T--WELL, HE MIGHT. REGARDLESS, HE'LL BE VERY, VERY INTERESTED TO TALK TO YOU.
"LIKE I SAID, YOU AND MR. BRANCH...
"...YOU HAVE A LOT IN COMMON.

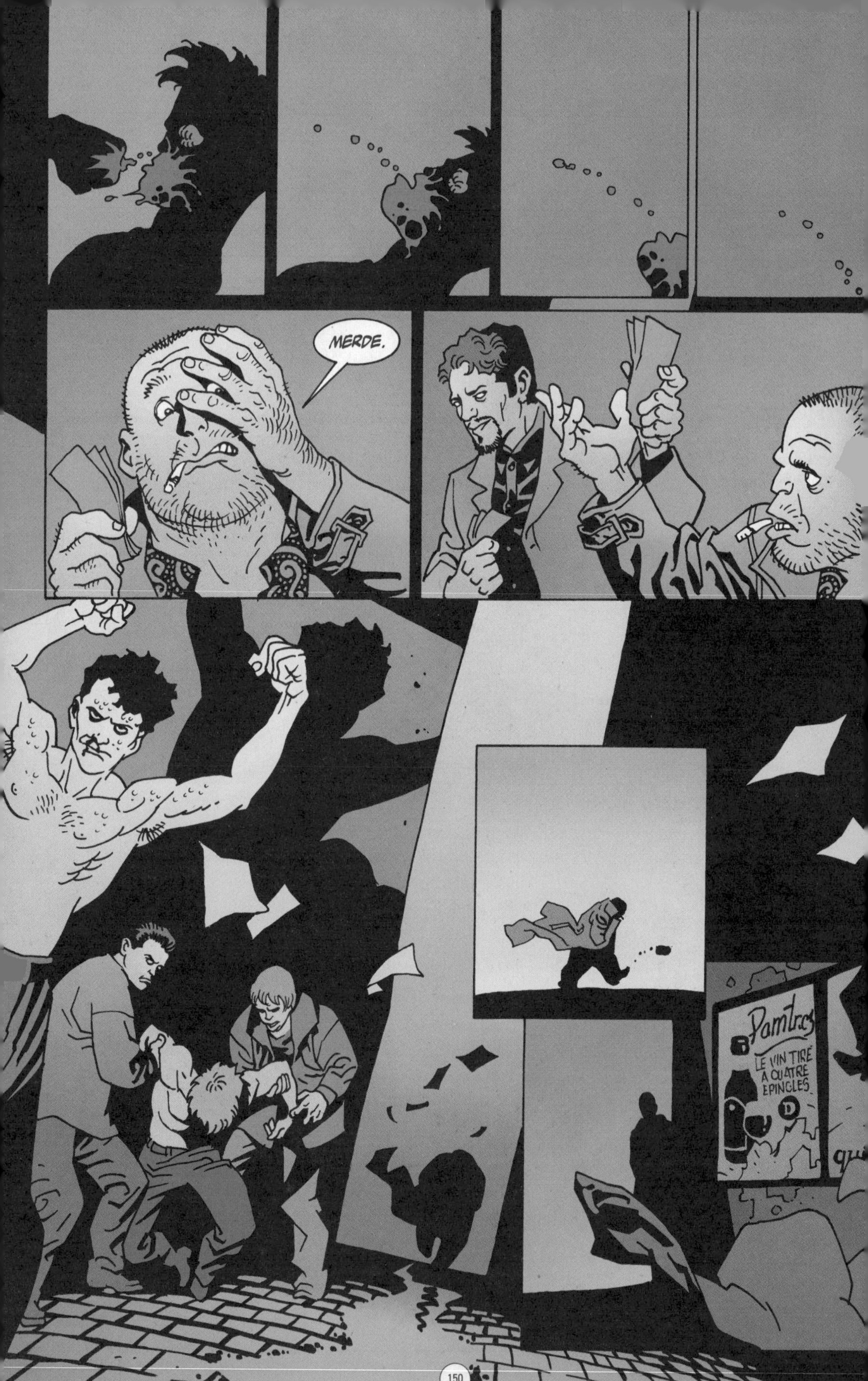
MERDE.
Pamtrcs
LE VIN TIRÉ
A QUATRE
EPINGLES
D

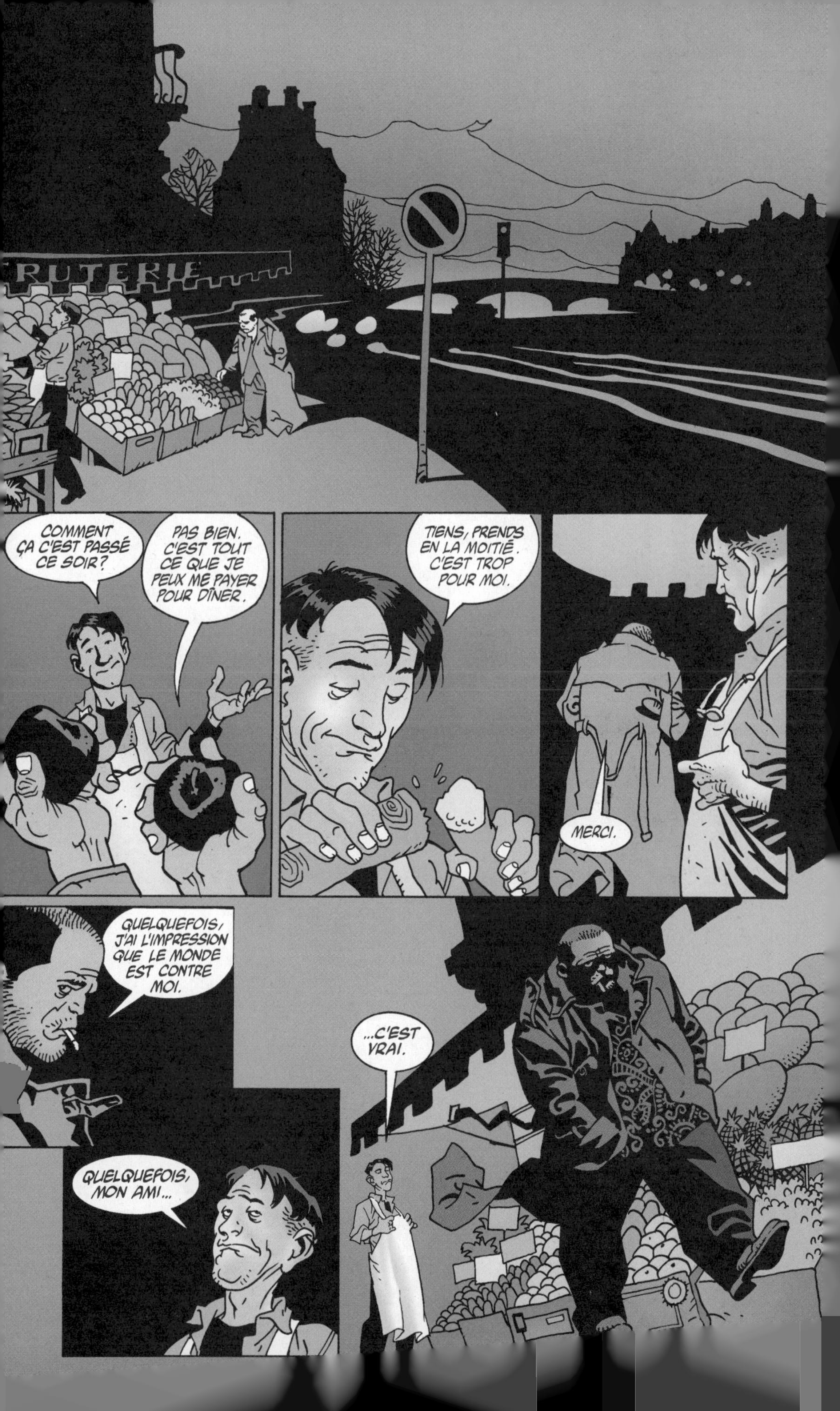
RUTERIE
COMMENT ÇA C'EST PASSÉ CE SOIR?
PAS BIEN. C'EST TOUT CE QUE JE PEUX ME PAYER POUR DÎNER.
TIENS, PRENDS EN LA MOITIÉ. C'EST TROP POUR MOI.
MERCI.
QUELQUEFOIS, J'AI L'IMPRESSION QUE LE MONDE EST CONTRE MOI.
QUELQUEFOIS, MON AMI...
...C'EST VRAI.

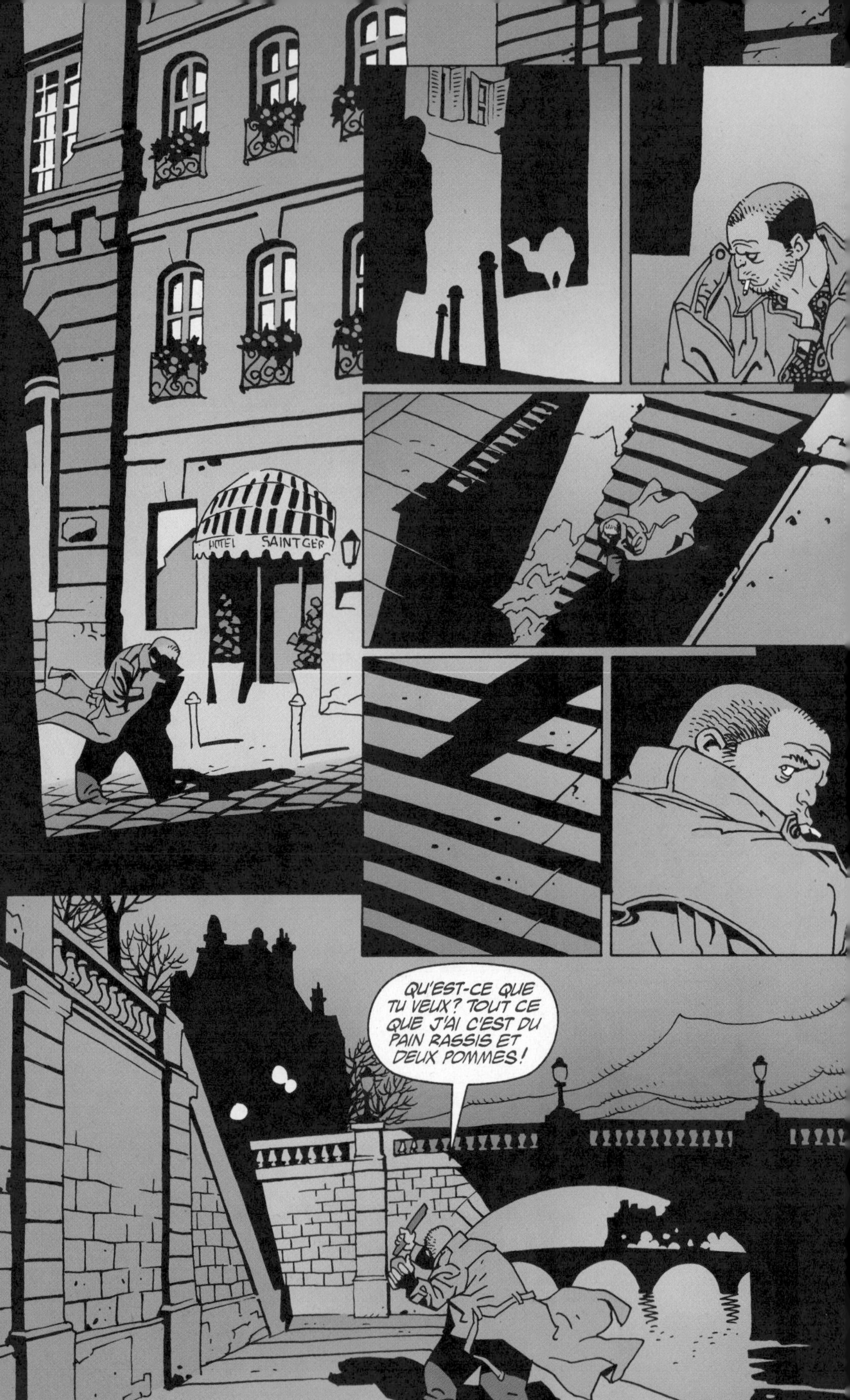
HOTEL SAINTGER
QU'EST-CE QUE TU VEUX? TOUT CE QUE J'AI C'EST DU PAIN RASSIS ET DEUX POMMES!

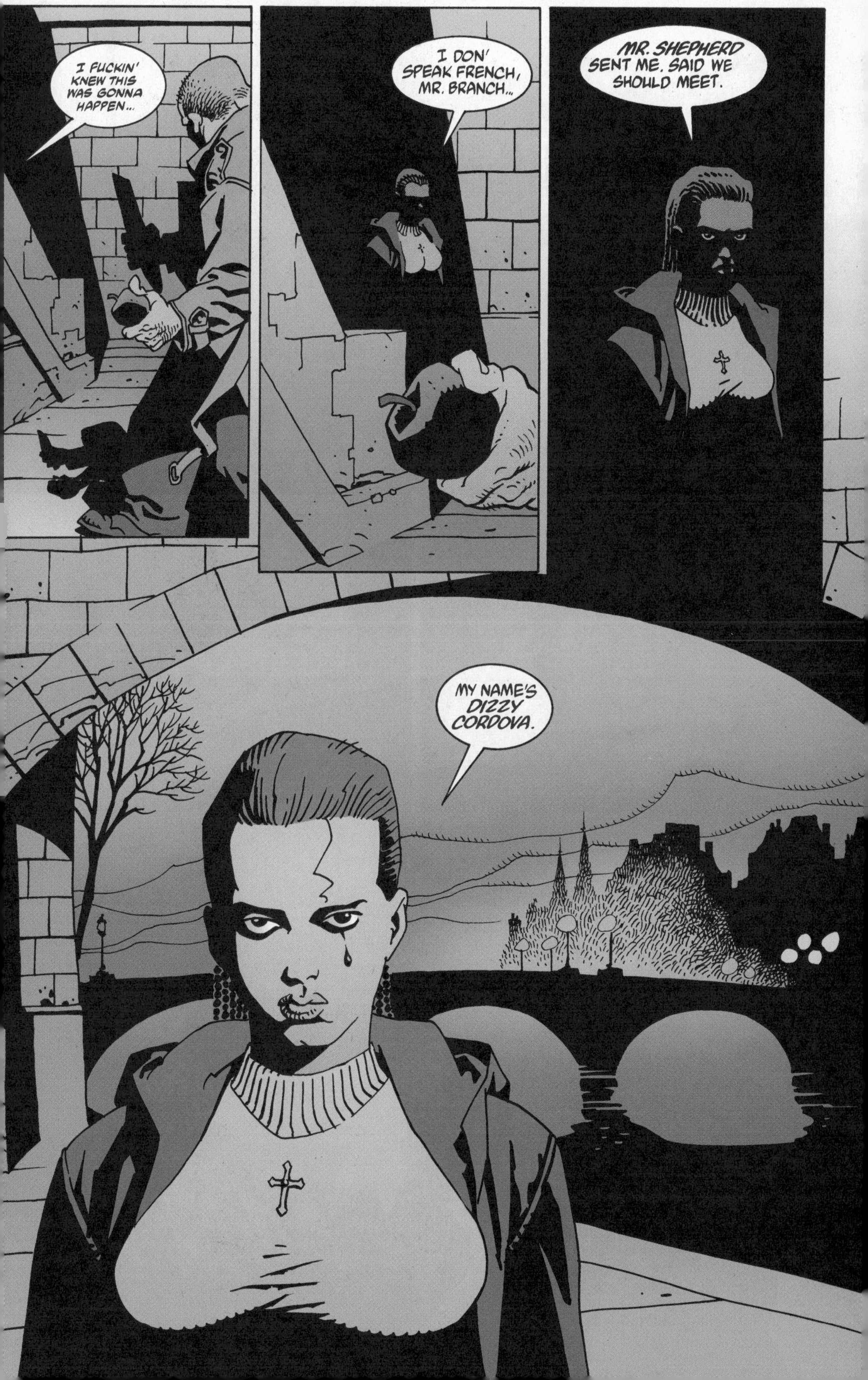
I FUCKIN' KNEW THIS WAS GONNA HAPPEN...
I DON' SPEAK FRENCH, MR. BRANCH...
MR. SHEPHERD SENT ME. SAID WE SHOULD MEET.
MY NAME'S DIZZY CORDOVA.

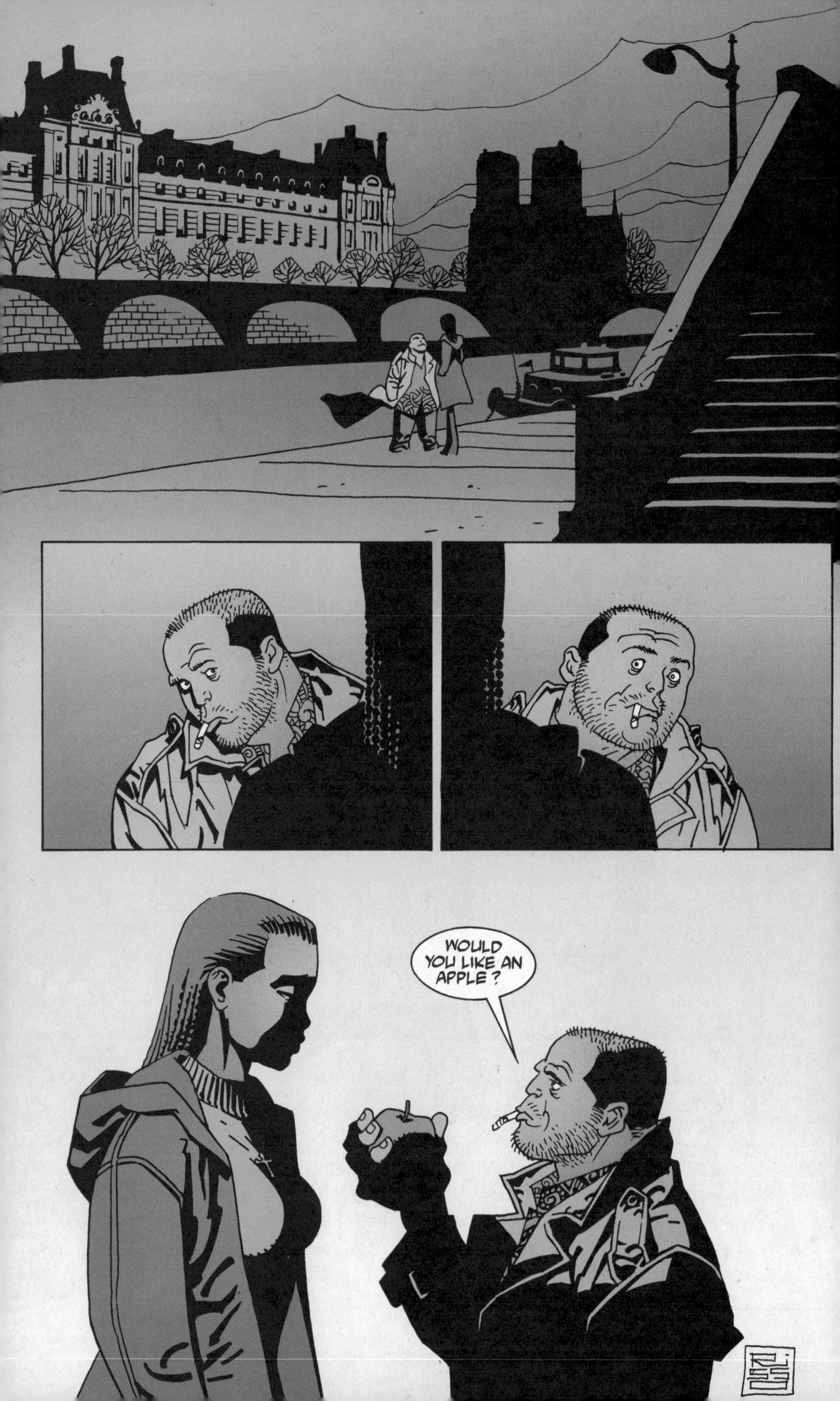
WOULD YOU LIKE AN APPLE?

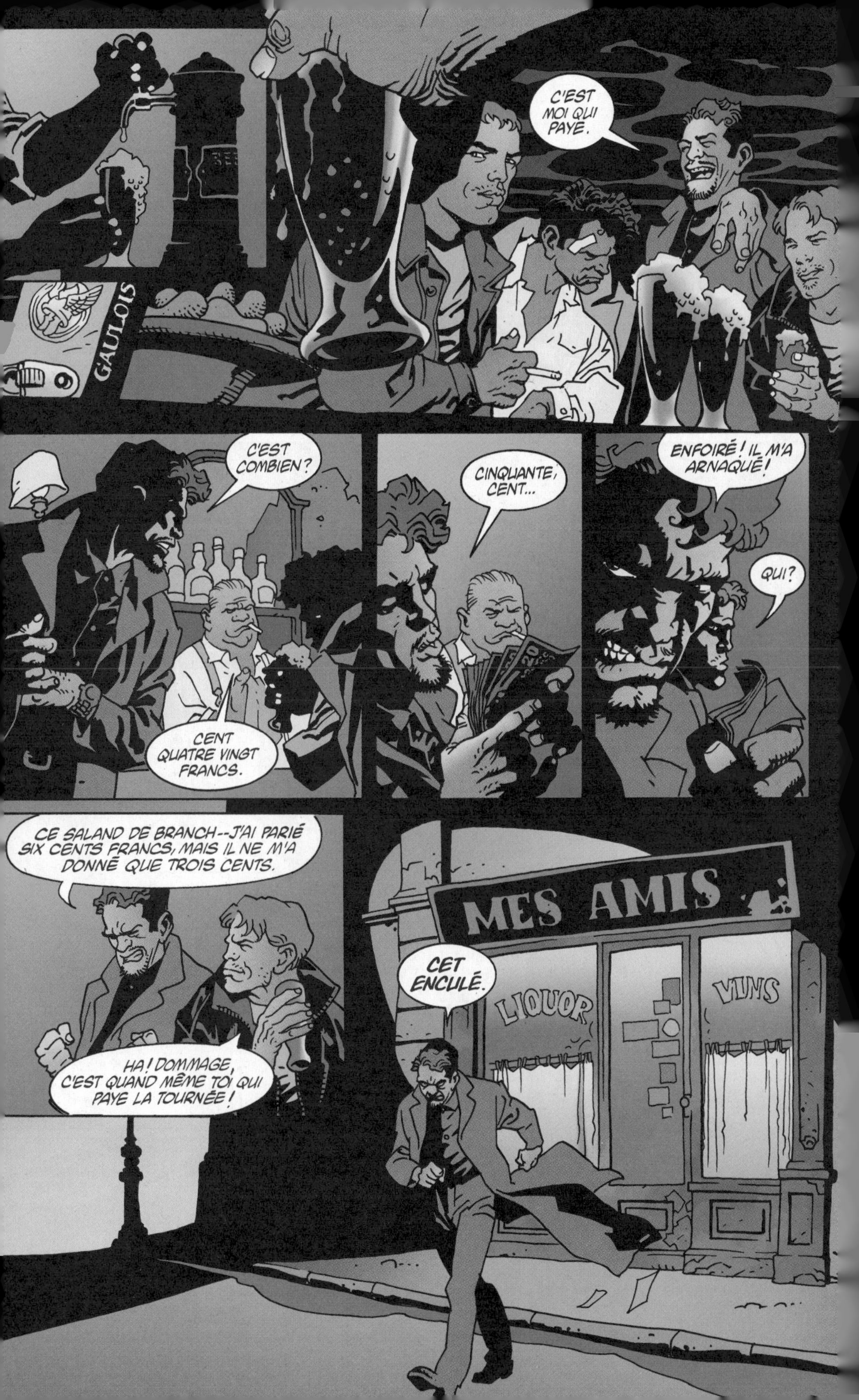
GAULOIS
C'EST MOI QUI PAYE.
C'EST COMBIEN?
CENT QUATRE VINGT FRANCS.
CINQUANTE, CENT...
ENFOIRÉ! IL M'A ARNAQUÉ!
QUI?
CE SALAND DE BRANCH--J'AI PARIÉ SIX CENTS FRANCS, MAIS IL NE M'A DONNÉ QUE TROIS CENTS.
HA! DOMMAGE, C'EST QUAND MÊME TOI QUI PAYE LA TOURNÉE!
MES AMIS
CET ENCULÉ.
LIQUOR
VINS

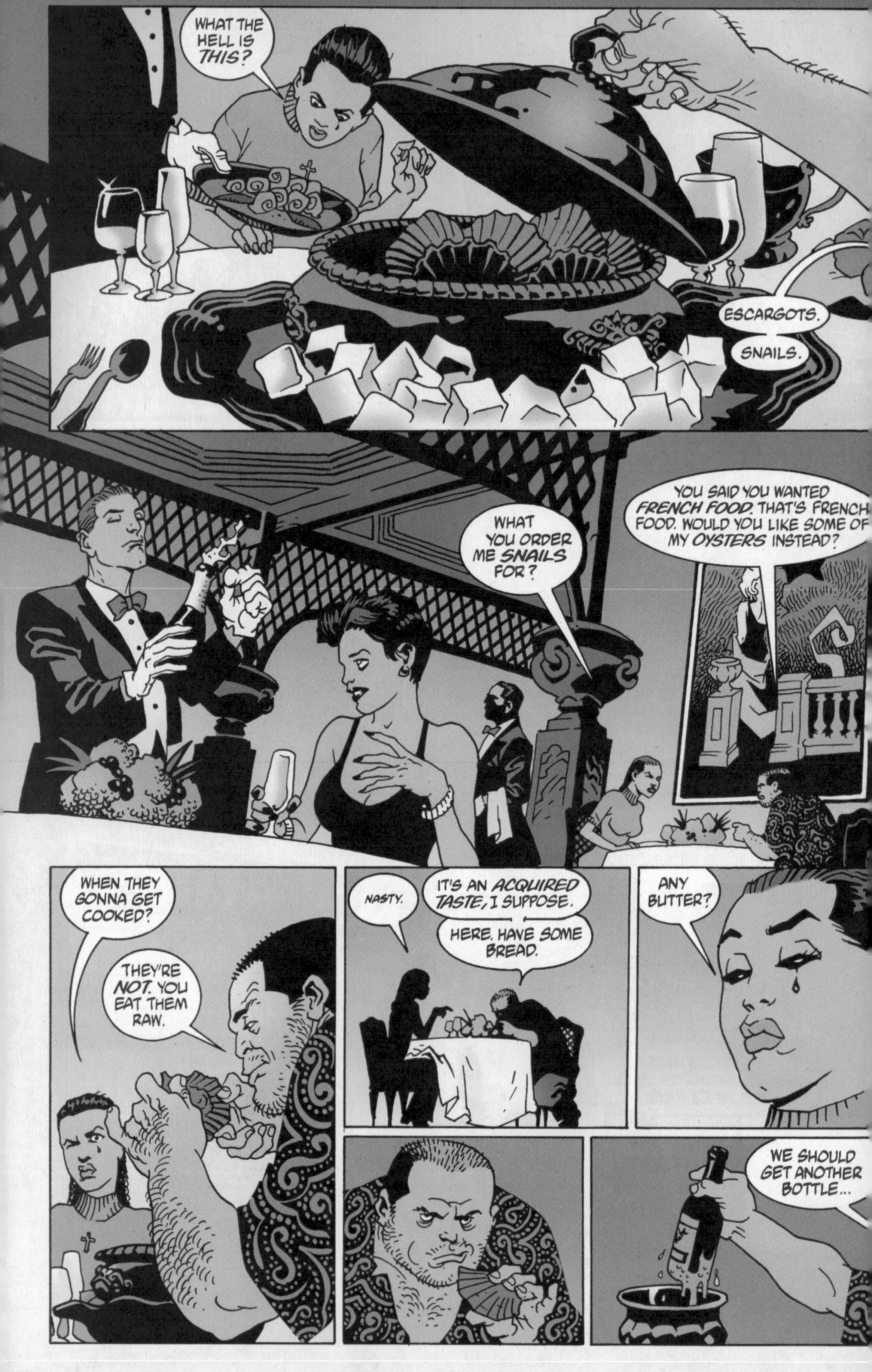

WHAT THE HELL IS THIS?
ESCARGOTS.
SNAILS.
WHAT YOU ORDER ME SNAILS FOR?
YOU SAID YOU WANTED FRENCH FOOD. THAT'S FRENCH FOOD. WOULD YOU LIKE SOME OF MY OYSTERS INSTEAD?
WHEN THEY GONNA GET COOKED?
THEY'RE NOT. YOU EAT THEM RAW.
NASTY.
IT'S AN ACQUIRED TASTE, I SUPPOSE.
HERE. HAVE SOME BREAD.
ANY BUTTER?
WE SHOULD GET ANOTHER BOTTLE...

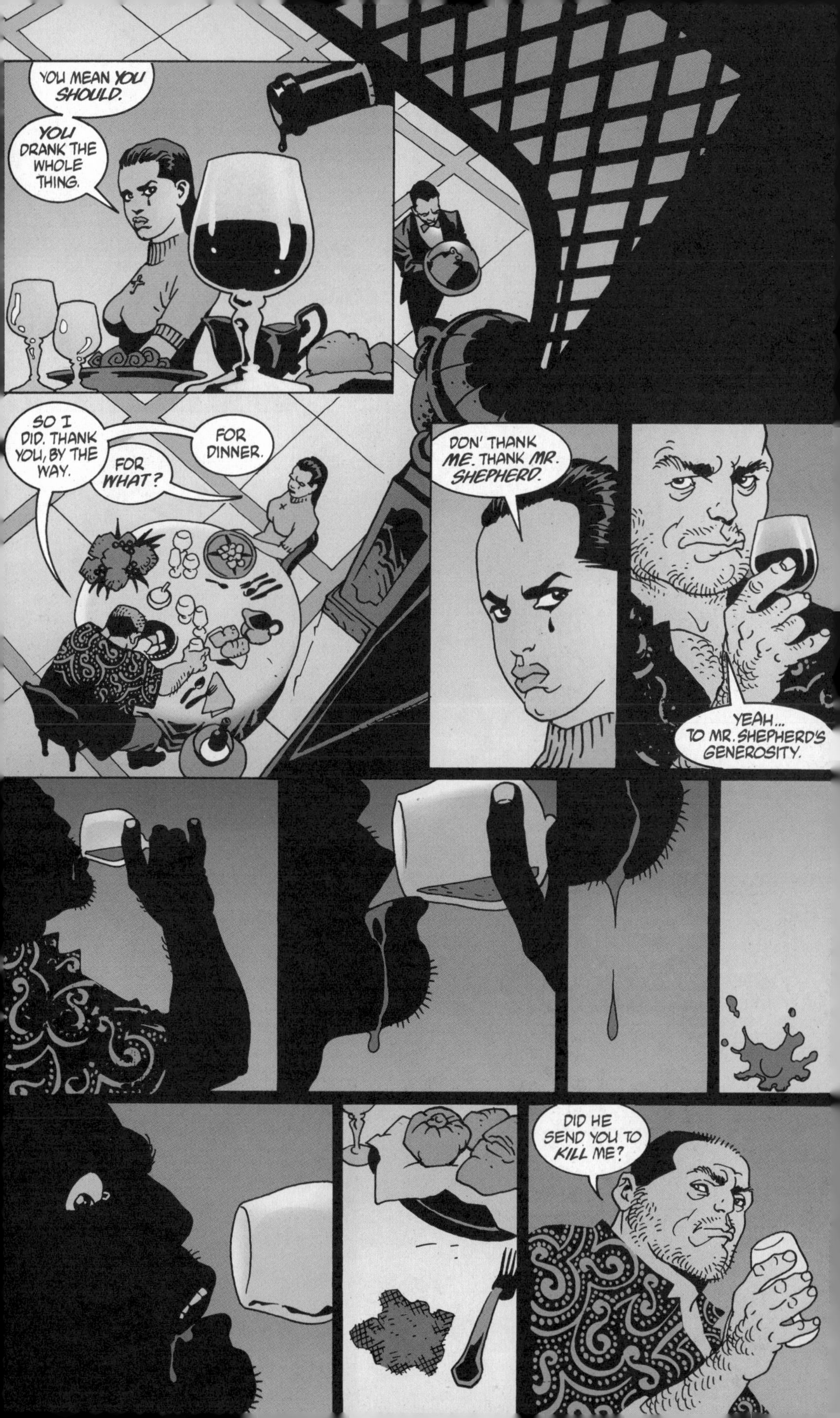
YOU MEAN YOU SHOULD.
YOU DRANK THE WHOLE THING.
SO I DID. THANK YOU, BY THE WAY.
FOR WHAT?
FOR DINNER.
DON' THANK ME. THANK MR. SHEPHERD.
YEAH... TO MR. SHEPHERD'S GENEROSITY.
DID HE SEND YOU TO KILL ME?

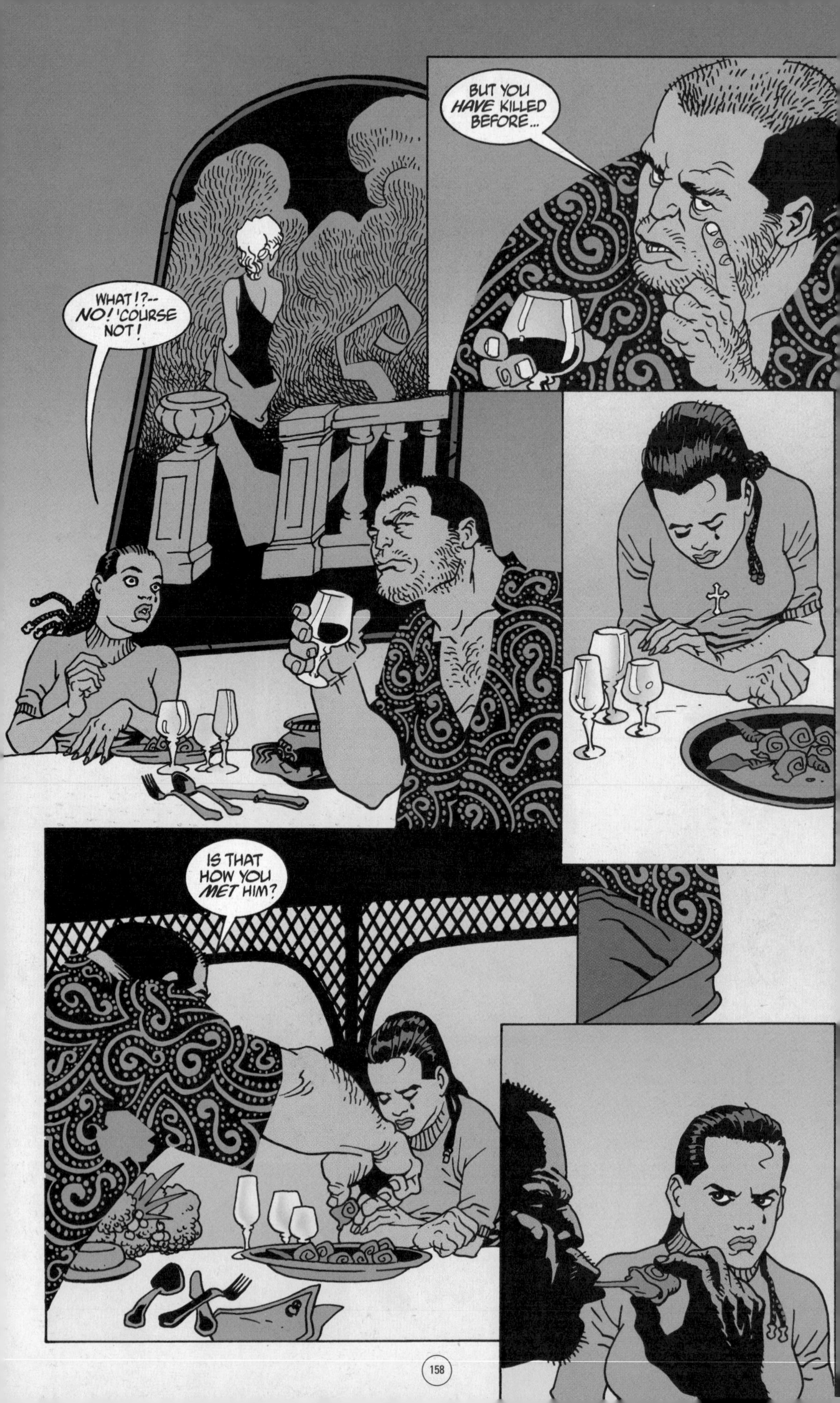
WHAT!?-- NO! 'COURSE NOT!
BUT YOU HAVE KILLED BEFORE...
IS THAT HOW YOU MET HIM?

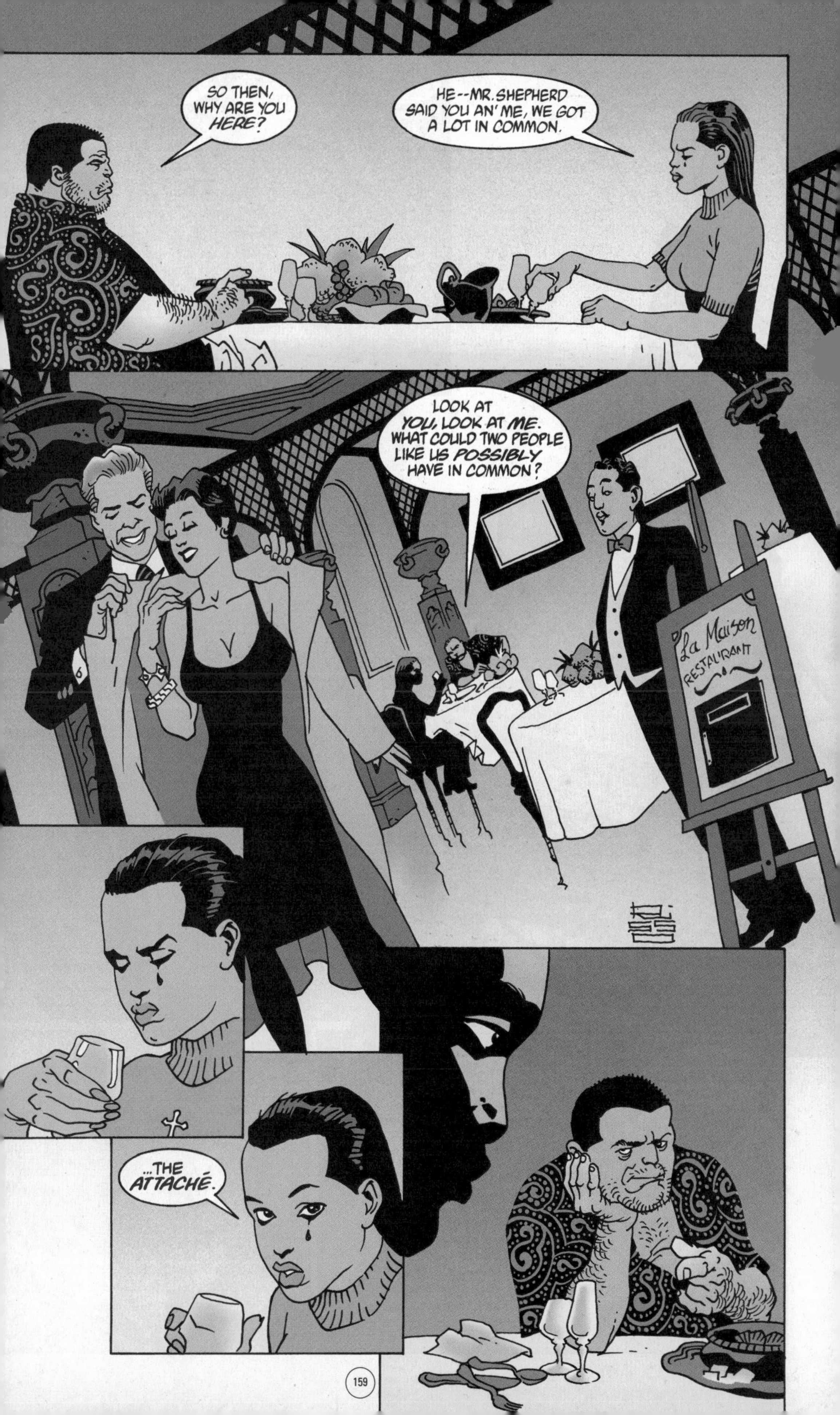
SO THEN, WHY ARE YOU *HERE?*
HE--MR. SHEPHERD SAID YOU AN' ME, WE GOT A LOT IN COMMON.
LOOK AT *YOU*, LOOK AT *ME*. WHAT COULD TWO PEOPLE LIKE US *POSSIBLY* HAVE IN COMMON?
La Maison
RESTAURANT
...THE *ATTACHÉ*.

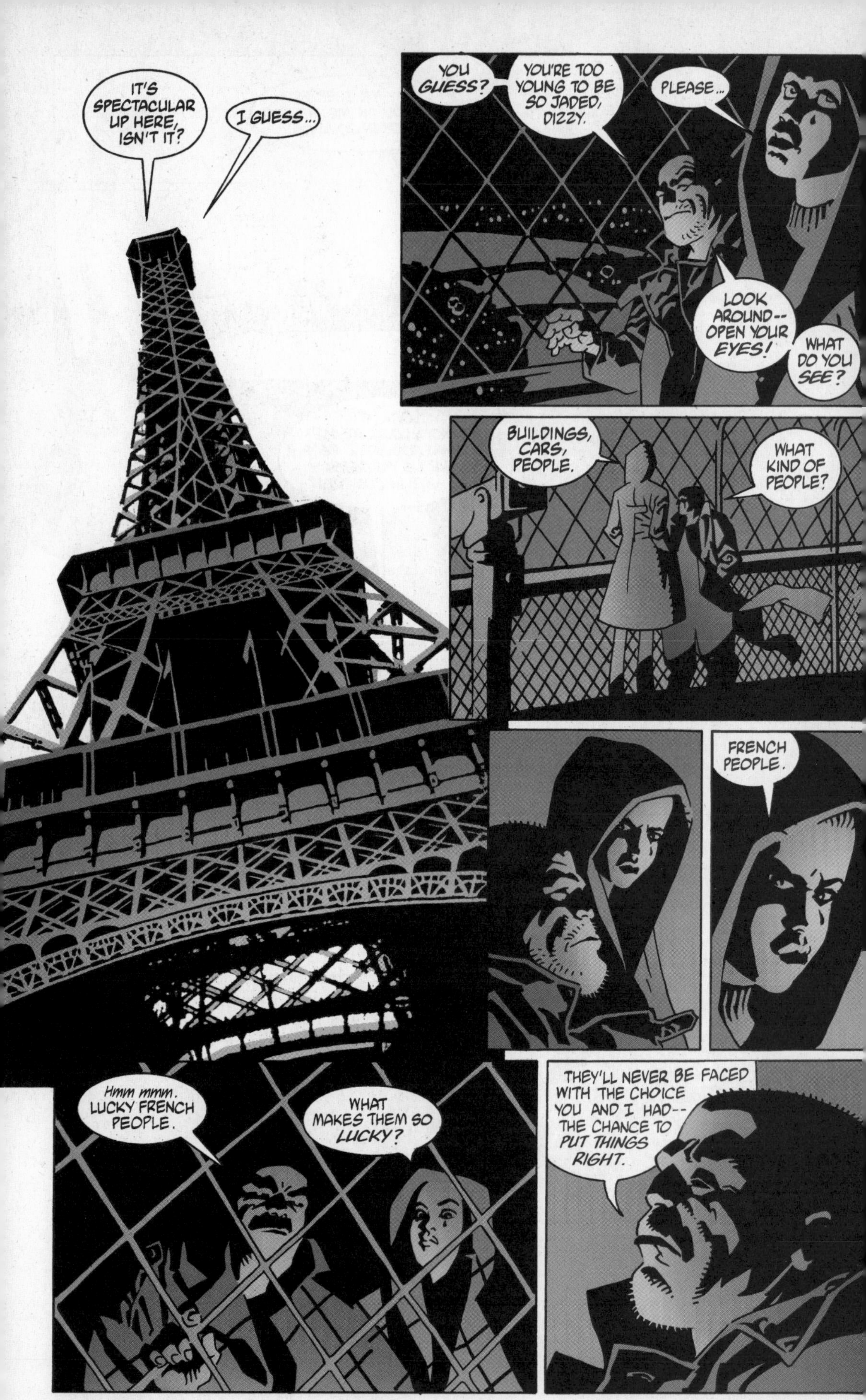
IT'S SPECTACULAR UP HERE, ISN'T IT?
I GUESS...
YOU GUESS?
YOU'RE TOO YOUNG TO BE SO JADED, DIZZY.
PLEASE...
LOOK AROUND-- OPEN YOUR EYES!
WHAT DO YOU SEE?
BUILDINGS, CARS, PEOPLE.
WHAT KIND OF PEOPLE?
FRENCH PEOPLE.
Hmm mmm. LUCKY FRENCH PEOPLE.
WHAT MAKES THEM SO LUCKY?
THEY'LL NEVER BE FACED WITH THE CHOICE YOU AND I HAD-- THE CHANCE TO PUT THINGS RIGHT.

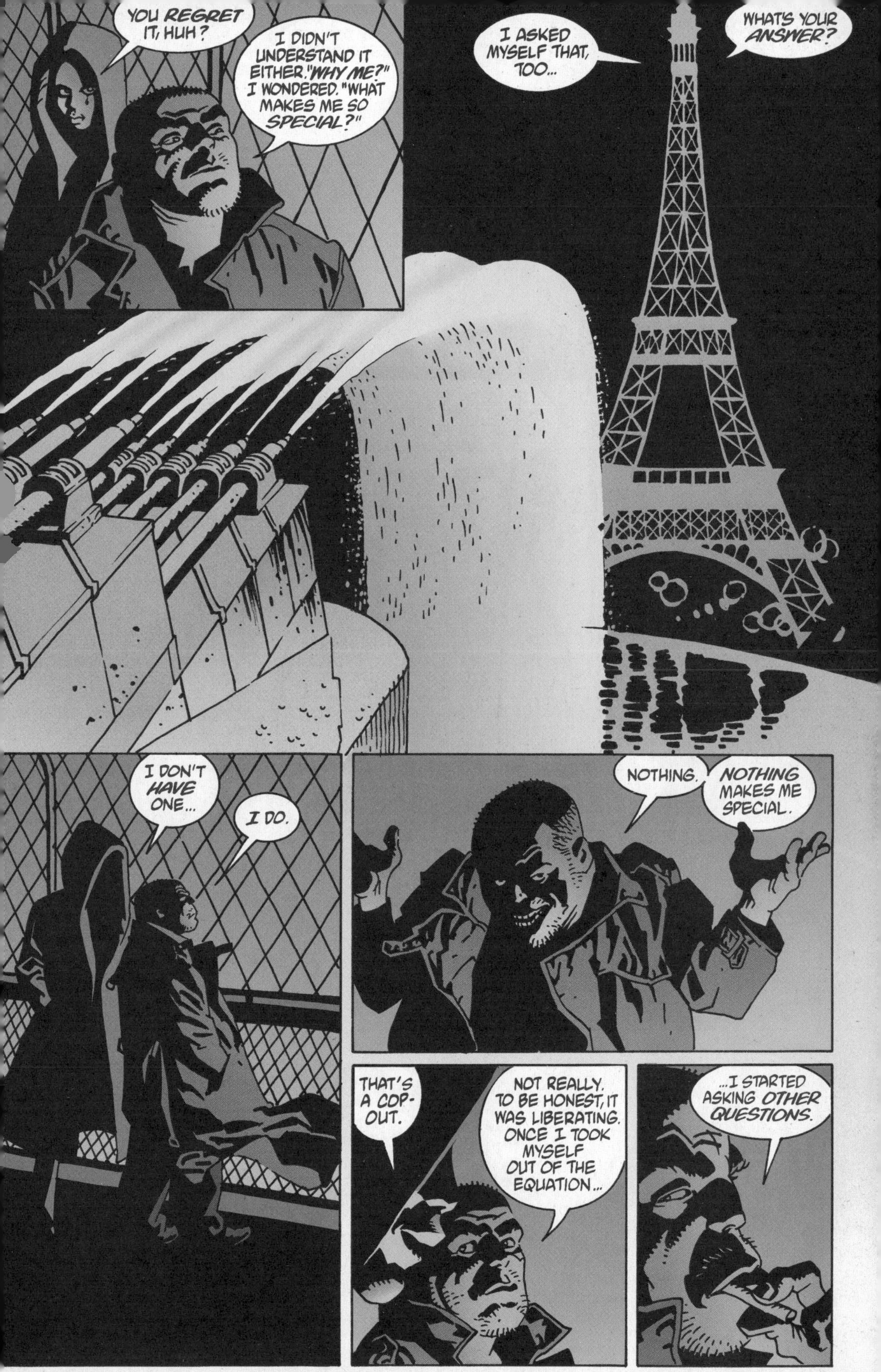
YOU REGRET IT, HUH?
I DIDN'T UNDERSTAND IT EITHER. "WHY ME?" I WONDERED. "WHAT MAKES ME SO SPECIAL?"
I ASKED MYSELF THAT, TOO...
WHAT'S YOUR ANSWER?
I DON'T HAVE ONE...
I DO.
NOTHING.
NOTHING MAKES ME SPECIAL.
THAT'S A COP-OUT.
NOT REALLY. TO BE HONEST, IT WAS LIBERATING. ONCE I TOOK MYSELF OUT OF THE EQUATION...
...I STARTED ASKING OTHER QUESTIONS.

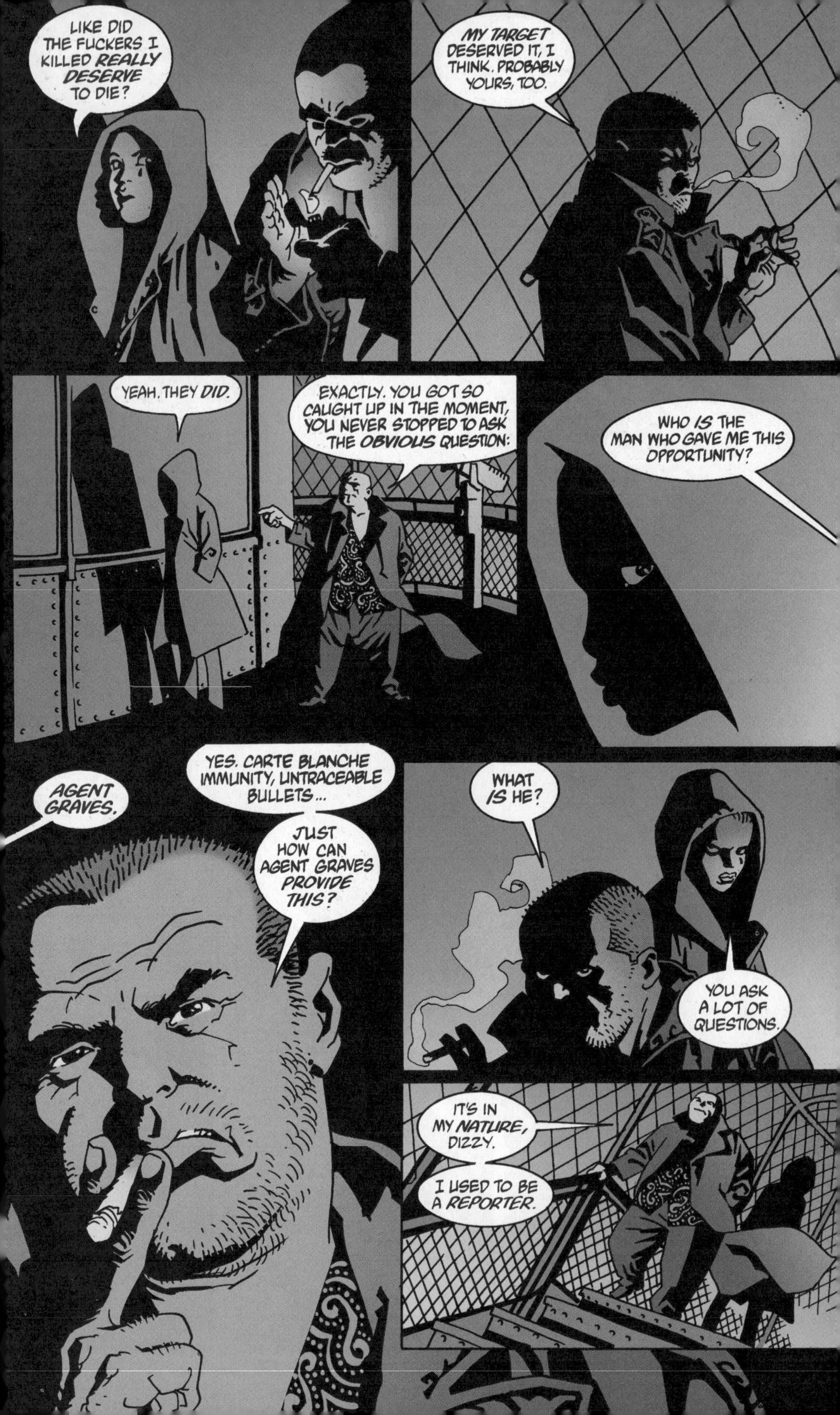
LIKE DID THE FUCKERS I KILLED *REALLY DESERVE* TO DIE?
MY TARGET DESERVED IT, I THINK. PROBABLY YOURS, TOO.
YEAH. THEY *DID*.
EXACTLY. YOU GOT SO CAUGHT UP IN THE MOMENT, YOU NEVER STOPPED TO ASK THE *OBVIOUS* QUESTION:
WHO *IS* THE MAN WHO GAVE ME THIS OPPORTUNITY?
AGENT GRAVES.
YES. CARTE BLANCHE IMMUNITY, UNTRACEABLE BULLETS...
JUST HOW CAN AGENT GRAVES *PROVIDE THIS?*
WHAT *IS* HE?
YOU ASK A LOT OF QUESTIONS.
IT'S IN MY *NATURE*, DIZZY.
I USED TO BE A *REPORTER*.

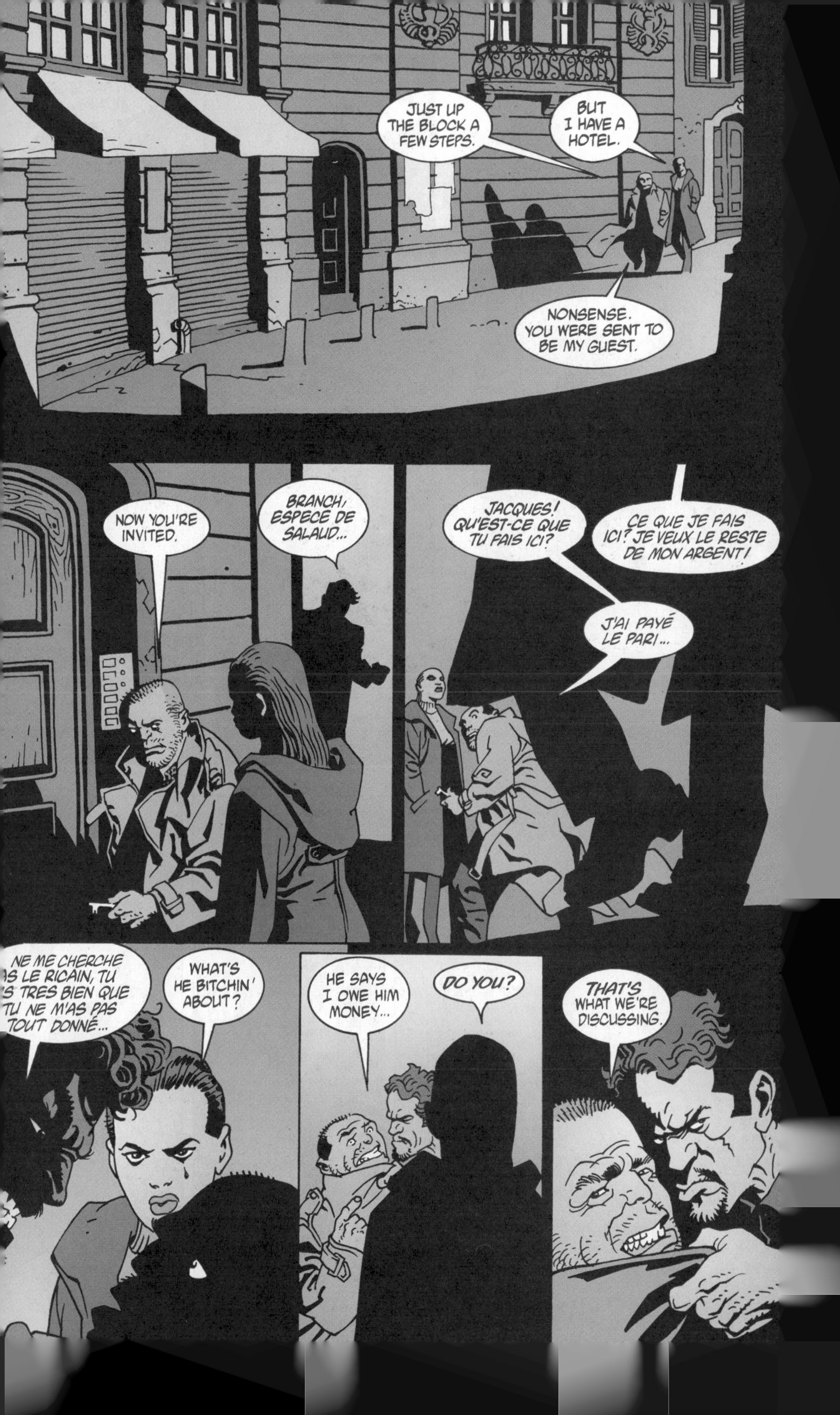
JUST UP THE BLOCK A FEW STEPS.
BUT I HAVE A HOTEL.
NONSENSE. YOU WERE SENT TO BE MY GUEST.
NOW YOU'RE INVITED.
BRANCH, ESPECE DE SALAUD...
JACQUES! QU'EST-CE QUE TU FAIS ICI?
CE QUE JE FAIS ICI? JE VEUX LE RESTE DE MON ARGENT!
J'AI PAYÉ LE PARI...
NE ME CHERCHE AS LE RICAIN, TU S TRES BIEN QUE TU NE M'AS PAS TOUT DONNÉ...
WHAT'S HE BITCHIN' ABOUT?
HE SAYS I OWE HIM MONEY...
DO YOU?
THAT'S WHAT WE'RE DISCUSSING.

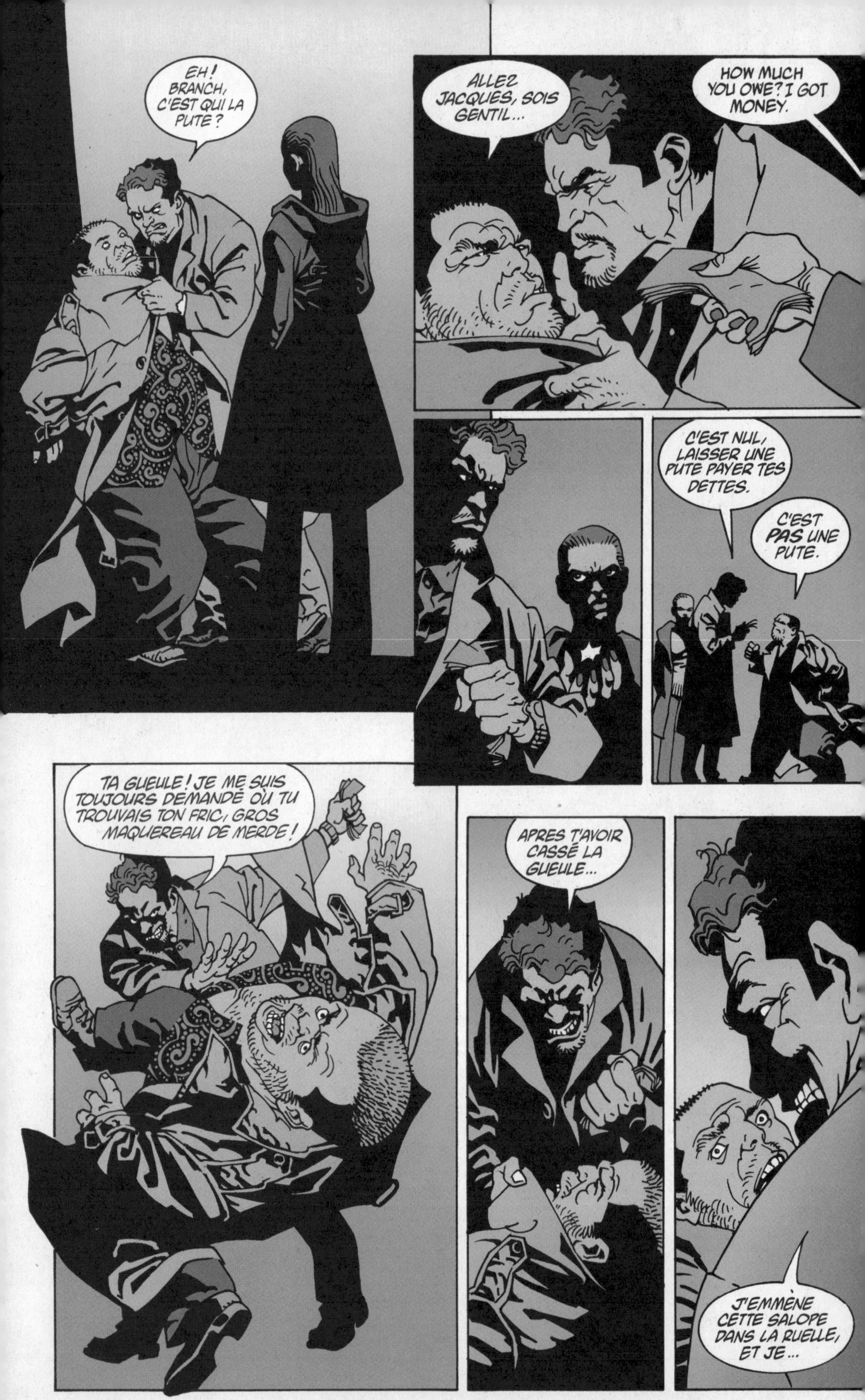

EH! BRANCH, C'EST QUI LA PUTE?
ALLEZ JACQUES, SOIS GENTIL...
HOW MUCH YOU OWE? I GOT MONEY.
C'EST NUL, LAISSER UNE PUTE PAYER TES DETTES.
C'EST PAS UNE PUTE.
TA GUEULE! JE ME SUIS TOUJOURS DEMANDÉ OÙ TU TROUVAIS TON FRIC, GROS MAQUEREAU DE MERDE!
APRES T'AVOIR CASSÉ LA GUEULE...
J'EMMÈNE CETTE SALOPE DANS LA RUELLE, ET JE...

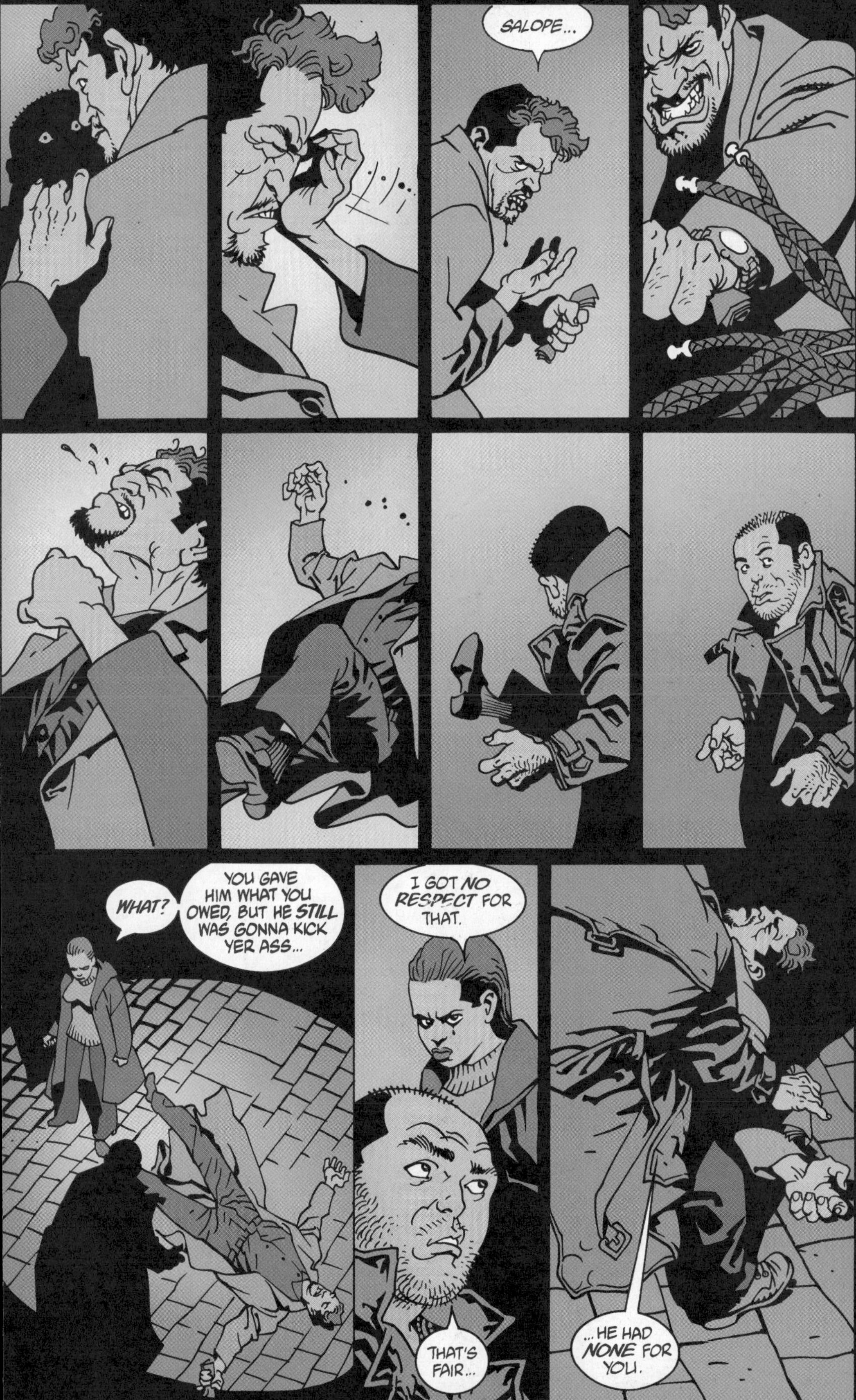
SALOPE...
WHAT?
YOU GAVE HIM WHAT YOU OWED, BUT HE STILL WAS GONNA KICK YER ASS...
I GOT NO RESPECT FOR THAT.
THAT'S FAIR...
...HE HAD NONE FOR YOU.

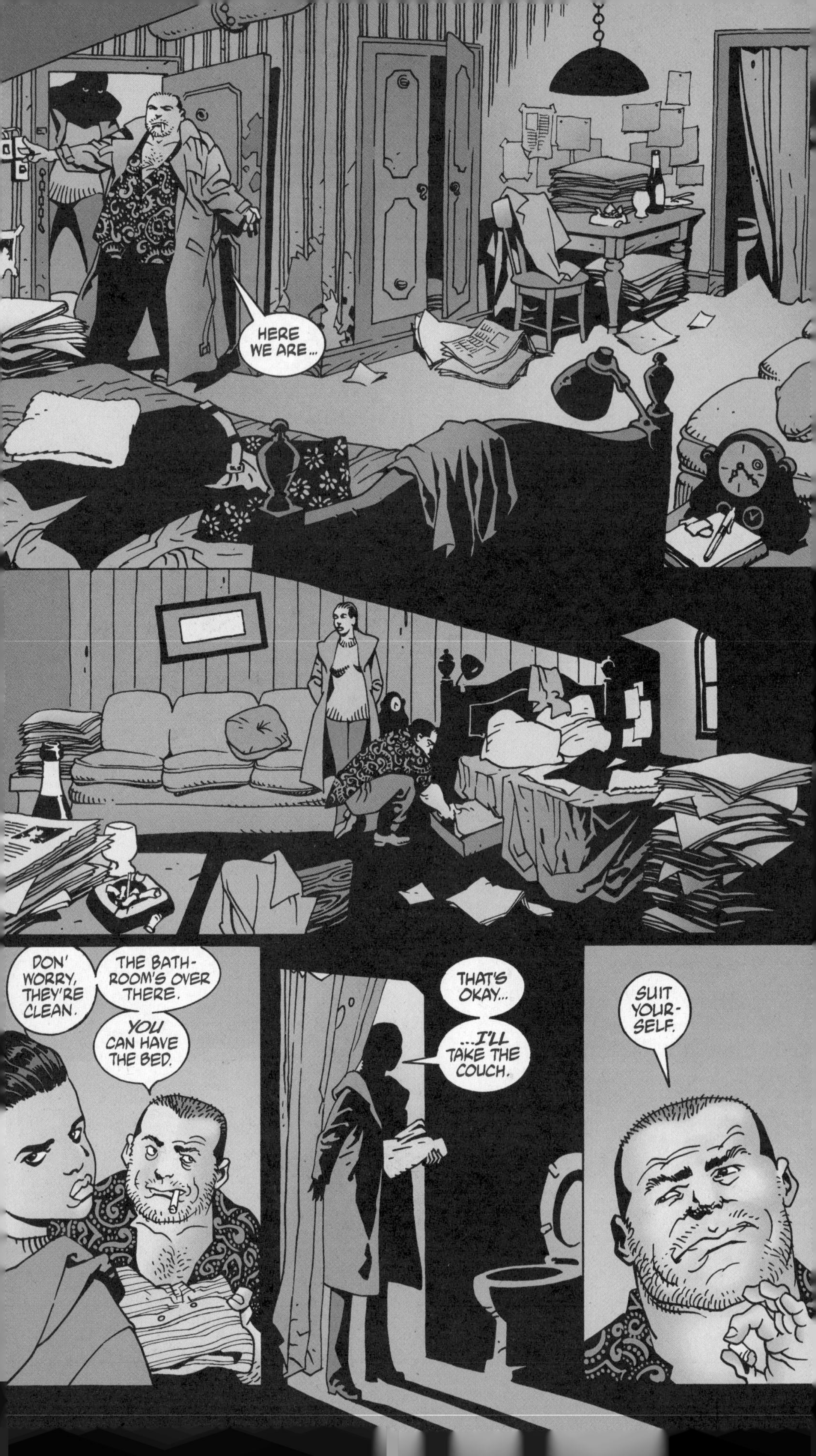
HERE WE ARE...
DON' WORRY, THEY'RE CLEAN.
THE BATH-ROOM'S OVER THERE.
YOU CAN HAVE THE BED.
THAT'S OKAY...
...I'LL TAKE THE COUCH.
SUIT YOUR-SELF.

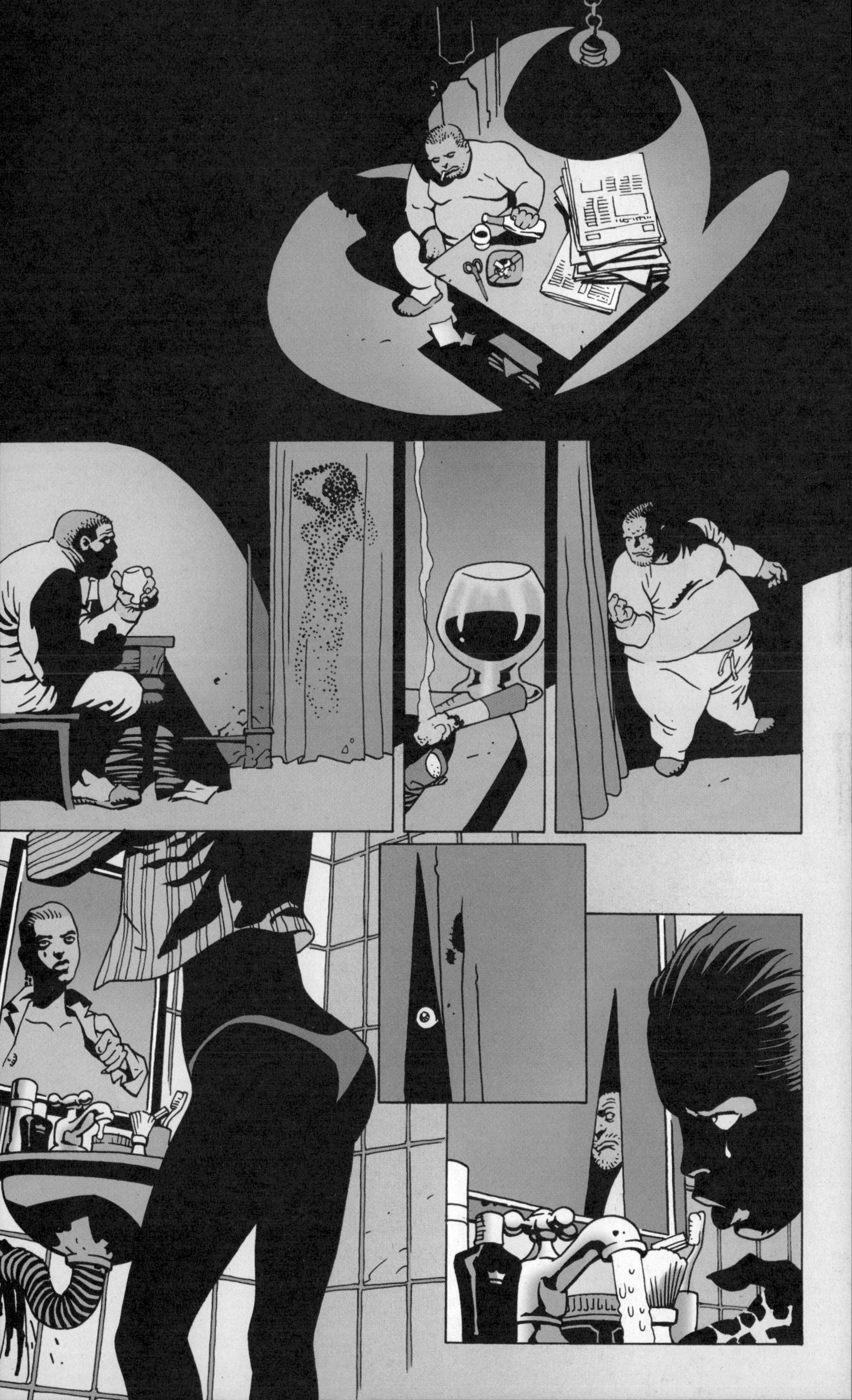

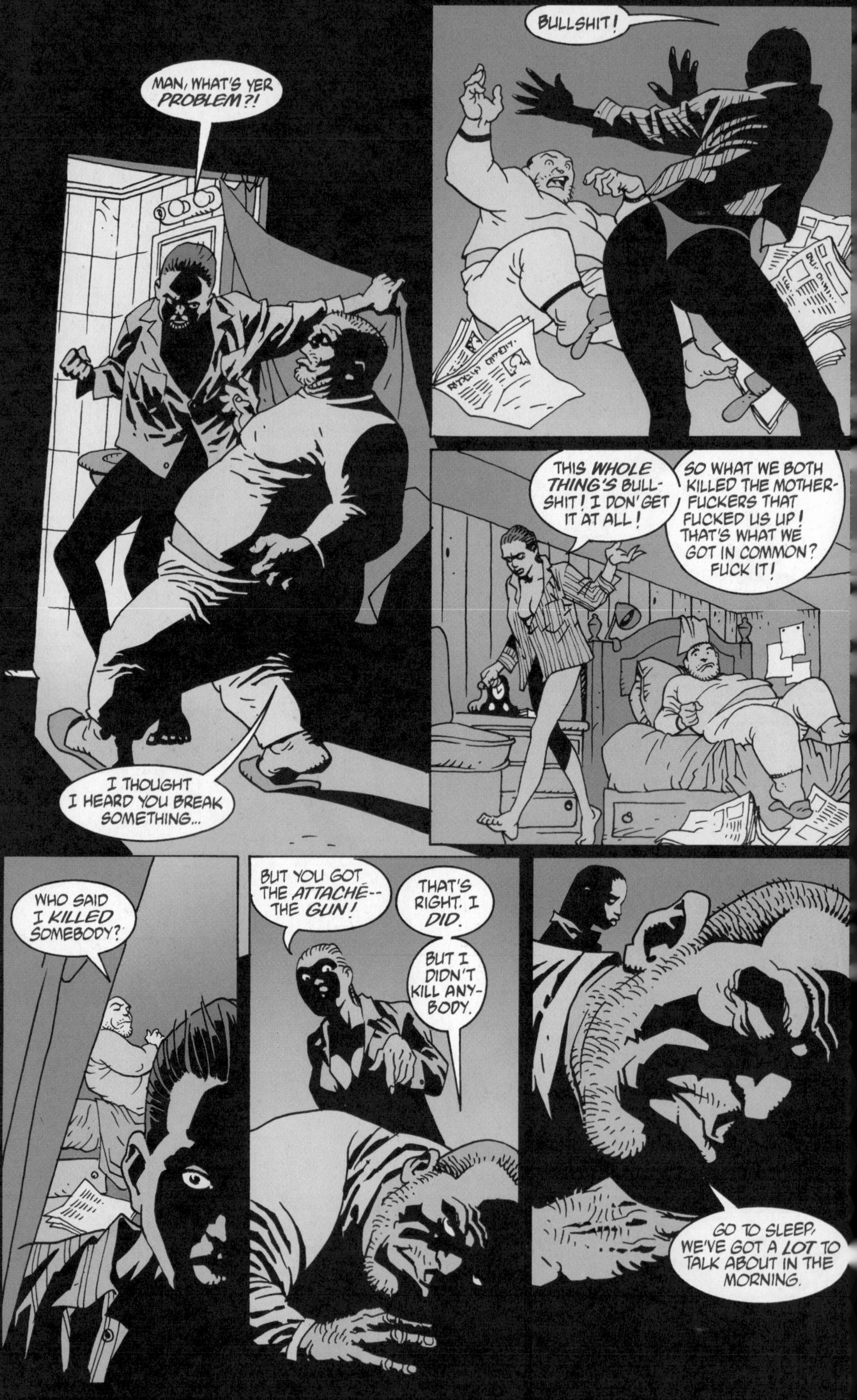
MAN, WHAT'S YER PROBLEM?!
I THOUGHT I HEARD YOU BREAK SOMETHING...
BULLSHIT!
THIS WHOLE THING'S BULLSHIT! I DON'T GET IT AT ALL!
SO WHAT WE BOTH KILLED THE MOTHERFUCKERS THAT FUCKED US UP! THAT'S WHAT WE GOT IN COMMON? FUCK IT!
WHO SAID I KILLED SOMEBODY?
BUT YOU GOT THE ATTACHÉ-- THE GUN!
THAT'S RIGHT. I DID.
BUT I DIDN'T KILL ANYBODY.
GO TO SLEEP, WE'VE GOT A LOT TO TALK ABOUT IN THE MORNING.

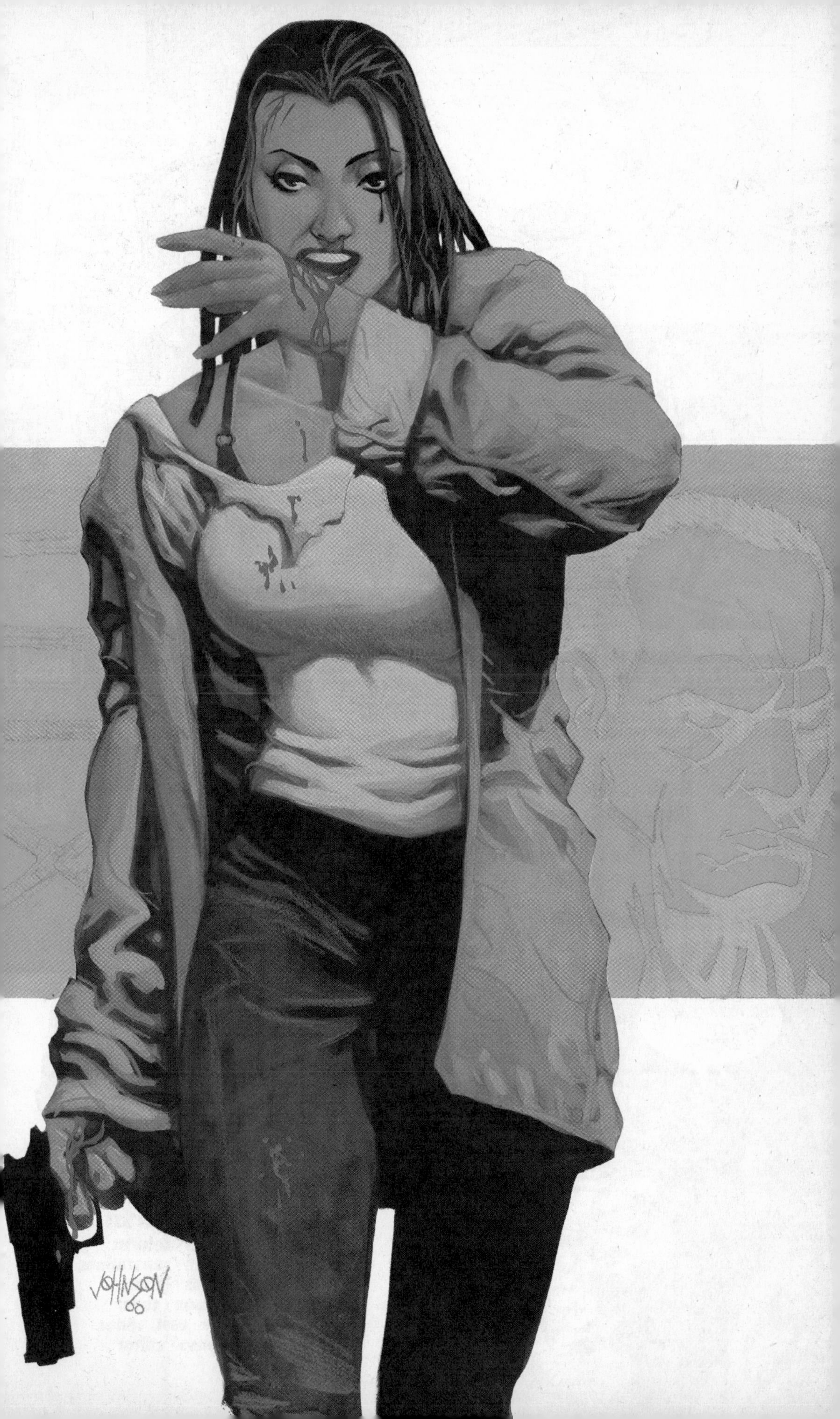
JOHNSON
00

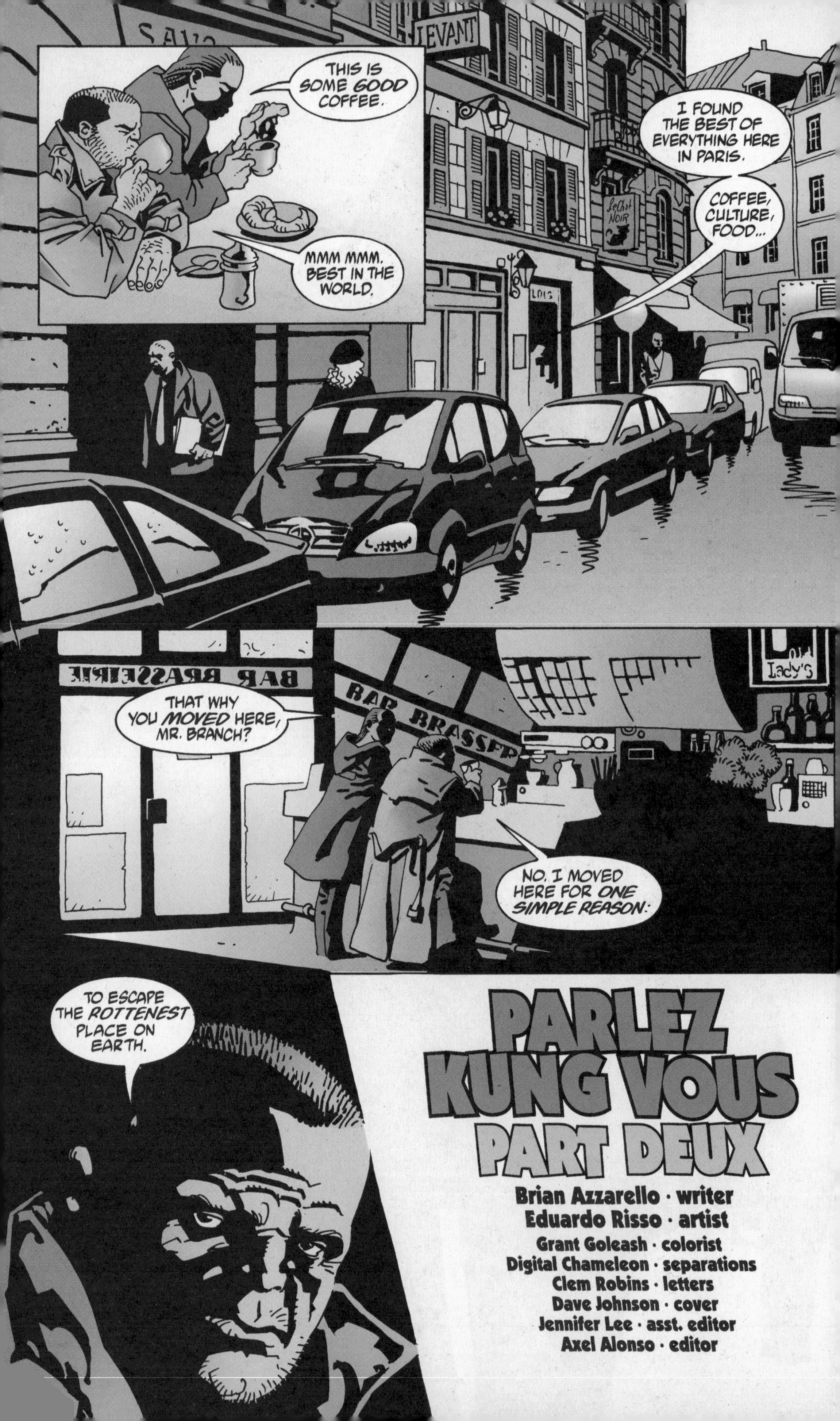
THIS IS SOME GOOD COFFEE.
MMM MMM. BEST IN THE WORLD.
I FOUND THE BEST OF EVERYTHING HERE IN PARIS.
COFFEE, CULTURE, FOOD...
THAT WHY YOU MOVED HERE, MR. BRANCH?
NO. I MOVED HERE FOR ONE SIMPLE REASON:
TO ESCAPE THE ROTTENEST PLACE ON EARTH.
PARLEZ KUNG VOUS PART DEUX
Brian Azzarello · writer
Eduardo Risso · artist
Grant Goleash · colorist
Digital Chameleon · separations
Clem Robins · letters
Dave Johnson · cover
Jennifer Lee · asst. editor
Axel Alonso · editor

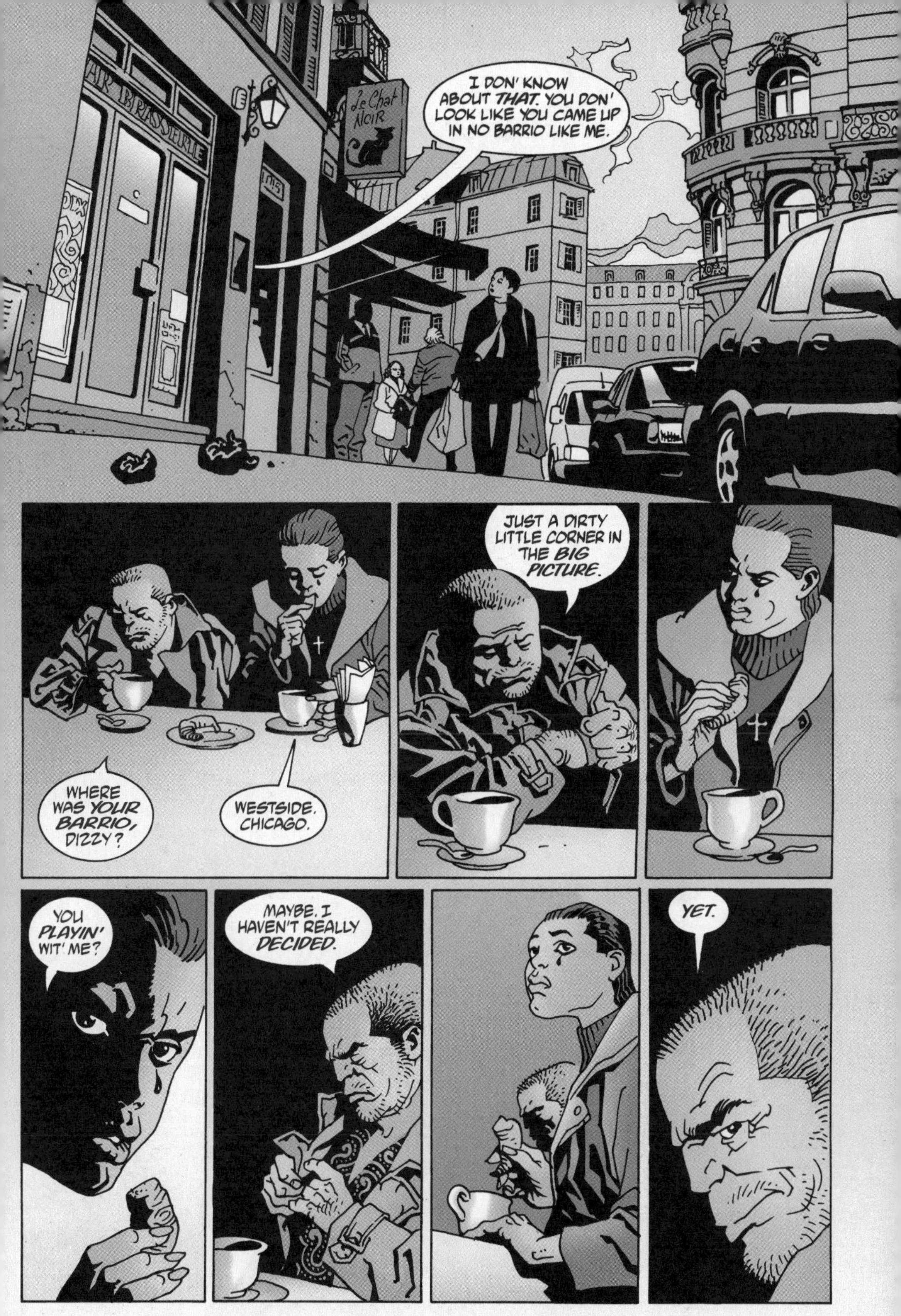

Le Chat Noir
I DON' KNOW ABOUT THAT. YOU DON' LOOK LIKE YOU CAME UP IN NO BARRIO LIKE ME.
WHERE WAS YOUR BARRIO, DIZZY?
WESTSIDE. CHICAGO.
JUST A DIRTY LITTLE CORNER IN THE BIG PICTURE.
YOU PLAYIN' WIT' ME?
MAYBE. I HAVEN'T REALLY DECIDED.
YET.

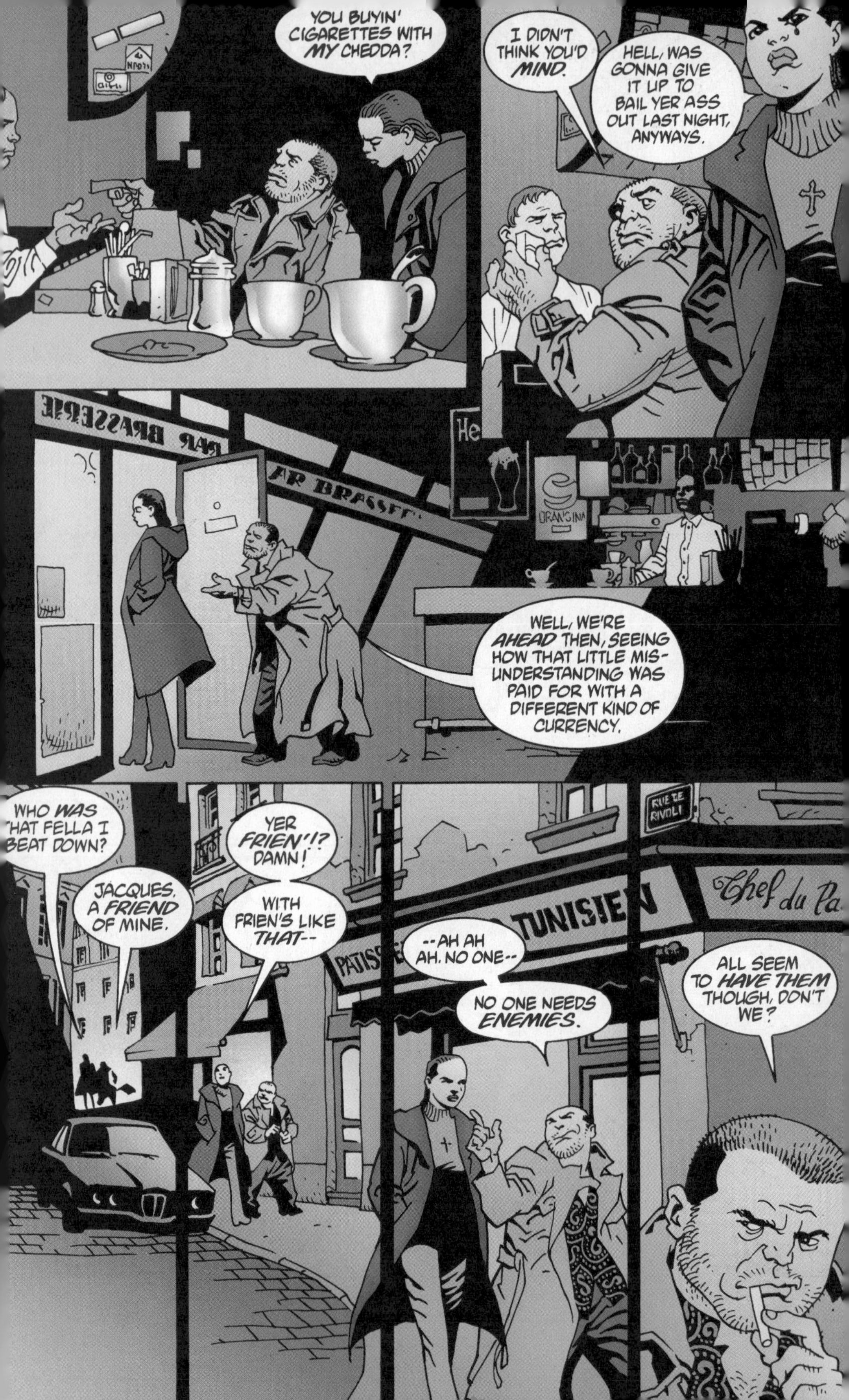

YOU BUYIN' CIGARETTES WITH *MY* CHEDDA?
I DIDN'T THINK YOU'D *MIND.*
HELL, WAS GONNA GIVE IT UP TO BAIL YER ASS OUT LAST NIGHT, ANYWAYS.
ORANGINA
WELL, WE'RE *AHEAD* THEN, SEEING HOW THAT LITTLE MIS-UNDERSTANDING WAS PAID FOR WITH A DIFFERENT KIND OF CURRENCY.
WHO *WAS* THAT FELLA I BEAT DOWN?
JACQUES. A *FRIEND* OF MINE.
YER *FRIEN'!?* DAMN!
WITH FRIEN'S LIKE *THAT*--
--AH AH AH. NO ONE--
NO ONE NEEDS *ENEMIES.*
TUNISIEN
ALL SEEM TO *HAVE THEM* THOUGH, DON'T WE?

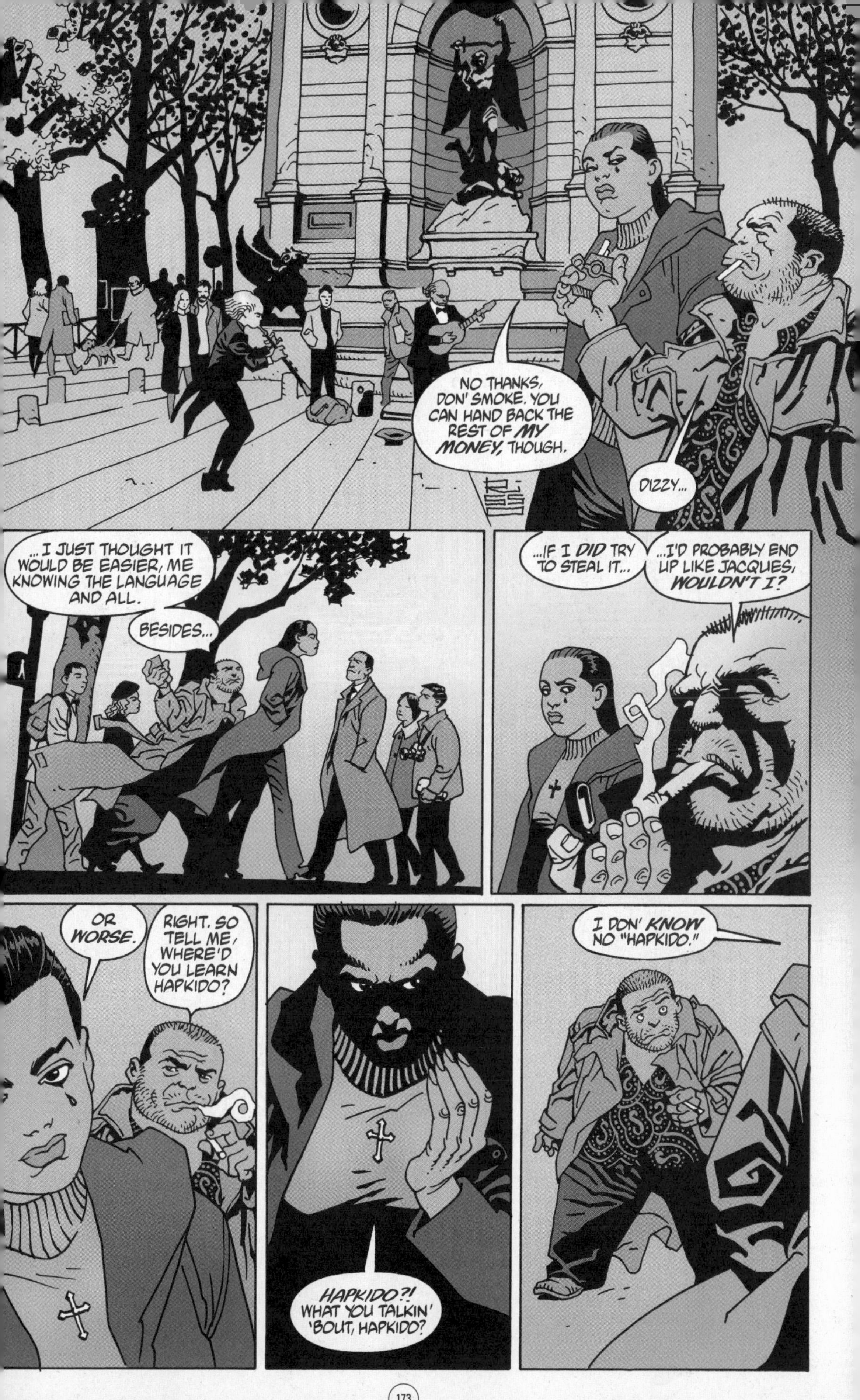
NO THANKS, DON' SMOKE. YOU CAN HAND BACK THE REST OF MY MONEY, THOUGH.
DIZZY...
...I JUST THOUGHT IT WOULD BE EASIER, ME KNOWING THE LANGUAGE AND ALL.
BESIDES...
...IF I DID TRY TO STEAL IT...
...I'D PROBABLY END UP LIKE JACQUES, WOULDN'T I?
OR WORSE.
RIGHT. SO TELL ME, WHERE'D YOU LEARN HAPKIDO?
HAPKIDO?! WHAT YOU TALKIN' 'BOUT, HAPKIDO?
I DON' KNOW NO "HAPKIDO."

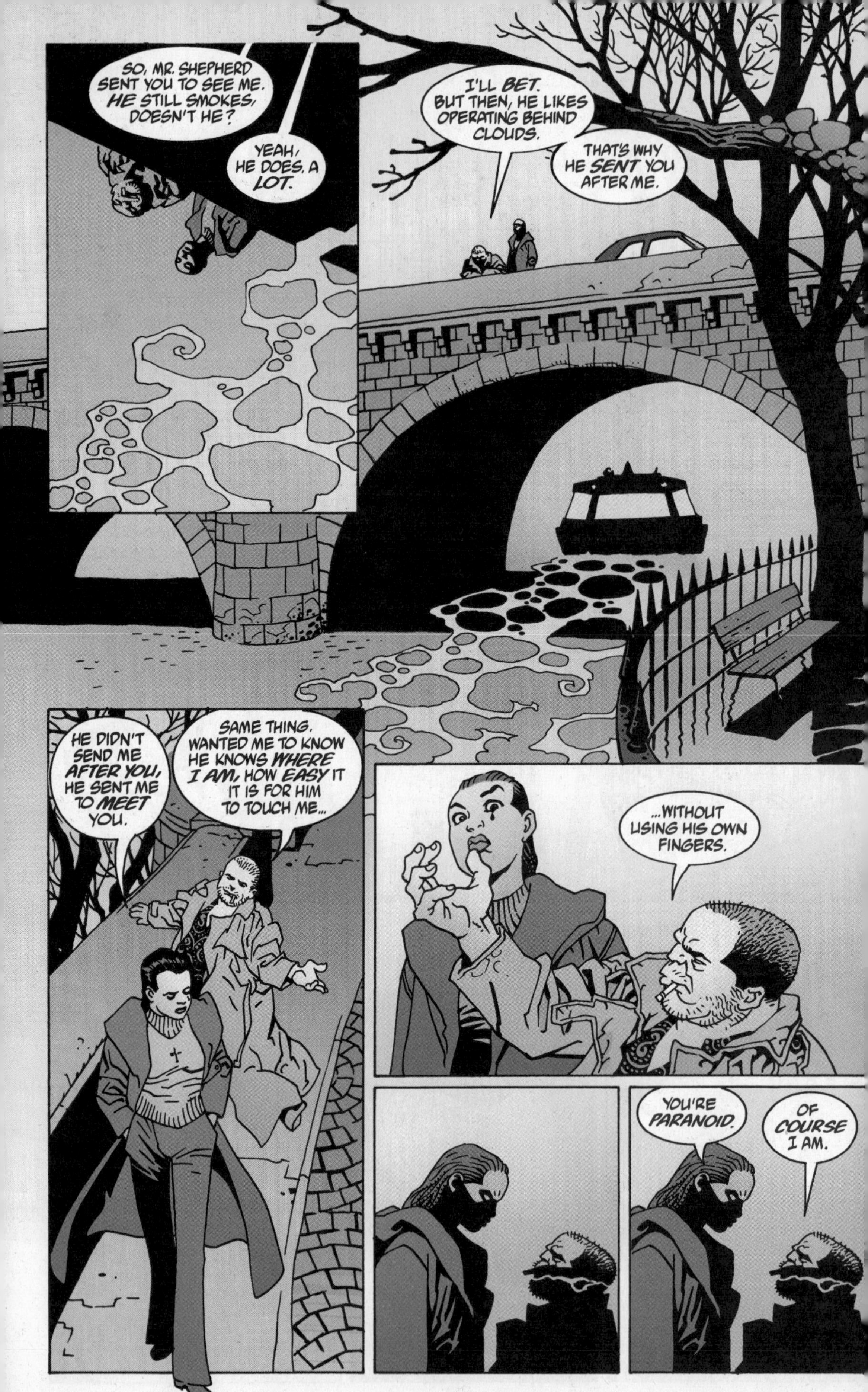

SO, MR. SHEPHERD SENT YOU TO SEE ME. HE STILL SMOKES, DOESN'T HE?
YEAH, HE DOES. A LOT.
I'LL BET. BUT THEN, HE LIKES OPERATING BEHIND CLOUDS.
THAT'S WHY HE SENT YOU AFTER ME.
HE DIDN'T SEND ME AFTER YOU, HE SENT ME TO MEET YOU.
SAME THING. WANTED ME TO KNOW HE KNOWS WHERE I AM, HOW EASY IT IT IS FOR HIM TO TOUCH ME...
...WITHOUT USING HIS OWN FINGERS.
YOU'RE PARANOID.
OF COURSE I AM.

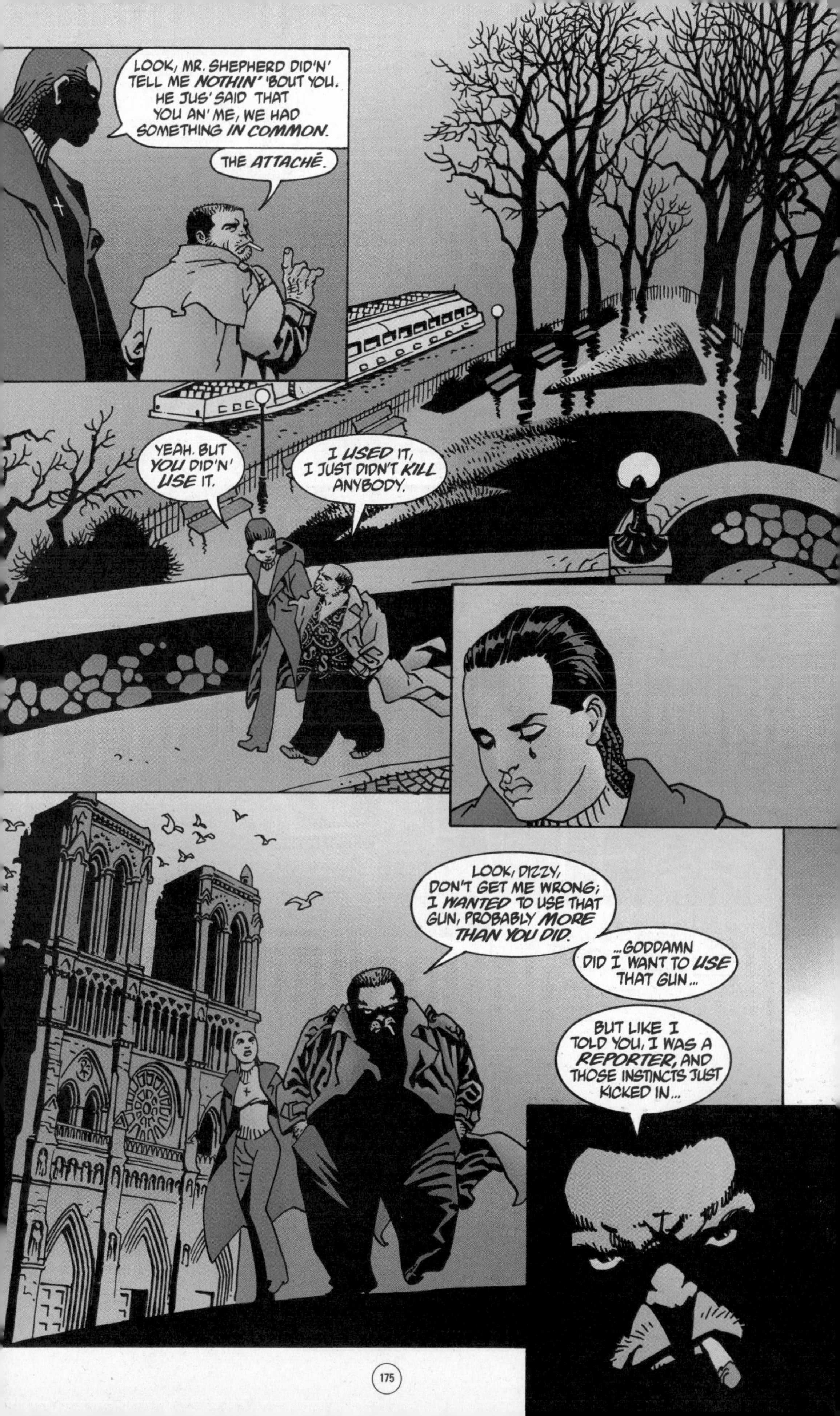
LOOK, MR. SHEPHERD DID'N' TELL ME NOTHIN' 'BOUT YOU. HE JUS' SAID THAT YOU AN' ME, WE HAD SOMETHING IN COMMON.
THE ATTACHÉ.
YEAH. BUT YOU DID'N' USE IT.
I USED IT, I JUST DIDN'T KILL ANYBODY.
LOOK, DIZZY, DON'T GET ME WRONG; I WANTED TO USE THAT GUN, PROBABLY MORE THAN YOU DID.
...GODDAMN DID I WANT TO USE THAT GUN...
BUT LIKE I TOLD YOU, I WAS A REPORTER, AND THOSE INSTINCTS JUST KICKED IN...

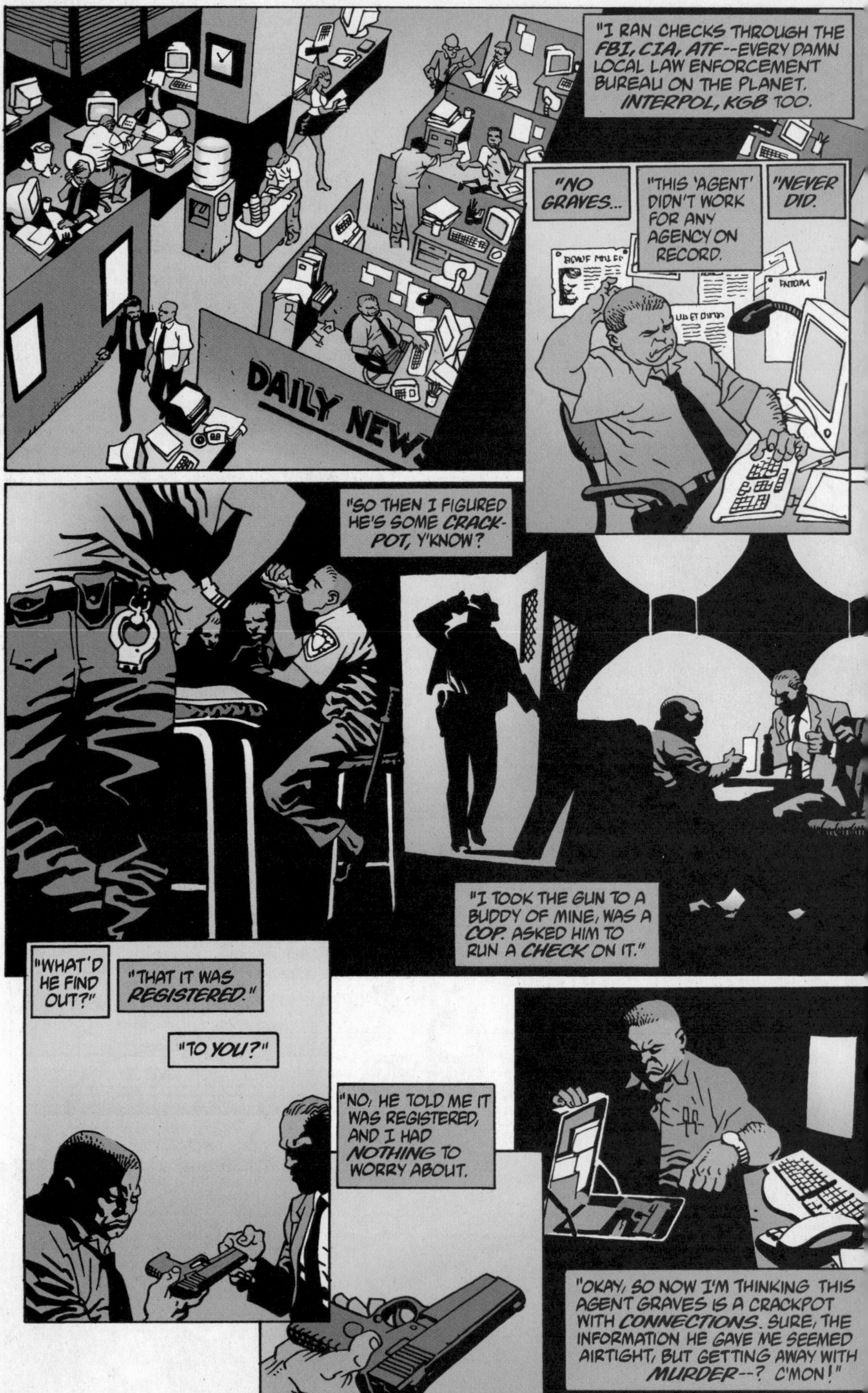

"I RAN CHECKS THROUGH THE FBI, CIA, ATF--EVERY DAMN LOCAL LAW ENFORCEMENT BUREAU ON THE PLANET. INTERPOL, KGB TOO.
DAILY NEWS
"NO GRAVES...
"THIS 'AGENT' DIDN'T WORK FOR ANY AGENCY ON RECORD.
"NEVER DID.
"SO THEN I FIGURED HE'S SOME CRACK-POT, Y'KNOW?
"I TOOK THE GUN TO A BUDDY OF MINE, WAS A COP. ASKED HIM TO RUN A CHECK ON IT."
"WHAT'D HE FIND OUT?"
"THAT IT WAS REGISTERED."
"TO YOU?"
"NO, HE TOLD ME IT WAS REGISTERED, AND I HAD NOTHING TO WORRY ABOUT.
"OKAY, SO NOW I'M THINKING THIS AGENT GRAVES IS A CRACKPOT WITH CONNECTIONS. SURE, THE INFORMATION HE GAVE ME SEEMED AIRTIGHT, BUT GETTING AWAY WITH MURDER--? C'MON!"

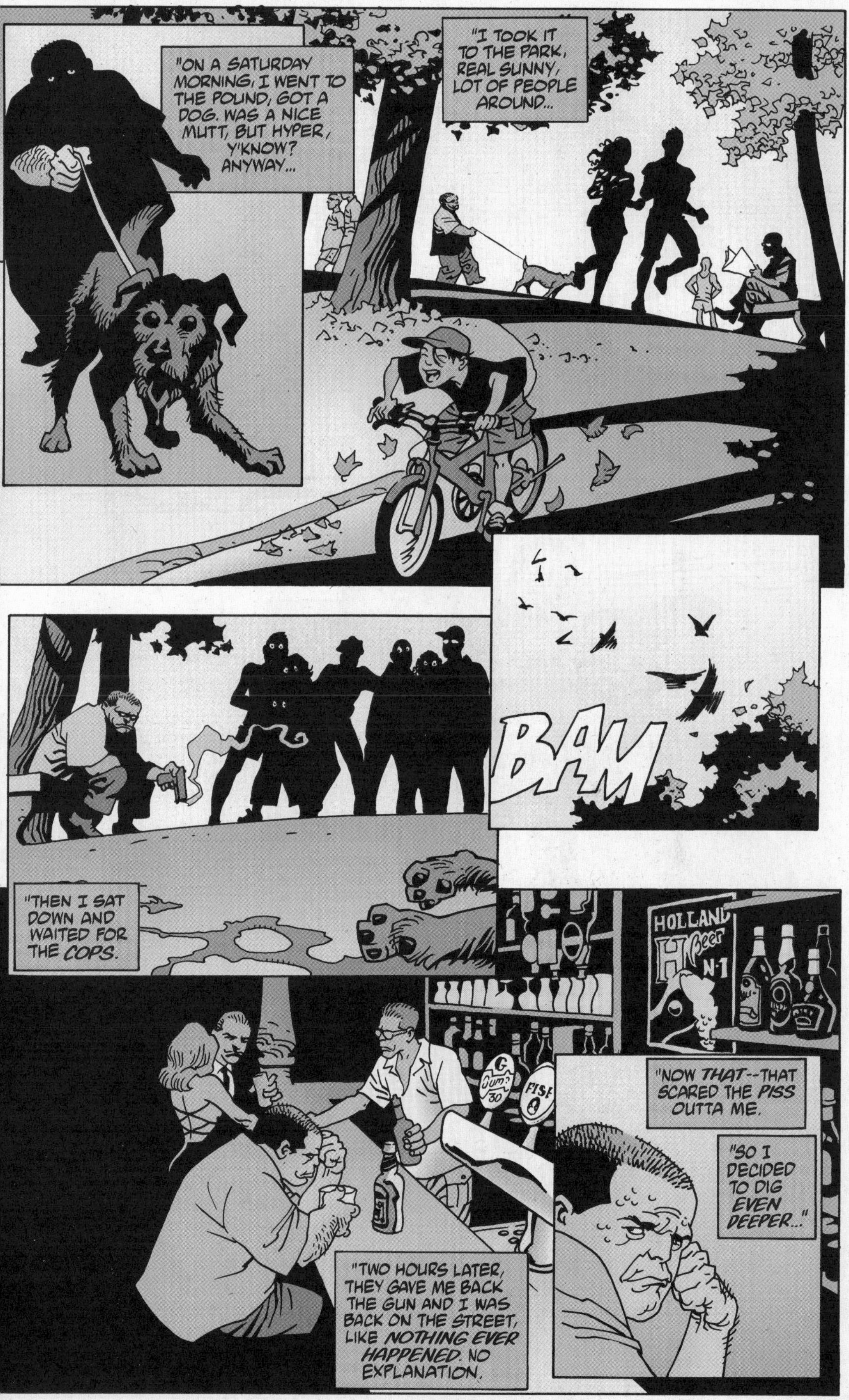

"ON A SATURDAY MORNING, I WENT TO THE POUND, GOT A DOG. WAS A NICE MUTT, BUT HYPER, Y'KNOW? ANYWAY...
"I TOOK IT TO THE PARK, REAL SUNNY, LOT OF PEOPLE AROUND...
BAM
"THEN I SAT DOWN AND WAITED FOR THE *COPS*.
HOLLAND
Beer
N-1
"NOW *THAT*--THAT SCARED THE *PISS* OUTTA ME.
"SO I DECIDED TO DIG *EVEN DEEPER*..."
"TWO HOURS LATER, THEY GAVE ME BACK THE GUN AND I WAS BACK ON THE STREET, LIKE *NOTHING EVER HAPPENED*. NO EXPLANATION.

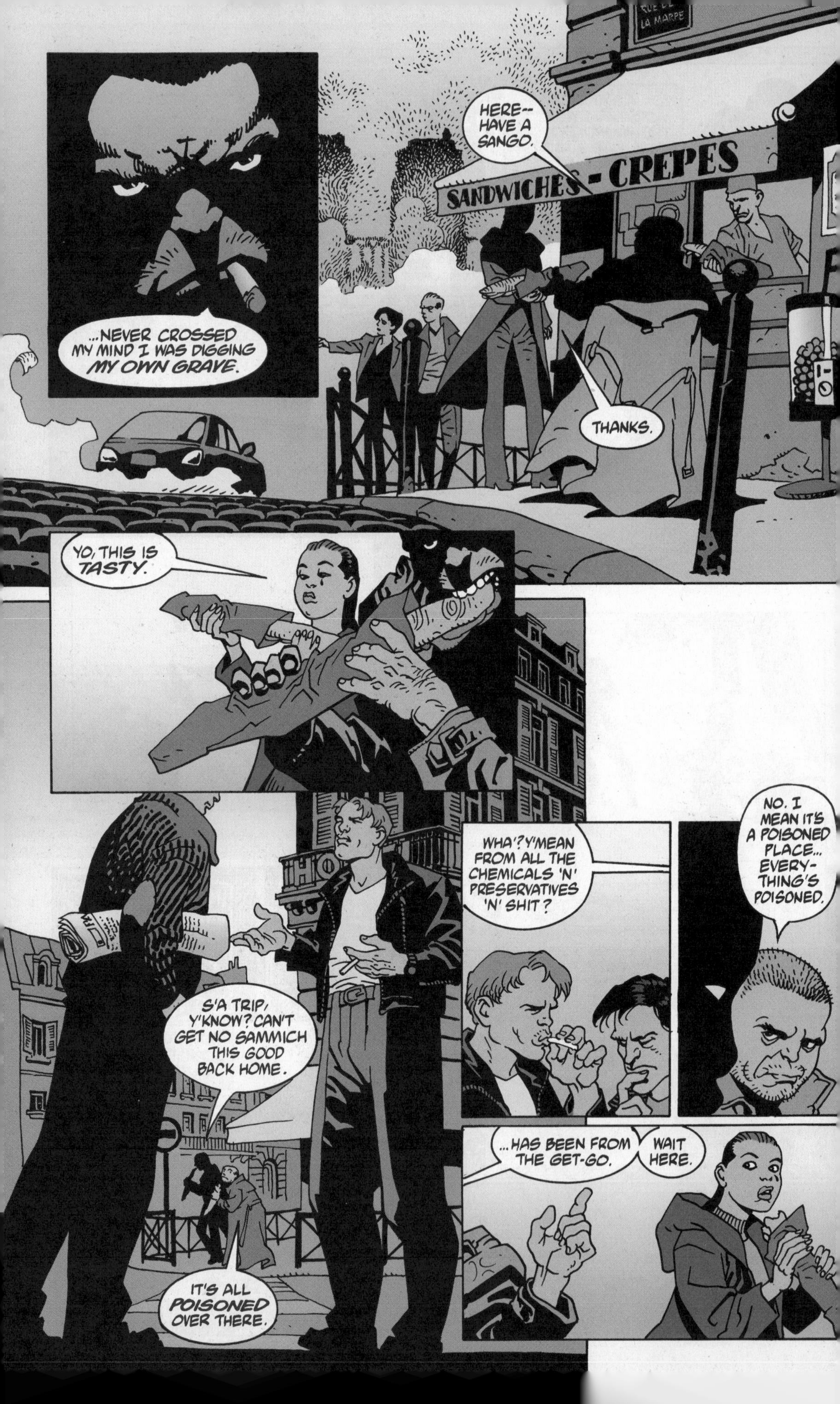
QUE DE
LA HARPE
...NEVER CROSSED MY MIND I WAS DIGGING MY OWN GRAVE.
HERE-- HAVE A SANGO.
SANDWICHES - CREPES
THANKS.
YO, THIS IS TASTY.
S'A TRIP, Y'KNOW? CAN'T GET NO SAMMICH THIS GOOD BACK HOME.
IT'S ALL POISONED OVER THERE.
WHA'? Y'MEAN FROM ALL THE CHEMICALS 'N' PRESERVATIVES 'N' SHIT?
NO. I MEAN IT'S A POISONED PLACE... EVERY-THING'S POISONED.
...HAS BEEN FROM THE GET-GO.
WAIT HERE.

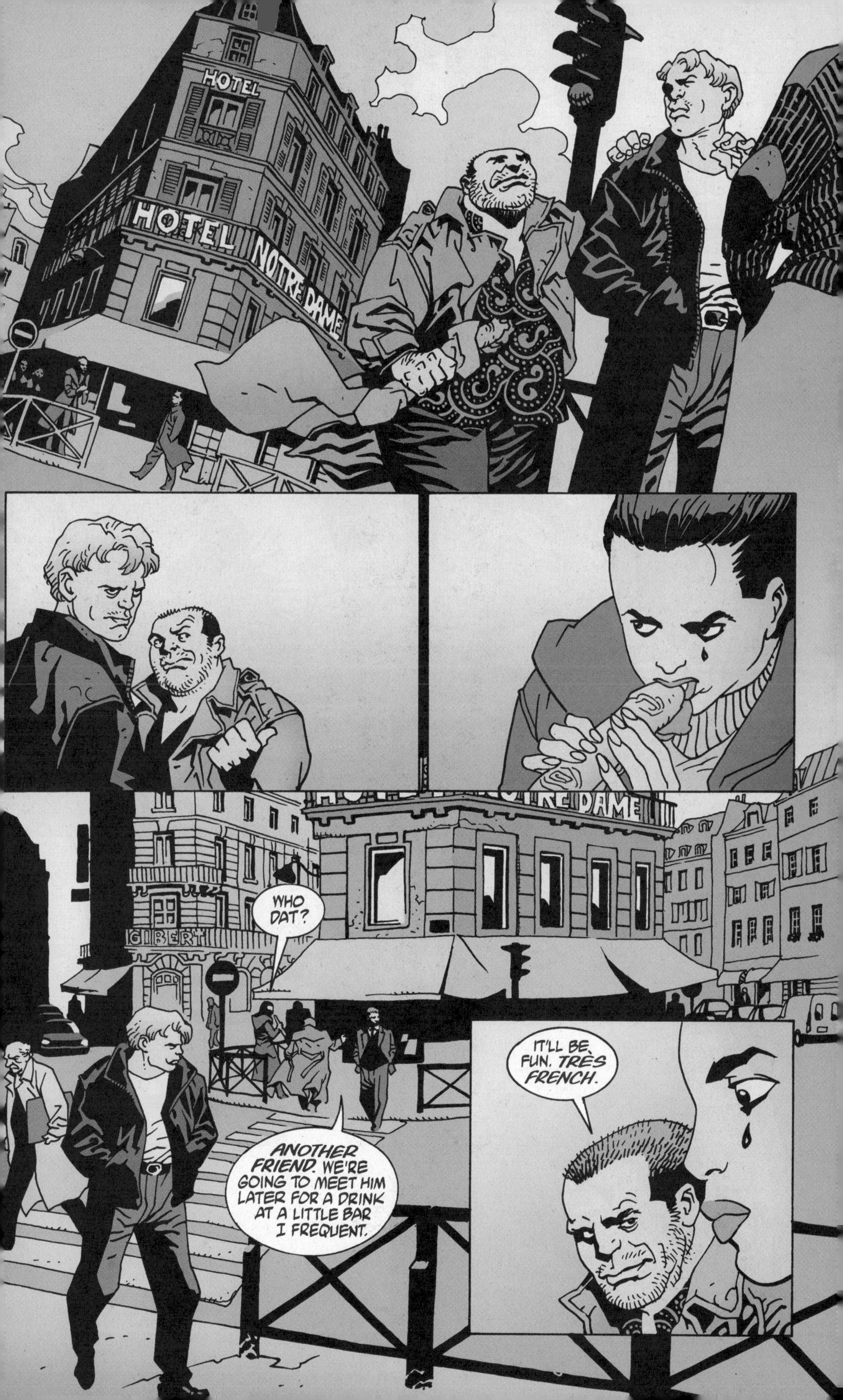
HOTEL
HOTEL NOTRE DAME
GIBERT
WHO DAT?
ANOTHER FRIEND. WE'RE GOING TO MEET HIM LATER FOR A DRINK AT A LITTLE BAR I FREQUENT.
IT'LL BE FUN. TRÈS FRENCH.

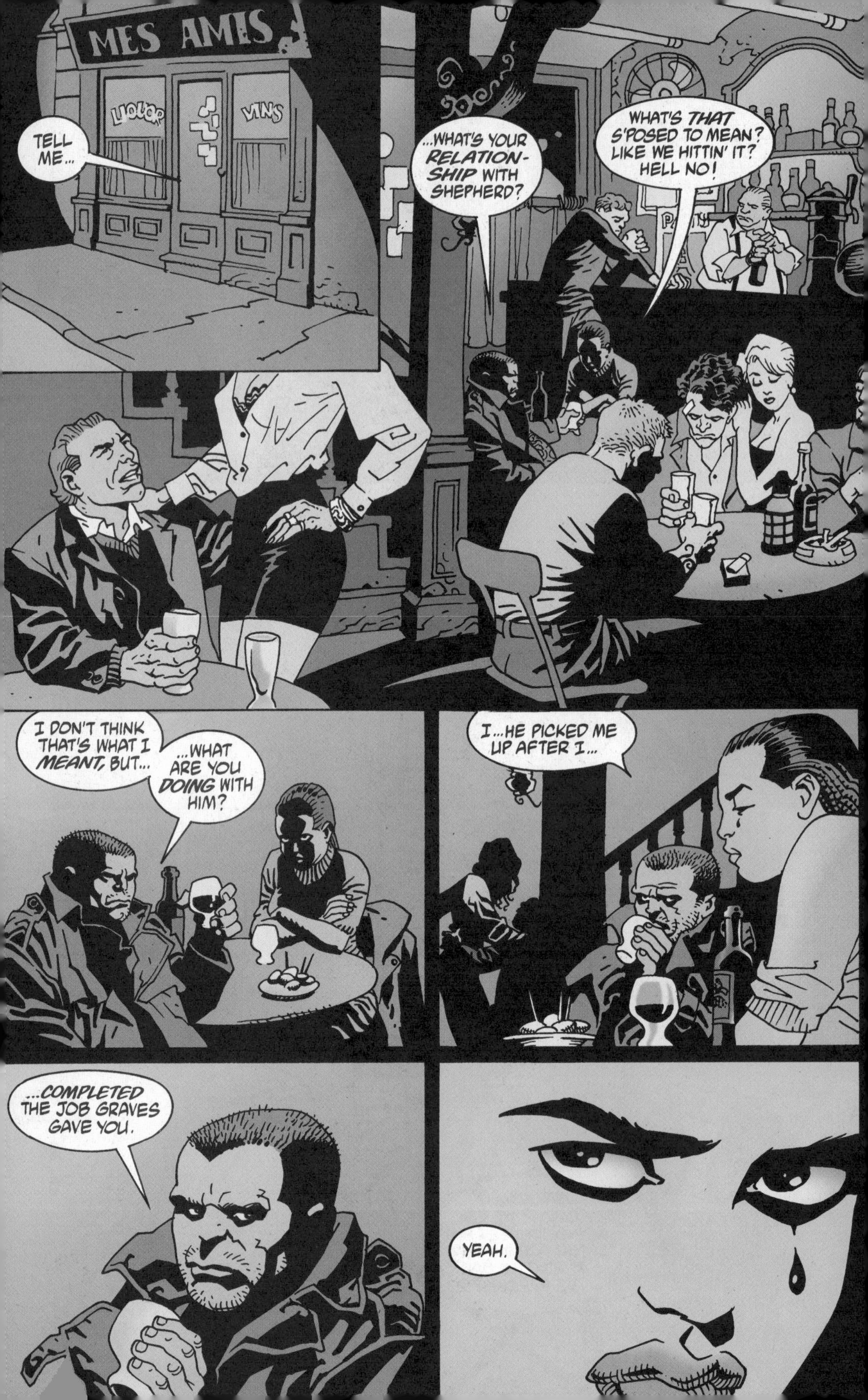

MES AMIS
LIQUEUR
VINS
TELL ME...
...WHAT'S YOUR RELATIONSHIP WITH SHEPHERD?
WHAT'S THAT S'POSED TO MEAN? LIKE WE HITTIN' IT? HELL NO!
I DON'T THINK THAT'S WHAT I MEANT, BUT...
...WHAT ARE YOU DOING WITH HIM?
I...HE PICKED ME UP AFTER I...
...COMPLETED THE JOB GRAVES GAVE YOU.
YEAH.

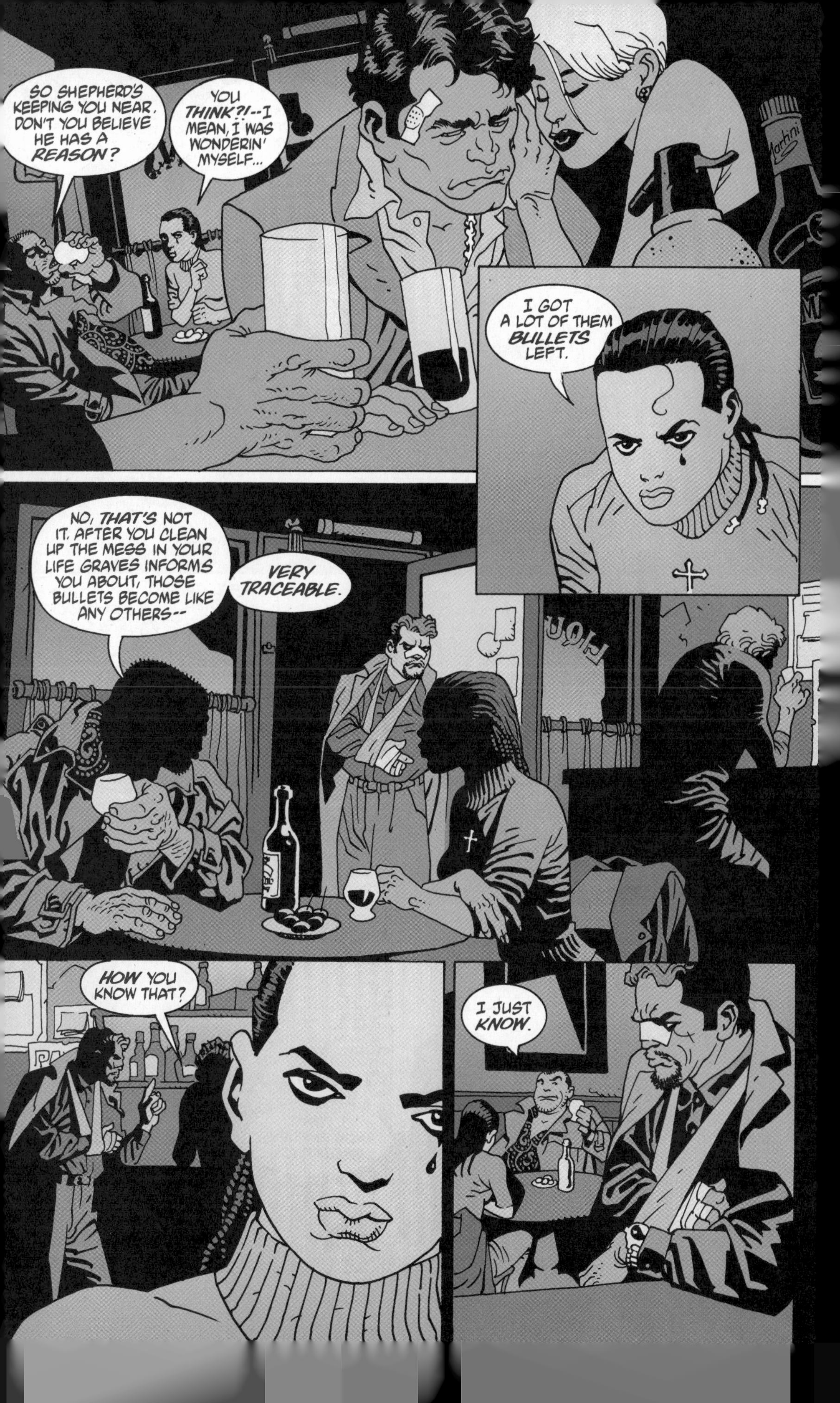
SO SHEPHERD'S KEEPING YOU NEAR. DON'T YOU BELIEVE HE HAS A REASON?
YOU THINK?!--I MEAN, I WAS WONDERIN' MYSELF...
I GOT A LOT OF THEM BULLETS LEFT.
NO, THAT'S NOT IT. AFTER YOU CLEAN UP THE MESS IN YOUR LIFE GRAVES INFORMS YOU ABOUT, THOSE BULLETS BECOME LIKE ANY OTHERS--
VERY TRACEABLE.
HOW YOU KNOW THAT?
I JUST KNOW.

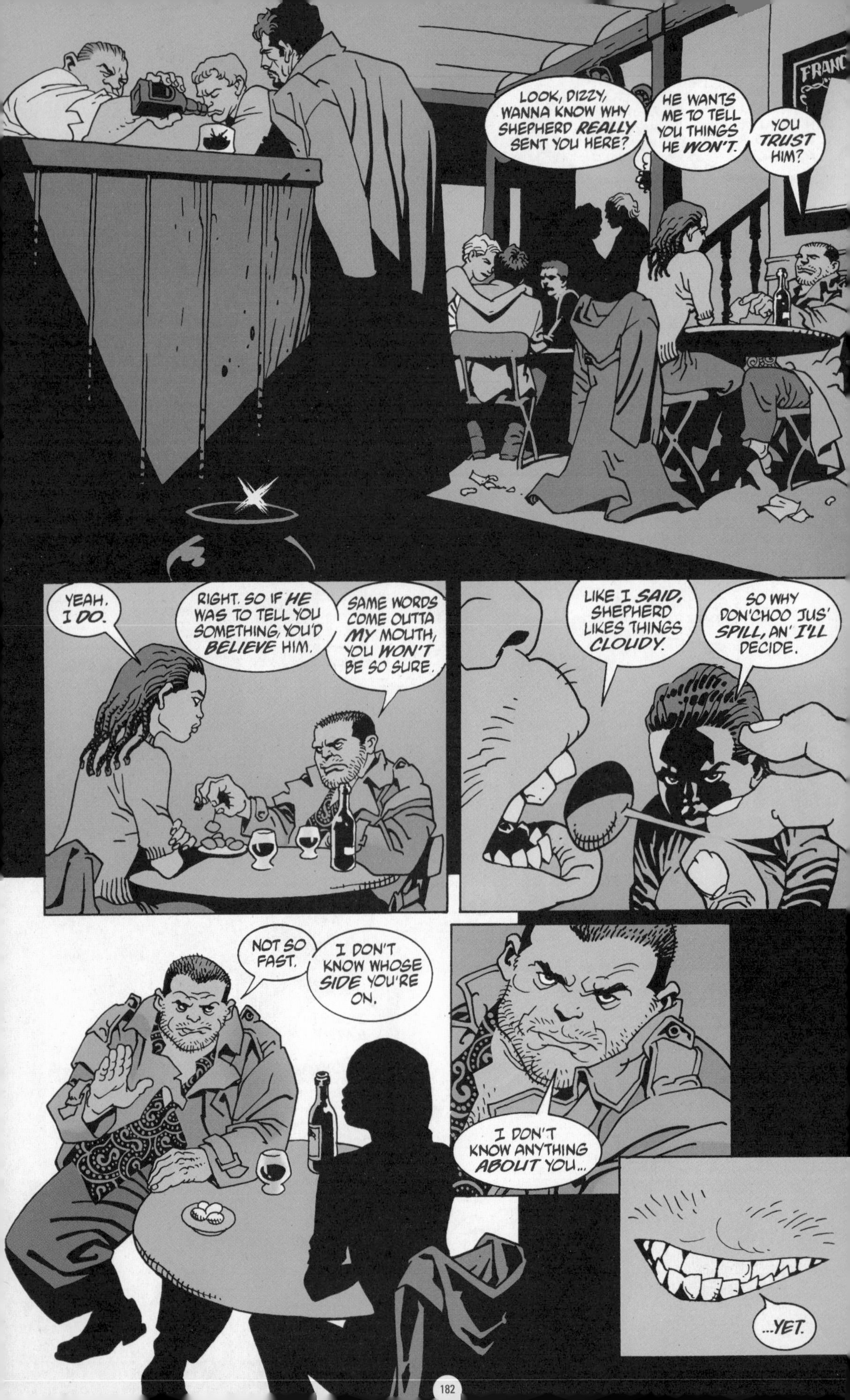

FRANC
LOOK, DIZZY, WANNA KNOW WHY SHEPHERD REALLY SENT YOU HERE?
HE WANTS ME TO TELL YOU THINGS HE WON'T.
YOU TRUST HIM?
YEAH. I DO.
RIGHT. SO IF HE WAS TO TELL YOU SOMETHING, YOU'D BELIEVE HIM.
SAME WORDS COME OUTTA MY MOUTH, YOU WON'T BE SO SURE.
LIKE I SAID, SHEPHERD LIKES THINGS CLOUDY.
SO WHY DON'CHOO JUS' SPILL, AN' I'LL DECIDE.
NOT SO FAST.
I DON'T KNOW WHOSE SIDE YOU'RE ON.
I DON'T KNOW ANYTHING ABOUT YOU...
...YET.

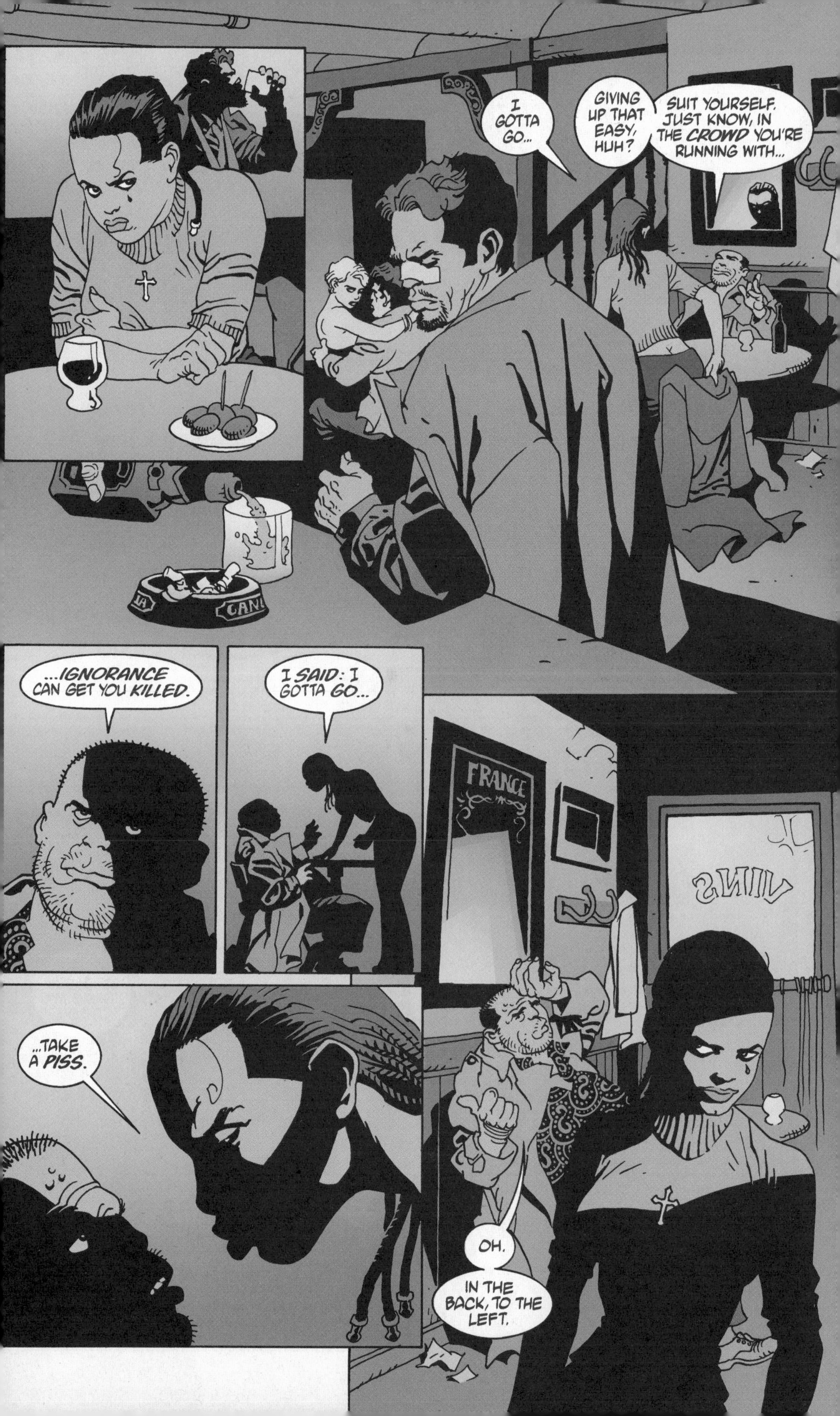
I GOTTA GO...
GIVING UP THAT EASY, HUH?
SUIT YOURSELF. JUST KNOW, IN THE CROWD YOU'RE RUNNING WITH...
...IGNORANCE CAN GET YOU KILLED.
I SAID: I GOTTA GO...
FRANCE
VINS
...TAKE A PISS.
OH.
IN THE BACK, TO THE LEFT.

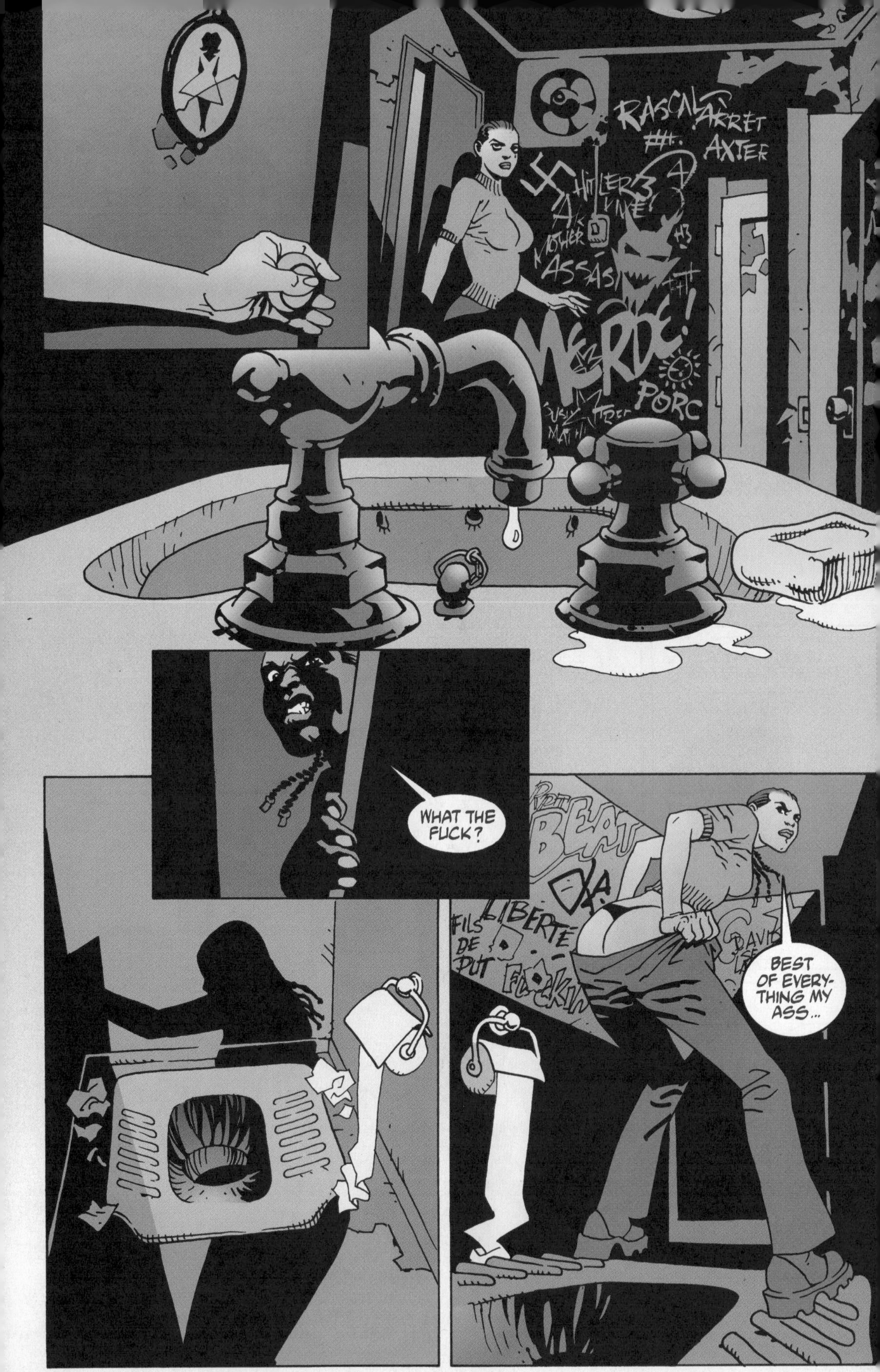
WHAT THE FUCK?
BEST OF EVERYTHING MY ASS...

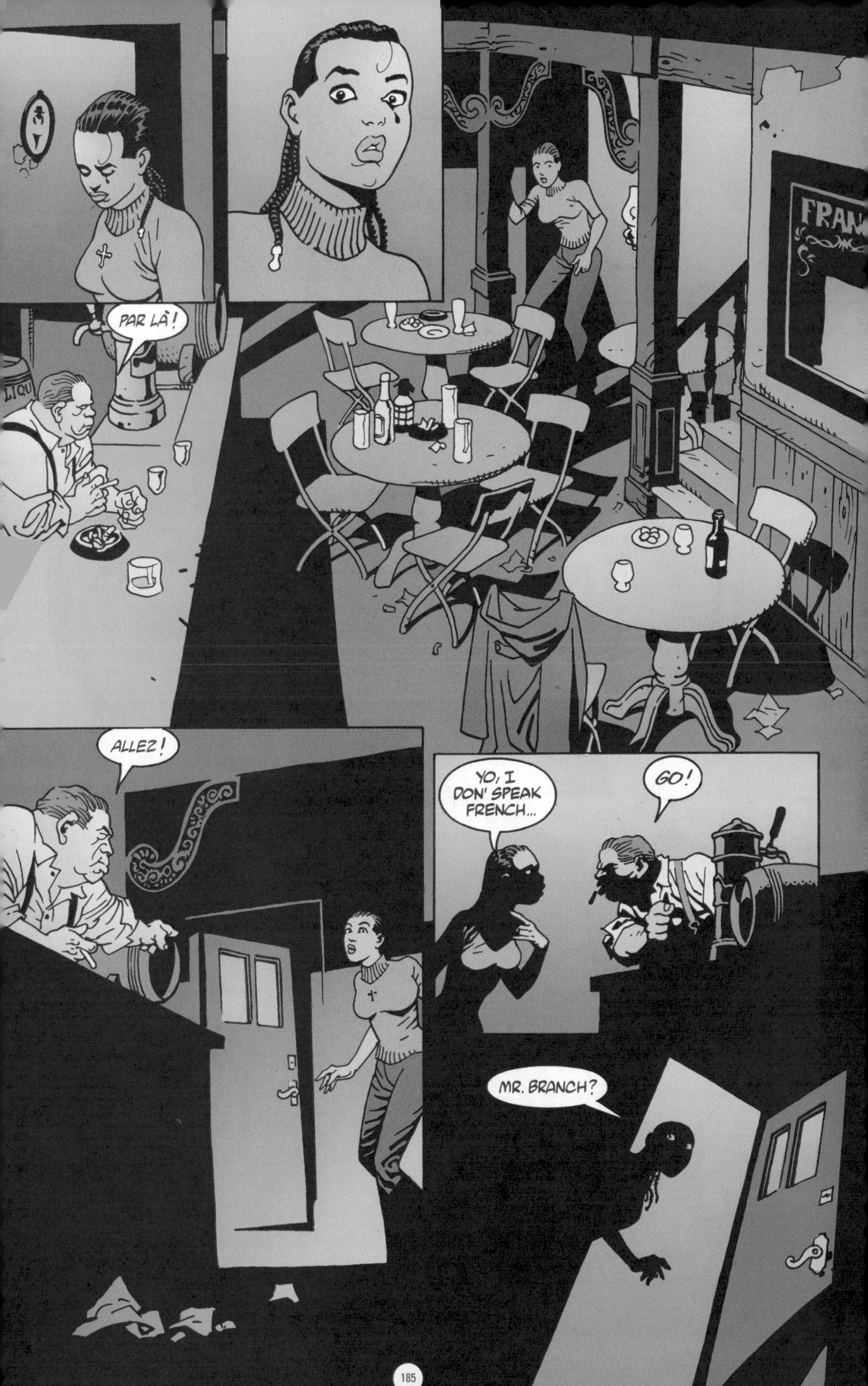
PAR LÀ!
FRAN
ALLEZ!
YO, I DON' SPEAK FRENCH...
GO!
MR. BRANCH?

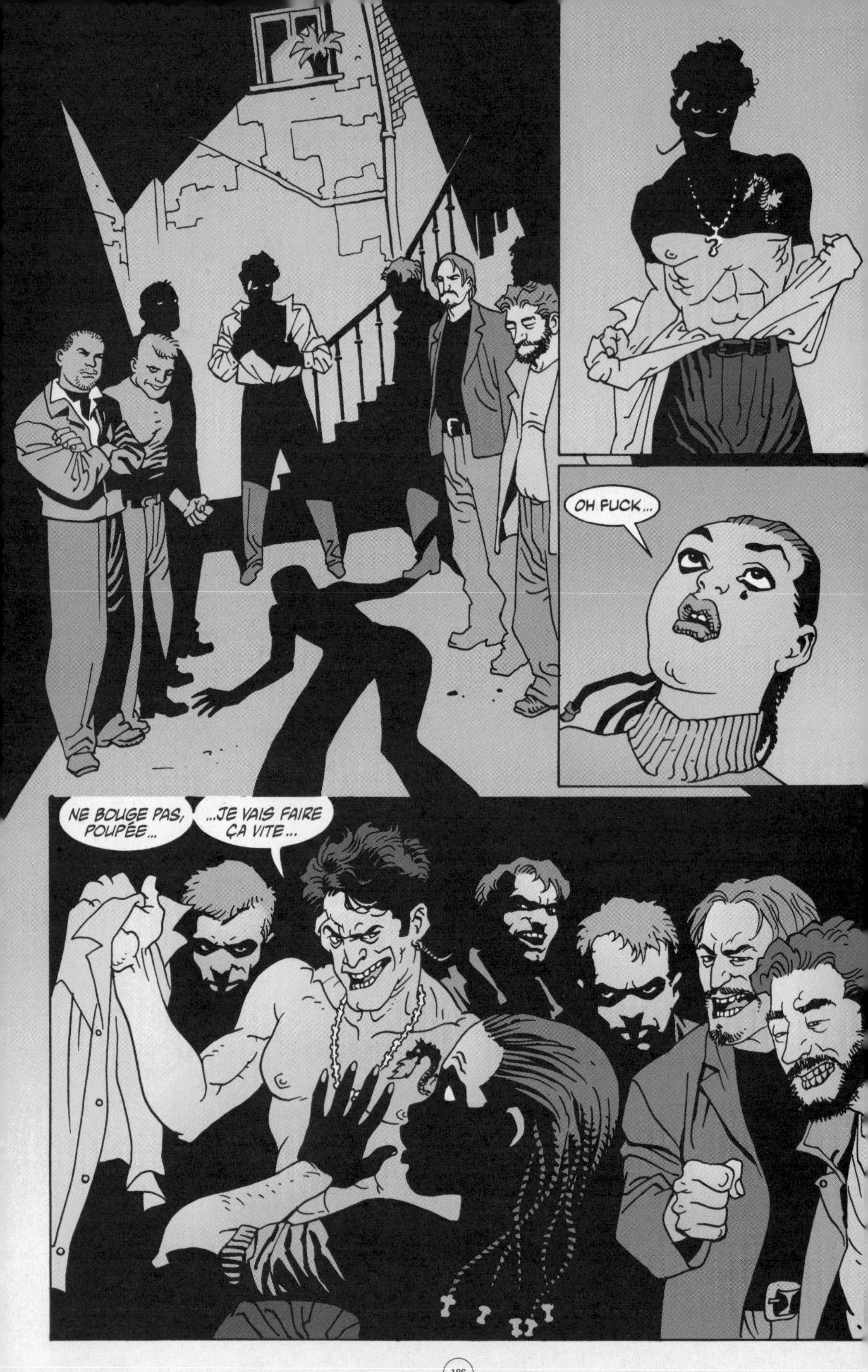
OH FUCK...
NE BOUGE PAS, POUPÉE...
...JE VAIS FAIRE ÇA VITE...

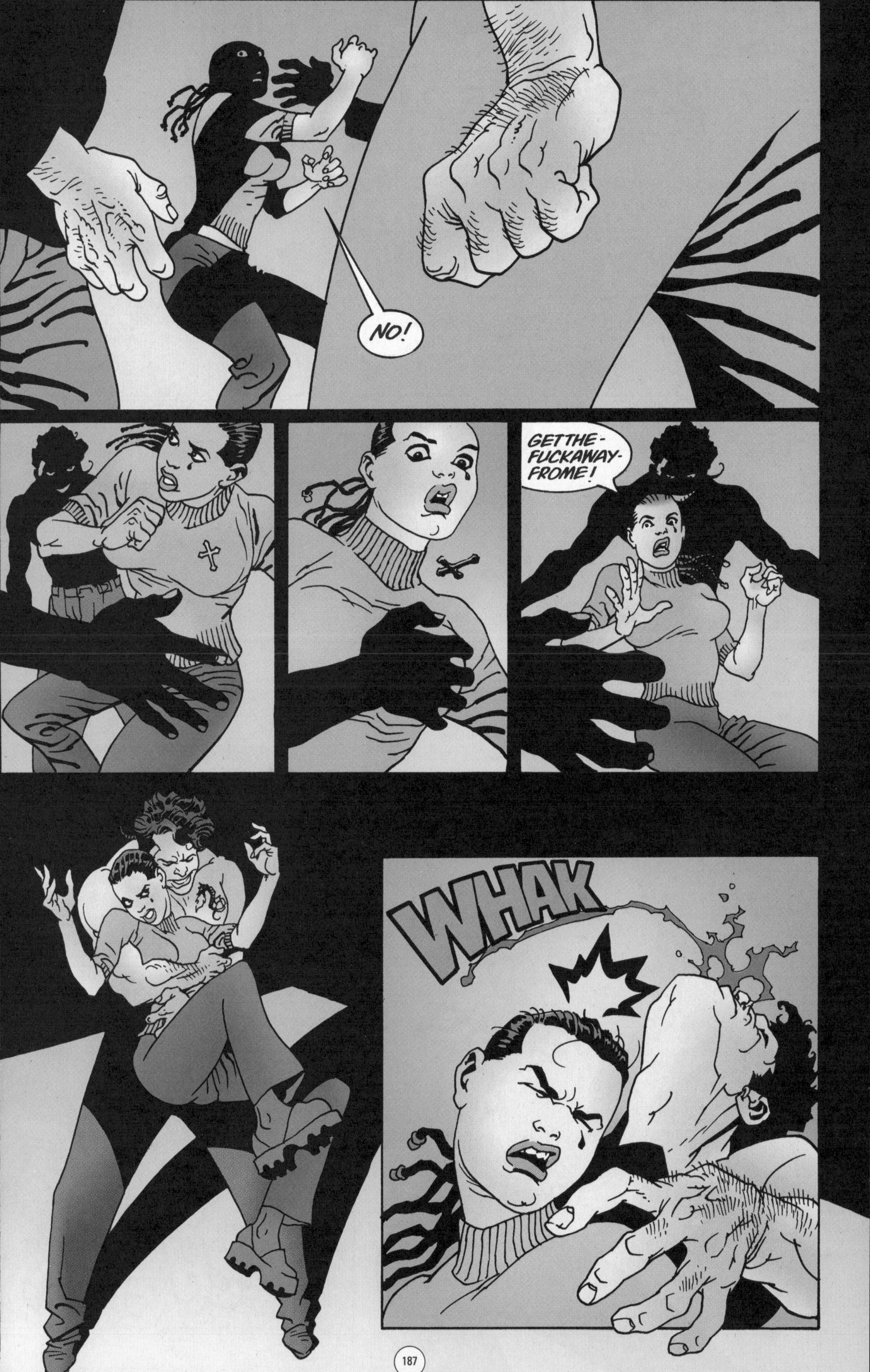
NO!
GET THE-FUCKAWAY-FROME!
WHAK

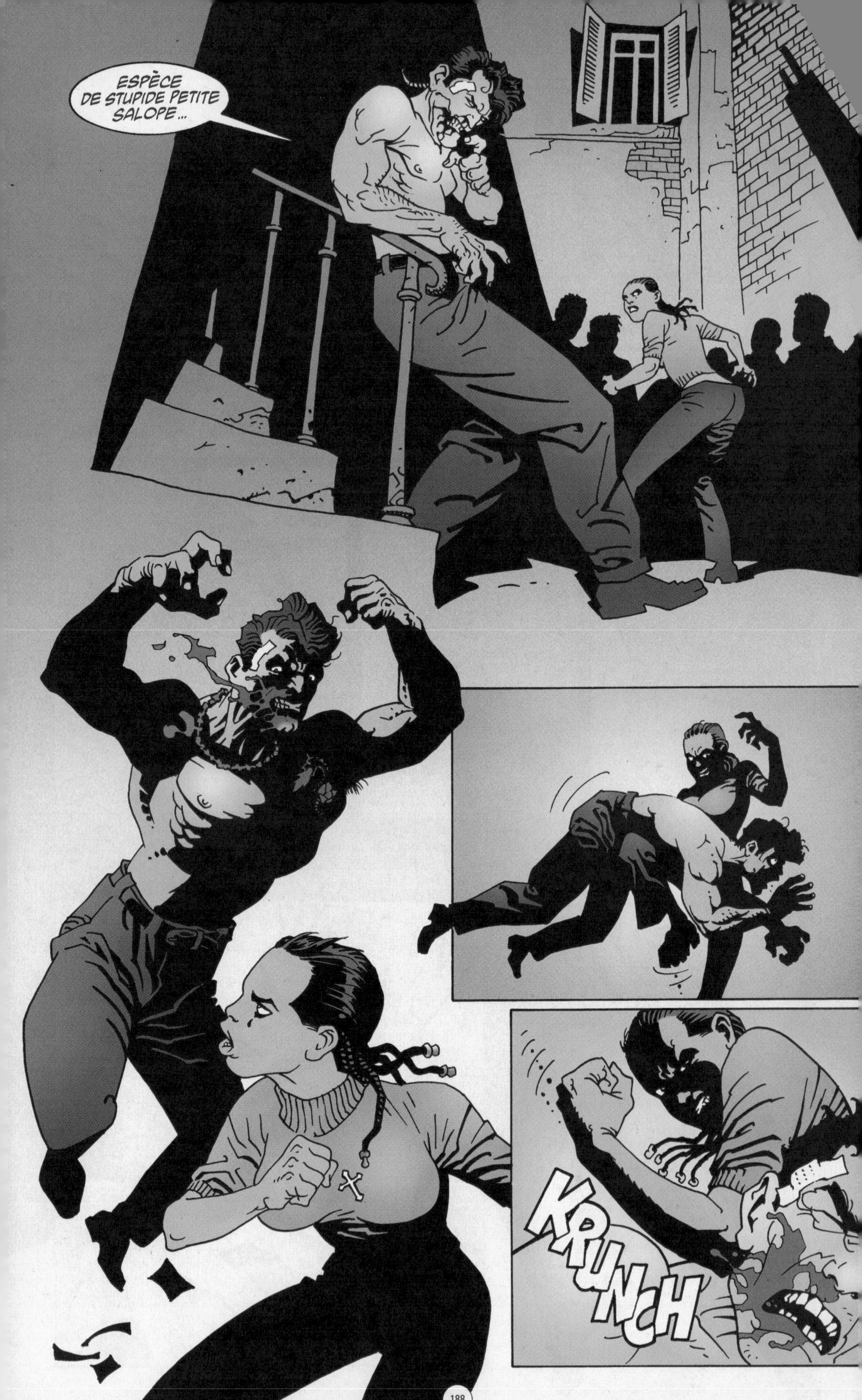
ESPÈCE DE STUPIDE PETITE SALOPE...
KRUNCH

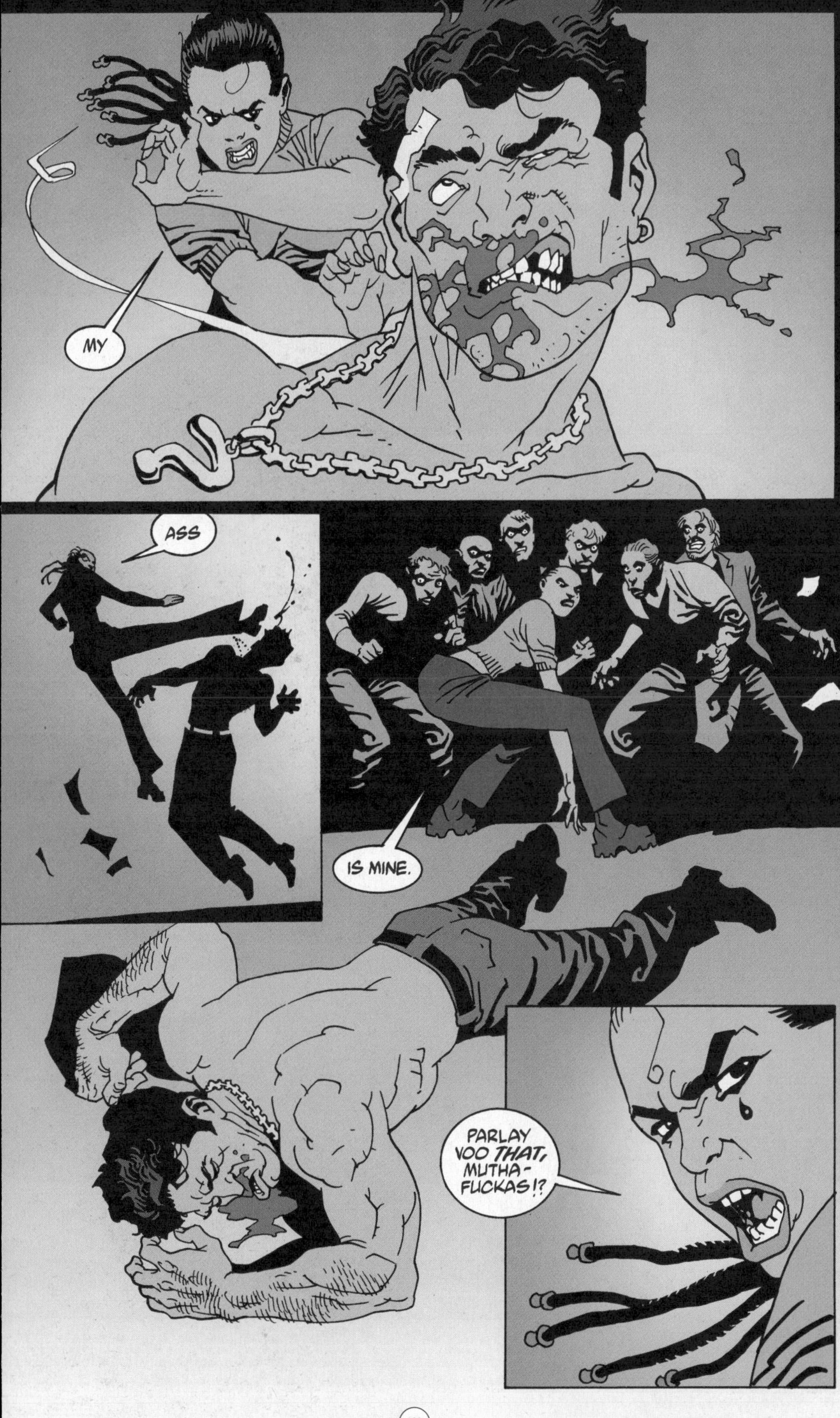
MY
ASS
IS MINE.
PARLAY VOO *THAT*, MUTHA-FUCKAS!?

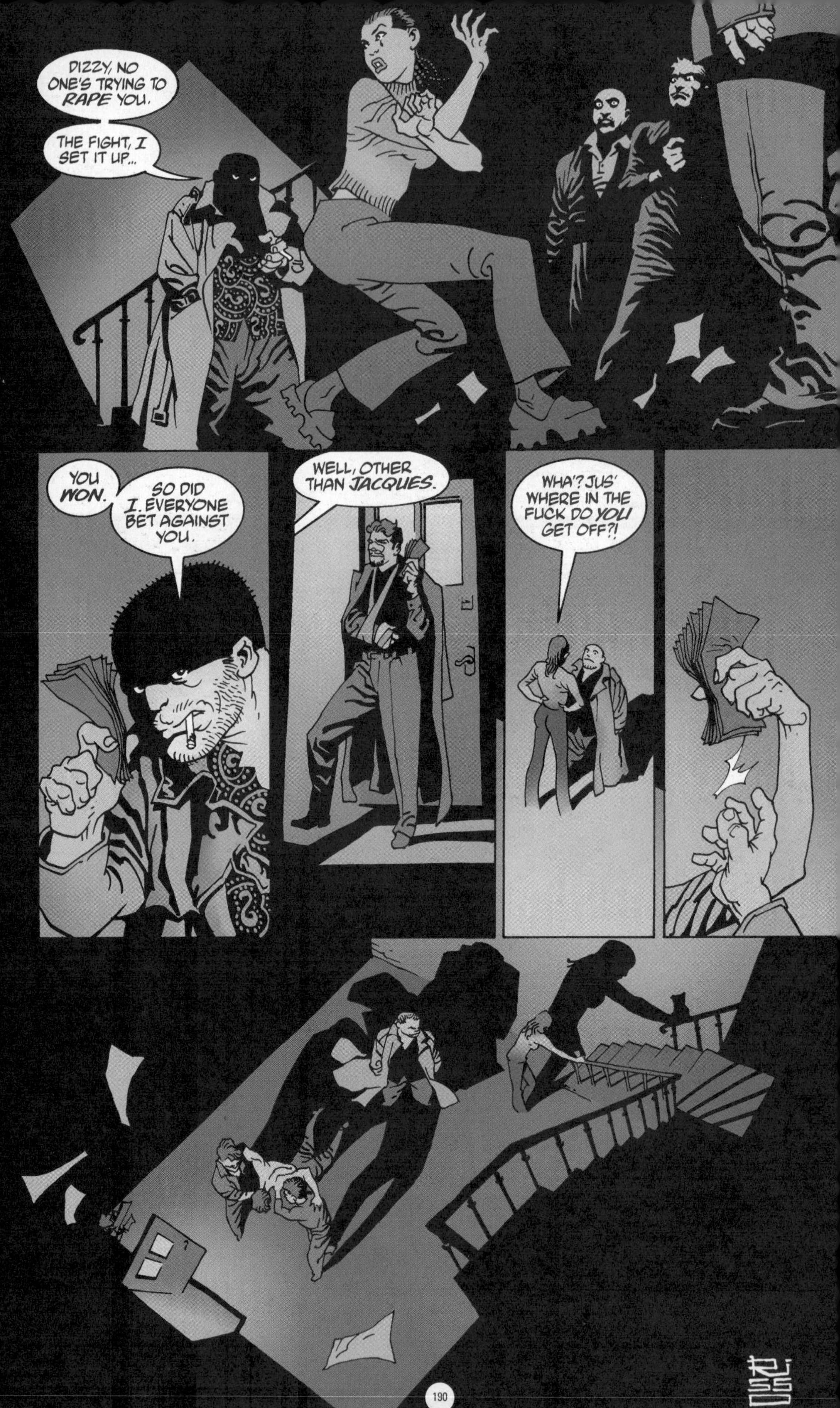
DIZZY, NO ONE'S TRYING TO RAPE YOU.
THE FIGHT, I SET IT UP...
YOU WON.
SO DID I. EVERYONE BET AGAINST YOU.
WELL, OTHER THAN JACQUES.
WHA'? JUS' WHERE IN THE FUCK DO YOU GET OFF?!
RISSO

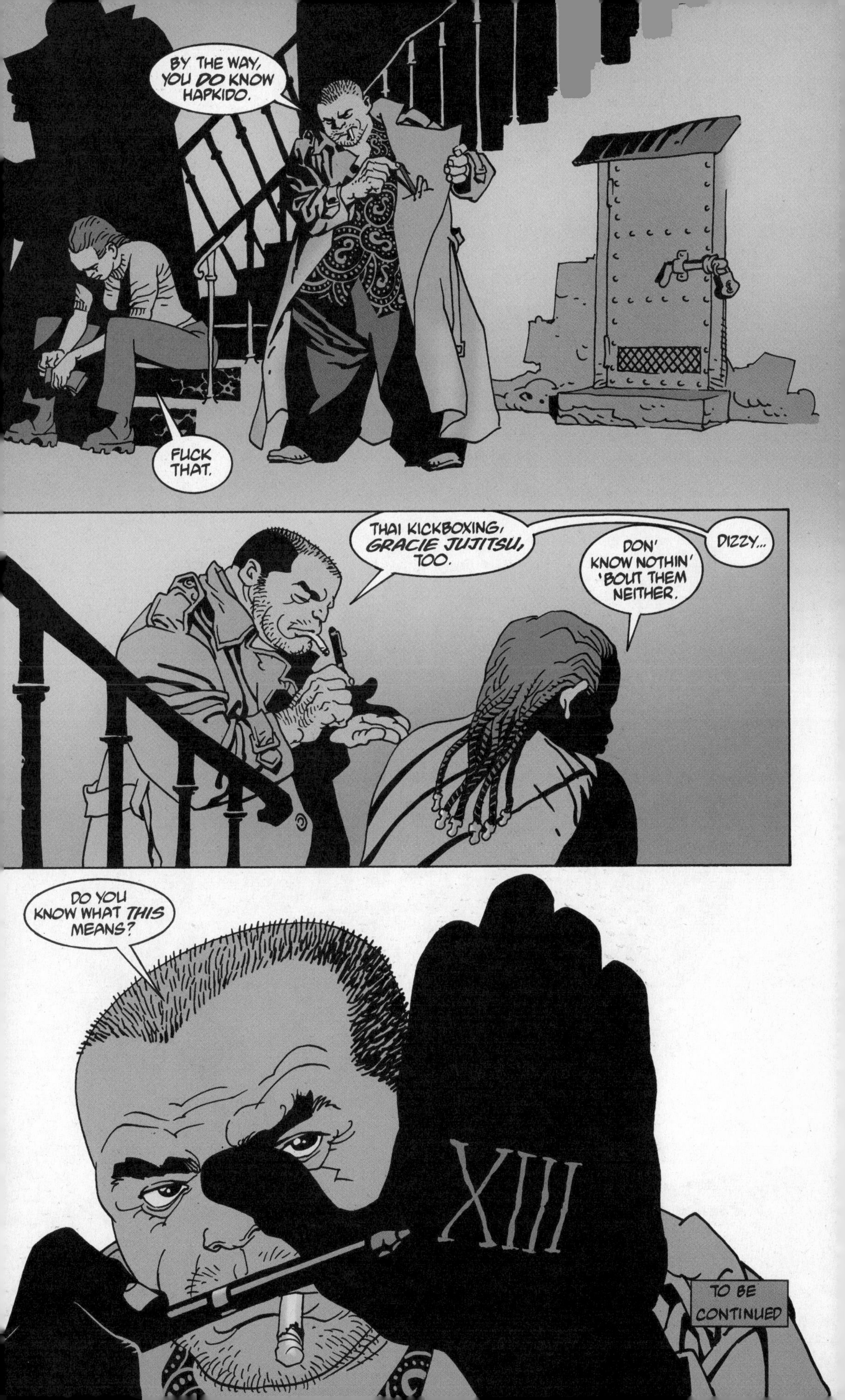
BY THE WAY, YOU *DO* KNOW HAPKIDO.
FUCK THAT.
THAI KICKBOXING, *GRACIE JUJITSU*, TOO.
DON' KNOW NOTHIN' 'BOUT THEM NEITHER.
DIZZY...
DO YOU KNOW WHAT *THIS* MEANS?
XIII
TO BE CONTINUED

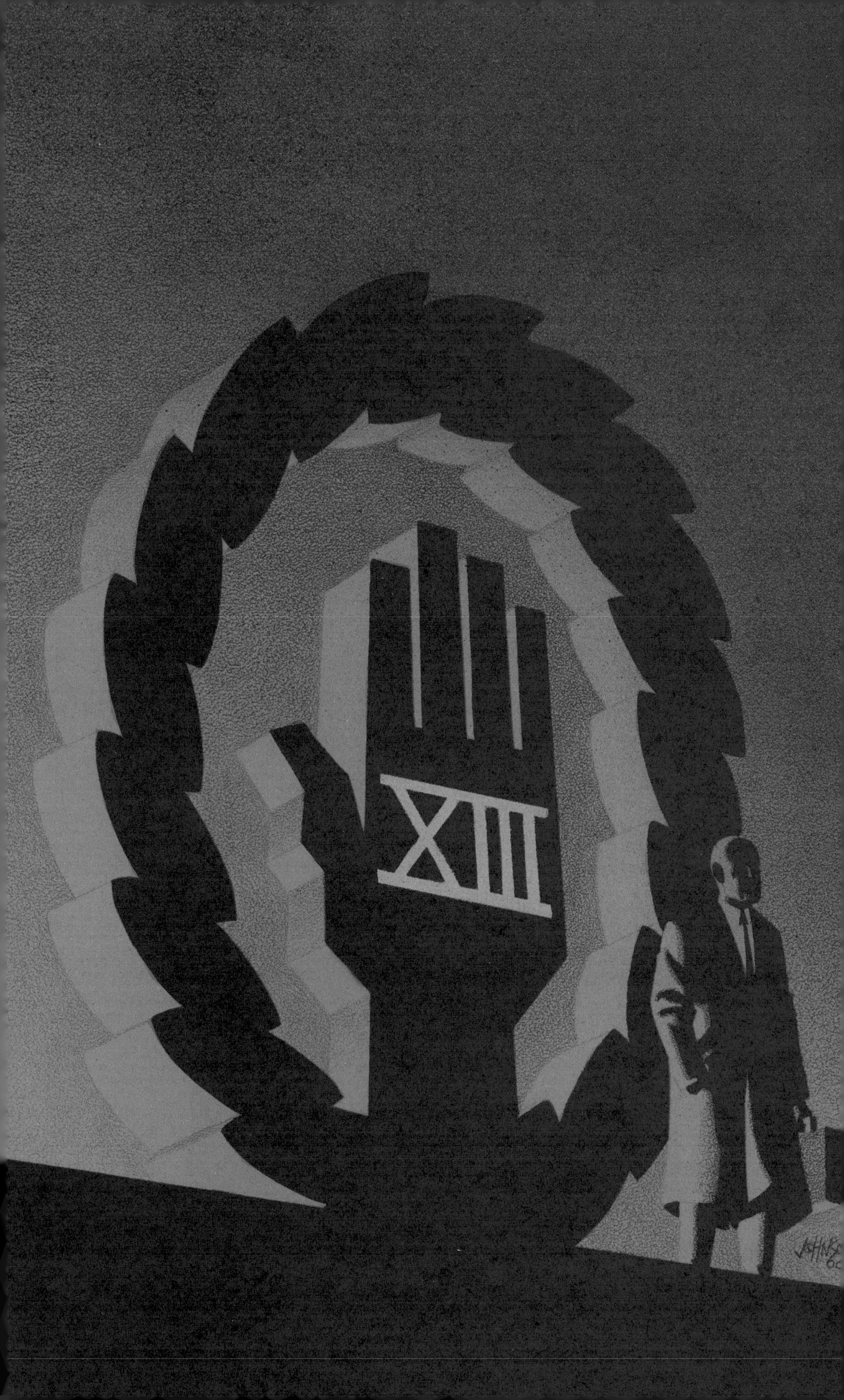
XIII

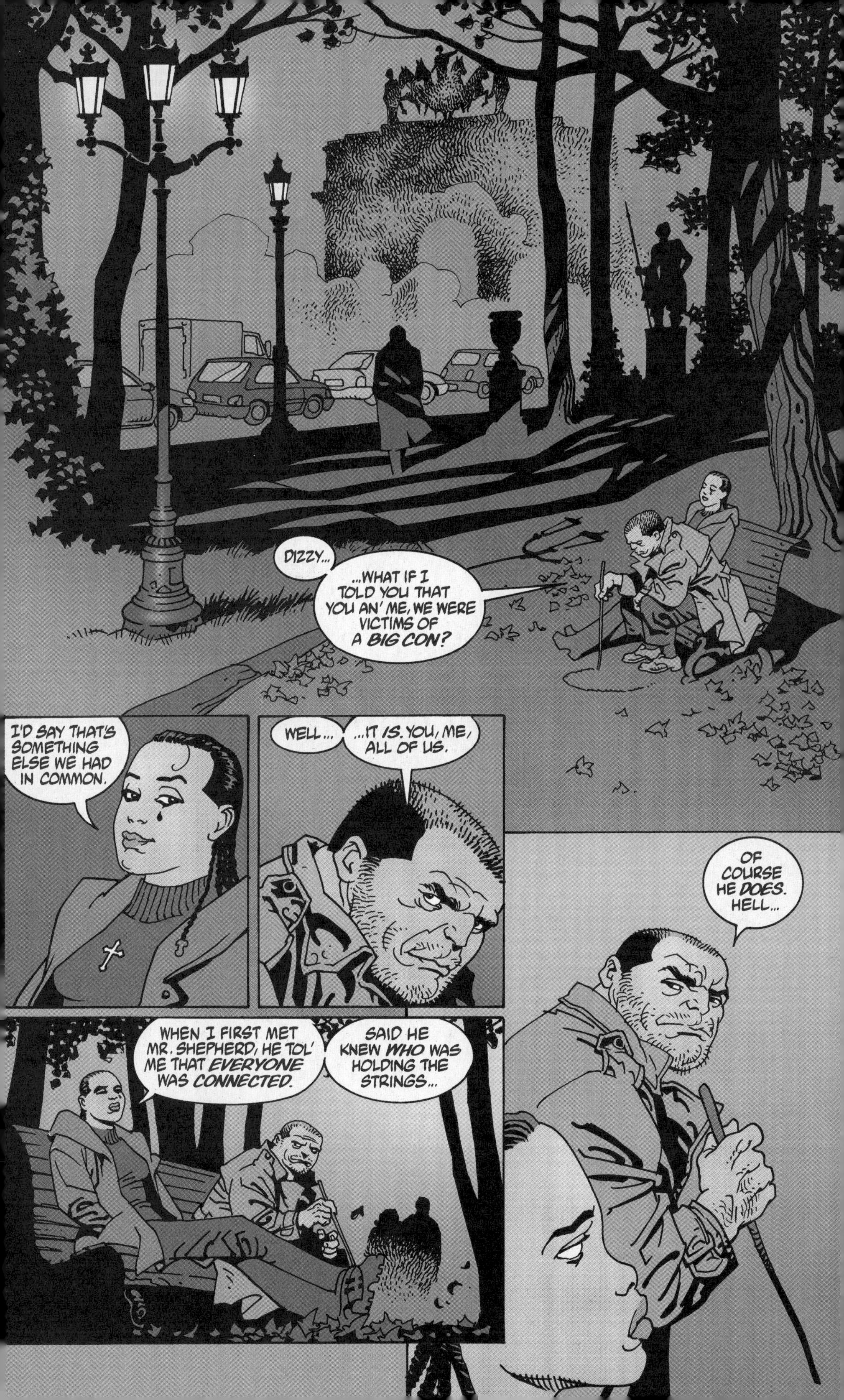
DIZZY...
...WHAT IF I TOLD YOU THAT YOU AN' ME, WE WERE VICTIMS OF A BIG CON?
I'D SAY THAT'S SOMETHING ELSE WE HAD IN COMMON.
WELL...
...IT IS. YOU, ME, ALL OF US.
WHEN I FIRST MET MR. SHEPHERD, HE TOL' ME THAT EVERYONE WAS CONNECTED.
SAID HE KNEW WHO WAS HOLDING THE STRINGS...
OF COURSE HE DOES. HELL...

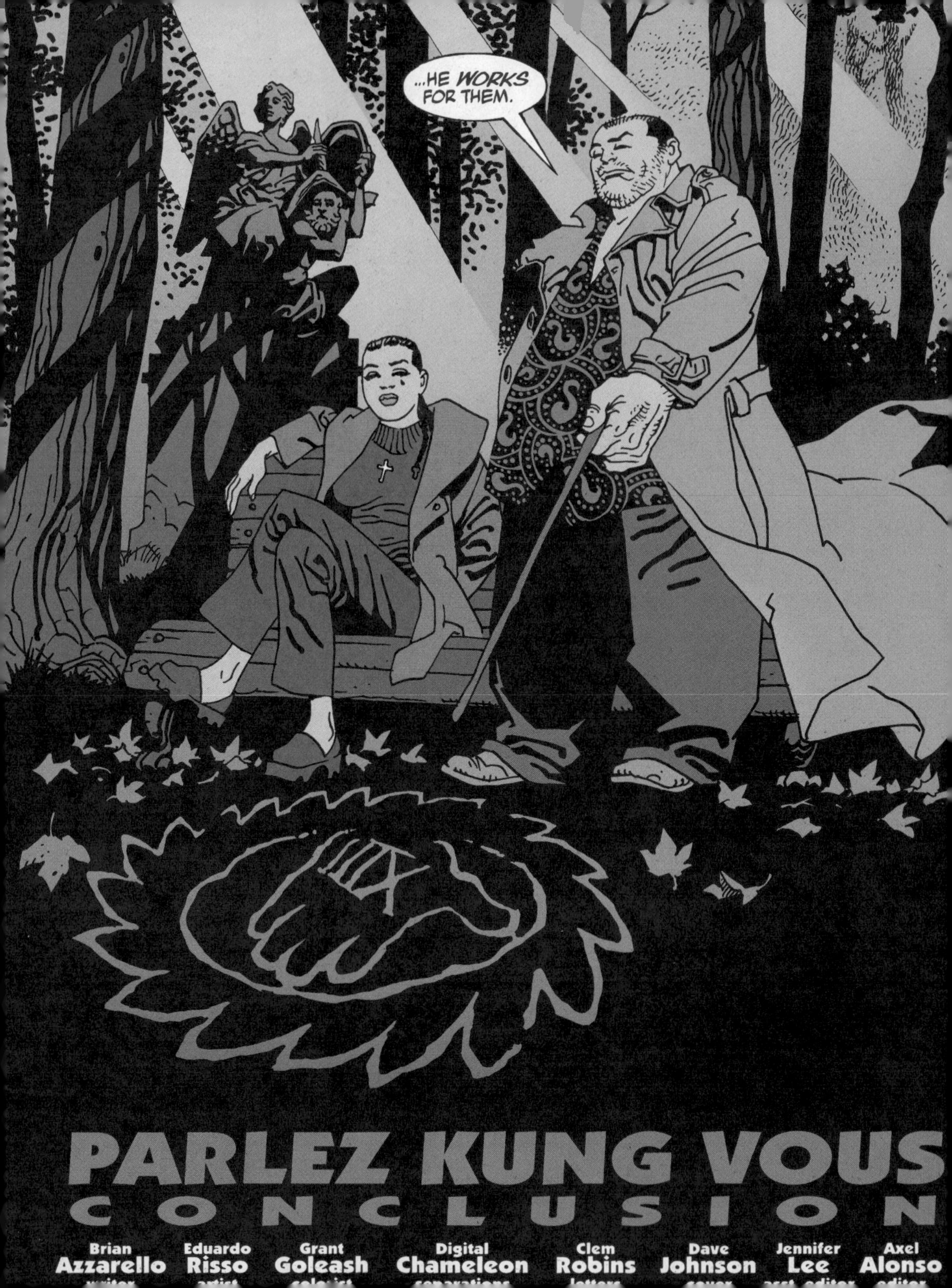
...HE WORKS FOR THEM.

PARLEZ KUNG VOUS
CONCLUSION

Brian Azzarello · Eduardo Risso · Grant Goleash · Digital Chameleon · Clem Robins · Dave Johnson · Jennifer Lee · Axel Alonso

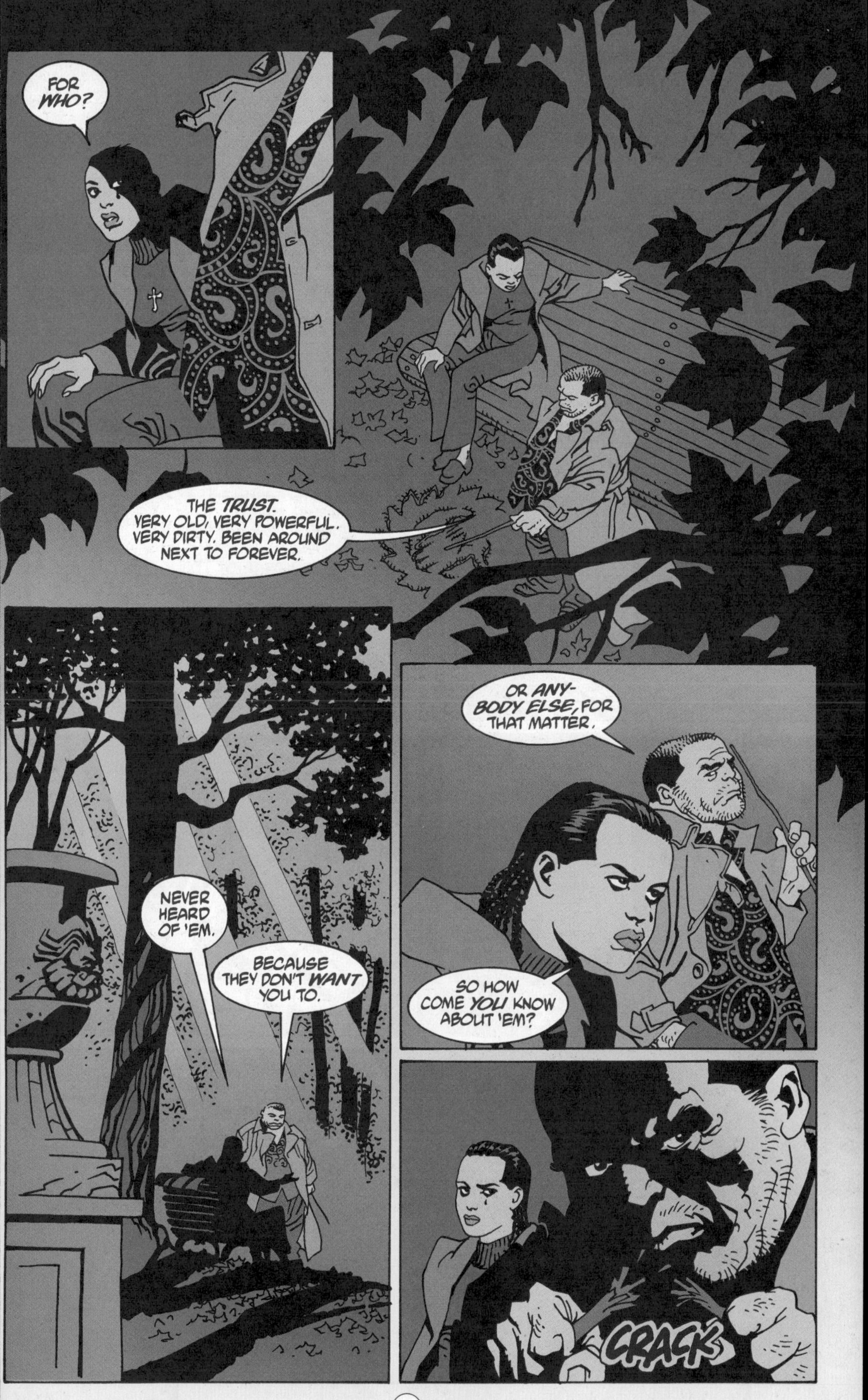
FOR WHO?
THE TRUST. VERY OLD, VERY POWERFUL. VERY DIRTY. BEEN AROUND NEXT TO FOREVER.
NEVER HEARD OF 'EM.
BECAUSE THEY DON'T WANT YOU TO.
OR ANYBODY ELSE, FOR THAT MATTER.
SO HOW COME YOU KNOW ABOUT 'EM?
CRACK

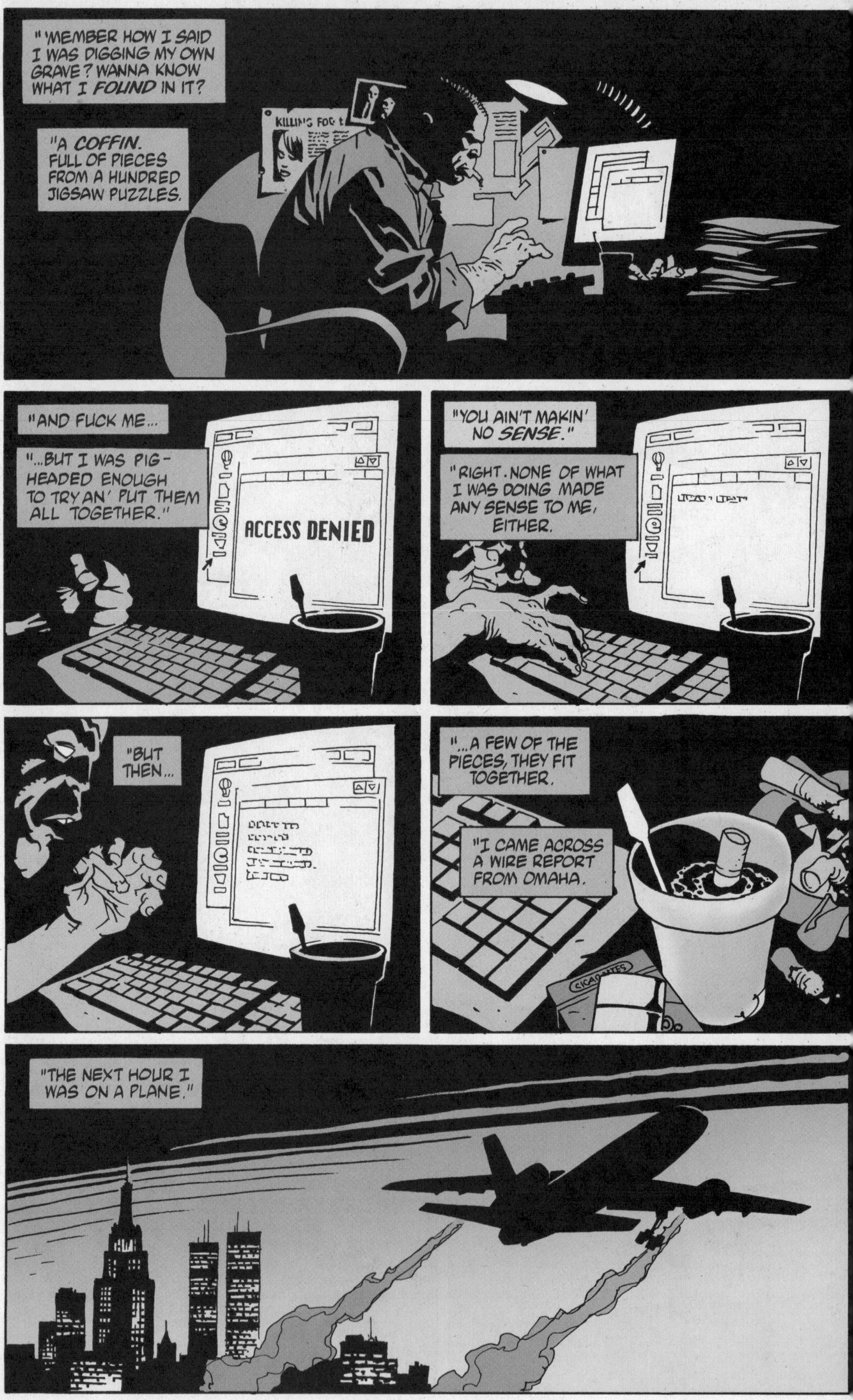
"'MEMBER HOW I SAID I WAS DIGGING MY OWN GRAVE? WANNA KNOW WHAT I FOUND IN IT?
"A COFFIN. FULL OF PIECES FROM A HUNDRED JIGSAW PUZZLES.
KILLING FOR
"AND FUCK ME...
"...BUT I WAS PIG-HEADED ENOUGH TO TRY AN' PUT THEM ALL TOGETHER."
ACCESS DENIED
"YOU AIN'T MAKIN' NO SENSE."
"RIGHT. NONE OF WHAT I WAS DOING MADE ANY SENSE TO ME, EITHER.
"BUT THEN...
"...A FEW OF THE PIECES, THEY FIT TOGETHER.
"I CAME ACROSS A WIRE REPORT FROM OMAHA.
"THE NEXT HOUR I WAS ON A PLANE."

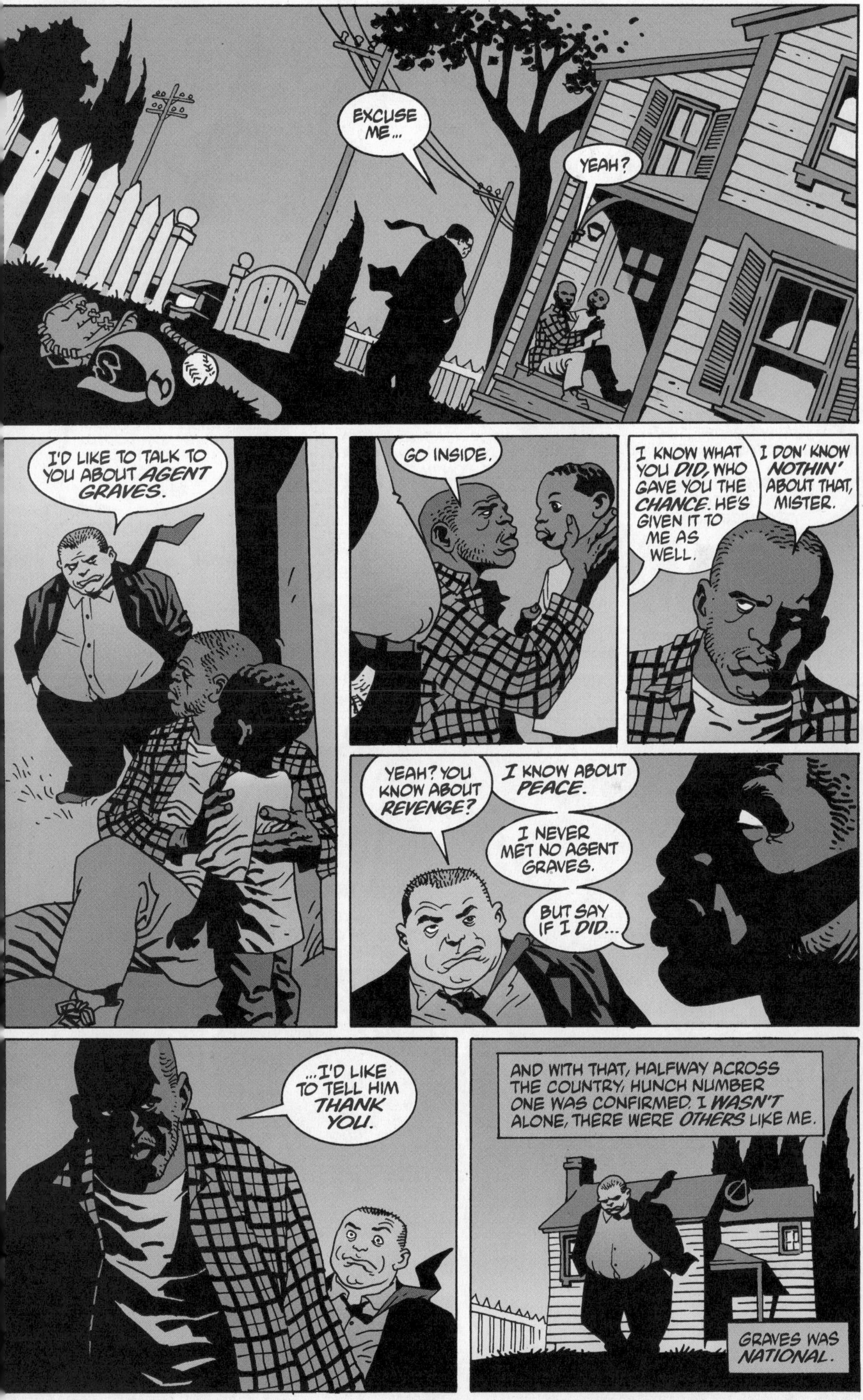
EXCUSE ME...
YEAH?
I'D LIKE TO TALK TO YOU ABOUT AGENT GRAVES.
GO INSIDE.
I KNOW WHAT YOU DID, WHO GAVE YOU THE CHANCE. HE'S GIVEN IT TO ME AS WELL.
I DON' KNOW NOTHIN' ABOUT THAT, MISTER.
YEAH? YOU KNOW ABOUT REVENGE?
I KNOW ABOUT PEACE.
I NEVER MET NO AGENT GRAVES.
BUT SAY IF I DID...
...I'D LIKE TO TELL HIM THANK YOU.
AND WITH THAT, HALFWAY ACROSS THE COUNTRY, HUNCH NUMBER ONE WAS CONFIRMED. I WASN'T ALONE, THERE WERE OTHERS LIKE ME.
GRAVES WAS NATIONAL.

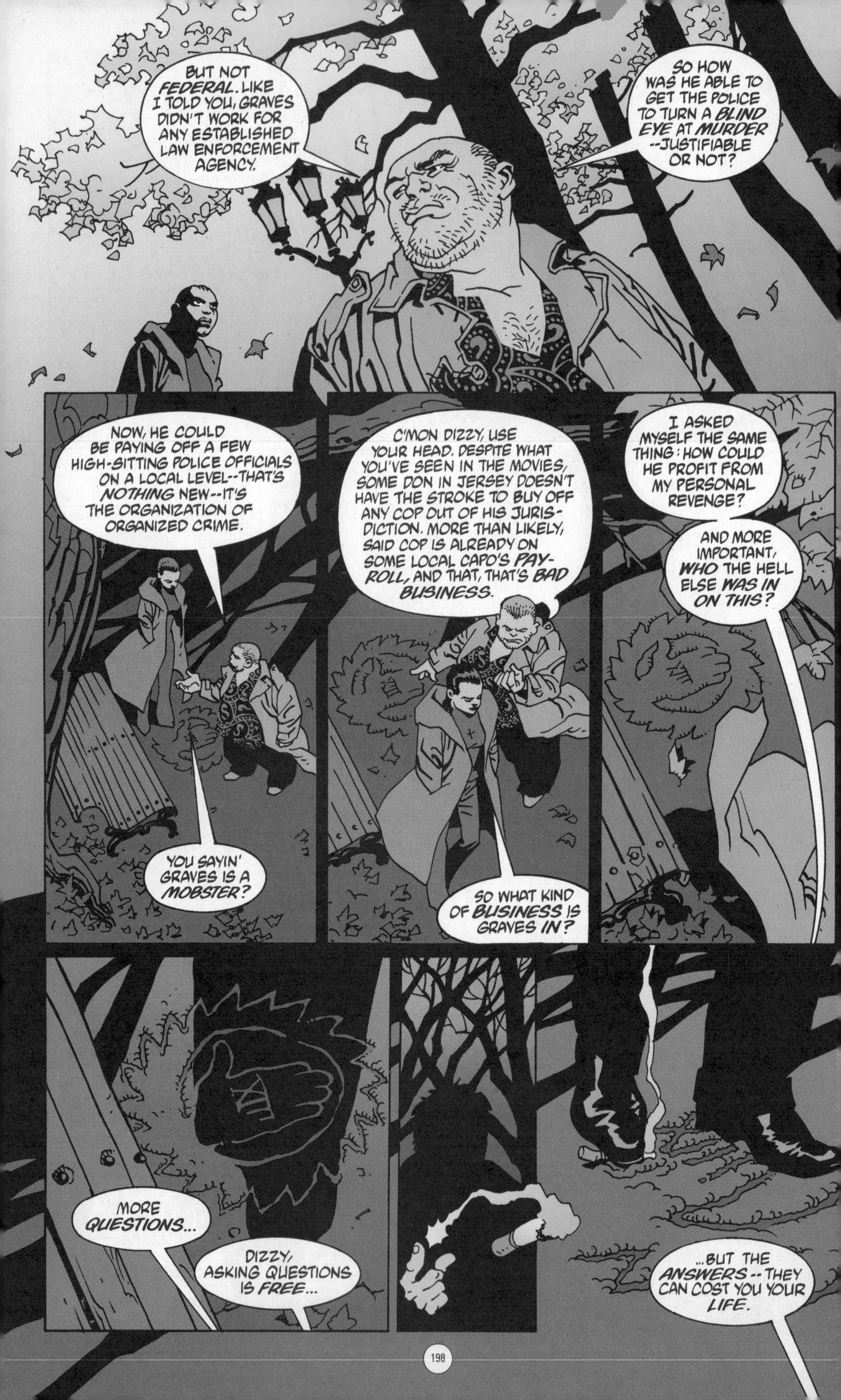

BUT NOT FEDERAL. LIKE I TOLD YOU, GRAVES DIDN'T WORK FOR ANY ESTABLISHED LAW ENFORCEMENT AGENCY.
SO HOW WAS HE ABLE TO GET THE POLICE TO TURN A BLIND EYE AT MURDER --JUSTIFIABLE OR NOT?
NOW, HE COULD BE PAYING OFF A FEW HIGH-SITTING POLICE OFFICIALS ON A LOCAL LEVEL--THAT'S NOTHING NEW--IT'S THE ORGANIZATION OF ORGANIZED CRIME.
YOU SAYIN' GRAVES IS A MOBSTER?
C'MON DIZZY, USE YOUR HEAD. DESPITE WHAT YOU'VE SEEN IN THE MOVIES, SOME DON IN JERSEY DOESN'T HAVE THE STROKE TO BUY OFF ANY COP OUT OF HIS JURIS-DICTION. MORE THAN LIKELY, SAID COP IS ALREADY ON SOME LOCAL CAPO'S PAY-ROLL, AND THAT, THAT'S BAD BUSINESS.
SO WHAT KIND OF BUSINESS IS GRAVES IN?
I ASKED MYSELF THE SAME THING: HOW COULD HE PROFIT FROM MY PERSONAL REVENGE?
AND MORE IMPORTANT, WHO THE HELL ELSE WAS IN ON THIS?
MORE QUESTIONS...
DIZZY, ASKING QUESTIONS IS FREE...
...BUT THE ANSWERS -- THEY CAN COST YOU YOUR LIFE.

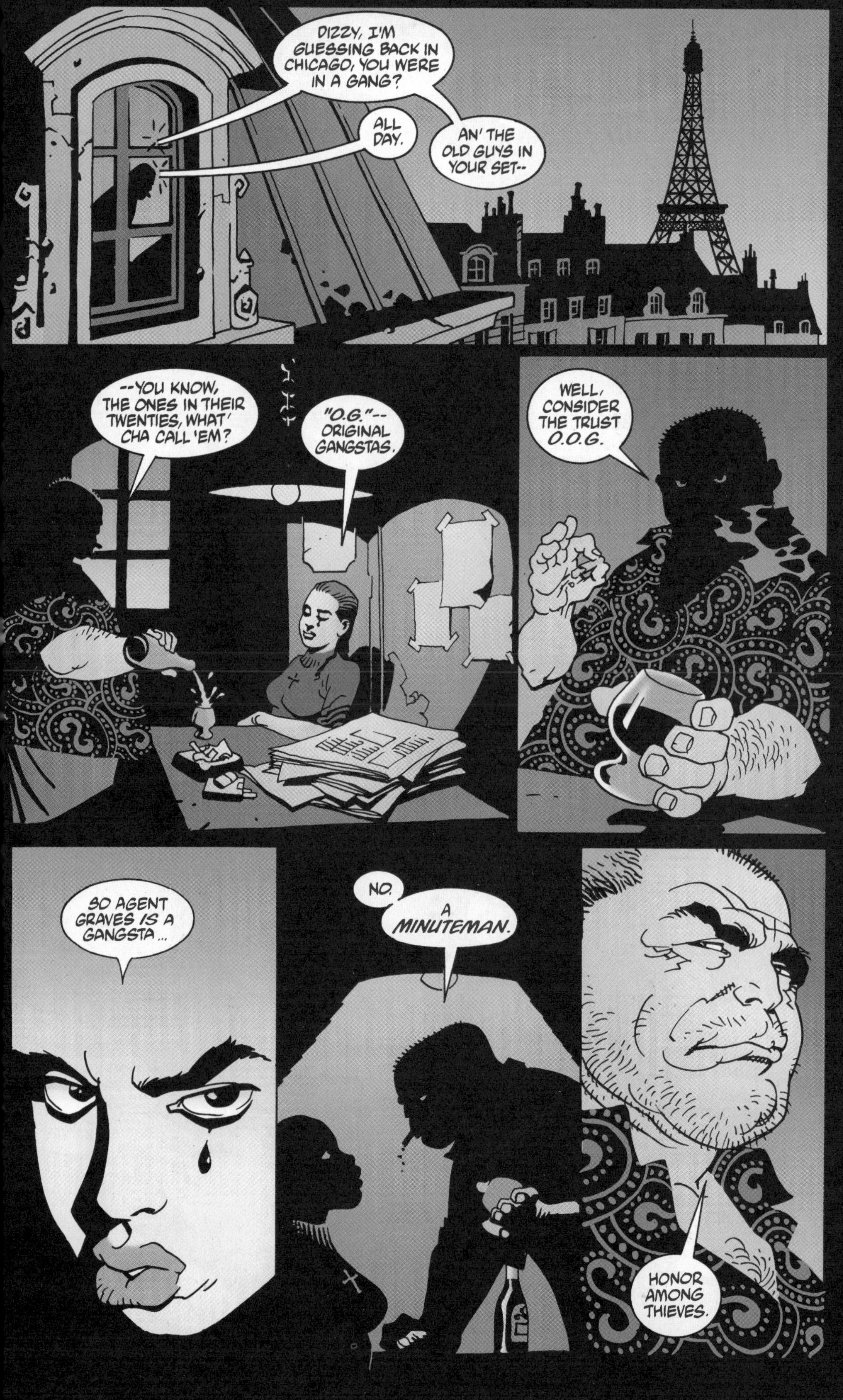

DIZZY, I'M GUESSING BACK IN CHICAGO, YOU WERE IN A GANG?
ALL DAY.
AN' THE OLD GUYS IN YOUR SET--
--YOU KNOW, THE ONES IN THEIR TWENTIES, WHAT'CHA CALL 'EM?
"O.G."-- ORIGINAL GANGSTAS.
WELL, CONSIDER THE TRUST O.O.G.
SO AGENT GRAVES IS A GANGSTA...
NO.
A MINUTEMAN.
HONOR AMONG THIEVES.

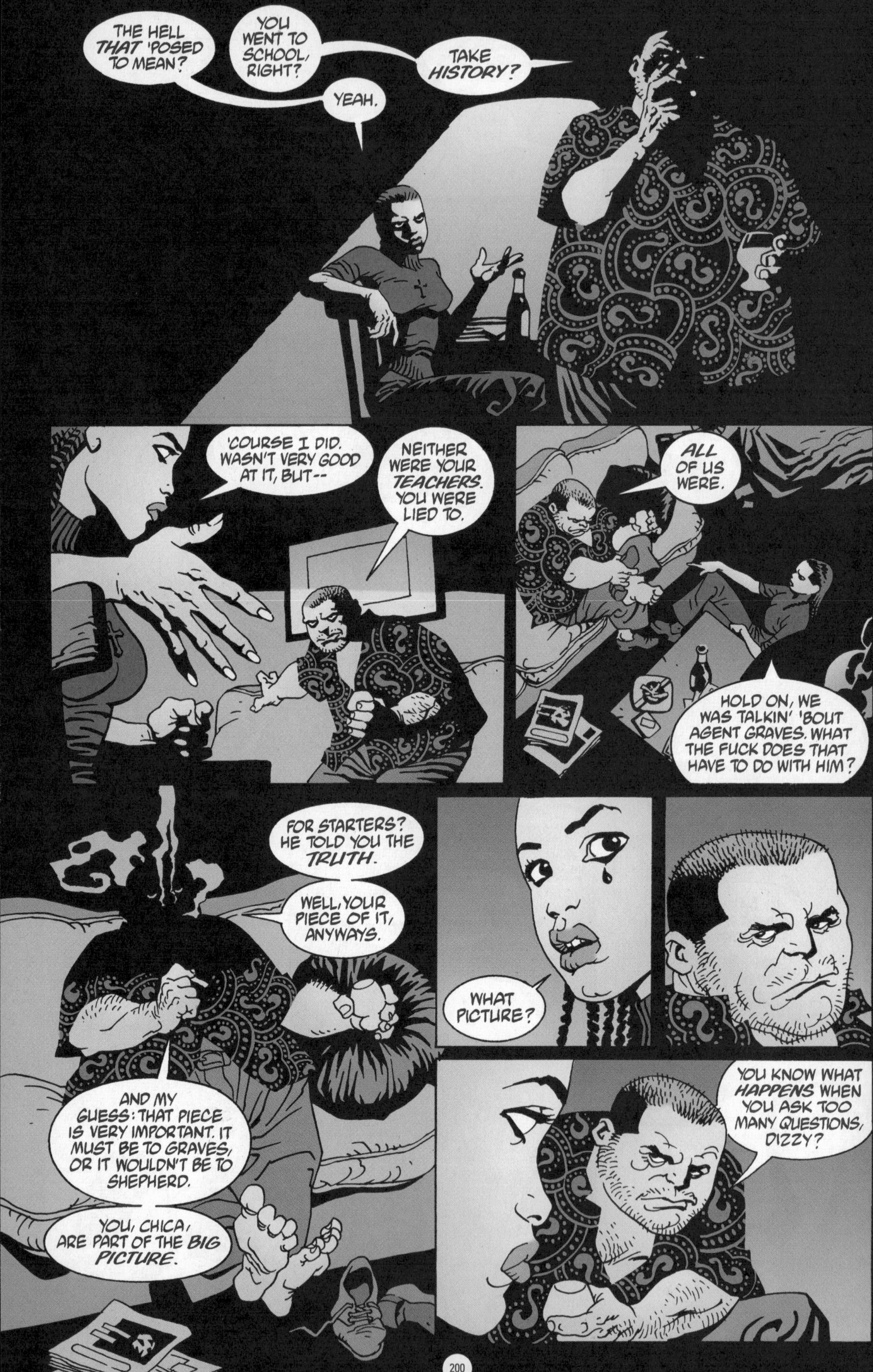

YOU WENT TO SCHOOL, RIGHT?
TAKE HISTORY?
THE HELL THAT 'POSED TO MEAN?
YEAH.
'COURSE I DID. WASN'T VERY GOOD AT IT, BUT--
NEITHER WERE YOUR TEACHERS. YOU WERE LIED TO.
ALL OF US WERE.
HOLD ON, WE WAS TALKIN' 'BOUT AGENT GRAVES. WHAT THE FUCK DOES THAT HAVE TO DO WITH HIM?
FOR STARTERS? HE TOLD YOU THE TRUTH.
WELL, YOUR PIECE OF IT, ANYWAYS.
AND MY GUESS: THAT PIECE IS VERY IMPORTANT. IT MUST BE TO GRAVES, OR IT WOULDN'T BE TO SHEPHERD.
YOU, CHICA, ARE PART OF THE BIG PICTURE.
WHAT PICTURE?
YOU KNOW WHAT HAPPENS WHEN YOU ASK TOO MANY QUESTIONS, DIZZY?

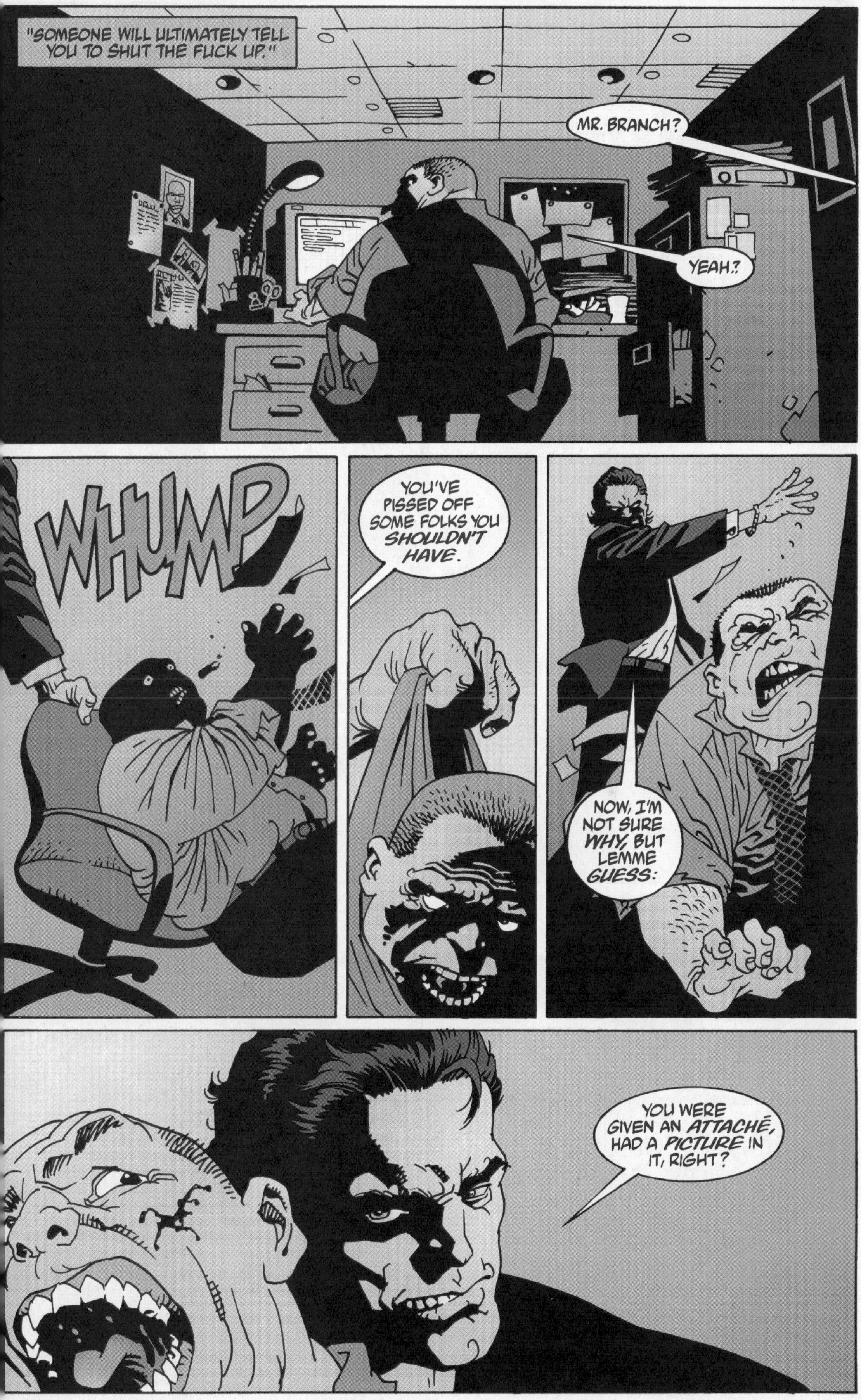
"SOMEONE WILL ULTIMATELY TELL YOU TO SHUT THE FUCK UP."
MR. BRANCH?
YEAH.?
WHUMP
YOU'VE PISSED OFF SOME FOLKS YOU *SHOULDN'T HAVE*.
NOW, I'M NOT SURE *WHY*, BUT LEMME *GUESS*:
YOU WERE GIVEN AN *ATTACHÉ*, HAD A *PICTURE* IN IT, RIGHT?

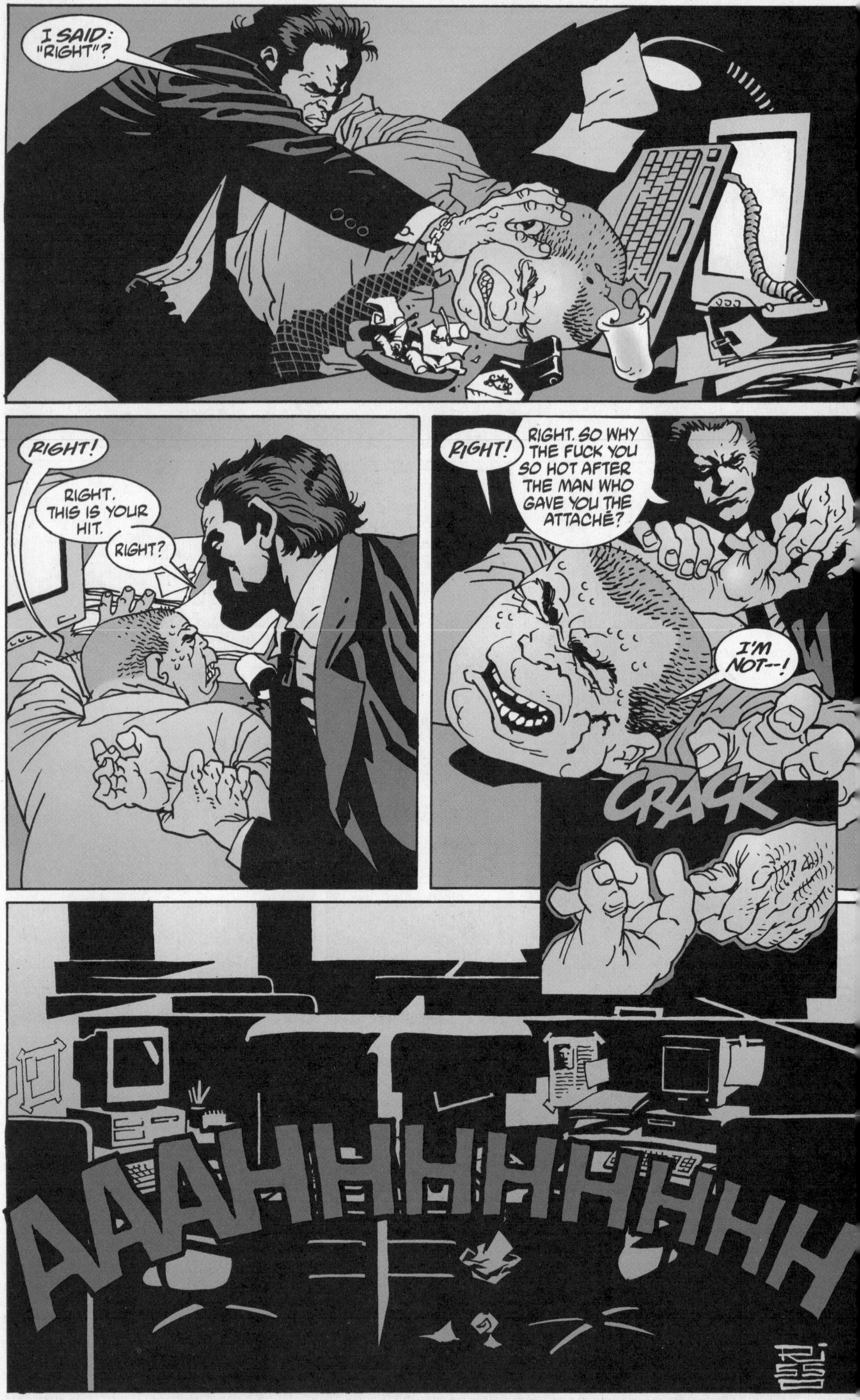
I SAID: "RIGHT"?
RIGHT!
RIGHT. THIS IS YOUR HIT.
RIGHT?
RIGHT!
RIGHT. SO WHY THE FUCK YOU SO HOT AFTER THE MAN WHO GAVE YOU THE ATTACHÉ?
I'M NOT--!
CRACK
AAAHHHHHHHHHH

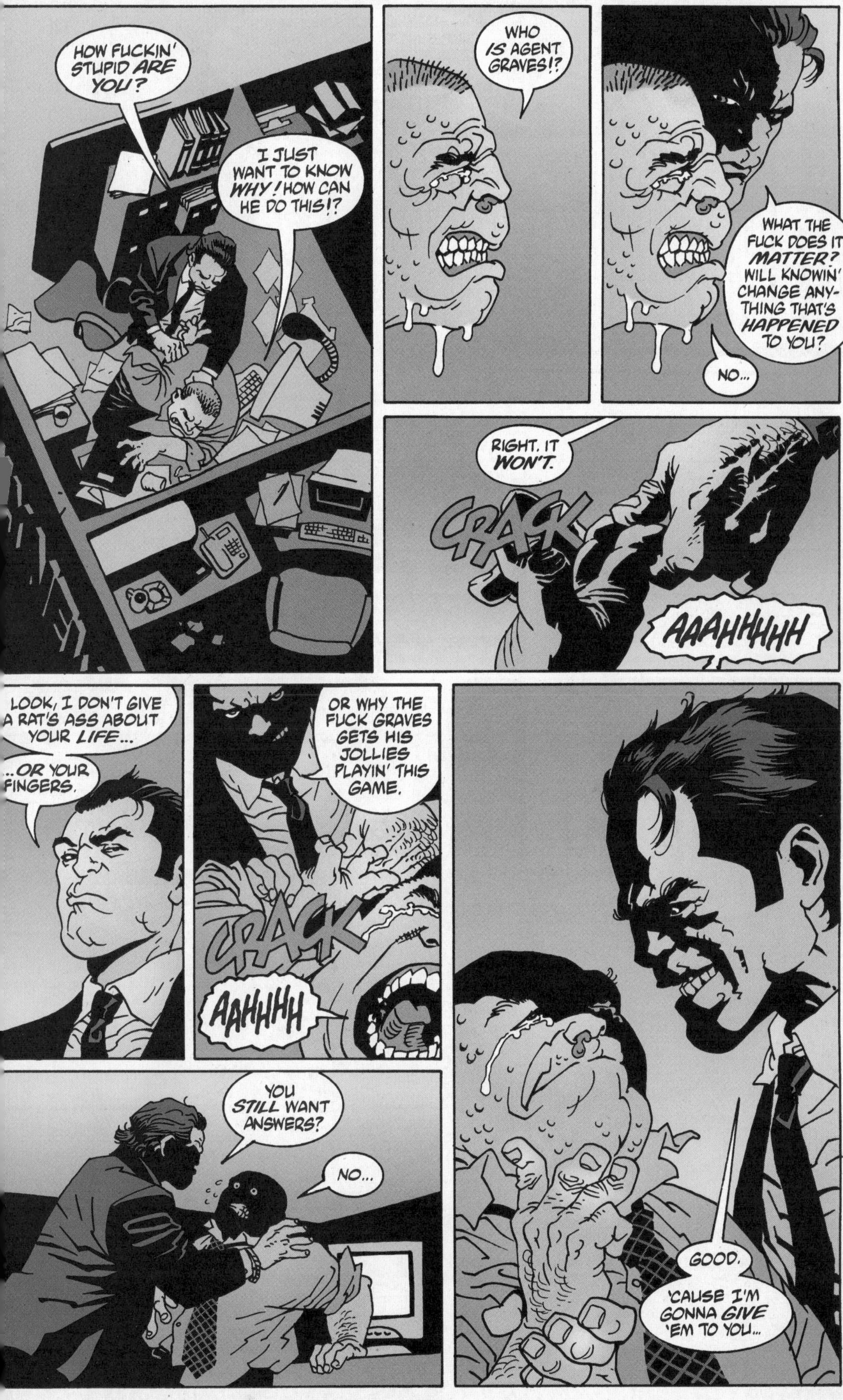
HOW FUCKIN' STUPID ARE YOU?
I JUST WANT TO KNOW WHY! HOW CAN HE DO THIS!?
WHO IS AGENT GRAVES!?
WHAT THE FUCK DOES IT MATTER? WILL KNOWIN' CHANGE ANYTHING THAT'S HAPPENED TO YOU?
NO...
RIGHT. IT WON'T.
CRACK
AAAHHHHH
LOOK, I DON'T GIVE A RAT'S ASS ABOUT YOUR LIFE...
...OR YOUR FINGERS.
OR WHY THE FUCK GRAVES GETS HIS JOLLIES PLAYIN' THIS GAME.
CRACK
AAHHHH
YOU STILL WANT ANSWERS?
NO...
GOOD.
'CAUSE I'M GONNA GIVE 'EM TO YOU...

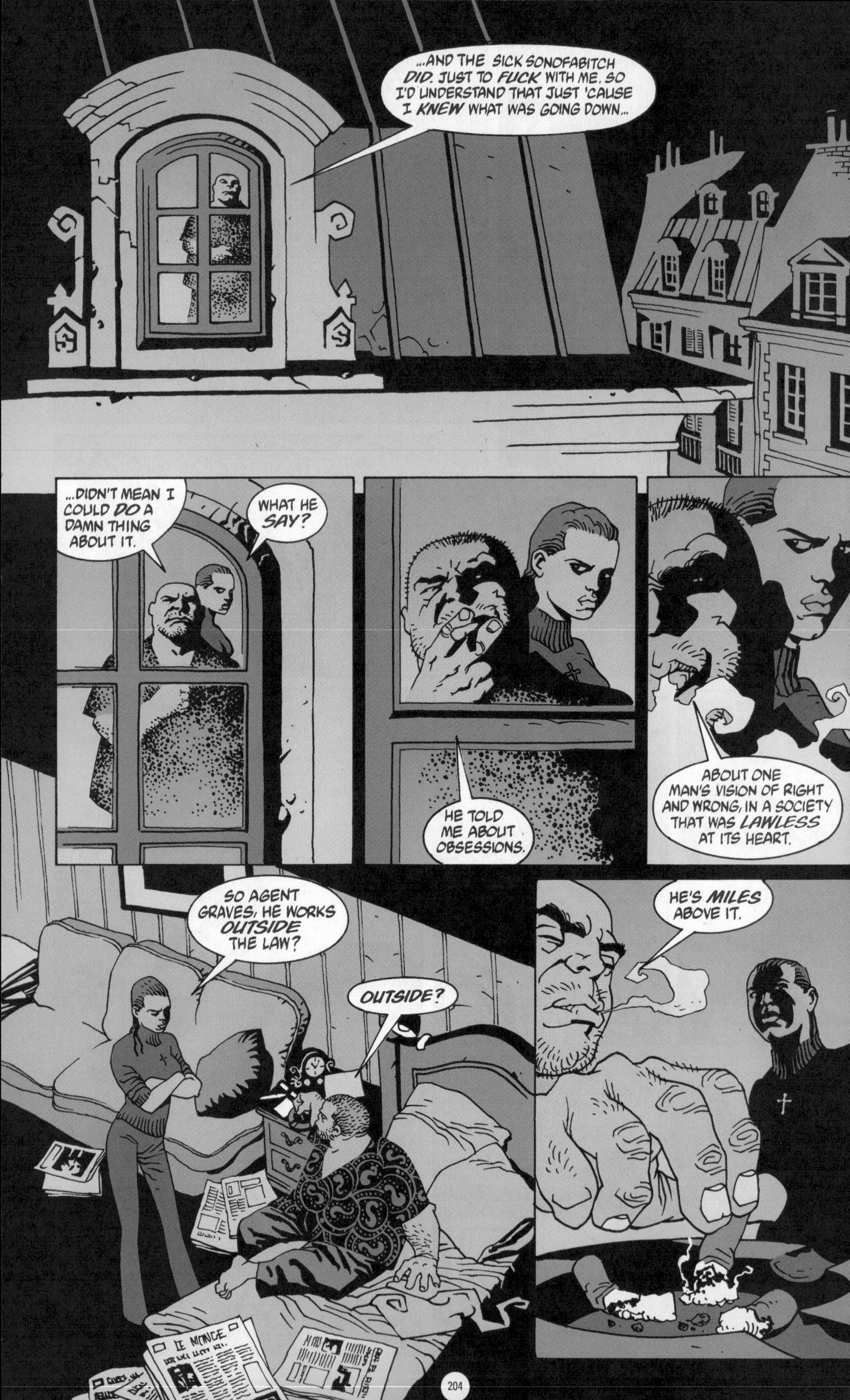
...AND THE SICK SONOFABITCH DID. JUST TO FUCK WITH ME. SO I'D UNDERSTAND THAT JUST 'CAUSE I KNEW WHAT WAS GOING DOWN...
...DIDN'T MEAN I COULD DO A DAMN THING ABOUT IT.
WHAT HE SAY?
HE TOLD ME ABOUT OBSESSIONS.
ABOUT ONE MAN'S VISION OF RIGHT AND WRONG, IN A SOCIETY THAT WAS LAWLESS AT ITS HEART.
SO AGENT GRAVES, HE WORKS OUTSIDE THE LAW?
OUTSIDE?
HE'S MILES ABOVE IT.
LE MONDE

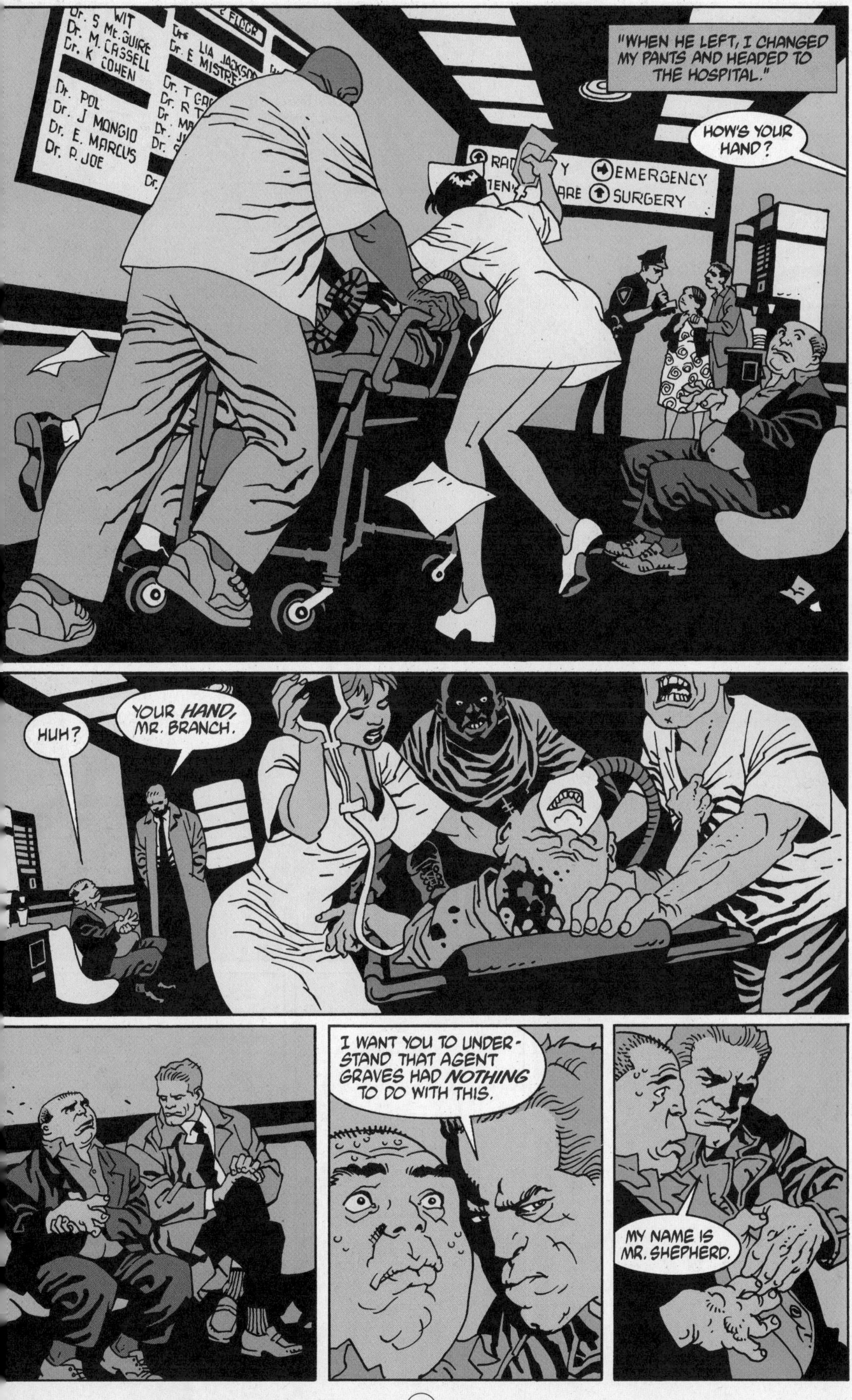
"WHEN HE LEFT, I CHANGED MY PANTS AND HEADED TO THE HOSPITAL."
HOW'S YOUR HAND?
EMERGENCY
SURGERY
HUH?
YOUR *HAND*, MR. BRANCH.
I WANT YOU TO UNDER-STAND THAT AGENT GRAVES HAD *NOTHING* TO DO WITH THIS.
MY NAME IS MR. SHEPHERD.

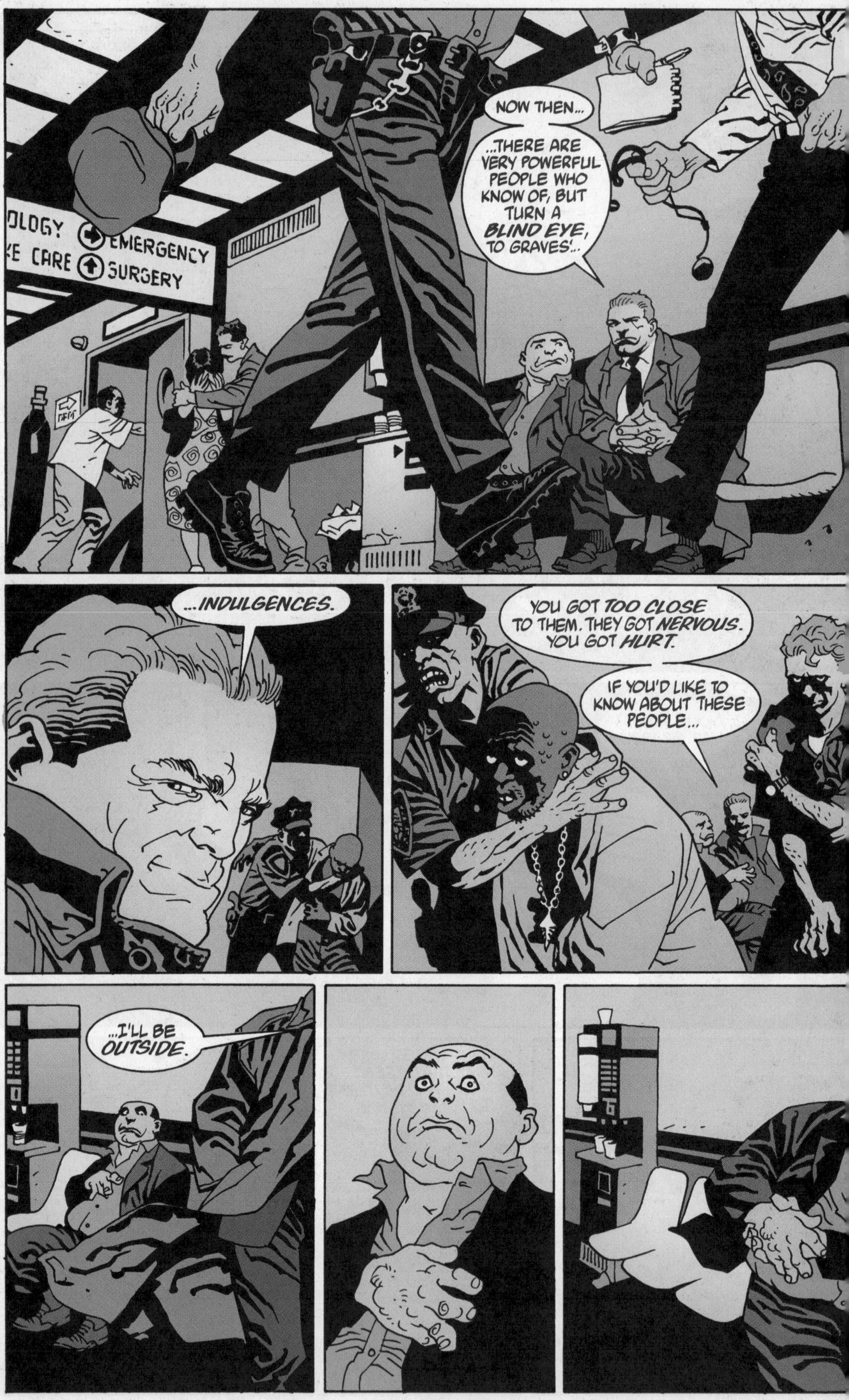
NOW THEN...
...THERE ARE VERY POWERFUL PEOPLE WHO KNOW OF, BUT TURN A BLIND EYE, TO GRAVES'...
EMERGENCY
SURGERY
...INDULGENCES.
YOU GOT TOO CLOSE TO THEM. THEY GOT NERVOUS. YOU GOT HURT.
IF YOU'D LIKE TO KNOW ABOUT THESE PEOPLE...
...I'LL BE OUTSIDE.

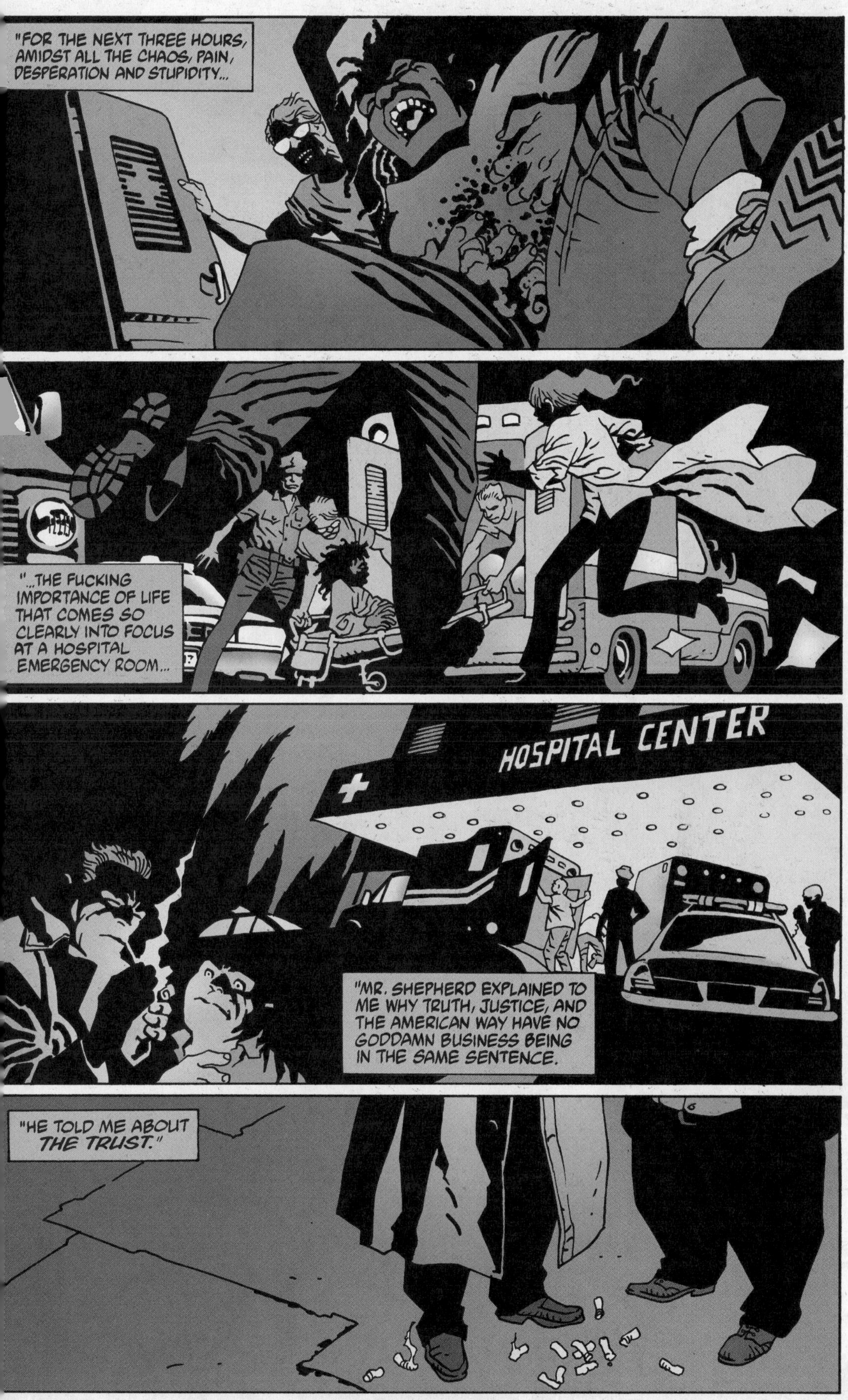
"FOR THE NEXT THREE HOURS, AMIDST ALL THE CHAOS, PAIN, DESPERATION AND STUPIDITY...
"...THE FUCKING IMPORTANCE OF LIFE THAT COMES SO CLEARLY INTO FOCUS AT A HOSPITAL EMERGENCY ROOM...
HOSPITAL CENTER
"MR. SHEPHERD EXPLAINED TO ME WHY TRUTH, JUSTICE, AND THE AMERICAN WAY HAVE NO GODDAMN BUSINESS BEING IN THE SAME SENTENCE.
"HE TOLD ME ABOUT *THE TRUST*."

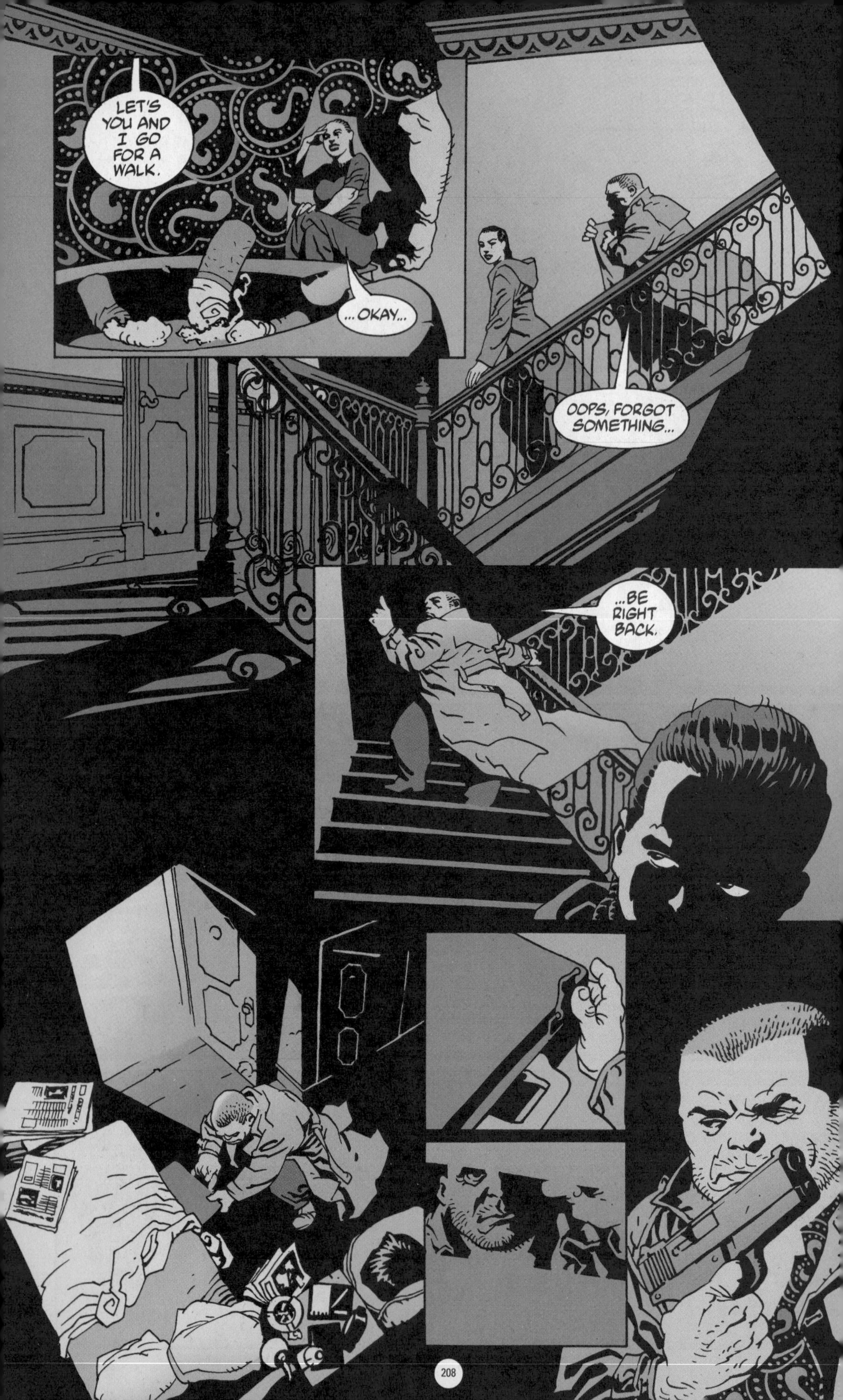
LET'S YOU AND I GO FOR A WALK.
...OKAY...
OOPS, FORGOT SOMETHING...
...BE RIGHT BACK.

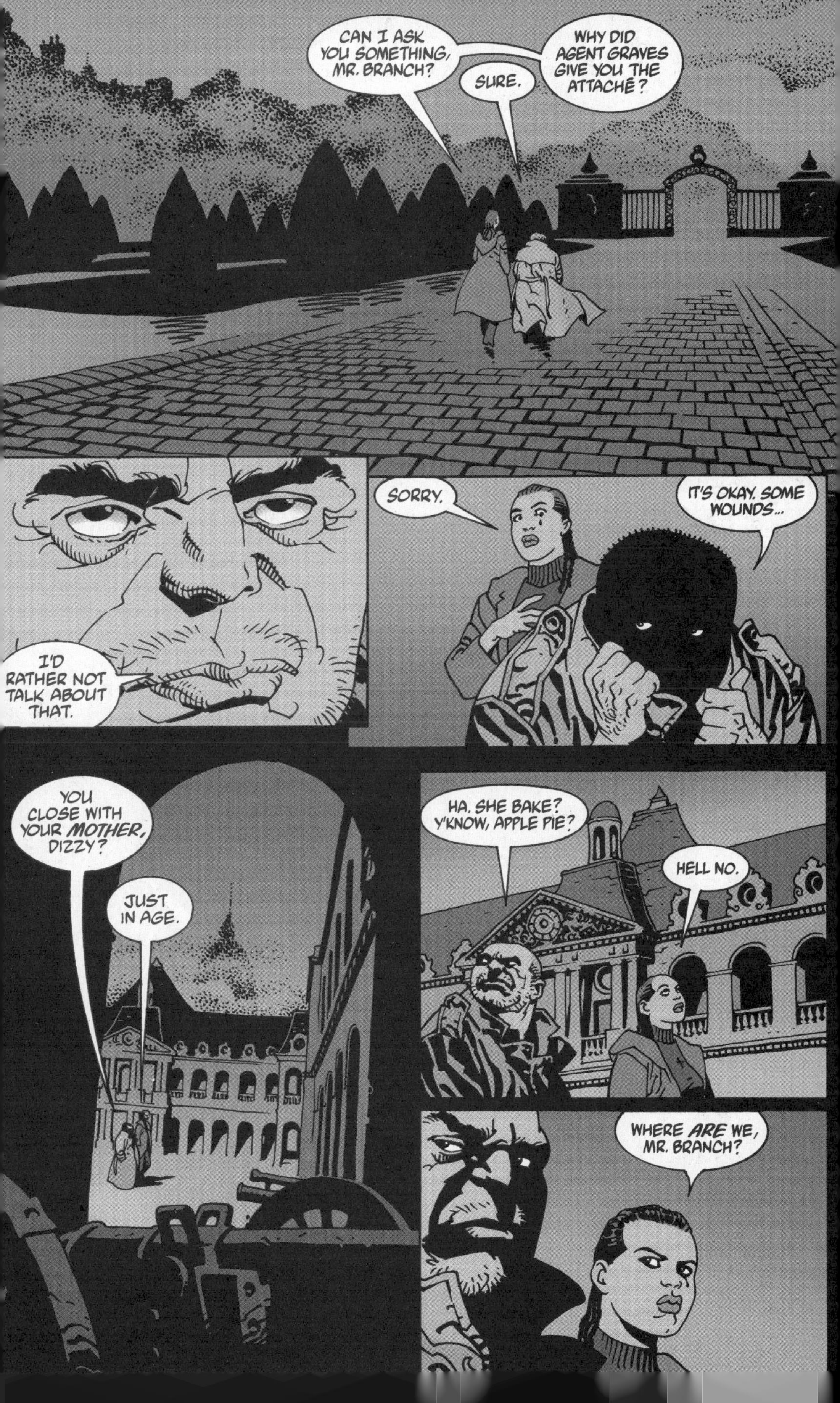
CAN I ASK YOU SOMETHING, MR. BRANCH?
SURE.
WHY DID AGENT GRAVES GIVE YOU THE ATTACHÉ?
I'D RATHER NOT TALK ABOUT THAT.
SORRY.
IT'S OKAY. SOME WOUNDS...
YOU CLOSE WITH YOUR MOTHER, DIZZY?
JUST IN AGE.
HA. SHE BAKE? Y'KNOW, APPLE PIE?
HELL NO.
WHERE ARE WE, MR. BRANCH?

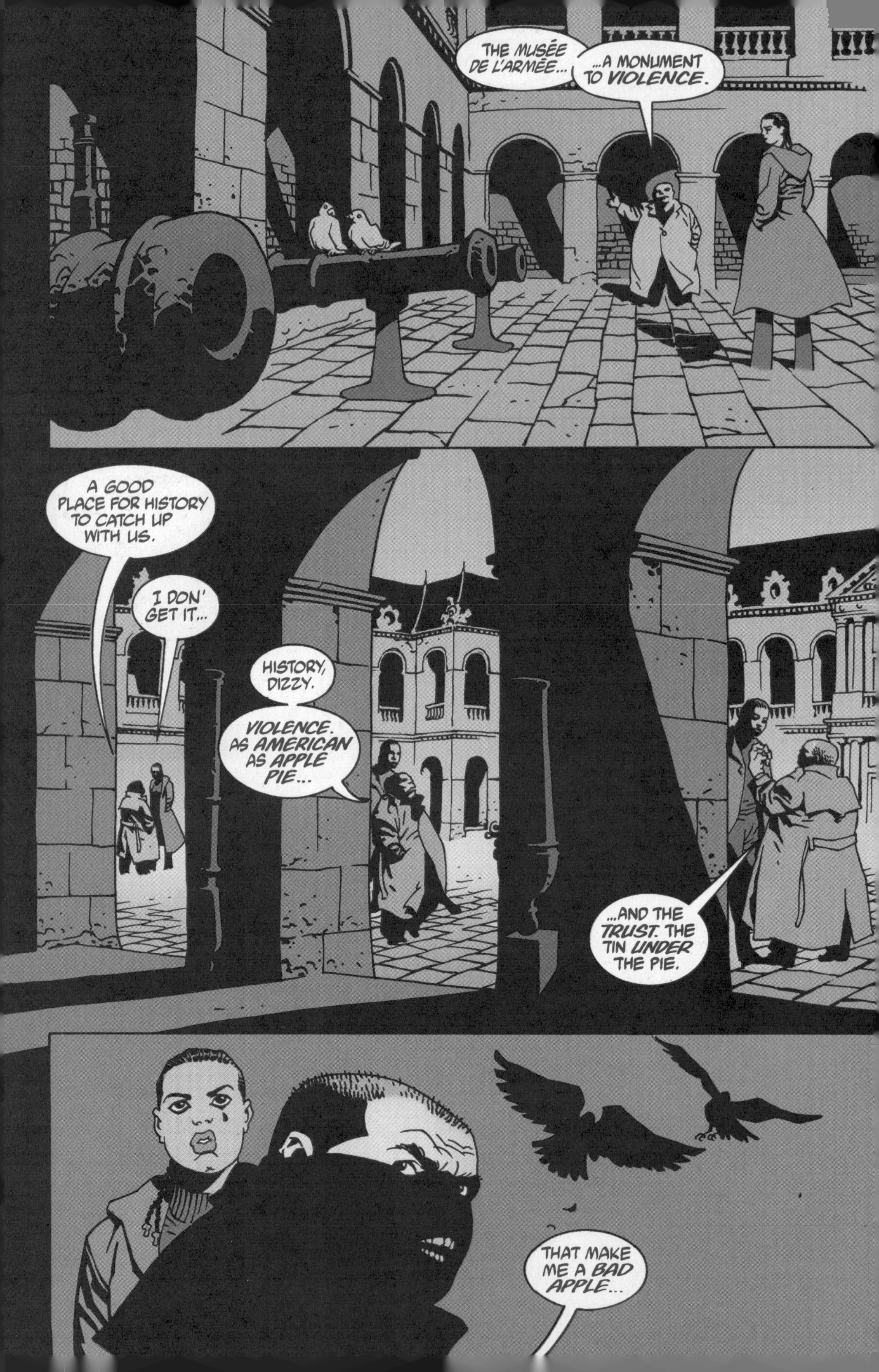
THE MUSÉE DE L'ARMÉE...
...A MONUMENT TO VIOLENCE.
A GOOD PLACE FOR HISTORY TO CATCH UP WITH US.
I DON' GET IT...
HISTORY, DIZZY.
VIOLENCE. AS AMERICAN AS APPLE PIE...
...AND THE TRUST. THE TIN UNDER THE PIE.
THAT MAKE ME A BAD APPLE...

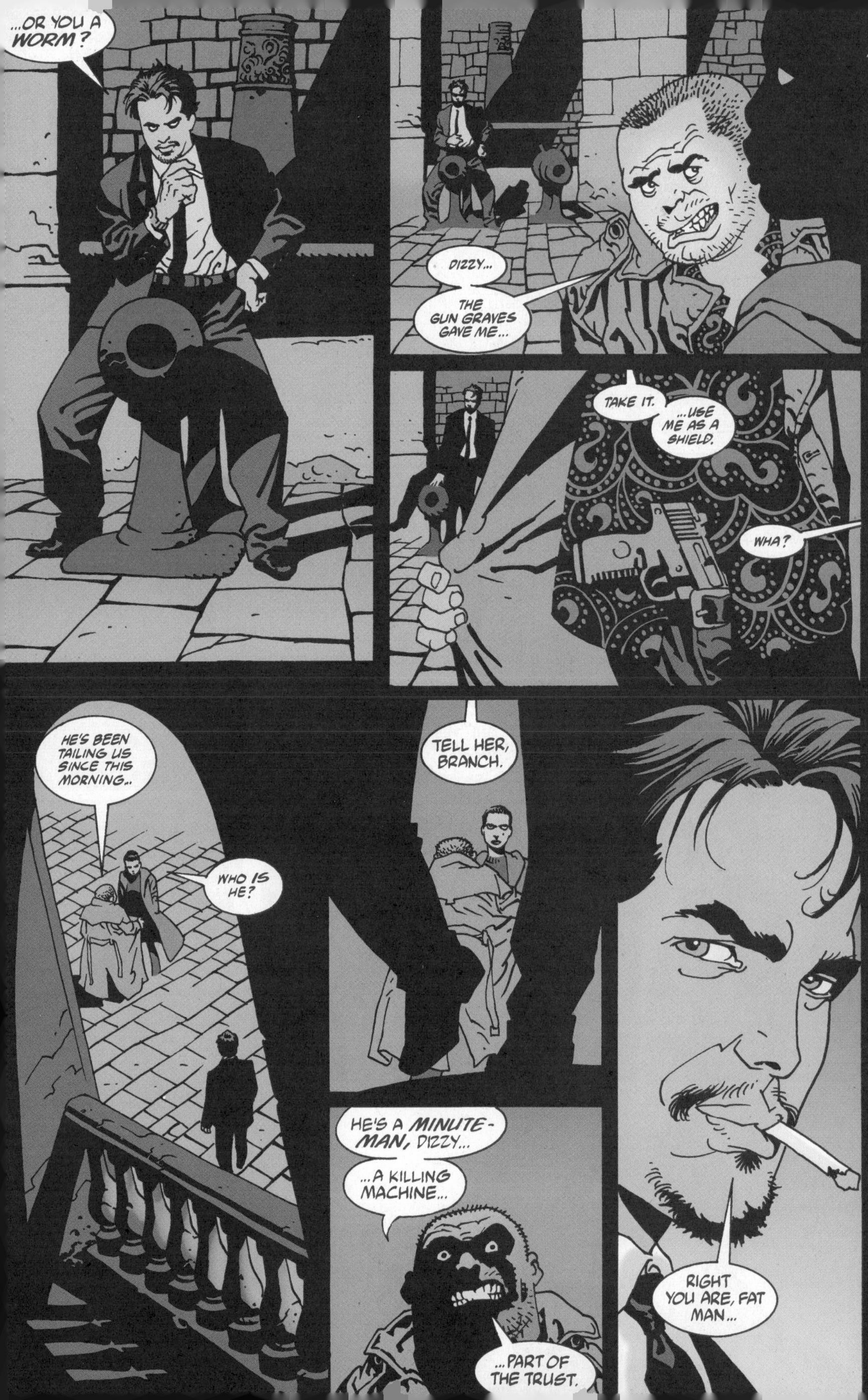

...OR YOU A WORM?
DIZZY...
THE GUN GRAVES GAVE ME...
TAKE IT.
...USE ME AS A SHIELD.
WHA?
HE'S BEEN TAILING US SINCE THIS MORNING..
WHO IS HE?
TELL HER, BRANCH.
HE'S A MINUTE-MAN, DIZZY...
...A KILLING MACHINE...
...PART OF THE TRUST.
RIGHT YOU ARE, FAT MAN...

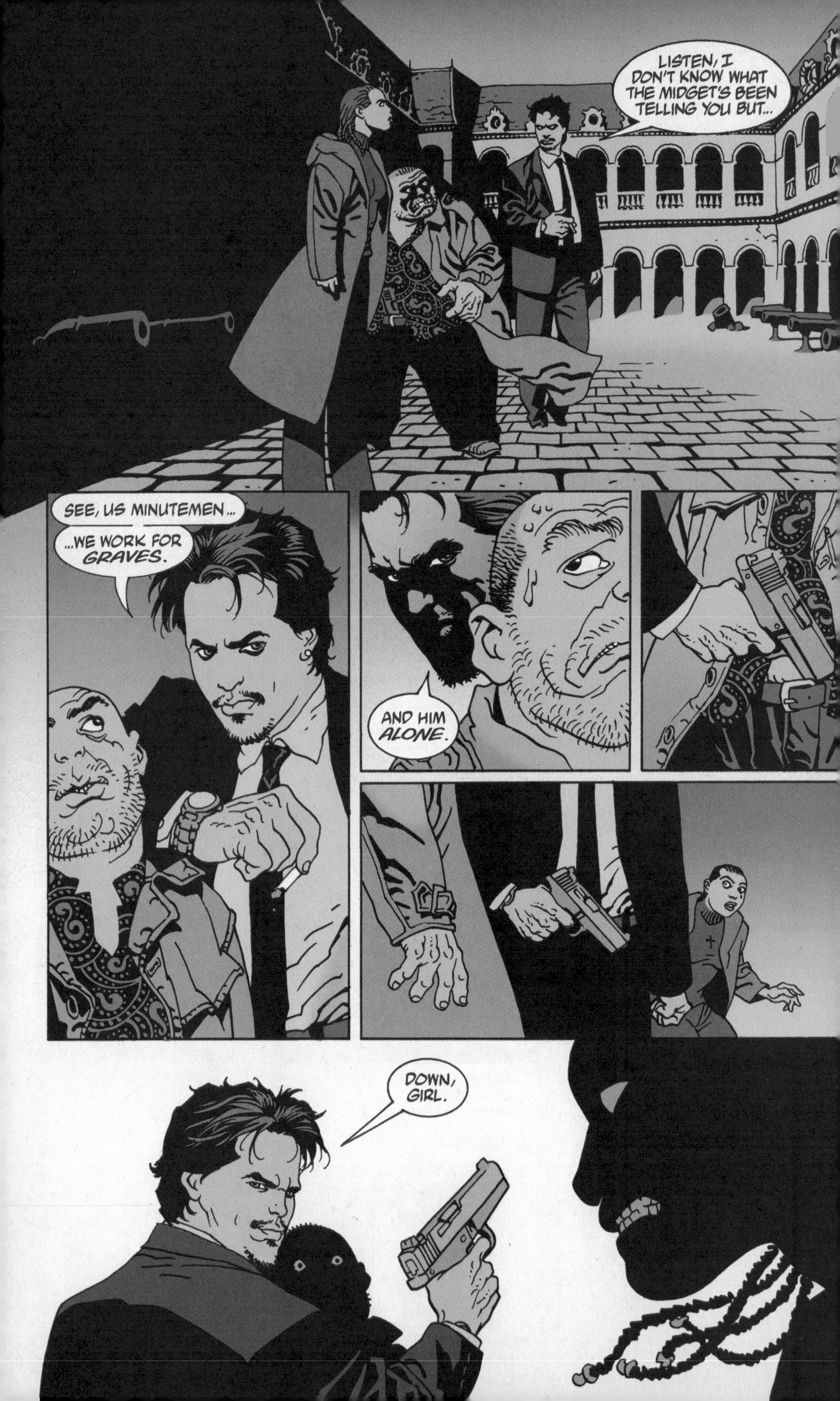

LISTEN, I DON'T KNOW WHAT THE MIDGET'S BEEN TELLING YOU BUT...
SEE, US MINUTEMEN...
...WE WORK FOR GRAVES.
AND HIM ALONE.
DOWN, GIRL.

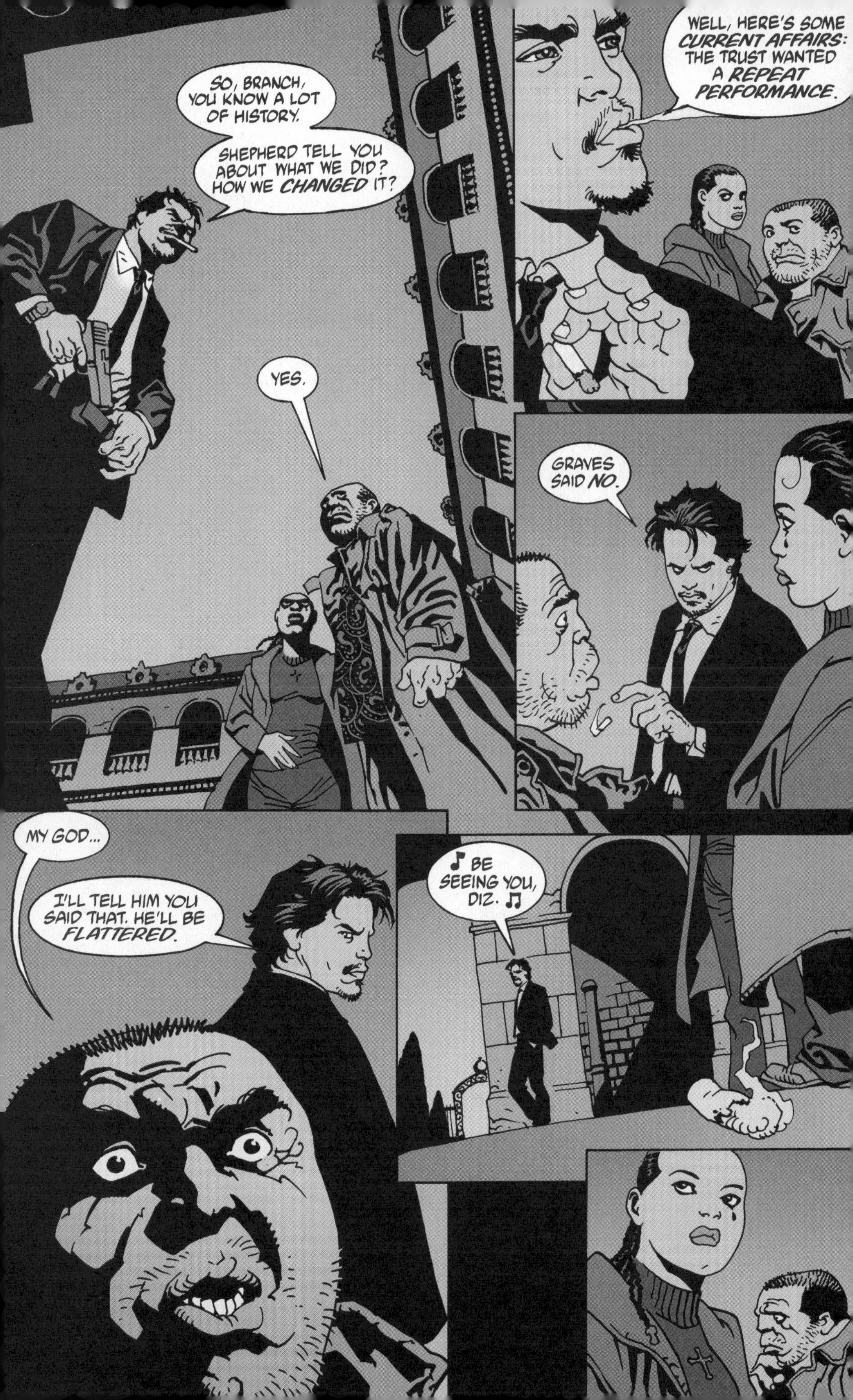
SO, BRANCH, YOU KNOW A LOT OF HISTORY.
SHEPHERD TELL YOU ABOUT WHAT WE DID? HOW WE CHANGED IT?
YES.
WELL, HERE'S SOME CURRENT AFFAIRS: THE TRUST WANTED A REPEAT PERFORMANCE.
GRAVES SAID NO.
MY GOD...
I'LL TELL HIM YOU SAID THAT. HE'LL BE FLATTERED.
♪ BE SEEING YOU, DIZ. ♫

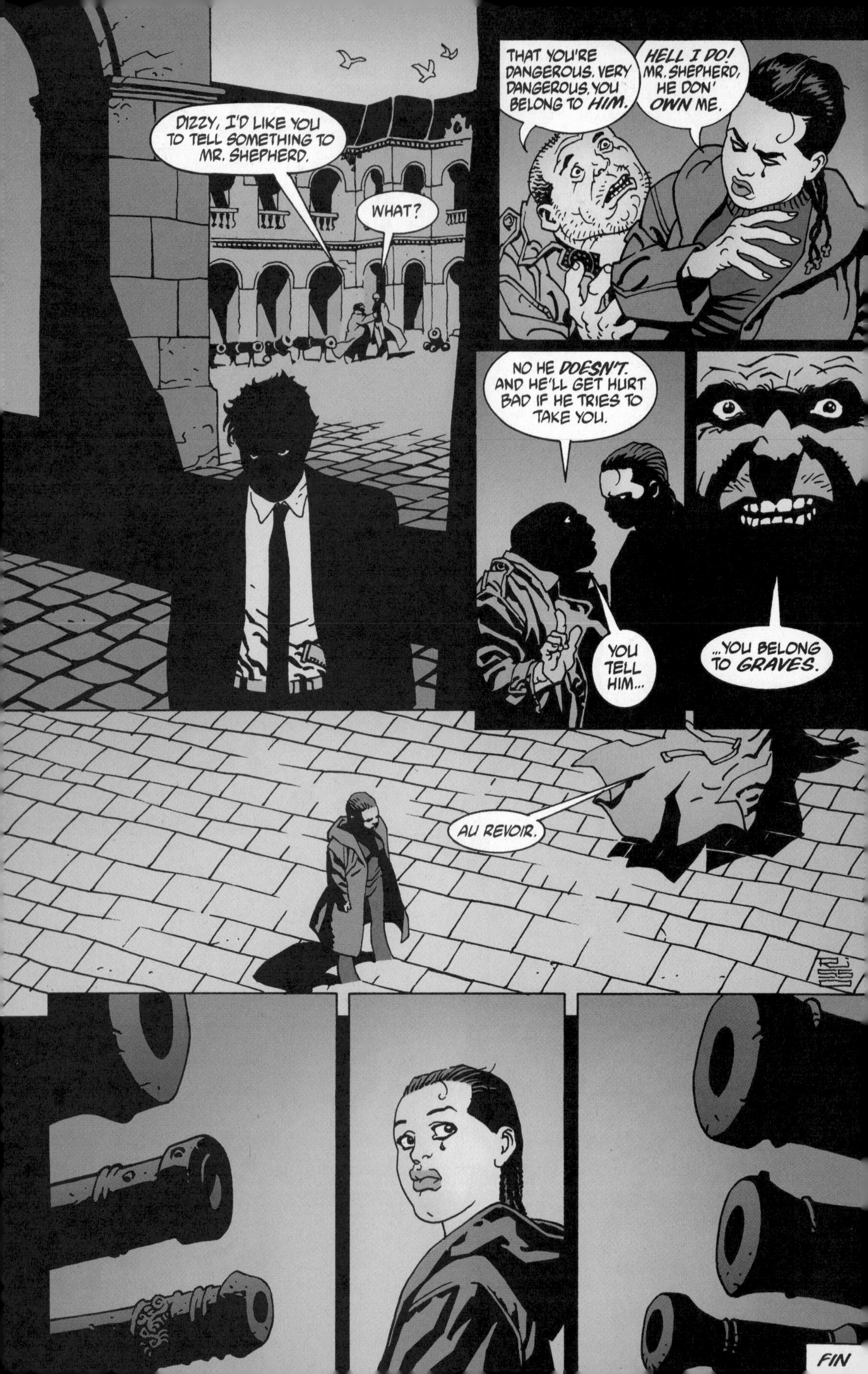

DIZZY, I'D LIKE YOU TO TELL SOMETHING TO MR. SHEPHERD.
WHAT?
THAT YOU'RE DANGEROUS. VERY DANGEROUS. YOU BELONG TO HIM.
HELL I DO! MR. SHEPHERD, HE DON' OWN ME.
NO HE DOESN'T. AND HE'LL GET HURT BAD IF HE TRIES TO TAKE YOU.
YOU TELL HIM...
...YOU BELONG TO GRAVES.
AU REVOIR.
FIN

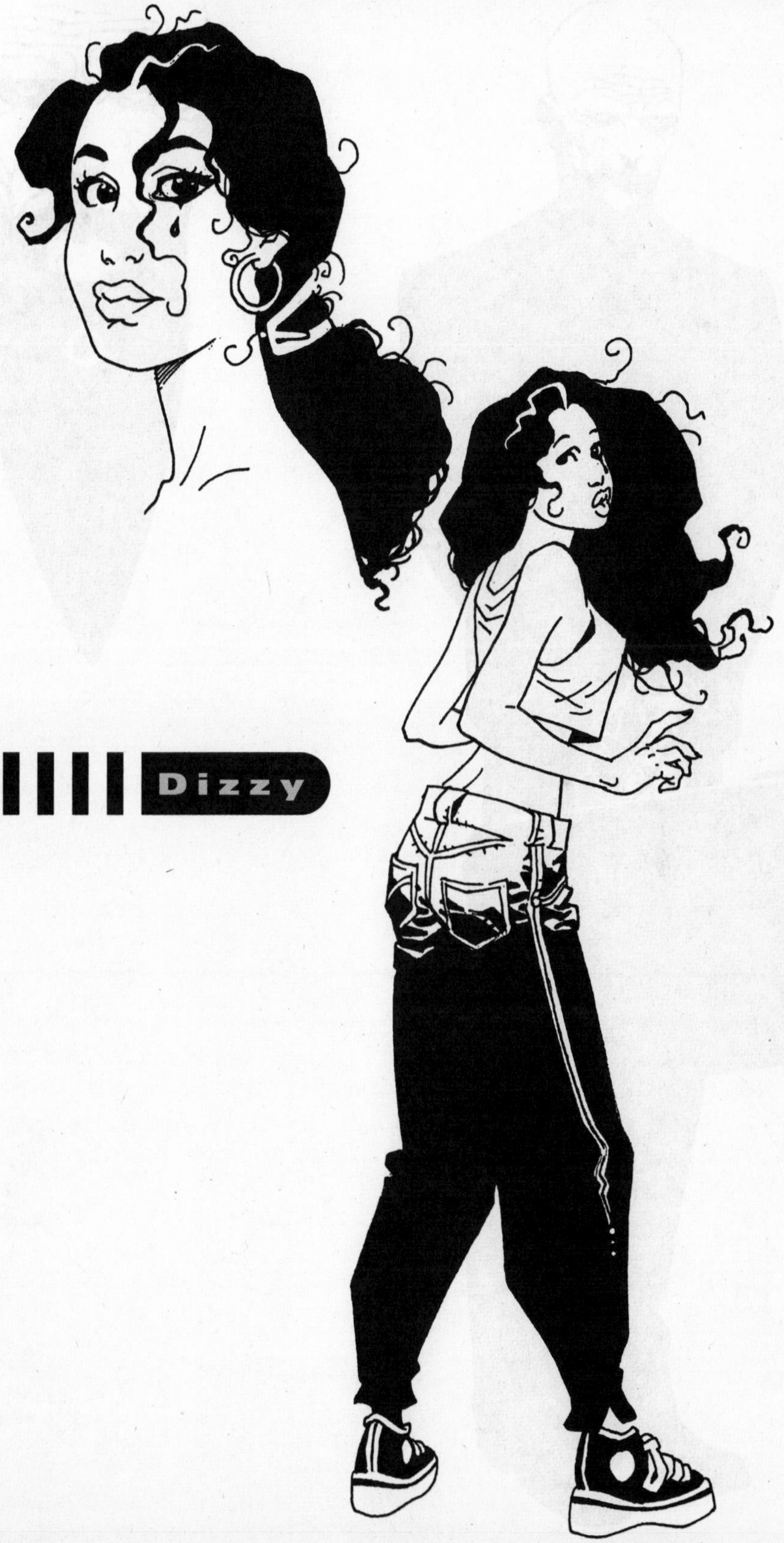

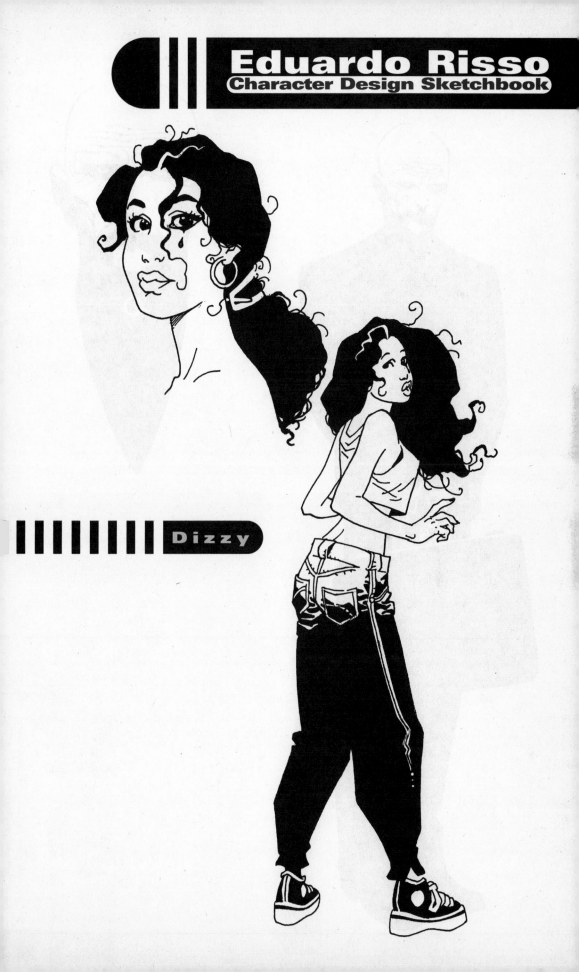

Dizzy

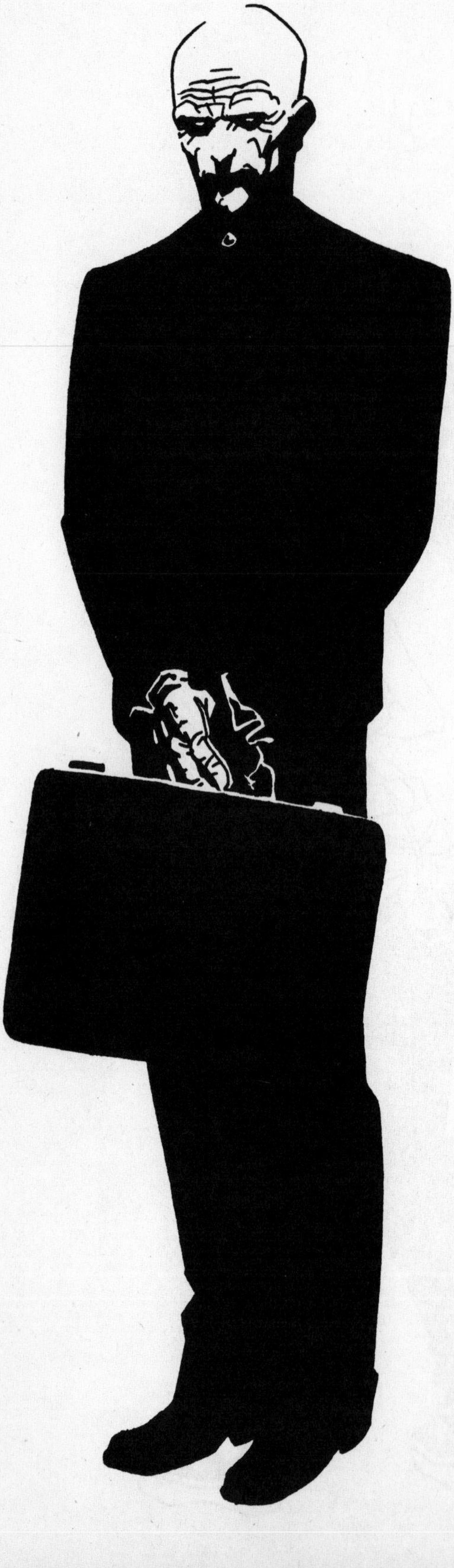

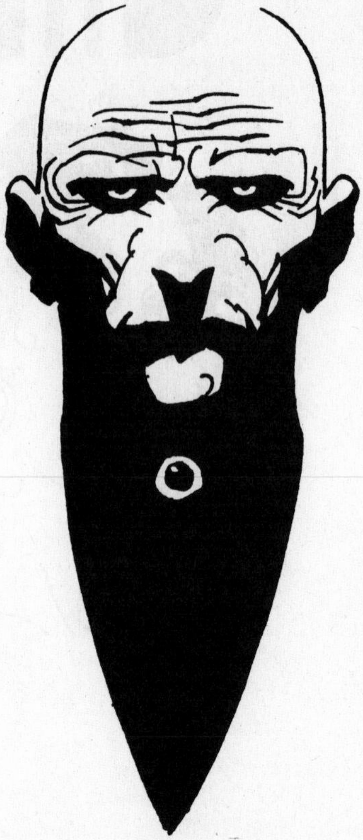

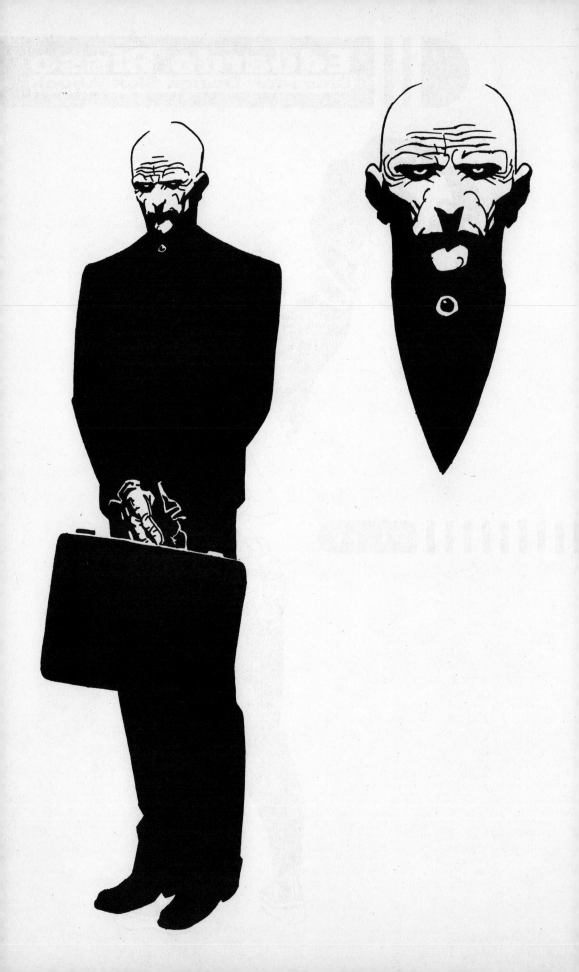

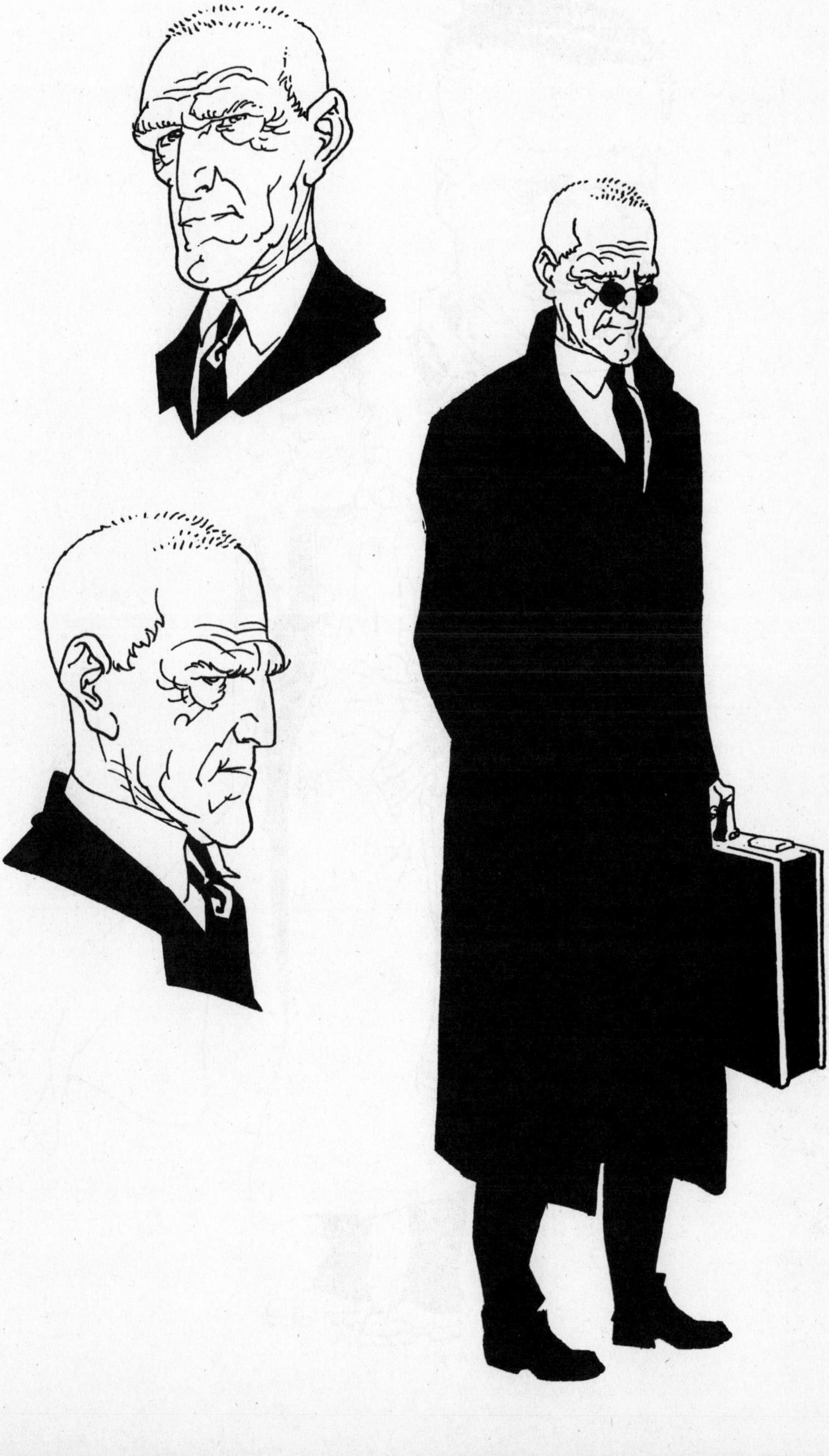

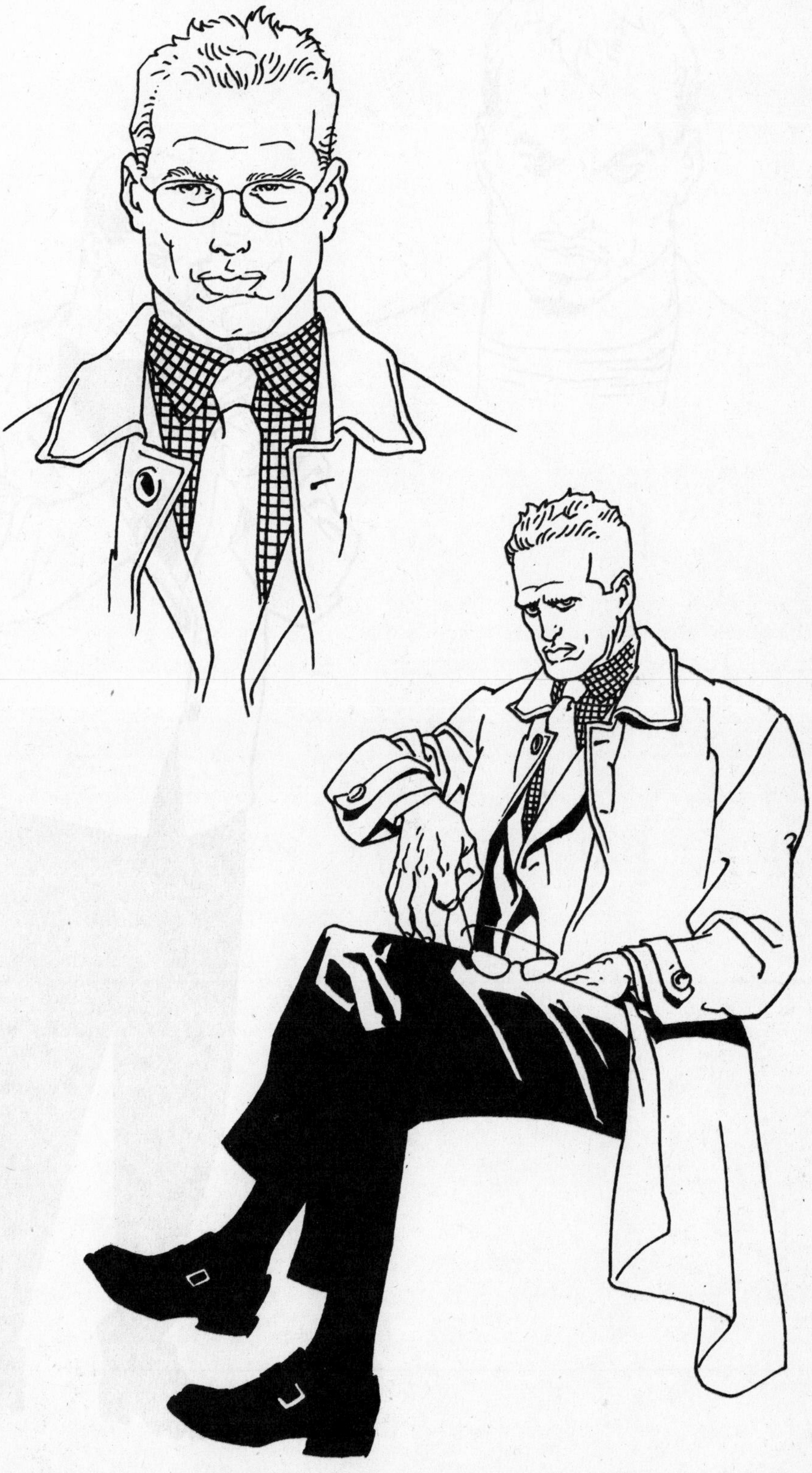

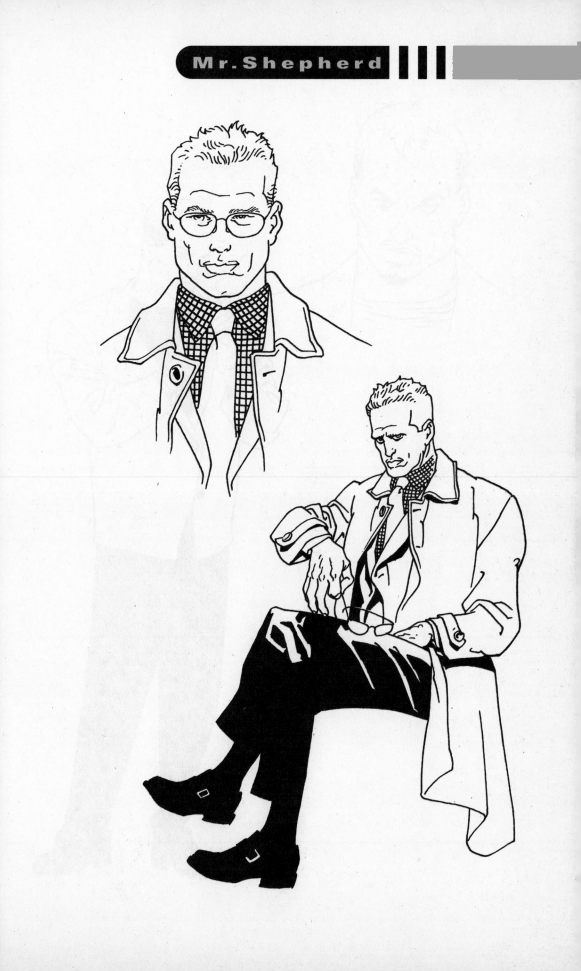

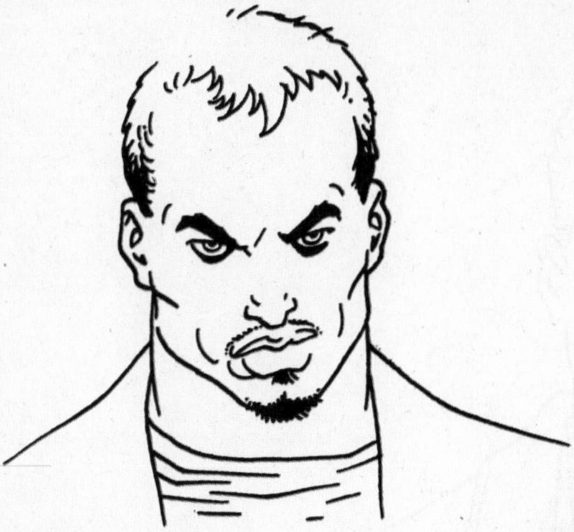

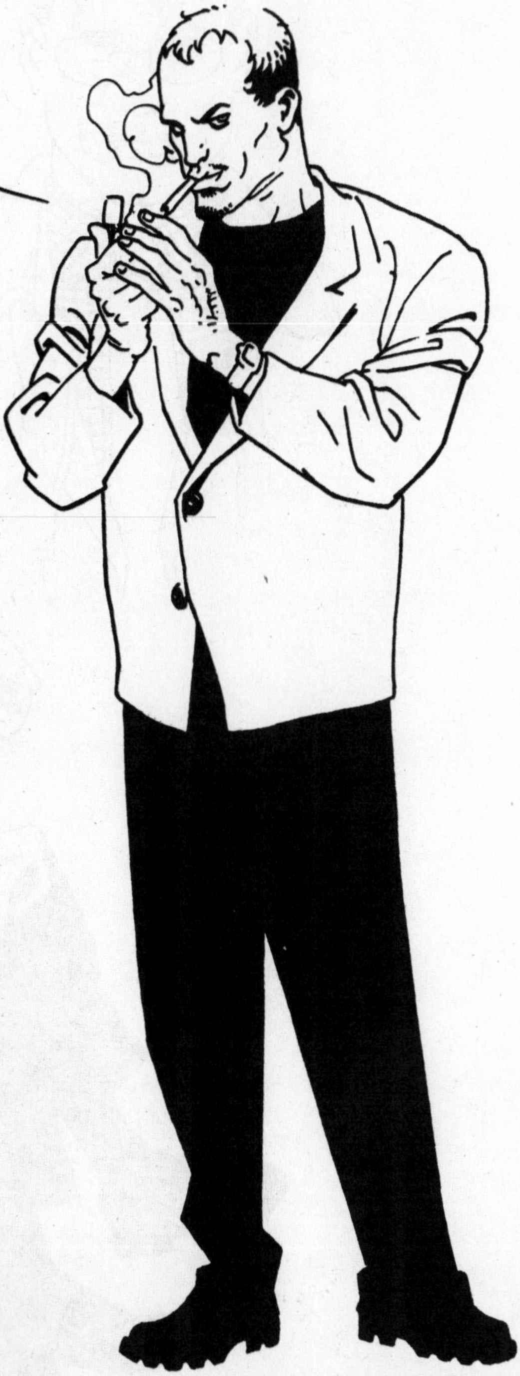

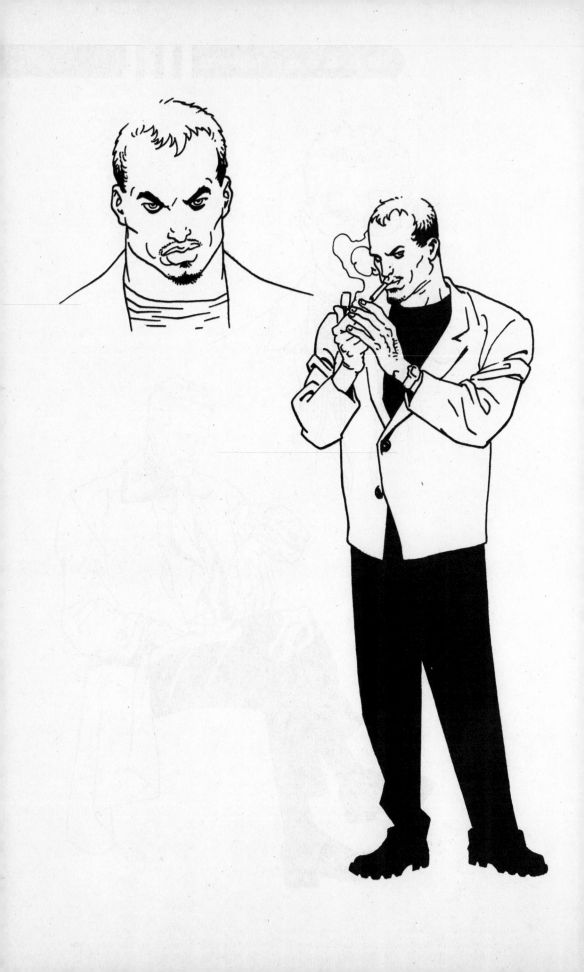

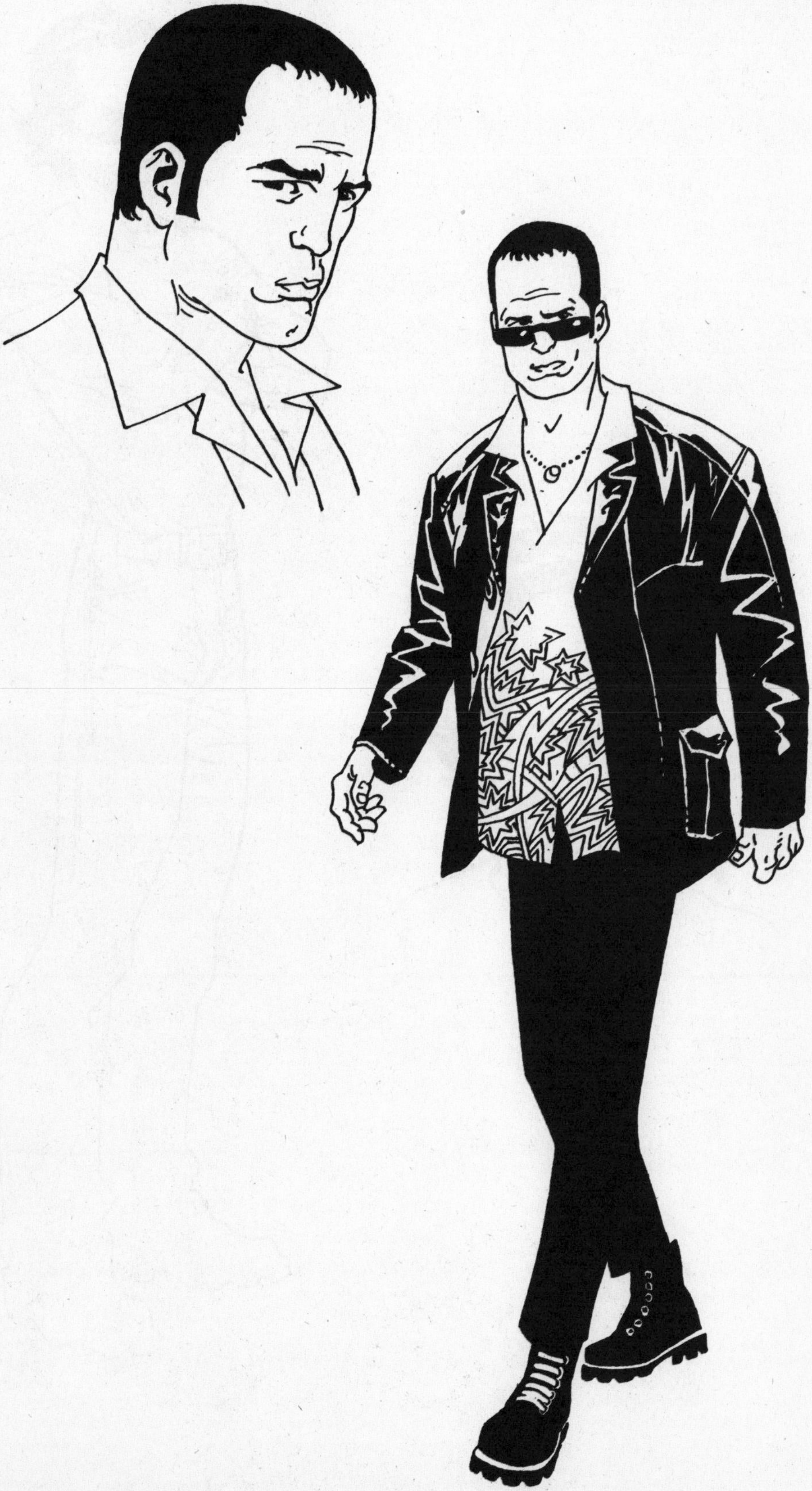

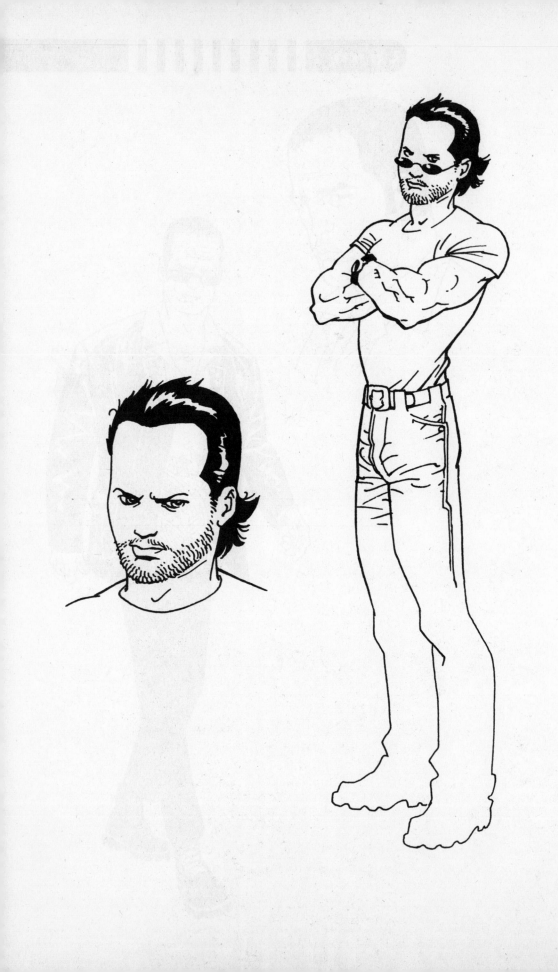

Cole Burns

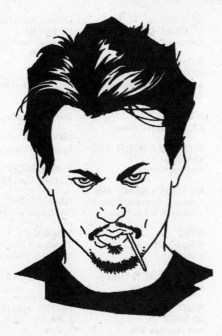

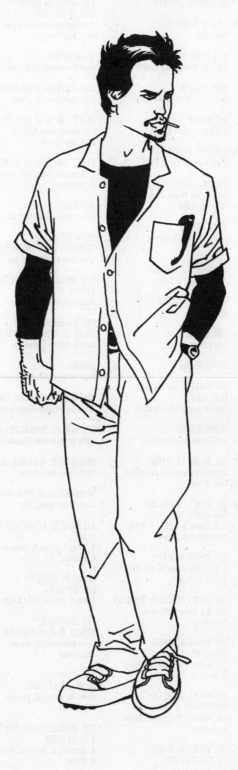

Look for these other Vertigo books:
All Vertigo titles are Suggested for Mature Readers

graphic novels

I DIE AT MIDNIGHT
Kyle Baker

KILL YOUR BOYFRIEND
Grant Morrison/Philip Bond/D'Israeli

MENZ INSANA
Christopher Fowler/John Bolton

MR. PUNCH
Neil Gaiman/Dave McKean

MYSTERY PLAY
Grant Morrison/Jon J Muth

TELL ME, DARK
Karl Edward Wagner/Kent Williams/
John Ney Rieber

TOXIC GUMBO
Lydia Lunch/Ted McKeever

VEILS
P. McGreal/S.J. Phillips/
J. Villarrubia/R. Guay

WHY I HATE SATURN
Kyle Baker

YOU ARE HERE
Kyle Baker

collections

**100 BULLETS: FIRST SHOT,
LAST CALL**
Brian Azzarello/Eduardo Risso

BLACK ORCHID
Neil Gaiman/Dave McKean

THE BOOKS OF FAERIE
Bronwyn Carlton/John Ney Rieber/
Peter Gross

**THE BOOKS OF FAERIE:
AUBERON'S TALE**
B. Carlton/J.N. Rieber/ P. Gross/
M. Buckingham/various

THE BOOKS OF MAGIC
N. Gaiman/J. Bolton/S. Hampton/
C. Vess/P. Johnson

THE BOOKS OF MAGIC: BINDINGS
John Ney Rieber/Gary Amaro/
Peter Gross

**THE BOOKS OF MAGIC:
SUMMONINGS**
J.N. Rieber/P. Gross/P. Snejbjerg/
G. Amaro/D. Giordano

**THE BOOKS OF MAGIC:
RECKONINGS**
J.N. Rieber/P. Snejbjerg/P. Gross/
J. Ridgway

**THE BOOKS OF MAGIC:
TRANSFORMATIONS**
John Ney Rieber/Peter Gross

**THE BOOKS OF MAGIC:
GIRL IN THE BOX**
John Ney Rieber/Peter Gross/
Peter Snejbjerg

BREATHTAKER
Mark Wheatley/Marc Hempel

THE COMPLEAT MOONSHADOW
J.M. DeMatteis/Jon J Muth

DEATH: THE HIGH COST OF LIVING
Neil Gaiman/Chris Bachalo/
Mark Buckingham

DEATH: THE TIME OF YOUR LIFE
N. Gaiman/C. Bachalo/M. Buckingham/
M. Pennington

DOG MOON
Robert Hunter/Timothy Truman

**DOOM PATROL:
CRAWLING FROM THE WRECKAGE**
Grant Morrison/Richard Case/various

**THE DREAMING: BEYOND THE
SHORES OF NIGHT**
Various writers and artists

**THE DREAMING: THROUGH THE
GATES OF HORN AND IVORY**
Various writers and artists

ENIGMA
Peter Milligan/Duncan Fegredo

HELLBLAZER: ORIGINAL SINS
Jamie Delano/John Ridgway/various

HELLBLAZER: DANGEROUS HABITS
Garth Ennis/William Simpson/various

HELLBLAZER: FEAR AND LOATHING
Garth Ennis/Steve Dillon

HELLBLAZER: TAINTED LOVE
Garth Ennis/Steve Dillon

**HELLBLAZER: DAMNATION'S
FLAME**
G. Ennis/S. Dillon/W. Simpson/
P. Snejbjerg

**HOUSE OF SECRETS:
FOUNDATIONS**
Steven T. Seagle/Teddy Kristiansen

**THE INVISIBLES:
BLOODY HELL IN AMERICA**
Grant Morrison/Phil Jimenez/
John Stokes

**THE INVISIBLES:
COUNTING TO NONE**
Grant Morrison/Phil Jimenez/
John Stokes

**THE INVISIBLES: SAY YOU WANT
A REVOLUTION**
G. Morrison/S. Yeowell/J. Thompson/
D. Cramer

**THE INVISIBLES:
KISSING MR. QUIMPER**
G. Morrison/C. Weston/I. Reis/various

**MICHAEL MOORCOCK'S
MULTIVERSE**
M. Moorcock/W. Simonson/J. Ridgway/
M. Reeve

MERCY
J.M. DeMatteis/Paul Johnson

**NEIL GAIMAN & CHARLES VESS'
STARDUST**
Neil Gaiman/Charles Vess

NEIL GAIMAN'S MIDNIGHT DAYS
N. Gaiman/T. Kristiansen/S. Bissette/
J. Totleben/M. Mignola/various

NEVADA
S. Gerber/P. Winslade/S. Leialoha/
D. Giordano

PREACHER: GONE TO TEXAS
Garth Ennis/Steve Dillon

**PREACHER: UNTIL THE END OF
THE WORLD**
Garth Ennis/Steve Dillon

PREACHER: PROUD AMERICANS
Garth Ennis/Steve Dillon

PREACHER: ANCIENT HISTORY
G. Ennis/S. Pugh/C. Ezquerra/R. Case

PREACHER: DIXIE FRIED
Garth Ennis/Steve Dillon

PREACHER: SALVATION
Garth Ennis/Steve Dillon

PREACHER: WAR IN THE SUN
Garth Ennis/Steve Dillon/
Peter Snejbjerg

THE SYSTEM
Peter Kuper

**SWAMP THING: SAGA OF THE
SWAMP THING**
Alan Moore/Steve Bissette/
John Totleben

SWAMP THING: LOVE AND DEATH
A. Moore/S. Bissette/J. Totleben/
S. McManus

SWAMP THING: ROOTS
Jon J Muth

TERMINAL CITY
Dean Motter/Michael Lark

**TRANSMETROPOLITAN:
BACK ON THE STREET**
Warren Ellis/Darick Robertson/various

**TRANSMETROPOLITAN:
LUST FOR LIFE**
Warren Ellis/Darick Robertson/various

**TRANSMETROPOLITAN: YEAR OF
THE BASTARD**
Warren Ellis/Darick Robertson/
Rodney Ramos

TRUE FAITH
Garth Ennis/Warren Pleece

UNCLE SAM
Steve Darnall/Alex Ross

UNKNOWN SOLDIER
Garth Ennis/Kilian Plunkett

V FOR VENDETTA
Alan Moore/David Lloyd

VAMPS
Elaine Lee/William Simpson

WITCHCRAFT
J. Robinson/P. Snejbjerg/M. Zulli/
S. Yeowell/T. Kristiansen

the Sandman library

**THE SANDMAN:
PRELUDES & NOCTURNES**
N. Gaiman/S. Kieth/M. Dringenberg/
M. Jones

THE SANDMAN: THE DOLL'S HOUSE
N. Gaiman/M. Dringenberg/M. Jones/
C. Bachalo/M. Zulli/S. Parkhouse

THE SANDMAN: DREAM COUNTRY
N. Gaiman/K. Jones/C. Vess/
C. Doran/M. Jones

**THE SANDMAN:
THE DREAM HUNTERS**
Neil Gaiman/Yoshitaka Amano

THE SANDMAN: SEASON OF MISTS
N. Gaiman/K. Jones/M. Dringenberg/
M. Jones/various

THE SANDMAN: A GAME OF YOU
Neil Gaiman/Shawn McManus/various

**THE SANDMAN:
FABLES AND REFLECTIONS**
Neil Gaiman/various

THE SANDMAN: BRIEF LIVES
Neil Gaiman/Jill Thompson/Vince Locke

THE SANDMAN: WORLDS' END
Neil Gaiman/various

THE SANDMAN: THE KINDLY ONES
N. Gaiman/M. Hempel/R. Case/various

THE SANDMAN: THE WAKE
N. Gaiman/M. Zulli/J. Muth/C. Vess

**DUSTCOVERS–
THE COLLECTED SANDMAN
COVERS 1989 - 1997**
Dave McKean/Neil Gaiman

THE SANDMAN COMPANION
Hy Bender

To find more collected editions and monthly comic books from DC Comics,
call 1-888-COMIC BOOK for the nearest comics shop or go to your local book store.

Visit us at www.dccomics.com

VER0011